THE PRENTICE HALL DIRECTORY OF
ONLINE EDUCATION RESOURCES

VICKI SMITH BIGHAM ▪ GEORGE BIGHAM

PRENTICE HALL
Paramus, New Jersey 07652

D0791697

Library of Congress Cataloging-in-Publication Data

Bigham, Vicki Smith.
     The Prentice Hall directory of online education resources / Vicki
Smith Bigham & George Bigham.
          p.   cm.
     Includes index.
     ISBN 0–13–618588–6
     1. Education—Computer network resources—Directories.
2. Internet (Computer network) in education—Directories.   3. World
Wide Web (Information retrieval system)—Directories.   I. Bigham,
George.   II. Title.
LB1044.87.B54   1998
025.06′37—dc21   98–15621
                                                                                              CIP

© 1998 by Prentice Hall, Inc.

Significant care and research has been devoted to ensuring that information provided is both accurate and current and additionally that Web sites listed have sound educational content. Given the dynamic nature of the Internet, the publisher and authors do not guarantee the accuracy or completeness of any information and are not responsible for errors or omissions or results obtained from use of the information.

Printed in the United States of America

10 9 8 7 6 5 4 3 2 1

ISBN 0-13-618588-6

ATTENTION: CORPORATIONS AND SCHOOLS

Prentice Hall books are available at quantity discounts with bulk purchase for educational, business, or sales promotional use. For information, please write to: Prentice Hall Career & Personal Development Special Sales, 240 Frisch Court, Paramus, NJ 07652. Please supply: title of book, ISBN, quantity, how the book will be used, date needed.

PRENTICE HALL
Paramus, NJ 07652

A Simon & Schuster Company

On the World Wide Web at http://www.phdirect.com

Prentice Hall International (UK) Limited, *London*
Prentice Hall of Australia Pty. Limited, *Sydney*
Prentice Hall Canada, Inc., *Toronto*
Prentice Hall Hispanoamericana, S.A., *Mexico*
Prentice Hall of India Private Limited, *New Delhi*
Prentice Hall of Japan, Inc., *Tokyo*
Simon & Schuster Asia Pte. Ltd., *Singapore*
Editora Prentice Hall do Brasil, Ltda., *Rio de Janeiro*

PREFACE

The Internet is somewhat like a magnificent and mysterious castle that has a multitude of rooms, many of which are full of precious treasures. These treasures are greater in number than one could likely ever find or count, let alone use, in a lifetime. But many offer tremendous value for those involved in teaching and learning, and they are the ones we most want to find.

When educators begin to explore the Internet in search of sites of value and interest to themselves or the students with whom they work, they typically find their own resources are finite. They are often limited in time as well as in the online search strategies and tools available or required to efficiently locate information to meet their specific needs. Most parents, and perhaps especially homeschooling parents, find their situation to be pretty much a parallel. Students learning to navigate the Internet may have more disposable time, but they too need to be able to easily find the information and resources they seek.

What is needed is a map of the castle and an inventory of some of its best treasures. *The Prentice Hall Directory of Online Education Resources* is intended to be that map—a toolkit for navigation, complete with directions and prime locations to visit and search, that will make it easy for you to locate information you need, connect with those who can provide suggestions and support, and discover new resources and ideas for teaching and learning. The *Directory* may be used by K-12 educators and specialists, homeschoolers, students, and their parents.

What kind of resources can you expect to find?

➤ Teaching ideas and lesson plans

➤ Instructional strategies and tips for classroom teachers and parents

➤ Free software and other resources available for downloading

➤ Information on educational standards and practices

➤ Research data for students

➤ Sites designed for kids

➤ Places to meet up with colleagues

➤ Online experts and discussion areas

➤ Funding information and assistance with grants

➤ Products and resources for those with special needs

➤ . . . and more!

The Prentice Hall Directory of Online Education Resources will serve as a perfect introduction to the Internet's education-related sources. For those already "surfing the

Net," it will likely target new Web sites of interest and additionally help organize resources in ways that will make them easy to share with others. Whether you are new to the Internet and online resources or an experienced Net navigator, *The Prentice Hall Directory of Online Education Resources* will help you quickly identify and review those Web sites that most closely match your needs and interests.

Vicki Smith Bigham
George Bigham

ABOUT THE AUTHORS

Vicki Smith Bigham has an extensive background in educational technology, with over 25 years of experience as a teacher, software developer, and administrator as well as professor of pre-service courses in technology integration. After teaching in Kansas and Texas schools for several years, she became a curriculum writer/software designer for the Dallas (Texas) Independent School District. Vicki then served, successively, as director of computer education at The Kinkaid School, coordinator for computer-based instruction at the Region IV Education Service Center, and director for technology and curriculum at The Briarwood School, all in Houston. A co-founder and past president of the Texas Computer Education Association and a past president of the International Society for Technology in Education, Vicki is presently managing partner in the consulting firm of Bigham Technology Solutions.

George Bigham is Vicki's resident techie, husband, and the other managing partner in Bigham Technology Solutions.

The Bighams work and live in Houston.

ACKNOWLEDGMENTS

Completing this book and Web site has been a true labor of love. Since we are both spouses and business partners, there were times when this project seemed to take over our lives (and there were a few times when it actually did!). But it has been a joy to explore and find sites that we have chosen to include in this *Directory*. It was all too often the case that we would find time escaping us as we became immersed in a particular site just discovered rather than moving on with the task at hand.

We had occasion many months ago to send e-mail to a local computer columnist describing our feelings that Web surfing was interesting and a lot of fun but that it could get in the way of a person's day job. His somewhat smug reply was, "Yes, unless it *is* your day job." Web surfing has been our "day job" and "night job" for the duration of this project. We have devoted a lot of time to research the project and compile this listing of sites. We hope that our work will save you time in searching for education-related information on the Internet.

We started this project by sending electronic mail to colleagues, business associates, and friends, asking them to identify some of their favorite sites, and we were rewarded with a number of good suggestions. Thanks to all of those who offered their favorites for our consideration.

One of the special gifts that has come our way as a result of this project has been meeting and working with Win Huppuch at Prentice Hall, a gentleman who has been such a delight to get to know and one of the most pleasant individuals we have ever had the pleasure of working with. Gratitude goes to him and his team for allowing us great latitude in defining what we wanted included in the *Directory* and for providing us with technical support.

Our warm thanks to Martha Muncrief, a friend and colleague for many years, who pitched in near the end of the project, did a lot of great work in a collapsed timeframe, and saved us from missing yet another deadline. Thanks also to Mary Wikoff, who assisted in particular with the special needs section and contributed to others as well. And thanks to Brian Hall, our good friend and serious Internet geek, who helped us get the most out of our computers, modems, and our ISP as we waded through untold numbers of Web sites in order to bring you the 1,000 best!

Our sincere thanks to all of these people, who supported us in the development of this product. And our thanks to one another for not letting this project interfere with our personal lives—on most days!

Vicki and George Bigham

CONTENTS

ABOUT THIS DIRECTORY OF ONLINE EDUCATION RESOURCES

Welcome to the Internet and its vast array of resources for education! If you are a teacher or other educator, a parent, or a student—or some combination—this *Directory* is for you. In it you will find suggestions for accessing online information and some definitions of terms you may have been wondering about. Most importantly, you will find a broad listing of over 1,000 sites with specific application to teaching and learning—with descriptions and commentary on each site.

Enjoy taking your first steps in exploring this expansive world of information available right at your fingertips. Or, if you have already ventured into cyberspace, cut down on your research time by quickly locating sites in the *Directory* that you can add to your current list of favorites.

Components of This Directory

The Prentice Hall Directory of Online Education Resources places in your hands:

> ### A PRINT DIRECTORY OF OVER 1,000 QUALITY EDUCATION-RELATED WEB SITES

The description that accompanies each site listing will help you determine whether you want to visit the site or not. If you decide it is a site that looks interesting, the Internet address for the site, the URL (Uniform Resource Locator), is noted.

> ### TIPS AND STRATEGIES FOR SUCCESSFUL INTERNET SEARCHING

The following introduction gives you a number of suggestions for how to use the Internet as a resource for teaching and learning as well as tips for managing student use and use by children getting online at home. At the end of this book you will also find a glossary of terms and a "how-to" guide to using what are the most common Web search engines.

> ### UPDATED, SEARCHABLE INFORMATION AVAILABLE ONLINE

Web sites change frequently. New ones are added every day, and sometimes sites that have been in existence are dropped for one reason or another. In addition to additions and deletions, the dynamic nature of the Internet fosters ongoing design and content changes to what is there at any given point in time. What you see today may well be modified or updated by tomorrow. You can receive updated information to the print information provided in this *Directory* by accessing its companion EdInfoSearch Web site. Also use the Web site to find exciting new sites we have found.

How to Use the Print Directory

For easy use, this book has been organized into the following sections:

About This Directory of Online Education Resources

This section, the one you are currently reading, explains how the *Directory* is organized, in print and online, and suggests how you can use Internet resources in the classroom or at home.

Curriculum Corner

Section 1, the largest section in the *Directory*, identifies sites that are appropriate for instruction and/or learning. These sites are possible resources for students as well as teachers and are broken down into the following subject areas, arranged alphabetically:

- Art
- Career and Technology Education
- Guidance and Counseling
- Foreign Language
- Health
- Language Arts
- Mathematics
- Music and Drama
- Science
- Social Studies
- Technology

Connecting with Colleagues

Section 2 helps you locate forums such as the "Teacher Talk Forum" sponsored by Indiana University, professional associations, and professional development sites for the dynamic sharing of information with colleagues all over the world.

Teaching Ideas

In Section 3, you'll find dozens of sites like "Teachers Helping Teachers," "Newton's Apple," and "The Curriculum Web Resource Center" featuring innovative lesson plans and management techniques and tools in all content areas.

Places for Parents

Section 4 focuses on online publications and other resources of special interest to parents and families, such as the U.S. Department of Education site "Helping Your Child Learn Science" and "Wizzywygs," a fun and informational "newsalogue" on computer.

Mostly for Kids

Section 5 takes you to sites offering plenty of fun (and learning) for kids, such as Mountain Lakes Software's "CyberKids," plus sources for assistance like "Homework Helper" and expert information on a host of topics.

Museums and Exhibits

The sites in Section 6 let you take a virtual tour of a variety of museums around the world, from the Musee du Louvre, Paris, to the Holocaust Memorial Museum in Washington, DC, to the Natural History Museum of Los Angeles County.

Online References

Section 7 identifies online versions of newspapers and magazines, such as *Time Daily*," encyclopedias, dictionaries, and other general reference works plus specialized style guides, electronic databases of quotations, software reviews, and more.

Grants and Funding

Section 8 leads you to sites like "Foundation Center Online" for information on funding opportunities and deadlines and provides easy access to necessary forms and publications.

Special Needs

The sites in Section 9 focus on a wide range of special needs, such as "LD Resources," a source of freeware relating to learning disabilities, and "Children and Adults with Attention Deficit Disorders," a site sponsored by CH.A.D.D.

Using the Internet

Section 10 features sites for learning about the Internet online, such as Cornell University's "CU-SeeMe Page," free videoconferencing software that works over the Internet and can be used to set up videoconferencing among student teams or classes.

Other Resources

The last section provides a list of terms and acronyms that are part of the "cyberspeak" relating to the Internet and a brief set of introductory instructions and suggestions to assist in your use of some of the Web search engines identified in this *Directory*.

The entry for each Web site in the *Directory* looks like the following. See what you will find in each listing:

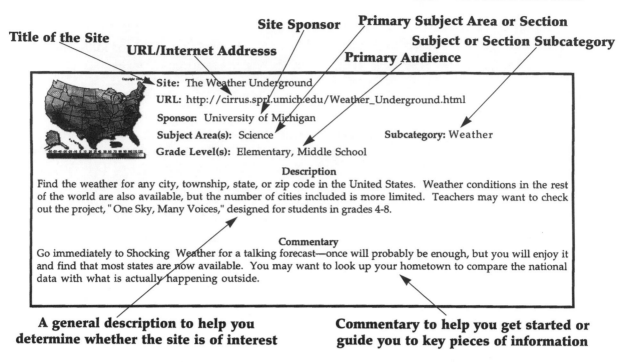

Title of the Site

URL/Internet Addresss

Site Sponsor

Primary Subject Area or Section

Subject or Section Subcategory

Primary Audience

Site: The Weather Underground

URL: http://cirrus.sprl.umich.edu/Weather_Underground.html

Sponsor: University of Michigan

Subject Area(s): Science   **Subcategory:** Weather

Grade Level(s): Elementary, Middle School

Description

Find the weather for any city, township, state, or zip code in the United States. Weather conditions in the rest of the world are also available, but the number of cities included is more limited. Teachers may want to check out the project, "One Sky, Many Voices," designed for students in grades 4-8.

Commentary

Go immediately to Shocking Weather for a talking forecast—once will probably be enough, but you will enjoy it and find that most states are now available. You may want to look up your hometown to compare the national data with what is actually happening outside.

A general description to help you determine whether the site is of interest

Commentary to help you get started or guide you to key pieces of information

The *Directory* gives you an extensive and rich set of education-related resources. However, it does not provide step-by-step instructions in how to become a proficient Internet navigator. If you are just getting started, you may wish to read one of the many books and guides currently available that provide an introduction to the Internet. One such guide is *Internet Adventures 1.2: Step-by-Step Guide to Finding and Using Educational Resources,* by Cynthia B. Leshin (Needham Heights, MA: Allyn & Bacon, 1996).

How to Use the Directory on the Internet Web Site

To access the companion online version of this *Directory,* EdInfoSearch, which will be updated at least quarterly, point your browser to its Web site at:

http://www.edinfosearch.com

We assume that you are a fairly nontechnical technology user but that you do already have a computer setup with a Web browser and an Internet connection through either a local Internet Service Provider (ISP) or an account with one of the online services that have Web browsers, such as America Online, CompuServe, Prodigy, the Microsoft Network, and others. Your connection can be a dial-up one via modem or a network connection, if you are fortunate enough to have one.

The usefulness of *The Prentice Hall Directory of Online Education Resources* is not related to *how* you are connected to the Internet or which Web browser you are using. Rather, it focuses on the information you can locate and use once that connection has been established.

A special area of the EdInfoSearch Web site at <http://www.edinfosearch.com> is available to purchasers of this printed *Directory* to get updates on Web sites listed in the book as well as to find new and exciting sites to visit that are not in the book.

And in the online directory, you can conduct searches on this directory database and quickly locate the Web sites that are of most interest to you.

What Exactly Is the Internet—and the World Wide Web?

The Internet is an enormous, worldwide network of computers and computer networks that was initiated by the U.S. military and universities to allow them to communicate on projects and distribute information. In the event of a national emergency, for example, if one site was eliminated, other sites would still have access to vital information needed.

In the mid-1980s, the National Science Foundation established five supercomputer centers for research and built a network that made them available to those who could not easily travel to the physical site. Over a couple of years, the network expanded until it became the fastest network in the United States. Corporations, large universities, and research centers began to make use of the network. And now, several years later, K-12 schools, other education agencies and institutions, public libraries, and the general public around the world are online.

The World Wide Web or, as it is often called, WWW or the Web, is the fastest growing part of the Internet—and the easiest to navigate. At one point in 1995, there were just over 50 sites on the Web. A year later, there were more than 50,000, and the numbers have been mushrooming since that time. These Web sites share a common language and access method, making it easy to point and click a computer mouse to navigate to selected sites. And once at the site, a user can find more than just text—graphics, sound, animation, video, and other forms of multimedia.

Who Contributes the Content Found on the Internet?

The Internet is somewhat like a vast library of information just waiting to be found and used. And on the Internet, anyone can actually provide the information or content. It will then be found in varied types and in varied formats. For this reason, it is important to have a discriminating eye when considering what to use or what to direct students or children to access.

One of the exciting aspects of the Internet is that it provides a vehicle for not only formal publishers, organizations, and research institutions to make information available online, but also for individuals such as students, teachers, parents, and anyone who wants to create and post information for others to see. With this wide range of people contributing information accessible via your computer, you obviously expect an equally wide range of quality of content. That is one of the reasons *The Prentice Hall Directory of Online Education Resources* will prove a valuable resource in identifying sites with quality information worth looking at to meet specific needs.

Why Should I Do This in My Classroom?

An unprecedented number of educators and students are communicating with colleagues and peers via the Internet. If you are an educator today or are talking with educators, you are hearing, "Internet, Internet, Internet." What's all the hype? Experience travel beyond classroom walls and see some of the exciting projects and products that are emerging daily for Internet use. See firsthand how the Internet and other types of telecommunications are opening up the world to teachers like yourself, giving them easy access to resources, information, and colleagues worldwide.

Teachers need to develop a critical eye as they view online resources for potential use in their classrooms. But they also need to become aware of the use of these resources as powerful enablers of learning. With this combined knowledge, they can see how online resources can contribute to student learning in certain areas and can better consider how to most effectively set up and then assess use of these resources in their classrooms.

Internet resources engage students in what they are learning. Students learn by doing, and when they can use the Internet to explore, they become active participants in the gathering, analyzing, organizing, and presenting of the information they find. These resources prove motivating for students—and their teachers. They are much like the media-oriented environment students are most accustomed to. Technology transforms the print information into an engaging set of links to stories, facts, ideas, pictures, places, and sounds available for the student to discover and explore. It provides students with the opportunity to learn by accomplishing real-world projects that include online research and interaction with experts. The students in our classrooms today will need to know how to locate and retrieve Internet resources and information both for their own lifelong learning as well as to be successful in the future workplace they will encounter.

And for you, the teacher, the Internet offers a wealth of resources outside your classroom walls and the walls of your campus, access to information and colleagues from around the world, tools to help you teach, lesson ideas and projects from teachers like yourself, and more. You are no longer confined to only the resources within your immediate reach. Via the computer and the Internet, the resources available to strengthen your instruction and support your own productivity are only a few keystrokes away.

You may well find what other teachers and students have discovered after a few successful experiences in navigating the Internet: that teaching and learning will forever be changed. You'll be able to collaborate with colleagues and share ideas. The Internet breaks down the walls of the classroom and allows you and your students to travel to places, interact with people, and access resources not available in any other way. And the information you find will be dynamic and up-to-date, sometimes to the minute.

Parents—What Do I Need to Know and Do?

As a parent, you will find a wealth of resources for yourself and your children on the Web—tips for parenting, ideas for activities to do with your children, engaging places for your children to explore on their own, and more.

You may wonder about the value of the Internet versus some of the stories you hear publicized regarding its negative aspects and the possibilities of what you or your children might encounter. It is true that some areas of the Internet are not intended for your own or any children. However, there are so many rich and valuable sites that your children can benefit from.

As you think about permitting your children to access the Net, compare it to letting them go to the movies or the mall on their own. You may not need to watch them every minute, but you should equip them with some sound rules and guidelines that will contribute to their safety, make them aware of what they can and cannot do. These guidelines should prepare them to handle the experience if they encounter information or sites that are other than you would find suitable.

There are a variety of parental control software products on the market, and you may choose to purchase one for your home. (Keep in mind that *no* product is foolproof!) However, as is true for much of parenting, you probably shouldn't just define the rules and leave it at that.

Monitor your children's use of the Internet and get to know the Web sites they are most interested in, just as you would want to know where they are going and who they are spending time with when they leave the house. Some parents identify the sites they want their children to use and require their children to ask if they want to link or go to a site not yet on the "approved list." Other parents set general guidelines and leave their children with some latitude for exploring. You, as a parent, must make that decision based on your child's age, interests, and your own goals for the activities your child is involved with online. Establish guidelines for usage time and activity based on what is comfortable for you.

Privacy is important to and for children, but supervision and parental involvement in your children's lives are important, too. As a general rule, don't give your children long periods of time completely unsupervised while they are online. Perhaps just having the computer in a fairly open area of your house rather than behind a closed door will be a way to feel comfortable about what your children are doing on their own—without having them feel you are constantly looking over their shoulder.

Do tell your children to never provide personal information online, such as full name, address, school name, phone number, or other personal data.

Use the information in this *Directory* to help you locate hundreds of sites that provide interesting, fun, and appropriate materials for your child—and a wealth of resources for you.

Short and Sweet for Students—A Few Basics

We've been talking to the adults here, but the majority of the sites referenced in this *Directory* are something you students will enjoy and use. And the good part is you often have more time to do this than we adults—we envy you that! Parents and teachers around you will be counting on you to show them the latest and greatest things you find while surfing the Net.

You're welcome to read any of the tips provided to teachers and parents above. Probably, though, you'd rather get past this reading and just get online. So only one basic message for you before you get going: If ever, while you are exploring new worlds of information and friends online, what you see or read just doesn't feel quite right to you, don't be embarrassed or worried to trust what you are feeling. Show what concerns you to a parent, teacher, or other adult you trust or just feel free to turn off the computer. *You* get to decide if something feels uncomfortable—that's your right, so always know that's something you can do.

Unraveling Those Internet Addresses

Addresses of Web sites in this *Directory* all begin with the following:

> http

"http" stands for "HyperText Transfer Protocol" and is an indication that the site is a hypertext document at the Internet address shown.

Punctuation marks such as periods, colons and forward slashes are simply Internet conventions for separating the parts of a URL (Uniform Resource Locator).

> http://www.

"www" means "World Wide Web." The Internet was originally character-based rather than graphics-based, and, at that time, most of the graphics-oriented material to be found was located in the "www" section of the Internet. Today, almost all of the sites you visit will be graphics-oriented, whether "www" appears in their URL or not.

> http://www.domain-name-address

The domain-name-address is the name of the host server computer where the information is located and also the address of the specific site or page on that computer. There should never be any spaces in this section (or any other section) of the URL.

> http://www.domain-name-address.ext

The last three characters of a URL tell you the type of organization hosting the site. Here is the current list of some of the types of organizations you will most often find:

.com	a commercial organization
.edu	an educational institution or agency
.gov	a government agency
.net	a network provider
.org	organizations and associations
.mil	a U.S. military agency

This "official" list contains some other extensions that identify types of organizations, and there is, at the time of this writing, discussion of expanding the current list even further.

We have made every attempt to verify that the addresses are current, but with the ever-changing nature of the Internet, you may find some that can't be accessed. Here are a few tips . . .

When you type in a URL, be sure to type it as it is given, including using capital letters or lowercase letters as indicated. This is important! And if you don't locate a site on the first try, try again—and check your spelling, just in case. Some of the URLs are fairly long, and it is easy to make a mistake.

You may get a message telling you that the site has moved to a new address—in that case, it will tell you what the new address is. And since Internet addresses often lead you to a section of a primary site and not the main page or home page, as the site is revised or updated, some of these addresses may change.

If your URL has been entered correctly and you still cannot access the site, one of the following may be the problem:

➤ The site may just be busy, with a lot of current traffic. Try again later.

➤ Keep in mind the dynamic nature of the Internet. The site may have merely gone away or eroded. It may have been old or not upgraded, and someone pulled it down.

➤ The site may have moved to a new address, but no link or indication of the new address is available. This is parallel to your moving to a new home and leaving no forwarding address.

➤ Sometimes, a site is being worked on or upgraded at the time you are trying to access it, and it will be only temporarily inaccessible. The server may be down. It is always a good idea to try again later before giving up on a site location.

A trick that sometimes works when a URL cannot be successfully accessed is to "simplify" the address by deleting the last part of the address down to what is called the "root directory" and trying again. For example, in the URL,

http://www.ed.gov/offices/OSERS/NIDRR/nidrr.html

deleting the last part of the URL and trying the root directory:

http://www.ed.gov

This may prove a successful way to begin your online navigation to the information you desire.

On Your Way

Enough of this! The best way to experience and enjoy the Internet is to get connected and get online. Use this *Directory* to quickly and easily identify the sites you want to visit. Be prepared for an exciting journey to the education-related treasures awaiting you and your colleagues, students, and children. Enjoy the voyage! We bet you'll be back often.

Vicki Smith Bigham
George Bigham

1 WWW CURRICULUM CORNER

This first section of the *Directory* identifies 444 Web sites that are appropriate for instruction and/or learning. Many of the sites are possible sources for students as well as teachers.

For easy use, the sites are presented according to subject area, arranged alphabetically. The following lists each area along with several of its subcategories. (When the sites in an area are very diverse, the subcategory is designated "Miscellaneous.")

➤ **ART:** Architecture, Art History, Drawing and Painting Origami, Photography

➤ **CAREER AND TECHNOLOGY:** Accounting, Business Information, Business Law, Computers, Construction, Engineering, Entrepreneurship, Finance, Home Economics, Marketing

➤ **FOREIGN LANGUAGE:** Arabic, ESL and Bilingual, French, German, Greek, Hindi, Indonesian, Italian, Japanese, Latin, Multiple Languages, Russian, Spanish, Vietnamese, Welsh

➤ **GUIDANCE AND COUNSELING:** Financial Aid for College, Getting into College, Locating a College, Online Coursework, Resources, World of Work

➤ **HEALTH:** Miscellaneous

➤ **LANGUAGE ARTS:** Literature, Miscellaneous, Poetry, Speaking, Vocabulary, Writing

➤ **MATHEMATICS:** Miscellaneous

➤ **MUSIC AND DRAMA:** Dance, Drama, Music

➤ **SCIENCE:** Astronomy and Space, Biology, Chemistry, Earth Science, Environment and Ecology, Miscellaneous, Physics, Weather

➤ **SOCIAL STUDIES:** Anthropology, Archaeology, Black History, Economics, U.S. Geography, U.S. Government, U.S. History, Women's Studies, World Geography, World Government, World History

➤ **TECHNOLOGY:** Computers

Section 01. Curriculum Corner

Site: Broadacre All-Wright-Site

URL: http://www.geocities.com/CapitolHill/2317/flw.html

Sponsor: Capitol Hill Neighborhood

Subject Area(s): Art   **Subcategory:** Architecture

Grade Level(s): Middle School, High School

Description
Frank Lloyd Wright, who lived from 1867 to 1959, was a prolific architect with close to 500 of his designs actually built. Find books he wrote as well as those written about him. The major feature of the site is the Architecture Guide with pages containing geographically organized links to over 120 of Wright's designs.

Commentary
Wright was the originator of many ideas that seem commonplace in our homes today, such as living rooms, carports, and open floor plans. Be sure to take a look at the Frank Lloyd Wright gas station, still in operation in Minnesota.

Site: Age of Enlightenment in the Paintings of France's National Museums

URL: http://mistral.culture.fr/lumiere/documents/files/imaginary_exhibition.html

Sponsor: Direction des Musees de France

Subject Area(s): Art   **Subcategory:** Art History

Grade Level(s): Middle School, High School

Description
History and exhibition of artwork are based on the Age of Enlightenment in France, from 1715 to 1799. During this time, France was experiencing domestic peace and economic prosperity, so the arts in all forms flourished. The reader can toggle between French and English.

Commentary
Students will find the history of the period quite interesting because of the liberal use of illustrations to communicate each concept. It is possible to view most of the major paintings from this period and also to read about them and learn where they are located. The short genealogy chart is helpful, since most of the rulers were named Louis or Marie.

Site: Art History on the Web

URL: http://www.dsu.edu/departments/liberal/artwork/ArtH.html

Sponsor: Dakota State University

Subject Area(s): Art   **Subcategory:** Art History

Grade Level(s): Elementary, Middle School

Description
This is a straightforward guide to art history with an emphasis on statues and architecture. The main sections are Greek classical, Etruscan, Hellenistic, Roman, early Christian, Byzantine, medieval, and Romanesque. Each main section contains photos with some annotation.

Commentary
All of the photos are black-and-white and can be expanded to fill the entire page. The number of examples in each section is limited, but this may be considered ideal if you are looking for an introduction to the period and/or a few important, key elements.

Section 01. Curriculum Corner

Site: Chesley Bonestell Art Gallery

URL: http://www.secapl.com/bonestell/Top.html

Sponsor: Chesley Bonestell Estate

Subject Area(s): Art   **Subcategory:** Art History

Grade Level(s): Middle School, High School

Description
Chesley Bonestell was born in 1888 and painted daily until his death at the age of 98. He had three successful careers in art, first as an architect and then as a special effects artist for movies. He began another in 1944 as an artist/illustrator of space flight and astronomical subjects. View sets of paintings on Earth, Mars, Jupiter, Saturn, the moon and stars.

Commentary
This is a privately owned art collection, so its inclusion on the Internet is the only way most people would ever see the paintings. Click on your favorite planet and enjoy a very different perspective of the galaxy.

Site: French Ministry of Culture

URL: http://www.culture.fr/index-en.html

Sponsor: Le Ministere de la culture

Subject Area(s): Art   **Subcategory:** Art History

Grade Level(s): Middle School, High School

Description
All of the text at this site can be viewed in either French or English. There is a news section (see images of recently discovered cave paintings), and one can visit the National Library or view archaeology documents. One section focuses on the Age of Enlightenment in the paintings of France's national museums. This site has won awards in France as an exemplary Web site.

Commentary
While the emphasis at this site is on art, there are many parts of it which will provide enrichment in the French classroom. One section, Christmas Traditions in France and Canada, includes current family and religious ceremonies but also offers information back to the Middle Ages.

Site: Gargoyles Then and Now

URL: http://ils.unc.edu/garg/garghp4.html

Sponsor: Jack Westerhoff and Beth Stevens

Subject Area(s): Art   **Subcategory:** Art History

Grade Level(s): Elementary, Middle School

Description
A gargoyle is a grotesquely carved human or animal figure found on an architectual structure. Gargoyles were originally designed to serve as a spout to throw rainwater clear of a building but later became primarily ornamental. They inhabited the great cathedrals of the Middle Ages and have many descendants.

Commentary
There is a great deal of history provided describing the origin of the gargoyle, but the real draw of this site is the giant collection of somewhat gross and ugly statues. One of the authors, from Duke University, has provided a map of current day use of gargoyles on campus.

13

Site: Great Artists

URL: http://www.ugrad.cs.jhu.edu/~baker/artpage.html

Sponsor: Brad Baker

Subject Area(s): Art   **Subcategory:** Art History

Grade Level(s): Middle School, High School

Description

The author of this site selects famous artists to feature. Currently showing are Vincent van Gogh, Claude Monet, and Paul Cezanne. In addition to displaying a wide collection of work from each artist, the site also provides links to bibliographical material.

Commentary

You can send a digital postcard of great art from this site. The author has provided a clock indicating the wait time to send each postcard...sometimes rather lengthy.

Site: World Art Treasures

URL: http://sgwww.epfl.ch/BERGER/index.html

Sponsor: J. E. Berger Foundation

Subject Area(s): Art   **Subcategory:** Art History

Grade Level(s): Middle School, High School

Description

There are 100,000 slides in this collection, all devoted to art, including the major civilizations such as Egypt, China, Japan, India, and Europe. In a novel approach, the curator builds a specific approach for each program as an attempt to give birth to a true art experience through a new technology. New programs are in preparation.

Commentary

"The Enchanted Gardens of the Renaissance" seems to beckon and is indeed worth exploring. The narrative explores gardens as parks, for hunting, to meditate, to contemplate as works of art, and simply for growing flowers.

Site: A Docent's Tour of Salvador Dali Resources

URL: http://www.empower.net/dali/dalimain.html

Sponsor: Merchant's Consulting Network (Florida)

Subject Area(s): Art   **Subcategory:** Drawing and Painting

Grade Level(s): Middle School, High School

Description

Salvador Dali was born in 1904, and during his very lengthy career as an artist, his work transitioned from Surrealist to Classical. This Web page of resources includes information about Dali's life, photographs of his Masterworks, information about his influences, and an index to resources.

Commentary

Eight of the roughly 20 Masterworks are included in the exhibition. Masterwork is a term coined by a Dali scholar to refer to paintings that are at least 5 feet in any one dimension. They are incredible...and if you are not an expert on modern art, you will find the extensive descriptions quite helpful.

Section 01. Curriculum Corner

Site: Art Galleries and Exhibits on the Web

URL: http://www.tristero.com/usa/tx/sa/gallery/arts.html

1205 ARTSPACE **Sponsor:** 1205 Artspace Gallery

Subject Area(s): Art   **Subcategory:** Drawing and Painting

Grade Level(s): Middle School, High School

Description
This site provides hundreds of links to exhibits and galleries. Some of those listed have an international flavor, such as Chinese, Filipino, Italian, Australian, Native American, and others. The majority of the links are art exhibits and include some that are physical sites as well as some that are Web-based only. The exhibits are arranged alphabetically and annotated for assisting the viewer in understanding the content.

Commentary
This represents a significantly large collection of art links. There are also links to individual artists, publications, jewelry, education, shows, and more. The emphasis here is on current, living artists, but included are a variety of others as well.

Site: Artist's Corner-Painting Lessons

URL: http://www.csi.nb.ca/safran/corner/

Sponsor: Barbara Safran Studios

Subject Area(s): Art   **Subcategory:** Drawing and Painting

Grade Level(s): Middle School, High School

Description
Barbara Safran provides some lessons in painting with watercolour, which she feels lends itself to many subtle effects. There is a discussion of the horizon line, of perspective, and then four watercolour lessons. Her goal is to provide information and showcase the techniques and unique effects possible with this medium.

Commentary
This is a wonderful site for the novice. Each aspect described is discussed in straightforward language, and the drawings help explain each step. You will want to look at the site while online, but you will also need a printed copy of materials and directions for your own work.

Welcome to **ArtServe**
THE AUSTRALIAN NATIONAL UNIVERSITY

Site: ArtServe

URL: http://rubens.anu.edu.au

Sponsor: The Australian National University

Subject Area(s): Art   **Subcategory:** Drawing and Painting

Grade Level(s): Middle School, High School

Description
This database contains more than 27,000 images of art and architecture, mainly from the Mediterranean Basin. It operates as a cost-recovery service, so that only a sampler of the images is available until a subscription fee is paid. There are reference works available and examples of student projects.

Commentary
This huge collection of images has a road map for navigating through the pages. In each subsection, only one painting is available, but there is a list of the remaining art from that artist. There is no search feature of the Sampler.

Section 01. Curriculum Corner

Site: Crayola Art Education

URL: http://www.crayola.com/art_education/

Sponsor: Binney & Smith

Subject Area(s): Art   **Subcategory:** Drawing and Painting

Grade Level(s): Elementary, Middle School, High School

Description

Binney & Smith, the Crayola folks, bring an informative and picturesque site to the Web. Click on Art Techniques, then choose a medium of interest—crayons, markers, paint or finger paint, pencils, modeling compound or dough, or others. Find special techniques for using the medium with examples to stimulate creativity. "Talk About Art!" is a teacher exchange area for ideas, art projects, lesson plans, and teaching tips.

Commentary

This is a beautiful site that students and teachers alike will appreciate. Teachers should be sure to click on Dream-Makers to learn about a program that provides art and elementary teachers a resource guide of thematic-based ideas. Teachers can submit students' artworks for possible inclusion in regional exhibitions.

Site: Escher Patterns

URL: http://www.sfc.keio.ac.jp/~aly/escher/escher.html

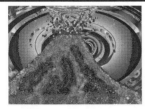

Sponsor: Yoshiaki Araki

Subject Area(s): Art   **Subcategory:** Drawing and Painting

Grade Level(s): Middle School, High School

Description

This site takes a number of Escher patterns and transposes them in bodypaint and other 3-D images. There are links to other Escher sites and information about a CD-ROM of pictures which is available for purchase.

Commentary

Cordon Art, who apparently owns the copyright to everything Escher ever made, is closing down many sites for copyright violations. This seems to be a good indication that better care should be taken with using pictures when the site says that permission must be requested first.

Site: Glenridge Middle School's Virtual Art Museum

URL: http://longwood.cs.ucf.edu:80/~MidLink/glenridge.hp.html

Sponsor: Glenridge Middle School

Subject Area(s): Art   **Subcategory:** Drawing and Painting

Grade Level(s): Elementary, Middle School

Description

These drawings and paintings seem to be done with several mediums, including the Brushstrokes program. Most are in color, but there are some black-and-white drawings—this selection is especially effective in the drawings of the church, tree, and snowfall.

Commentary

This site is somewhat slow to load, because all of the paintings are page size and additionally because a complete section is loaded at once. The kids represented on these pages are very talented and would like to receive paintings back from other students.

Section 01. Curriculum Corner

Site: Kids Art Museum

URL: http://www.skr.or.jp/~aka/7_kidsart/

Sponsor: Kodomo Bijutsukan

Subject Area(s): Art   **Subcategory:** Drawing and Painting

Grade Level(s): Preschool, Elementary

Description

Since most of the site is in Japanese, it is appropriate for the nonreader. There are four main sections, and only one title when opened, Collaborations Works, is in English, but each has further subsections. Exploration is intuitive as one moves from room to room and examines pictures drawn by kids.

Commentary

This is fun if you relax and enjoy the unexpected. It is easy to navigate, even if you can't read any Japanese. The pictures are great and can usually be expanded to page size. There are some solid works, maybe origami, and an occasional English word.

Site: Leonardo da Vinci

URL: http://www.leonardo.net/museum/main.html

Sponsor: Leonardo Internet

Subject Area(s): Art   **Subcategory:** Drawing and Painting

Grade Level(s): Middle School, High School

Description

The original Renaissance Man, Leonardo da Vinci, was a painter, designer, scientist, futurist, and thinker. The gallery features four wings: oil paintings, engineering and futurist designs, drawings and sketches, and a historical exhibit about the life and times of da Vinci.

Commentary

Although born in 1452, Leonardo da Vinci seems to grow in popularity as the years pass. Take a look at his most famous paintings, "Mona Lisa" and "The Last Supper," but don't neglect to explore the gallery with futuristic designs. His helicopter design might not have worked, but consider when it was designed!

Site: Paintings of Vermeer

URL: http://www.cacr.caltech.edu/~roy/vermeer

Sponsor: Roy Williams Clickery

Subject Area(s): Art   **Subcategory:** Drawing and Painting

Grade Level(s): Middle School, High School

Description

Johannes (Jan) Vermeer lived his short life (1632 – 1675) in Delft with very little known about his history. His paintings have limited scope of subject matter but are fascinating because of the intricate combination of light, color, proportion, and scale. The Webmaster allows us to peruse the collection by physical location, chronological order, popularity, or just by browsing thumbnail paintings.

Commentary

The thumbnail copies are a great way to get an overview of the entire collection. When you select any one of the pictures, you see a larger version plus a discussion of the artistic qualities worth noting. The popularity of the paintings was determined by viewer access during a selected period last year. "The Girl with a Pearl Earring" was the winner.

Section 01. Curriculum Corner

Site: Peace in Pictures Project

URL: http://www.macom.co.il/peace/pic1/index.html

Sponsor: Macom Networking (Jerusalem)

Subject Area(s): Art   **Subcategory:** Drawing and Painting

Grade Level(s): Elementary

Description

The "Peace in Pictures" project invites children of all ages from around the world to draw their impressions of peace. The pictures are then placed on the Internet for everyone to view and enjoy—and to inspire us.

Commentary

There are dozens of children's drawings from around the world. A few classes also sent poems to accompany the pictures. Most pictures have no title or explanation. You may select a picture from the list of young artists who are grouped by country.

Site: The Adventures of Tiger the Kitten

URL: http://www.tigerthekitten.com/index.html

Sponsor: Hub-Boy

Subject Area(s): Art   **Subcategory:** Drawing and Painting

Grade Level(s): Preschool, Elementary

Description

This Web site is dedicated to Tiger the Kitten and features many illustrations of him. There is music, animation, and a variety of activities in which to participate. You will find approximately 40 drawings, each with a theme—all charming and clever.

Commentary

All of the drawings are done using fairly simple computer tools, which may inspire you to try your hand at illustration. Some personal favorites to check out are "Tiger, asleep, in the Land of Giant Fruit" and the animation "It's a bird! It's a plane".

Site: Virtual Museums

URL: http://www.vol.it/UK/EN/ARTE/ingvirtual.html

Sponsor: Video On Line

Subject Area(s): Art   **Subcategory:** Drawing and Painting

Grade Level(s): Middle School, High School

Description

This site provides easy access to links of thirteen art centers and/or monographic studies which the Webmaster has compiled. Each "virtual museum" exists only on the Internet. The listing ranges from classical favorites such as Renoir to modern painters such as Salvador Dali and includes the work of Christo.

Commentary

One especially intriguing link is to Art Crimes. This is actually a site of graffiti which has been photographed before being erased or painted over. The site is divided into city walls, trains, articles, and graffiti shows. Be patient—as the art is hosted from around the world, downloading time is variable.

Section 01. Curriculum Corner

Site: WebMuseum, Paris

URL: http://watt.emf.net/louvre/

Sponsor: Nicolas Pioch

Subject Area(s): Art   **Subcategory:** Drawing and Painting

Grade Level(s): Middle School, High School

Description
The curator of this site has posted thousands of famous paintings which can be indexed by artist or theme. There are hundreds of artists arranged in alphabetical order, and the themes index provides another way of examining the paintings, such as the Italian Renaissance and the Northern Renaissance collections. Enjoy a variety of exhibits and architectural sites in Paris.

Commentary
The Tres Riches Heures is the classic example of a medieval book of hours. Because the book was prepared between 1412 and 1416, it is in poor condition and only available for viewing on the Web. Glorious and magnificent, this type of site certainly seems to justify the very existence of the Internet!

Site: Jasper's Guide to Paperfolding Instructions

URL: http://www.cytex.com/go/jasper/origami/tutorial/techniques.html

Sponsor: John Paulsen

Subject Area(s): Art   **Subcategory:** Origami

Grade Level(s): Elementary, Middle School, High School

Description
Step-by-step directions are given here for creating nine origami art pieces. The egg crate shown in the logo is the only example of a simple model and should take approximately 5–10 minutes. The remaining pieces are classified as low intermediate, intermediate, and high intermediate.

Commentary
If you need a little inspiration to try this technique, go over to Jasper's Original Menagerie. He presents his favorite models from real life and dozens of examples of how they have been depicted through paperfolding. You will love the animals!

Site: Joseph Wu's Origami Page

URL: http://www.datt.co.jp/Origami/index.html

Sponsor: Joseph Wu

Subject Area(s): Art   **Subcategory:** Origami

Grade Level(s): Elementary, Middle School

Description
Origami is the Japanese art of paper folding; the faces in the page's logo were created and folded from paper. Find comments on much of the art work and a selection of new items of worth. There are photo galleries, links to other pages, and directions for construction of your own origami masterpieces.

Commentary
You may be inspired to try your hands at paper folding after viewing the photo gallery. The Creatures of Myth created and folded by Joseph Wu himself are marvelous. If you decide to try origami, there are files and diagrams to guide you in your own creations.

Section 01. Curriculum Corner

Site: Ansel Adams

URL: http://bookweb.cwis.uci.edu:8042/AdamsHome.html

Sponsor: University of California

Subject Area(s): Art　　　　　　　　　　**Subcategory:** Photography

Grade Level(s): Middle School, High School

Description

Ansel Adams, the photographer, was commissioned to produce a "current portrait" of the University of California for the Centennial celebration in 1968. Two annotated biographies provide links to other photographs in his collection. Adams had a long time association with the Sierra Club and is famous for photography of Yosemite National Park and redwood trees.

Commentary

All photographs are in black-and-white and are magnificent. For the individual interested in art and/or ecology, this is a delightful site. Adams' career spanned more than 50 years, and he continues to be an inspiration to young photographers.

Site: HyperVision

URL: http://www.magic.ca/magicmedia/hypervision.html

Sponsor: Magic Online Services

Subject Area(s): Art　　　　　　　　　　**Subcategory:** Photography

Grade Level(s): Middle School, High School

Description

HyperVision is an electronic gallery which supports the work of local and international artists. It makes art available to Internet users 24 hours a day, seven days a week. Artists describe the inspiration for their work and what they used to take the pictures—then you can view the photographs. Click on the smaller picture to enlarge it.

Commentary

The developers of this site invite artists to contact HyperVision about showing their work in this way. They also describe clearly their philosophy against use of the art for other purposes. It should be interesting for students to view varied work and discover the goal or mood or setting the photographer was trying to capture.

Site: LIFE Remembers Alfred Eisenstaedt

URL: http://pathfinder.com/@@78PMsnK3awEAQC@f/Life/eisie/eisie.html

Sponsor: Life Magazine

Subject Area(s): Art　　　　　　　　　　**Subcategory:** Photography

Grade Level(s): Middle School, High School

Description

Alfred Eisenstaedt immigrated to the United States in 1935 and landed a job as one of the first staff photographers for LIFE magazine. He is often referred to as the father of photojournalism. This collection of his photographs spans 50 years and includes his most celebrated cover photos.

Commentary

Many may not be familiar with the name of Alfred Eisenstaedt, but we have all seen his famous photograph of the V-J Day Kiss. It is also interesting to look at the other cover photographs, some of celebrities and others of ordinary Americans.

Section 01. Curriculum Corner

Site: White House News Photographers' Association (WHNPA)

URL: http://www.whnpa.org/~whnpa/

Sponsor: White House News Photographers' Association

Subject Area(s): Art   **Subcategory:** Photography

Grade Level(s): Middle School, High School

Description
The Member Gallery features the work of a different photographer each month or so. Many photographers have worked with several presidents so that their work provides a historical timeline. There is a link to other photojournalism sites which will be useful to the serious photographer.

Commentary
This site is still under development, which is good news. The Member Gallery is so fascinating that it should be expanded for a more extensive look at our presidents at work and at leisure. Check in every couple of months to see how it evolves.

Site: Accounting Resources on the Internet

URL: http://raw.rutgers.edu/raw/internet/internet.html

Sponsor: State University of New Jersey at Rutgers

Subject Area(s): Career and Technology Ed.   **Subcategory:** Accounting

Grade Level(s): High School

Description
This home page is part of a larger site dealing with accounting in all of its aspects. The index includes links to categories in the Big Six accounting firms, professional associations, journals, finance, taxation, education, audit and law, government, publishers, software, and corporate SEC filings.

Commentary
This site is probably of most interest to the business student who is considering accounting as a career choice. It may actually be of help to the future accountant to see what members of the profession consider as the greatest entertainment sites on line.

Site: Big Book - A Whole New Kind of Yellow Pages

URL: http://www.bigbook.com

Sponsor: American Business Information, Inc.

Subject Area(s): Career and Technology Ed.   **Subcategory:** Business Information

Grade Level(s): Middle School, High School

Description
This site hosts a directory of over 16 million U.S. businesses. It is searchable by category, name of business, and/or location, down to a specific zip code. Once a business has been selected, find driving directions and a map to the business location. Visitors who register on the site can "vote" for or against a specific business based on their experience with firm.

Commentary
This is an excellent site to use for many business education projects, including market research. How many restaurants are there in a certain zip code? How many service stations? It will be easy to show how to do targeted mailings by type of business and location. Business profiles and credit reports are also available.

Site: BusinessWeek Online

URL: http://www.businessweek.com/

Sponsor: McGraw-Hill Companies

Subject Area(s): Career and Technology Ed.   **Subcategory:** Business Information

Grade Level(s): High School

Description

Business Week is a best-selling business magazine, much of which is online at this site, together with significant additional resources. There are daily briefings, archives, computer reviews, quotes and portfolios, executive programs, online stories, and much more.

Commentary

In addition to reprints of articles, there are graphs and charts which will be of interest to many students. There are searchable archives which date back to 1991 for the report-writer interested in longitudinal data. This is a very commercial site, but it is clear about areas in which you will need to pay a fee.

Site: Inc. Online

URL: http://www.inc.com/virtualconsult/databases/

Sponsor: Goldhirsh Group

Subject Area(s): Career and Technology Ed.   **Subcategory:** Business Information

Grade Level(s): High School

Description

This Web site for growing companies provides searchable business information databases. These databases include yellow pages, glossaries of financial and marketing terms, demographics, business and computer consultants, zip code directories, franchise finders, and more. Tables of content and selected articles are available from *Inc. Magazine*.

Commentary

The student enrolled in an occupational course will find much of general interest at this site. There is access to both national and some local news, with the opportunity to have a conversation with some consultants in businesses in which you might have an interest.

**Larry's
InfoPOWER Pages
" *Knowledge is Power* "**

Site: Larry's InfoPOWER Pages

URL: http://www.clark.net/pub/lschank/web/business.html

Sponsor: Larry Schankman

Subject Area(s): Career and Technology Ed.   **Subcategory:** Business Information

Grade Level(s): High School

Description

Librarian Larry Schankman has several lists of resources including this one in Business and Economics Resources. The table of contents includes sections on the top five all-purpose sites, business resources, consumer services, numeric data, economics page, reference resources, and stocks and mutual funds.

Commentary

A large number of resources are included here, all annotated. Some of the links are searchable; others provide articles and news of interest. Mr. Schankman states that he no longer has time to maintain and add to this site, but it will remain active—and everything seems to function well at this point.

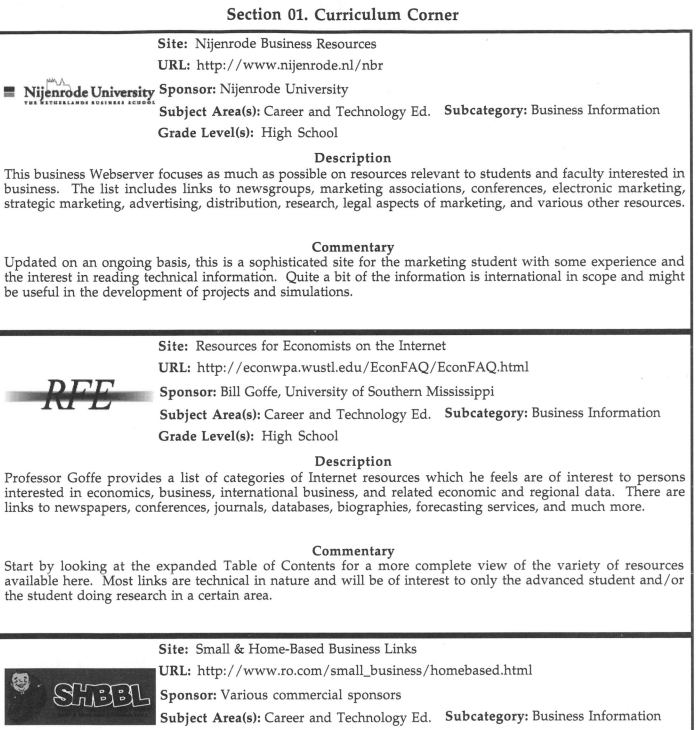

Site: Nijenrode Business Resources

URL: http://www.nijenrode.nl/nbr

Sponsor: Nijenrode University

Subject Area(s): Career and Technology Ed.   **Subcategory:** Business Information

Grade Level(s): High School

Description
This business Webserver focuses as much as possible on resources relevant to students and faculty interested in business. The list includes links to newsgroups, marketing associations, conferences, electronic marketing, strategic marketing, advertising, distribution, research, legal aspects of marketing, and various other resources.

Commentary
Updated on an ongoing basis, this is a sophisticated site for the marketing student with some experience and the interest in reading technical information. Quite a bit of the information is international in scope and might be useful in the development of projects and simulations.

Site: Resources for Economists on the Internet

URL: http://econwpa.wustl.edu/EconFAQ/EconFAQ.html

Sponsor: Bill Goffe, University of Southern Mississippi

Subject Area(s): Career and Technology Ed.   **Subcategory:** Business Information

Grade Level(s): High School

Description
Professor Goffe provides a list of categories of Internet resources which he feels are of interest to persons interested in economics, business, international business, and related economic and regional data. There are links to newspapers, conferences, journals, databases, biographies, forecasting services, and much more.

Commentary
Start by looking at the expanded Table of Contents for a more complete view of the variety of resources available here. Most links are technical in nature and will be of interest to only the advanced student and/or the student doing research in a certain area.

Site: Small & Home-Based Business Links

URL: http://www.ro.com/small_business/homebased.html

Sponsor: Various commercial sponsors

Subject Area(s): Career and Technology Ed.   **Subcategory:** Business Information

Grade Level(s): High School

Description
This hotlist was designed for individuals who want to own a small or home-based business. It includes links to pages on franchises, business opportunities, small business reference material, information to help run and market a small or home-based business, newsgroups, searching tools, services for small business, and more.

Commentary
Distributive education students will find the sections on direct marketing and multi-level marketing useful. Students enrolled in all types of occupational programs will be interested in the diversity of resources available for those who eventually want to own a business rather than work for someone else.

Section 01. Curriculum Corner

Site: The Better Business Bureau

URL: http://www.bbb.org/

Sponsor: Better Business Bureau

Subject Area(s): Career and Technology Ed.   **Subcategory:** Business Information

Grade Level(s): High School

Description

Better Business Bureaus are private non-profit organizations supported largely by membership dues paid by business and professional groups in each Bureau's service area. This Web site contains articles about their primary activities which are providing reports on business firms, providing information about charity groups, resolving consumers' disputes with businesses, and promoting ethical business standards.

Commentary

The resource library provides a wide variety of helpful publications and other information for both consumers and businesses. Home economics students may be interested in the guidelines for children's advertising. Check out the address of the BBB closest to you.

Site: U.S. Business Advisor

URL: http://www.business.gov/

Sponsor: U.S. Department of Commerce

Subject Area(s): Career and Technology Ed.   **Subcategory:** Business Information

Grade Level(s): High School

Description

The U.S. Business Advisor exists to provide business with one-stop access to federal government information, services, and transactions to make the relationship between business and government more productive. There are general information sections organized as common questions, tools, and news of interest to the business community. In addition, the reader can browse the categories or do a keyword search.

Commentary

The news is not quite as current as one would expect but still contains useful information. Check out the article entitled "Department of Labor's Employer's Guide to Teen Worker Safety." There are six categories in the Browse section with dozens of links.

Site: Welcome to Madalyn!

URL: http://www.udel.edu/alex/mba/main/netdir2.html

Sponsor: University of Delaware MBA Program students

Subject Area(s): Career and Technology Ed.   **Subcategory:** Business Information

Grade Level(s): High School

Description

Topics with links at this site are accounting, corporate information, current business news, economics, entrepreneurship, ethics, finance, international business, law, management, marketing, technology, operations, quality, search tools, and career information. There is also a section on how to cite electronic resources in papers.

Commentary

For students considering a business degree and eventual MBA, there is an online tour of the department at the University of Delaware. Some handy features of this site are that the number of links follows each topic plus there is a brief description of the contents of each link.

Section 01. Curriculum Corner

Site: LAWS.COM: A Compendium of Law Resources

URL: http://www.laws.com/resource.html

Sponsor: Law Offices of Dennis Spencer Kahane (CA)

Subject Area(s): Career and Technology Ed.   **Subcategory:** Business Law

Grade Level(s): High School

Description

The resources at this site are organized into the broad groups of United States, Canada, and International. Under each group, there is general information, plus resources regarding federal and state/provincial governments whenever appropriate. There are multinational directories with extensive information about the other English-speaking countries.

Commentary

This is a very specialized site with little information of general use. Because of that, the student who might be interested in laws and regulations affecting certain types of businesses will find this the logical starting place for that search.

Site: LawTalk - Business Law and Personal Finance

URL: http://www.law.indiana.edu/law/bizlaw.html

Sponsor: Indiana University School of Law

Subject Area(s): Career and Technology Ed.   **Subcategory:** Business Law

Grade Level(s): High School

Description

This collection of topics related to business law contains items such as business structures, environmental regulations, forming a corporation, health insurance, corporate responsibility, and investment opportunities. The section on personal finance includes inspecting bank statements, credit card errors, stolen credit cards, living wills, and bounced checks.

Commentary

LawTalk appears to be done completely in audio. This is a slower connection but rather interesting to actually hear a voice discussing the issue. Because the clips are short, this presents a superficial treatment of the subject—but no reading!

Site: Careers in Computing

URL: http://www.tcm.org/resources/cmp-careers/cnc-topdrawer.html

Sponsor: The Computer Museum Network

Subject Area(s): Career and Technology Ed.   **Subcategory:** Computers

Grade Level(s): Middle School, High School

Description

Students interested in computer-related careers can start here and link to "Career Research on the Web" or to the "Careers in Computing" page, which is divided into five areas: support, hardware, software, education & research, and computer-assisted.

Commentary

There is a special section on "Links for Women and Girls" that will be of interest to female students considering a career in the computer industry. The Computer Museum has partnered via this site with The Monster Board to allow easy online searching for jobs by type and geographic location.

Site: AEC Info

URL: http://www.aecinfo.com/

Sponsor: AEC InfoCenter

Subject Area(s): Career and Technology Ed.   **Subcategory:** Construction

Grade Level(s): High School

Description

This Web site is centered around the disciplines of architecture, engineering, construction, and home building. There are sections on building products, support services, software, hardware, government and authorities, news, and interactive forums.

Commentary

There is quite a bit of advertising at this site, but you should also find some information of use. Read about the solar power systems being used for the athletes' village in Sydney for the upcoming Olympics—the world's largest solar project. Check out the cool sites in each of the four disciplines and see a house being built in three days.

Site: Better Homes & Gardens Home Improvement Encyclopedia

URL: http://www.bhglive.com/homeimp/docs/index.html

Sponsor: Books That Work

Subject Area(s): Career and Technology Ed.   **Subcategory:** Construction

Grade Level(s): High School

Description

Home maintenance topics covered include home improvement basics, house structure, decks, plumbing, electrical, yard structures, landscape, tool dictionary, and project calculators. There is an extensive glossary for assistance in understanding terms which have been used on the site or in other home repair situations.

Commentary

All information presented is unique to this site and ranges from suggestions and topics for beginners to more advanced information. For some topics, there are easy-to-follow steps for completing the project. There is quite a bit of advertising, but it doesn't really get in the way of the retrieval of information.

Site: Builder Online

URL: http://www.builderonline.com

Sponsor: Hanley-Wood, Inc.

Subject Area(s): Career and Technology Ed.   **Subcategory:** Construction

Grade Level(s): High School

Description

Affliated with the magazine *Builder,* this site contains information useful to laypeople and professionals in the building trades. There are sections on news, products, an architects' spot, discussions, remodeling, links to other Web sites, and more.

Commentary

Updated daily, this attractive Web page provides a continuing flow of articles and products related to the housing industry. Start with the latest issue of *Builder* magazine, which has a lot of articles and pictures online. Looking at the print pictures will never be the same after visiting this site. Stand in the middle of the room and watch it slowly move until you have viewed every side of the room.

Site: BuilderWeb

URL: http://www.builderweb.com/

Sponsor: BuilderWeb

Subject Area(s): Career and Technology Ed.   **Subcategory:** Construction

Grade Level(s): High School

Description

The mission of this site is to provide the building industry with a site which links to all major kitchen design and manufacturing industry participants as well as trade magazines and associations. Links are provided according to categories such as bath, builder, closet, deck, home center, kitchen, landscape, office furniture, and windows and doors.

Commentary

This is a fairly new site, still under development. There is some useful information with the promise of more to come. Check it out occasionally to see how it is developing.

Site: Building Materials and Wood Technology

URL: http://www.umass.edu/bmatwt/

Sponsor: University of Massachusetts at Amherst

Subject Area(s): Career and Technology Ed.   **Subcategory:** Construction

Grade Level(s): High School

Description

The University of Massachusetts prepares students as professional managers of the companies that manufacture, distribute and use building materials. This Web page contains information about the curriculum, feature articles, career path, and related links to manufacturers, wholesalers, and retailers.

Commentary

Students may find the "Ask the Experts" section useful or may want to proceed directly to the Web links. Topics covered there are associations, products, construction, energy efficiency, building codes, educational institutions, publications, and assorted link pages. The section on Covered Bridges is fascinating!

Site: Construction Trade Resources

URL: http://www.educationindex.com/construct/

Sponsor: College View

Subject Area(s): Career and Technology Ed.   **Subcategory:** Construction

Grade Level(s): High School

Description

The Education Index aims to provide learners and educators with access to the best educational Web sites for a variety of subjects and lifestages. This listing of construction trade resources contains links, arranged alphabetically, with brief annotations regarding each link.

Commentary

Updated on an ongoing basis, this is a great site for the student interested in the construction trades. You might also wish to explore the "Lifestage" section which provides links to resources for individuals at various points in the career development process. Move back and forth to explore the various sections included here.

Site: Home and Design Online

URL: http://www2.hdo.com/

Sponsor: Telescan, Inc.

Subject Area(s): Career and Technology Ed.   **Subcategory:** Construction

Grade Level(s): High School

Description

Called a magazine for innovative home design, this site includes information pertaining to home plans, housing products, housing professionals, housing trades, featured articles, forums, homes for sale, a chat room, and the ability to search the site.

Commentary

This somewhat poorly designed Web page begs for a 50" monitor in order to avoid the excessive scrolling of frames. But the ability to search the house plans for various features is the compensating feature at this site which building trade students might find quite useful. Some high quality photographs are included.

No Graphic Found

Site: HVAC/R Sites on the World Wide Web

URL: http://www.elitesoft.com/sci.hvac/hvac.html

Sponsor: Paul Milligan

Subject Area(s): Career and Technology Ed.   **Subcategory:** Construction

Grade Level(s): High School

Description

This Usenet group of Heating, Ventilating, and Air Conditioning professionals maintains this site with the links organized into categories such as automation, commercial sites, refrigeration and ozone, desiccants, industry groups, publications, schools, related specialties, and other links. The hot links are placed in these categories as one of the members has time to perform this task.

Commentary

There are intriguing titles in the hot links, such as sustainable architecture, but a lot of commercial information also. The organization is somewhat loose and it will require some work by the student to locate appropriate resources, but there are certainly many kinds of them here.

Site: Online Learning Environment (O.L.E.)

URL: http://www.geocities.com/Baja/8205/robotenter.html

Sponsor: Ed Schmidt, Putnam County High School

Subject Area(s): Career and Technology Ed.   **Subcategory:** Engineering

Grade Level(s): High School

Description

Designed by a teacher as a part of his Technology/Engineering curriculum, this site is aimed at students in grades 9–12 enrolled in science, junior engineering, and/or technology. Among the topics included are robotics, lasers, hovercraft, wind energy, solar energy, fiber-optics, superconductors, satellites, tidal power, helicopters, geothermal energy, and much more.

Commentary

There are a lot of sounds and movies at this site, so be patient while the page is loading. There are dozens of fascinating topics, making this a really great site for technically oriented students. Many sections are designed for serious study with quizzes at the end. There is a great deal of information about future study in these fields, too.

Section 01. Curriculum Corner

Site: Canadian Youth Business Foundation

URL: http://www.cybf.ca

Sponsor: The Canadian Youth Business Foundation

Subject Area(s): Career and Technology Ed.   **Subcategory:** Entrepreneurship

Grade Level(s): High School

Description

The Canadian Youth Business Foundation is a nonprofit, private-sector initiative designed to provide mentoring, business support and lending to young Canadian entrepreneurs who are creating new businesses. There are weekly features, resources, a loan program, and quick tips.

Commentary

Students may want to start with the quick tips or the advice section. There is an opportunity to sign up online to connect with a mentor. The resource list is divided by those which are on the Web and those across Canada. There is an interesting article posted on how to use trade exhibits to the best advantage.

Site: Clearinghouse on Entrepreneurship Education (CELCEE)

URL: http://www.celcee.edu/

Sponsor: Center for Entrepreneurial Leadership

Subject Area(s): Career and Technology Ed.   **Subcategory:** Entrepreneurship

Grade Level(s): High School

Description

CELCEE collects, indexes, abstracts, and disseminates information about entrepreneurship education. The intent is to make the rich array of materials related to entrepreneurship education more accessible. This is part of the ERIC database but also includes related links.

Commentary

"Entrepreneurship education is the process of providing individuals with the concepts and skills to recognize opportunities that others have overlooked, and to have the insight and self-esteem to act where others have hesitated." This is a tall order, but there is certainly a wide variety of information sources listed here. The database provides only general searching help, so you need to know what you are looking for.

Site: CNNfn

URL: http://www.cnnfn.com/

Sponsor: Cable News Network

Subject Area(s): Career and Technology Ed.   **Subcategory:** Finance

Grade Level(s): Middle School, High School

Description

As a part of CNN, the financial network specializes in business news with a link to the main site. Regular features include hot stories, markets, small business information, resources, briefings, stock quotes, traveling for business, chat room, and a search capacity.

Commentary

Updated several times daily, this is a dependable source of information about the stock market and other breaking business news. Some stories are presented in brief form; other articles contain the full story. All are written in an easy-to-read format. The section entitled "Hot Stories" is a good starting point on this Web page.

Section 01. Curriculum Corner

Site: Consumer Price Index Calculator

URL: http://woodrow.mpls.frb.fed.us/economy/calc/cpihome.html

Sponsor: Federal Reserve Bank of Minneapolis

Subject Area(s): Career and Technology Ed.   **Subcategory:** Finance

Grade Level(s): Middle School, High School

Description

The Consumer Price Index (CPI) is the ratio of the value of a basket of goods in the current year to the value of the same basket of goods in an earlier year. It measures the average level of prices of the goods and services typically consumed by an urban American family. The site also contains information about inflation rates and a link to the Bureau of Labor Statistics.

Commentary

The calculations are quite simple—type in two years and you can compare prices for those two years. An interesting example is used to compare movie prices for the years in which your parents were teenagers with those of today. You will see that the price for some goods and services is increasing far ahead of inflation (like movies), but other prices are far slower (like the price of eggs).

Site: Edustock

URL: http://tqd.advanced.org/3088

Sponsor: Advanced Network & Services

Subject Area(s): Career and Technology Ed.   **Subcategory:** Finance

Grade Level(s): High School

Description

Edustock is an educational Web page designed to teach what the stock market is and how it can work for you. It includes tutorials on the stock market and how to pick strong stocks plus information on a select group of companies. There is a free realtime (actually 20 minute delayed time) stock market simulation.

Commentary

Created by high school students for the ThinkQuest competition ("Best Entry" award winner), this exemplifies the capability and energy in our young people. The Stock Market tutorial is clearly organized, and it is possible to skip over topics with which you might already be familiar.

FinanCenter

Site: FinanCenter

URL: http://www.financenter.com/

Sponsor: FinanCenter, Inc.

Subject Area(s): Career and Technology Ed.   **Subcategory:** Finance

Grade Level(s): High School

Description

This private, for-profit company provides personal finance calculators and related information in the following categories: homes, autos, credit lines, credit cards, budgeting, saving, insurance, investing, and retirement. Each topic contains a variety of calculators.

Commentary

This site contains most of the areas taught in consumer education. The calculators can be a little complex at first but keep working with them. You may find it helpful to print out the results for further study. The section on "What's it worth to reduce my spending?" might provide some motivation for budgeting.

Section 01. Curriculum Corner

Site: Good News Bears Stock Market Project

URL: http://www.ncsa.uiuc.edu/edu/rse/RSEyellow/gnb.html

Sponsor: UISES

Subject Area(s): Career and Technology Ed.   **Subcategory:** Finance

Grade Level(s): Middle School, High School

Description

This Web-based Interactive Stock Market Learning Project for students includes an overview, purpose and objectives, teacher resources, student resources and Web resources. The project revolves around an interactive stock market competition between classmates using realtime stock market data from the New York Stock Exchange and NASDAQ.

Commentary

This project is still free and available online. Plans are underway, however, to change the interface, make the simulation more sophisticated (and appropriate for high school through college students), and to charge a fee. There is still lots of useful information here for both students and teachers.

Site: InvestSmart

URL: http://library.advanced.org/10326/

Sponsor: Advanced Network & Services

Subject Area(s): Career and Technology Ed.   **Subcategory:** Finance

Grade Level(s): High School

Description

In the interactive stock market simulation, each "player" is given $100,000 to invest in over 5,000 companies. Other features include investment basics and lessons, easy setup for classes or investment clubs, a "Group Directory" view of each student portfolio, research capability of stocks, and a benchmark of each portfolio.

Commentary

This simulation was developed by students for the ThinkQuest competition. The reader should begin with the investment basics and lessons before proceeding to the simulation. Make sure that you check out the real-life examples of three teenagers who got started investing.

Site: Lemonade Stand

URL: http://www.littlejason.com/lemonade/index.html

Sponsor: Jason Mayans

Subject Area(s): Career and Technology Ed.   **Subcategory:** Finance

Grade Level(s): Middle School

Description

The objective of this Web version of the classic supply and demand simulation is to make money. Players must decide how much lemonade to make, how much to charge for each cup, and how much to spend on advertising. Players must consider some random variables such as weather and construction blockage.

Commentary

After registering for the game (only for the purpose of scorekeeping), each lemonade stand owner is given $5.00 to start off, with 25 days to make as much money as possible. This is a fun game—and many readers will not have seen the original computer simulation—but it still offers some practical learning about supply, demand, and profit.

Section 01. Curriculum Corner

Site: NETworth Insider

URL: http://networth.galt.com/www/home/insider/insider.html

Sponsor: Quicken

Subject Area(s): Career and Technology Ed.   **Subcategory:** Finance

Grade Level(s): High School

Description

The NETworth Insider is a source for finding information relevant to personal investing and financial management. Resources include an explanation of types of investments, economic resources, and other general information. The glossary will be helpful to both students and teachers. The database is searchable by keywords.

Commentary

There are many advertisements on this site but no hard sells. As might be expected, information is totally up-to-date. There are stock quotations and currency exchange rates available.

Site: Quote.Com

URL: http://www.quote.com/

Sponsor: Quote.com

Subject Area(s): Career and Technology Ed.   **Subcategory:** Finance

Grade Level(s): High School

Description

This private corporation provides financial market data to Internet users which includes current quotes on stock, options, commodity futures, mutual funds, and indices. In addition, there is business news, earnings forecasts and reports, company profiles, and other assorted news.

Commentary

This home page loads slowly because of the large number of advertisements with motion. That said, it is still a nicely organized site which provides information in an easy-to-find format. The Investor's Almanac is interesting as is the constantly changing information about stocks and other business news.

Site: The Best Finance Sites on the World Wide Web

URL: http://www.bev.net/education/schools/admin/finance-hot-spots.html

Sponsor: Larry W. Arrington

Subject Area(s): Career and Technology Ed.   **Subcategory:** Finance

Grade Level(s): High School

Description

Listed in alphabetical order, these links are described so that the reader can choose the items of interest. The emphasis is on personal finance, which would be useful to almost everyone, with topics such as investments, saving, financial aid for college, a financial encyclopedia, income tax assistance, guides to banking, and connections to several publications.

Commentary

The "best" sites are accompanied with a listing of their awards, and there is a further grouping of runner-up sites. Your Life, depicted in the logo, is one of several links which are ideal for new investors and/or individuals beginning to learn about managing financial affairs.

Section 01. Curriculum Corner

The Mortgage Calculator

Site: The Mortgage Calculator

URL: http://www.ibc.wustl.edu/ibc/mort.html

Sponsor: Hugh Chou

Subject Area(s): Career and Technology Ed.   **Subcategory:** Finance

Grade Level(s): High School

Description

A form is given for entering appropriate data so that your total mortgage and monthly payments will be calculated. The developer also has this and various other calculator programs available as downloadable software.

Commentary

There is a variety of additional calculators which students and adults might find interesting, such as tuition savings, how much house can you afford, and simple savings. Entering the values is very easy but would probably be of interest only to mature students.

The Young Investor Website

Site: The Young Investor Website

URL: http://www.younginvestor.com/

Sponsor: Liberty Financial

Subject Area(s): Career and Technology Ed.   **Subcategory:** Finance

Grade Level(s): Middle School, High School

Description

The Young Investor Website is a place to learn about money and perhaps earn some. The reader registers by age and selects a tour guide. The program branches from there to provide options for reading, question-answer, investment games, and other information.

Commentary

A companion parent site is somewhat commercial by encouraging parents in investments for their children but also offers an interesting forum for parents with Dr. Tightwad. The site has attractive graphics and some sound.   You may want to download the publication "A Young Investor's Guide To Annual Reports."

Site: World Bank Group

URL: http://www.worldbank.org

Sponsor: The World Bank

Subject Area(s): Career and Technology Ed.   **Subcategory:** Finance

Grade Level(s): High School

Description

The World Bank was organized in 1946 and continues to expand. Lending to developing countries for education alone has exceeded $1 billion per year. The extensive library of articles includes such topics as agriculture, economics and trade, environment, finance and private sector development, and human resources and poverty.

Commentary

Since this site is updated even on weekends, news is always current. For research purposes, there is data on all countries in regard to GNP and other economic and socioeconomic indices. Searches can be done by keyword also.

Section 01. Curriculum Corner

Site: WWW Virtual Library: Finance

URL: http://www.cob.ohio-state.edu/dept/fin/overview.html

Sponsor: The Ohio State University

Subject Area(s): Career and Technology Ed.   **Subcategory:** Finance

Grade Level(s): High School

Description

The university's Department of Finance maintains this site for academia and investors. The index includes categories such as banks, exchanges, world market, insurers, investment banks, current quotes, market news, and specialized sections for investors, researchers, students, executives, and educators.

Commentary

The "For Students" section is oriented primarily for college students. You will have better luck examining the "New Links" and "Popular Sites" sections from the index. The Dow of Pooh is fun to read; otherwise, this is mostly serious business and investment information.

Site: Aunt Edna's Kitchen

URL: http://www.cei.net/~terry/auntedna/

Sponsor: Terry and Edna Campbell

Subject Area(s): Career and Technology Ed.   **Subcategory:** Home Economics

Grade Level(s): High School

Description

The cooking utilities include descriptions of various spices, ingredient substitutions, food equivalant tables, temperature conversions, fractions/decimal equivalents, and the conversions for U.S., metric, and imperial units. There is also a recipe file, nutrition information from the United States Department of Agriculture, and links to other sites.

Commentary

Food service students (and others interested in food preparation) will find both useful and just-for-fun information at this site. The recipes look terrific—Aunt Edna is keen on desserts but doesn't let you forget about vegetables and main dishes.

Site: Consumer Information Center

URL: http://www.pueblo.gsa.gov/

Sponsor: U.S. General Services Administration

Subject Area(s): Career and Technology Ed.   **Subcategory:** Home Economics

Grade Level(s): Middle School, High School

Description

The full text version of hundreds of the best federal consumer publications are available here, online and free. There are sections on children, food and nutrition, health, housing, money management, federal programs, consumer resources, and other items of general interest.

Commentary

Updated daily, this site contains information that for the most part is serious and useful, with an occasional touch of humor such as the list of the top ten uses for a moldy fruitcake. In addition to the standard features, it is possible to search the site for information which may not be readily identifiable in the categories.

Site: FabricLink

URL: http://www.FabricLink.com/

Sponsor: FabricLink

Subject Area(s): Career and Technology Ed.   **Subcategory:** Home Economics

Grade Level(s): High School

Description

FabricLink is an educational resource and communication link developed for the textile/apparel/retail industry and its consumers. The major sections include a consumer guide, fabric university (fiber, fabrics, and clothing care), and a retailer's forum. There is also an online expert to answer questions related to purchase and care of textiles.

Commentary

The "What's New" section contains not only specific textile information but articles of interest to almost everyone. There is a stain removal chart and an article on the sport-specific socks worn by the NBA and NFL. Marketing students may want to examine the retailing section.

Site: Learn2 Set a Table

URL: http://learn2.com/06/0608/0608.html

Sponsor: Panmedia

Subject Area(s): Career and Technology Ed.   **Subcategory:** Home Economics

Grade Level(s): Middle School, High School

Description

General home economics and food service students will find a step-by-step lesson with diagrams for the bare basics of tablesetting, the standard placesetting, the formal placesetting, variations of formal placesetting, and adapting to special circumstances. Related tutorials include carving a turkey, choosing a wine, serving champagne, and sharpening a knife.

Commentary

Information is presented in such a clever and colorful manner that you might forget that it is actual essential learning for correct food service. There are useful hints on organization and guidelines for determining the type of placesetting appropriate to the occasion.

Site: Top Marketing Tips, Tricks & Techniques

URL: http://www.disclosure.com/marketing/toptricks.html

Sponsor: Disclosure

Subject Area(s): Career and Technology Ed.   **Subcategory:** Marketing

Grade Level(s): High School

Description

The marketing tips and techniques are divided into nine sections: advertising, direct marketing, marketing management, promotions, public relations, sales, telemarketing, trade shows, and marketing law. Each of these sections links to a variety of articles under each topic.

Commentary

Although this site does not appear to be maintained any longer, the existing information is still quite useful. The articles are straightforward and practical but totally lacking in graphics or attention-getting devices. These tips will help you write better ads and brochures and make an impact on customers.

Section 01. Curriculum Corner

Site: Arabic Program

URL: http://philae.sas.upenn.edu/Arabic/arabic.html

Sponsor: University of Pennsylvania

Subject Area(s): Foreign Language   **Subcategory:** Arabic

Grade Level(s): High School

Description

There are many resources for the teacher interested in starting an Arabic language program for older adolescents and/or adults.   Software for learning Arabic can be downloaded, but some Arabic audio lessons are online (after downloading the RealAudio player, which is also online).

Commentary

The music and QuickTime movie sections are still experimental and have some problems in their use.   The Picture Album from the Islamic World is, however, ready for use and magnificent. There are paintings and frescoes from dozens of countries. This is not designed as a travel site, but it is certainly motivational as one.

Site: EFLWEB

URL: http://www.u-net.com/eflweb

Sponsor: Intec Publishing

Subject Area(s): Foreign Language   **Subcategory:** ESL and Bilingual

Grade Level(s): High School

Description

EFLWEB is an online magazine for those teaching and learning English as a Foreign Language. The site is available in French, Spanish, Italian, German, and Portuguese. There is a bookshop and software store online for purchases in addition to product reviews and directories.

Commentary

Students will probably head first for the Learning Resources—links to sites to support the learning of English. Some of the links are a little puzzling—travel and life in Belize? Other links are more obviously appropriate for help in writing and using idioms, both American and British.

Site: ARTFL Project

URL: http://humanities.uchicago.edu/ARTFL/ARTFL.html

Sponsor: University of Chicago

Subject Area(s): Foreign Language   **Subcategory:** French

Grade Level(s): High School

Description

Collaboration between French and American universities has resulted in the translation and/or preservation of many documents. Among the works found at this site are an encyclopedia, several dictionaries, the French Bible, medieval documents, early Dante manuscripts, and search capacity for many other documents.

Commentary

Several documents are present in trial version to examine the issues of making them available on the Internet. Not to be missed are the illuminated manuscripts, especially the Book of Hours. This glorious page, done around 1360, is made even more interesting by the knowledge that technology is essential for the average person to view it.

Section 01. Curriculum Corner

Site: English and French Language Resources

URL: http://www.wfi.fr/volterre/home.html

Sponsor: Linda Thalman

Subject Area(s): Foreign Language   **Subcategory:** French

Grade Level(s): High School

Description

Written in both English and French, this site provides resources for English learners and teachers who are working on French as well as for French learners and teachers who wish to learn more English. There is information about foreign language conferences, links to travel sites, search capacity, and a What's New section.

Commentary

This site appears to be updated monthly but also offers a free subscription to the VolTerre newsletter. The What's New section has dozens of new links for both students and teachers. The main focus of the site is learning and teaching English (for French speakers), but this provides some rich resources in reverse.

Site: Le Cordon Bleu Restaurant

URL: http://sunsite.unc.edu/expo/restaurant/restaurant.html

Sponsor: Le Cordon Bleu, Inc.

Subject Area(s): Foreign Language   **Subcategory:** French

Grade Level(s): Middle School, High School

Description

Le Cordon Bleu dates back to 1827 with the publication of a Cordon Bleu cookbook. By 1895 there was a weekly publication in which famous chefs gave advice and discussed the pleasures of the table. The following year, cookery courses began and continue to flourish today in order to promote the fine art of French cooking.

Commentary

There isn't actually a great deal of French here, but students will find menus for the entire week in French, with translation in English. This imaginary restaurant was inspired by the world-famous cooking school which has trained chefs from more than 50 countries.

Site: Tennessee Bob's Famous French Links

URL: http://www.utm.edu/departments/french/french.html

Sponsor: Tennessee Bob Peckham

Subject Area(s): Foreign Language   **Subcategory:** French

Grade Level(s): High School

Description

Now in its 2nd edition, this supersite claims more than 5,000 links to everything French. The main headings are Finding New Francophone Sites, Books and Literature, Art and General Culture, History of France and the French-Speaking World, Virtual Francophone Tourism, the French Language, Press and Radio/TV, Education in French-Speaking Schools, and French across the Curriculum.

Commentary

If you are at all interested in France and/or French, there will be plenty to capture your attention in this grouping of links. Annotations would have helped, but often the title alone provides a good clue to the content of the link. Links are in both English and French—the title of the link is obviously a good clue. "Reading a French Newspaper" is both fun and useful.

Section 01. Curriculum Corner

Site: The French Page

URL: http://philae.sas.upenn.edu/French/french.html

Sponsor: University of Pennsylvania

Subject Area(s): Foreign Language **Subcategory:** French

Grade Level(s): High School

Description

There are six lessons on French history and civilization to be found here. In each lesson, there are ten annotated slides. When you click on the speaker, you are able to both read the French description of the slide and hear it read to you.

Commentary

There is no English support at this site—everything is in French. However, the slides are beautiful and even for those with a little knowledge of the French language, it is possible to determine much of what is being discussed. It helps greatly to be able to both read and hear the French.

Site: German Internet Project

URL: http://www.uncg.edu/~lixlpurc/GIP/

Sponsor: Andreas Linxl, University of North Carolina at Greensboro

Subject Area(s): Foreign Language **Subcategory:** German

Grade Level(s): Middle School, High School

Description

The project is a group of resources for German studies clustered under six headings: German Studies Trails, Elementary Exercises in German, Exercises for All Levels of German, KinderWeb, Multimedia Language Center, and a German Culture Course. For teachers of German, there are further resources for inservice and personal development.

Commentary

This is a great site because of the expertise of the Webmaster and his ability to combine his personality with the selections. You will need to know at least a little German in order to navigate well, but you certainly don't have to be proficient. No matter what your level, go straight for the KinderWeb. You did know that "Kinder" is German!

Site: Germany, Austria, Switzerland

URL: http://www.geocities.com/Athens/1446

Sponsor: Frau Hogan, Pt. Pleasant High School

Subject Area(s): Foreign Language **Subcategory:** German

Grade Level(s): Middle School, High School

Description

This page provides links to major cities, German literature, newspapers, magazines, language resources, and European information. The list is scrollable and provides links to resources in German and English. There are no annotations, so it is necessary to explore and use the bookmark when something proves interesting.

Commentary

Jetzt, a German magazine for teens, is presented online. There are lots of links to geography, travel, and culture sites which might be useful in preparing reports. Many sites are available in both German and English—for most, you are on your own with the German language.

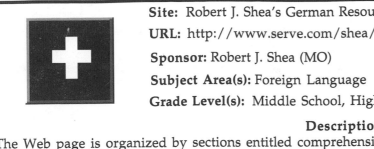

Site: Robert J. Shea's German Resources

URL: http://www.serve.com/shea/germany.html

Sponsor: Robert J. Shea (MO)

Subject Area(s): Foreign Language   **Subcategory:** German

Grade Level(s): Middle School, High School

Description
The Web page is organized by sections entitled comprehensive pages; Internet in Germany; news, info, and tourism; news and culture; computer applications; German language instruction; entertainment and freetime; and miscellaneous. The scrollable lists have brief annotations and sometimes pictures to help preview before following a link.

Commentary
There are extensive directions to take here, but follow a wonderful link to a site of customs, traditions, and origins of holidays—many of these are German, but other countries and cultures are included as well. Also don't miss the link to The German Way, with extensive information about books, cinema, travel, photos, etc.

Site: Saarbruekcer Zeitung Newsline

URL: http://www.sz-sb.de/

Sponsor: Saarbruekcer Zeitung Newsline

Subject Area(s): Foreign Language   **Subcategory:** German

Grade Level(s): High School

Description
This news service from Germany provides up-to-the-minute information about different news categories from a variety of locations. The site is written entirely in German.

Commentary
Not only is this site current, it is actually a day ahead of us! You really must be able to read German fluently to reap much from this site, although for students and teachers of the language, it is a find.

Site: Hellenistic Greek Linguistics Pages

URL: http://www.entmp.org/HGrk/

Sponsor: James K. Tauber

Subject Area(s): Foreign Language   **Subcategory:** Greek

Grade Level(s): High School

Description
Hellenistic Greek was the dialect spoken between 300 B.C. and 600 A.D. The resources at this site are provided for a scholarly study of the Hellenistic Greek language, including the New Testament. There is a Greek grammar reference, fonts, bibliographies, and software.

Commentary
Most of the references are scholarly in nature and will likely be useful to the student trying to decipher old Greek texts.

Site: Hindi Program

URL: http://philae.sas.upenn.edu/Hindi/HindiProgram.html

Sponsor: University of Pennsylvania

Subject Area(s): Foreign Language   **Subcategory:** Hindi

Grade Level(s): Middle School, High School

Description
Designed by a Hindi professor at the University of Pennsylvania, this site contains many audio lessons for use in teaching. The remainder of the site consists of links to photography albums of Northern India.

Commentary
The University of Pennsylvania was the first institution in the United States to offer language instruction in Hindi and other South Asian languages after World War II. Students interested in architecture will also find this site interesting. The small picture attached is of the Dilwara Temple of Jains which dates back from 1030 BC. All of the pictures are annotated with the builder, if known, and the location.

Site: PERMIAS NYC

URL: http://www.nyc.permias.org/

Sponsor: Indonesian Students Association

Subject Area(s): Foreign Language   **Subcategory:** Indonesian

Grade Level(s): High School

Description
The Indonesian Students Association provides information about upcoming events, university programs, archives, and current news. The site is in a mixture of languages, but the main menus are in English.

Commentary
The links provided here are especially interesting. Check out the Indonesian home page with information about batik, a beautiful handmade cloth unique to the region, and wonderful pictures of the flowers grown there.

Site: Learn to Speak Italian

URL: http://www.eat.com/learn-italian/

Sponsor: Lipton, Inc.

Subject Area(s): Foreign Language   **Subcategory:** Italian

Grade Level(s): Middle School, High School

Description
There are six lessons provided at this site, including conversation for a happy family, useful phrases, travel, food, romance, and an Italian folk tale. The quality of the sound is excellent and offered are a variety of words and sentences for practice.

Commentary
The Learn to Speak Italian site is a great deal of fun. So what if all the old world recipes start with a jar of Ragu spaghetti sauce—you still get a nice feel for the language. "Rispetta sempre la tua mamma."

Section 01. Curriculum Corner

Site: Akatsukayama High School

URL: http://www.kobe-cufs.ac.jp/kobe-city/cityoffice/57/050/akatsuka/home.html

Sponsor: Board of Education, Kobe, Japan

Subject Area(s): Foreign Language   **Subcategory:** Japanese

Grade Level(s): High School

Description
The home page for this school in Kobe, Japan, is written entirely in excellent English with verbal comments and writings contributed by the students. The tour of the school features the building, with cherry trees in bloom, and takes you through the school year to picture students engaged in various activities.

Commentary
Pick the location first so that you will have an idea of where Kobe is located in relation to the rest of Japan. This is an impressive site! There are just a few well-chosen links that help you have a better idea about the food eaten on a daily basis as well as for holidays, and you can visit other local schools, too.

Site: Irasshai Launch Pad

URL: http://www.ceismc.gatech.edu/irasshai/culwww/toc.html

Sponsor: Georgia Public Broadcasting

Subject Area(s): Foreign Language   **Subcategory:** Japanese

Grade Level(s): Middle School, High School

Description
Links at this site are listed alphabetically under the categories of architecture, arts, business, culinary treats, culture-pop, culture and tradition, ecology and environment, education, geography, geology, government, history, language, life in Japan, media, meteorology, music, pets, recreation, science and technology, sports, student work, and travel information.

Commentary
This is surely one of the best language sites available! Most of the information is available in Japanese, with English translation. The picture of the koban was taken from one of the student's works; these are tiny police stations scattered throughout the country.

Site: Kabuki for Everyone

URL: http://www.fix.co.jp/kabuki/kabuki.html

Sponsor: National Theater

Subject Area(s): Foreign Language   **Subcategory:** Japanese

Grade Level(s): Middle School, High School

Description
Kabuki is a traditional form of Japanese theater founded early in the 17th century. It is a sophisticated, stylized form of theater which continues to be an important part of the Japanese culture. This site contains kabuki sounds, a makeup demonstration, and articles about Kabuki's history with summaries of plays.

Commentary
Since women's roles are played by men, the makeup demonstration is especially interesting. There is up-to-the-minute information about the theater schedule and links to other sites involving Japanese theater. Although there is almost no Japanese language on this site, it does provide a nice feel for this aspect of the culture.

Section 01. Curriculum Corner

Site: OROPPAS

URL: http://210.132.56.150/OROPPAS/HomePage2.html

Sponsor: Inner City OROPPAS

Subject Area(s): Foreign Language   **Subcategory:** Japanese

Grade Level(s): Elementary, Middle School

Description

This is a primarily Japanese site, but some sections have an English version. The Art Gallery and Concert are both available in English. Current newspapers, bookstore, and information about television are in Japanese only.

Commentary

The graphics are charming, and the site seems intended for very young children, based on the drawings alone. However, most of the site requires quite a bit of reading...and a great deal of Japanese literacy. There is a request for help from anyone who can assist in turning the other sections into English.

Site: Travelers' Japanese with Voice

URL: http://www.ntt.co.jp/japan/japanese/

Sponsor: Nippon Telegraph and Telephone Company

Subject Area(s): Foreign Language   **Subcategory:** Japanese

Grade Level(s): Middle School, High School

Description

This tutorial in Japanese is divided into pronunciation, essential expressions, vehicles, "asking the way," restaurants, and shopping. Each section provides the opportunity to practice many different phrases after hearing them spoken.

Commentary

There is really only one link—and it is a major one. Japanese Information contains extensive information about the country and is available in both Japanese and English. Be sure to hear the national anthem, check out sumo wrestling, and browse the travel section for some motivation to learn Japanese.

Site: A Course in Latin

URL: http://hydra.perseus.tufts.edu/cgi-bin/text?lookup=ag+gram.+toc

Sponsor: Allen and Greenough

Subject Area(s): Foreign Language   **Subcategory:** Latin

Grade Level(s): High School

Description

The Table of Contents for this course includes letters and sounds, words and their forms, the sentence syntax, parts of speech, and construction of the three cases in Latin.

Commentary

James J. O'Donnell has provided the link to this site; he teaches a class in Medieval Latin at the University of Pennsylvania. You may want to move backwards to his site at http://ccat.sas.upenn.edu:80/jod/ for additional resources in medieval studies.

Section 01. Curriculum Corner

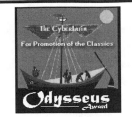

Site: The Latin Page

URL: http://www.geocities.com/Athens/Acropolis/3773

Sponsor: University of Nebraska, Lincoln

Subject Area(s): Foreign Language   **Subcategory:** Latin

Grade Level(s): Middle School, High School

Description

Designed as classroom aids for 7–12 Latin teachers and their students, the site contains lesson plans with background material on architecture, the Roman army, and the Roman forum. In addition, there is a collection of links with Latin content such as dictionaries, the Bulfinch's Mythology, interactive games, sound clips, and information about organizations for individuals interested in the classics.

Commentary

Unfortunately, many of the links appear to be closed—and you may have wanted to hear Elvis sing in Latin—but there is still an extensive amount of material. There are many sounds, music, graphics, software to download, and games.

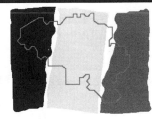

Site: Belgian Federal Government Online

URL: http://belgium.fgov.be/

Sponsor: Federal Information Service, Belgium

Subject Area(s): Foreign Language   **Subcategory:** Multiple Languages

Grade Level(s): High School

Description

Find information about the country of Belgium, its people, its Council of Ministers, cities and communes, and more.

Commentary

Begin your search by clicking on a button (Nederlands, Français, Deutsch, or English) to indicate the language you prefer. Even if you choose English, in subcategories, you will encounter some of the information only available in languages other than English.

Site: Berlitz: Helping the World Communicate

URL: http://www.berlitz.com/whatsnew.html

Sponsor: Berlitz International, Inc.

Subject Area(s): Foreign Language   **Subcategory:** Multiple Languages

Grade Level(s): Elementary, Middle School, High School

Description

This site offers foreign language tapes, phrasebooks, and more for sale but also has fun activities and informative resources available for free. Check out Kid Talk for games for kids and tips for parents or teachers. And in the Cafe Berlitz, you can check out current news from around the world, post or read questions and responses on the bulletin board, or perhaps test your knowledge of the world by taking a culture quiz.

Commentary

There are some resources for a wide range of ages here—from dictionary pictures that can be printed and colored, to jokes in a variety of languages, to brain teasers to figure out, to tips for parents as they help their kids master languages.

Section 01. Curriculum Corner

Site: Bienvenidos Bienvenus Welcome

URL: http://www.geocities.com/athens/acropolis/1506

Sponsor: Jim (high school Spanish teacher) and Crew

Subject Area(s): Foreign Language   **Subcategory:** Multiple Languages

Grade Level(s): Middle School, High School

Description

The foreign languages included at this site are French, German, and Spanish. For each language, there is a set of links plus another section dealing specifically with newspapers and magazines. There are general foreign language resources plus projects and homework help for students. New sections are added for holidays and special events.

Commentary

Winner of many awards and updated frequently, this is a valuable site for both students and teachers. There are supervised chat rooms available for students in Spanish and the opportunity for adding a free Web page to the site. This site is a little slow to load, but worth the wait.

Site: CALL Lab

URL: http://www.tcom.ohiou.edu/OU_Language/

Sponsor: Ohio University

Subject Area(s): Foreign Language   **Subcategory:** Multiple Languages

Grade Level(s): Middle School, High School

Description

Languages sponsored here include primarily French, German, Japanese, Spanish and English (ESL/EFL). Students will find documents in the chosen language from newspapers and books, with emphasis on travel, music, museums, cooking, and the language itself.

Commentary

Teachers will find an extensive, well-organized list of resources divided into those which are appropriate for teachers of any language and those which are language-specific. Student resources might be used alone or incorporated into lessons.

Site: Cultures of the Andes

URL: http://www.andes.org

Sponsor: Ada and Russ Gibbons

Subject Area(s): Foreign Language   **Subcategory:** Multiple Languages

Grade Level(s): Middle School, High School

Description

Quechua is the language of the Indians who live in the Andes Mountains of South America, particularly Peru and Bolivia. Using both Spanish and /or English, the reader can become familar with the Quechua language through songs, jokes, dances, poetry, expressions, riddles, and some basic lessons.

Commentary

There are lots of photographs here, and every attempt has been made to present the language in a fun-to-learn manner. Some basic trivia: When the Peace Corps was first begun in the '60s, they used Quechua to test the language-learning capabilities of future Volunteers—on the correct assumption that none of them had been exposed to this language.

Section 01. Curriculum Corner

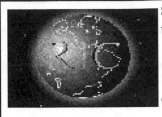

Site: Dictionaries & Translators

URL: http://rivendel.com/~ric/resources/dictionary.html

Sponsor: Riverdell International Communications

Subject Area(s): Foreign Language   **Subcategory:** Multiple Languages

Grade Level(s): High School

Description

The centerpiece of this site is the current dictionaries for dozens of languages. There are also multilingual dictionaries, indexes, software, and online translation and language course services. There are language chat sites offered for many countries.

Commentary

Because of the enormous databases involved, this site operates very slowly, but it has some wonderful capabilities. Uni-Verse is a multilingual realtime chat which lets you use the translators at this site to communicate across the world—unbelievable!

Site: European Home Page

URL: http://s700.uminho.pt/europa.html

Sponsor: Jose Miranda

Subject Area(s): Foreign Language   **Subcategory:** Multiple Languages

Grade Level(s): Middle School, High School

Description

An outline map of Europe is overlaid with flags from different countries. By clicking on the flag, the reader is moved to the home page of that country and then to various other links. Most sites have some English available, but the flavor of the country comes through best in the native language.

Commentary

Cultural and travel information is grouped into a separate site with maps; the icon for this page shows the location of Slovenija in relation to the rest of Europe.

Site: Foreign Language Exercises on the Web

URL: http://www.uncg.edu/~lixlpurc/publications/MLCexerc.html

Sponsor: Andreas Linxl, University of North Carolina at Greensboro

Subject Area(s): Foreign Language   **Subcategory:** Multiple Languages

Grade Level(s): Middle School, High School

Description

Based at the Multimedia Language Center at the University of North Carolina, Mr. Linxl used his expertise to examine the World Wide Web for the best examples of foreign language exercises for elementary to advanced levels of proficiency. The examples involve language, literature, and culture in French, German, Greek, Hebrew, Italian, Japanese, Latin, Russian, and Spanish.

Commentary

There are additional links to language education, including some resources for ESL. This is not an exhaustive listing of links but rather just a few chosen in each language category, based on the author's judgment.

Section 01. Curriculum Corner

Site: Foreign Language Resources on the Web

URL: http://www.itp.berkeley.edu/~thorne/HumanResources.html

Sponsor: Steve Thorne, Berkeley Language Center

Subject Area(s): Foreign Language   **Subcategory:** Multiple Languages

Grade Level(s): Middle School, High School

Description

This resource list is presented as a starting point for examining the thousands of foreign language resources available on the Web. The author has been selective in listing resources in the following languages: Arabic, Chinese, Czech, French, German, Hebrew, Italian, Latin, Middle English, Portuguese, Russian, Scandinavian languages, South Asian languages, Spanish, Swahili, Tagalog, Turkish, and Yiddish.

Commentary

Well-organized and annotated, the primary interest here is on language, with culture and travel information being secondary. There are many sound files for listening, fonts to download in many languages, and information about learning and teaching different languages.

Site: Foreign Languages for Travelers

URL: http://insti.physics.sunysb.edu/~mmartin/languages/languages.html

Sponsor: The Travlang Company

Subject Area(s): Foreign Language   **Subcategory:** Multiple Languages

Grade Level(s): Middle School, High School

Description

Over 50 languages are offered for learning at this site. A menu of flags from each country is presented with the language written in the native tongue and in English. After selecting a language, the learner is offered a category of words and phrases to choose for pronouncing.

Commentary

This private site has gone public because of the growing interest in learning a foreign language. It is helpful for assistance in actually learning language for travel but is also fun just to listen to little bits of other languages. The sound capability is terrific; you have time to hear the word or phrase three times and practice your pronunciation in between the speech.

Site: Language Learning Resource Center

URL: http://ml.hss.cmu.edu/llrc/

Sponsor: Carnegie Mellon University

Subject Area(s): Foreign Language   **Subcategory:** Multiple Languages

Grade Level(s): High School

Description

The Language Learning Resource Center is a function of the Department of Modern Languages. There is a media catalog for each language describing the resources of the university. There is also information about courses and services to the community.

Commentary

Most useful to the teachers or students who access this home page are the language links, grouped by individual languages and a category of language-related resources. Readers of the page are invited to add their own link.

Site: Sara Jordan Presents

URL: http://www.sara-jordan.com/edu-mart

Sponsor: Jordan Music Productions

Subject Area(s): Foreign Language   **Subcategory:** Multiple Languages

Grade Level(s): Elementary, Middle School

Description

These educational resources are for kids, parents, and teachers. Online resources include a coloring book, lullabies from around the world, classrooms online, snacks from around the world, and links to cool sites for kids. Resources are selected and annotated under each category.

Commentary

This site is really multicultural rather than multilingual, but it does provide a nice flavor of countries around the world. Coloring pages and coloring cartoons can be downloaded from many countries for use off line. Some material is available for purchase.

Site: The Applied Linguistics Virtual Library

URL: http://alt.venus.co.uk/VL/AppLingBBK/welcome.html

Sponsor: Birkbeck College, University of London

Subject Area(s): Foreign Language   **Subcategory:** Multiple Languages

Grade Level(s): High School

Description

The list of indexes available at this site includes teaching and research institutions, conferences and seminars, data archives, electronic journals, print journals, publishers, electronically available papers, and other resources.

Commentary

This is a site for serious language students and/or those interested in exploring careers in linguistics. The section of Web courses is still under development and hopefully will be useful to students interested in exploring this field further.

Site: The Linguist List

URL: http://www.emich.edu/~linguist/

Sponsor: Eastern Michigan University

Subject Area(s): Foreign Language   **Subcategory:** Multiple Languages

Grade Level(s): High School

Description

This site presents information about the profession, research, publications, pedagogy, computer support, language resources, and links to linguistic sites. Teachers will find announcements regarding conferences and new publications in their field.

Commentary

Many of the pedagogical references relate to college courses, but there is still sufficient information to interest teachers at all levels. "Sounds of the World's Animals" is a delightful link that would be useful in teaching ESL students as well as foreign languages.

Section 01. Curriculum Corner

Site: Transparent Language

URL: http://www.transparent.com/

Sponsor: Transparent Language, Inc.

Subject Area(s): Foreign Language   **Subcategory:** Multiple Languages

Grade Level(s): Middle School, High School

Description

Twelve languages are supported at this Web page. The reader selects from the following languages: English, French, German, Italian, Latin, Chinese, Portuguese, Japanese, Russian, Swedish, Spanish, and Dutch. Under each language is a listing of products to teach that language and links to culture, food and drink, and travel in that area.

Commentary

While this is an obviously commercial site, the company provides far more than information about its own products. The culture, food, and travel sections are extensive and cover many countries (if the language is spoken in more than one country).

No Graphic Found

Site: Universal Survey of Languages

URL: http://www.teleport.com/~napoleon/

Sponsor:

Subject Area(s): Foreign Language   **Subcategory:** Multiple Languages

Grade Level(s): Middle School, High School

Description

This is a demonstration project which the author hopes will be expanded to include many of the world's languages. There are numerous languages on this site—from Afrikan and Arabic to Spanish and Tamil. Each language group is represented by native speakers so that students can hear dialects.

Commentary

It will be interesting for students to compare languages and dialects. For example, the French student can easily compare "standard French" with "Louisiana French Creole." You will find a mailing list to subscribe to if you are interested in discussion of the creation of cross-platform standards for electronic dictionaries.

Site: VCU Trail Guide to International Sites & Language Resources

URL: http://www.fln.vcu.edu/

Sponsor: Robert Godwin-Jones, Virginia Commonwealth University

Subject Area(s): Foreign Language   **Subcategory:** Multiple Languages

Grade Level(s): Middle School, High School

Description

There are activities and information available in French, German, Italian, Russian, and Spanish. Links to resources in other languages are organized into categories, as well as general references for language learning and teaching of foreign languages.

Commentary

The sound and light shows are fun, since you will be able to hear real people in a variety of languages. Trail guides are available in the five major languages, and they provide wonderful and varied resources for anyone with an interest in the language and/or country of origin.

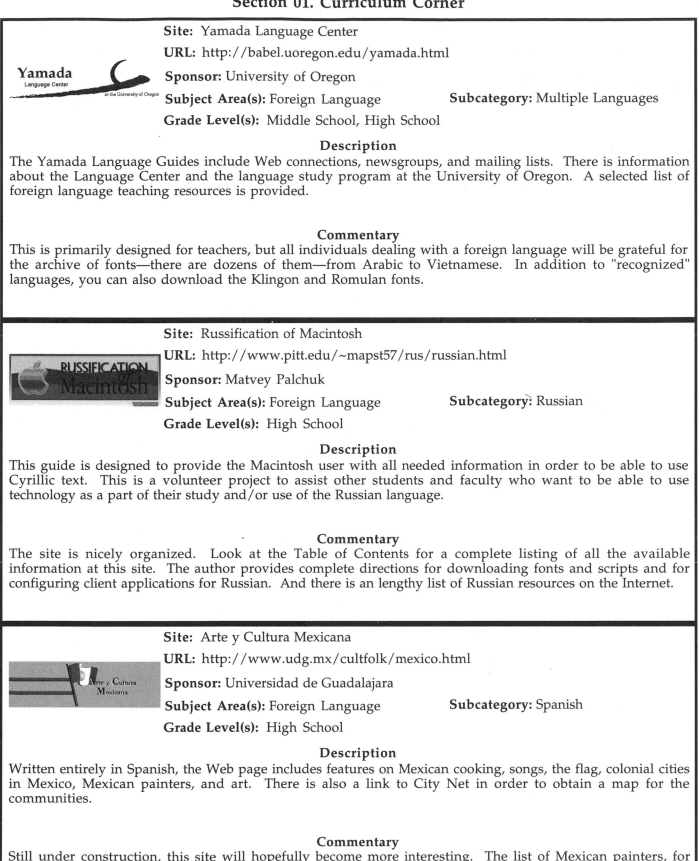

Site: Yamada Language Center

URL: http://babel.uoregon.edu/yamada.html

Sponsor: University of Oregon

Subject Area(s): Foreign Language   **Subcategory:** Multiple Languages

Grade Level(s): Middle School, High School

Description

The Yamada Language Guides include Web connections, newsgroups, and mailing lists. There is information about the Language Center and the language study program at the University of Oregon. A selected list of foreign language teaching resources is provided.

Commentary

This is primarily designed for teachers, but all individuals dealing with a foreign language will be grateful for the archive of fonts—there are dozens of them—from Arabic to Vietnamese. In addition to "recognized" languages, you can also download the Klingon and Romulan fonts.

Site: Russification of Macintosh

URL: http://www.pitt.edu/~mapst57/rus/russian.html

Sponsor: Matvey Palchuk

Subject Area(s): Foreign Language   **Subcategory:** Russian

Grade Level(s): High School

Description

This guide is designed to provide the Macintosh user with all needed information in order to be able to use Cyrillic text. This is a volunteer project to assist other students and faculty who want to be able to use technology as a part of their study and/or use of the Russian language.

Commentary

The site is nicely organized. Look at the Table of Contents for a complete listing of all the available information at this site. The author provides complete directions for downloading fonts and scripts and for configuring client applications for Russian. And there is an lengthy list of Russian resources on the Internet.

Site: Arte y Cultura Mexicana

URL: http://www.udg.mx/cultfolk/mexico.html

Sponsor: Universidad de Guadalajara

Subject Area(s): Foreign Language   **Subcategory:** Spanish

Grade Level(s): High School

Description

Written entirely in Spanish, the Web page includes features on Mexican cooking, songs, the flag, colonial cities in Mexico, Mexican painters, and art. There is also a link to City Net in order to obtain a map for the communities.

Commentary

Still under construction, this site will hopefully become more interesting. The list of Mexican painters, for example, contains a brief bibliography but no paintings. The lovely photograph of a restaurant incites interest in the food, but very little information is there.

Section 01. Curriculum Corner

Site: I Touch the Future...I Teach!

URL: http://geocities.com/Athens/4444

Sponsor: Coqui (WI)

Subject Area(s): Foreign Language   **Subcategory:** Spanish

Grade Level(s): Middle School, High School

Description

Spanish links include countries and regions, education and information, food and recipes, music and art, newspapers and magazines, plus personal pages. There is also an extensive group of Educator links, arranged alphabetically, many with the same name.

Commentary

Under "Music and Art" you will find dozens of sites involving pop and ancient culture. It's a highly selective group. There is Gloria Estefan and Luis Miguel, but no Alejandro Fernandez—just a matter of taste or access. Because of the extensive number of links, expect to find quite a few which will not open.

Site: SBCC's Spanish Department Home Page

URL: http://www.sbcc.cc.ca.us/academic/spanish/spanish.html

Sponsor: Spanish Department, Santa Barbara City College

Subject Area(s): Foreign Language   **Subcategory:** Spanish

Grade Level(s): High School

Description

The Spanish language resources are divided into the following sections: cultural information, search engines in Spanish, news about Spanish-speaking countries, magazines, literature, tools, sports, radio stations, CIA information, and US State Department travel advisories. The cultural information is further divided into Central and South America, the Caribe, Mexico, and Spain.

Commentary

There are lots of photographs and music at these sites, which is helpful in examining the cultural diversity of the Spanish-speaking nations. The painting for the logo is Mayan, but there are many modern cultural items included, too. Students who read Spanish well will find the magazine, books, and sports links interesting.

Site: Spanish Alphabet

URL: http://mac94.ralphbunche.rbs.edu/spanish.html

Sponsor: Ralph Bunche School

Subject Area(s): Foreign Language   **Subcategory:** Spanish

Grade Level(s): Preschool, Elementary

Description

Ralph Bunche School is a multicultural, multilingual school in New York City. This site showcases a project of the early grades in which they have drawn pictures to match the Spanish alphabet letter, written a sentence, and signed with their names.

Commentary

There is a very nice picture of a gato (cat) and one students will especially enjoy of zapatos (shoes). Some of the letters are still missing, so perhaps you would like to try doing an alphabet picture of your own. The school home page has other information which may also be of interest.

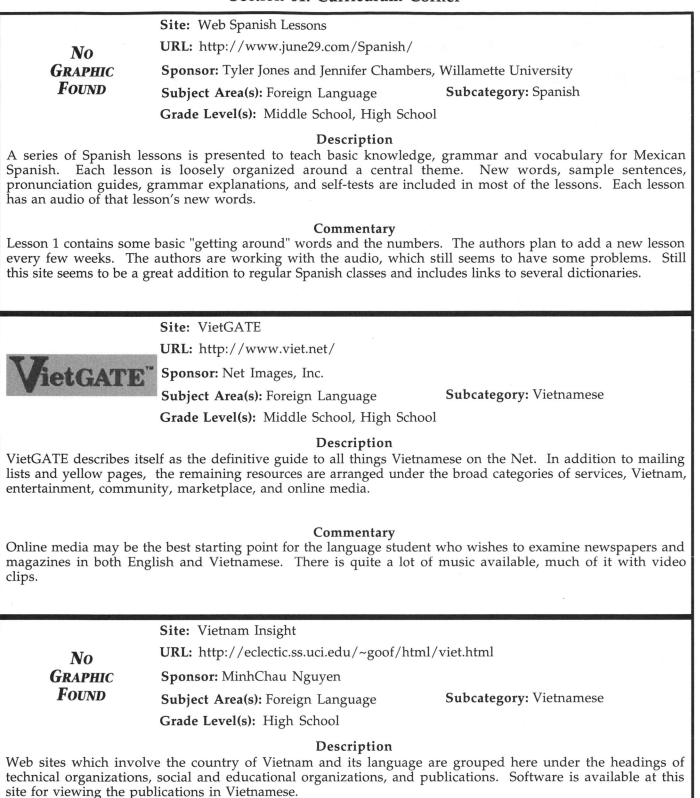

No Graphic Found

Site: Web Spanish Lessons

URL: http://www.june29.com/Spanish/

Sponsor: Tyler Jones and Jennifer Chambers, Willamette University

Subject Area(s): Foreign Language   **Subcategory:** Spanish

Grade Level(s): Middle School, High School

Description

A series of Spanish lessons is presented to teach basic knowledge, grammar and vocabulary for Mexican Spanish. Each lesson is loosely organized around a central theme. New words, sample sentences, pronunciation guides, grammar explanations, and self-tests are included in most of the lessons. Each lesson has an audio of that lesson's new words.

Commentary

Lesson 1 contains some basic "getting around" words and the numbers. The authors plan to add a new lesson every few weeks. The authors are working with the audio, which still seems to have some problems. Still this site seems to be a great addition to regular Spanish classes and includes links to several dictionaries.

VietGATE™

Site: VietGATE

URL: http://www.viet.net/

Sponsor: Net Images, Inc.

Subject Area(s): Foreign Language   **Subcategory:** Vietnamese

Grade Level(s): Middle School, High School

Description

VietGATE describes itself as the definitive guide to all things Vietnamese on the Net. In addition to mailing lists and yellow pages, the remaining resources are arranged under the broad categories of services, Vietnam, entertainment, community, marketplace, and online media.

Commentary

Online media may be the best starting point for the language student who wishes to examine newspapers and magazines in both English and Vietnamese. There is quite a lot of music available, much of it with video clips.

No Graphic Found

Site: Vietnam Insight

URL: http://eclectic.ss.uci.edu/~goof/html/viet.html

Sponsor: MinhChau Nguyen

Subject Area(s): Foreign Language   **Subcategory:** Vietnamese

Grade Level(s): High School

Description

Web sites which involve the country of Vietnam and its language are grouped here under the headings of technical organizations, social and educational organizations, and publications. Software is available at this site for viewing the publications in Vietnamese.

Commentary

Vietnam Insight is a monthly publication in English which provides news and cultural information. Unfortunately a number of the links are closed (it appears to be maintained by a college student), but there are several items from which to choose.

Section 01. Curriculum Corner

Site: A Welsh Course

URL: http://www.cs.brown.edu/fun/welsh/Welsh.html

Sponsor: Mark Nodine

Subject Area(s): Foreign Language   **Subcategory:** Welsh

Grade Level(s): Middle School, High School

Description
This is an online, beginning course in Welsh, with emphasis on developing conversational skills in Welsh as it is currently spoken. The Table of Contents provides information about the various lessons and the appendices.

Commentary
The course is being reworked with frames and, hopefully, some sounds. The extensive charts on vowel pronunciation are only for true linguists. Much more interesting are the many links to Wales which provide a great motivation for actually learning some Welsh.

Site: Educaid University

URL: http://www.educaid.com/index_nn.html

Sponsor: Educaid

Subject Area(s): Guidance and Counseling   **Subcategory:** Financial Aid for College

Grade Level(s): High School

Description
Educaid offers government and private loans for all levels of education from parents of students in private elementary school to medical students. Features include how to get into college, financial aid information, and an online debt management seminar. Educaid On-Line offers the opportunity to view loan information through the Web site by entering the student's Social Security number and birth date.

Commentary
High school students and their parents can access lots of useful information here that is free. Counselors will find the Financial Aid Professionals page helpful. Check the News and Regulations section for legal updates and EdLines, an online quarterly newsletter. Free brochures and loan applications may be requested in bulk through the Communicate With Us page.

Site: FAFSA on the Web

URL: http://www.fafsa.ed.gov/

Sponsor: U.S. Department of Education

Subject Area(s): Guidance and Counseling   **Subcategory:** Financial Aid for College

Grade Level(s): Middle School, High School

Description
"FAFSA" is the acronym for Free Application for Federal Student Aid. From this Web site, students can apply for federal financial aid online. This site is well-organized and easy to use. Visit the "Supported Browsers" section to check whether secure transactions can work, then the "What you need to fill out this form" section to find out what information is needed, and complete the step-by-step process to submit an application.

Commentary
Other online information available here includes the "Families Guide to the 1997 Tax Cuts for Education," "Finding Out about Financial Aid," "Applying for Federal Student Aid," and the "Guide to Defaulted Student Loans," which describes options for resolving problems that occur when student loans go into default.

Section 01. Curriculum Corner

Site: Office of Postsecondary Education

URL: http://www.ed.gov/offices/OPE/

Sponsor: U.S. Department of Education

Subject Area(s): Guidance and Counseling   **Subcategory:** Financial Aid for College

Grade Level(s): High School

Description
The Office of Postsecondary Education offers information for students seeking financial assistance. The Financial Aid for Students page provides financial aid guides, application materials and other financial aid information. There are also pages for Financial Aid Professionals, News and Highlights, Exploring the Web, and Funding for Institutions.

Commentary
Families should note that the Families' Guide to the 1997 Tax Cuts for Education outlines tax benefits for parents who are sending or planning to send their children to college, including information on the HOPE Scholarship tax credit, Lifetime Learning tax credit, and other benefits and tax cuts available.

Site: Student Guide 1997-98

URL: http://www.ed.gov/prog_info/SFA/StudentGuide/

Sponsor: U.S. Department of Education

Subject Area(s): Guidance and Counseling   **Subcategory:** Financial Aid for College

Grade Level(s): Middle School, High School

Description
The Student Guide is the most comprehensive resource on student financial aid from the U.S. Department of Education. Grants, loans, and work-study are the three major forms of student financial aid available through the federal Student Financial Assistance Programs. Updated each year, The Student Guide tells students about the programs and how to apply for them.

Commentary
This site also has a link to FAFSA, a Web site where students can apply for aid electronically. Students may additionally contact the Federal Student Aid Information Center. It is open Monday through Friday, from 8:00 am to 8:00 pm (Eastern Time) at 1-800-4-FED-AID (1-800-433-3243) .

Site: The Financial Aid Information Page

URL: http://www.finaid.org/

FinAid The Financial Aid Information Page   **Sponsor:** National Association of Student Financial Aid Administrators

Subject Area(s): Guidance and Counseling   **Subcategory:** Financial Aid for College

Grade Level(s): Middle School, High School

Description
This site consists of a comprehensive collection of links to every conceivable resource involving student financial aid. The site is organized into sections on navigation, assistance, tools, discussion, sources of aid, loans, government/schools, special interest, and other.

Commentary
One important link on this page is to "FAFSA," the Department of Education's "Free Application for Federal Student Aid" Web site, where students can apply online for federal financial aid. There are also links to searchable online databases of scholarships and fellowships.

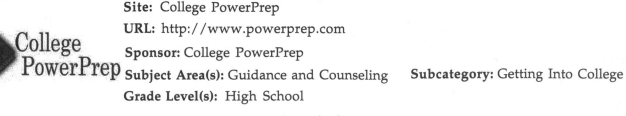

Site: College PowerPrep

URL: http://www.powerprep.com

Sponsor: College PowerPrep

Subject Area(s): Guidance and Counseling   **Subcategory:** Getting Into College

Grade Level(s): High School

Description
Visit this site to find lessons, quizzes, and resources to assist you in mastering the SAT test. Start by clicking on SAT Labs to check out the resources there. A new SAT Tip of the Day is featured at the site each day. Be aware that some of the software offered here must be purchased, but there is also a lot of free downloadable software and online activities and resources you can take advantage of.

Commentary
Be sure to check out the College Advice button for help in determining which college is best for you, for junior or senior year timetables for getting everything in, for College Board strategies, and for financial aid information.

Site: Fishnet

URL: http://www.jayi.com/Open.html

Sponsor: The College Guide

Subject Area(s): Guidance and Counseling   **Subcategory:** Getting into College

Grade Level(s): High School

Description
Fishnet is an electronic guide for students preparing to go to college. Students can build a profile of themselves and then send it to colleges of interest. College search and financial aid information is available, and you can complete an application to be sent online.

Commentary
In addition to the very helpful college and financial information, you may find some of the articles useful. "Finding a Perfect Fit" offers some excellent advice for students considering colleges as does "What College Viewbooks Don't Show You."

Site: TESTPREP.COM™

URL: http://www.testprep.com

Sponsor: Stanford Testing Systems, Inc.

Subject Area(s): Guidance and Counseling   **Subcategory:** Getting into College

Grade Level(s): High School

Description
Get ready for the SAT! TESTPREP.COM™ claims to be the only Web site on the Internet with free and complete online test preparation for the SAT test. The site includes individual diagnosis of math and verbal skills and practice lessons with over 700 problems. Additional tests to be posted to this site include the ACT and several post-graduate exams.

Commentary
The instructions are easy to read and understand. Visitors must register with TESTPREP.COM before using the site. In order to have individual skills analyzed, students must acquire and complete the College Board booklet *Taking the SAT-I*, available from high school counselors (usually free) and have completed test at hand to transfer answers to the electronic answer sheet.

Site: Instituciones Educativas Americanas

URL: http://www.sc.ehu.es/unis_americanas.html

 Sponsor: Universidad del Pais Vasco

Subject Area(s): Guidance and Counseling   **Subcategory:** Locating a College

Grade Level(s): High School

Description

Search for information on U.S. colleges and universities. The site provides a comprehensive alphabetical list of links to schools, some of which offer an electronic application that can be printed and completed or actually completed and electronically transmitted. Some schools will respond to e-mailed questions.

Commentary

This is a good resource for high school students who are researching potential colleges or universities to attend. There are also links to the U.S. Department of Education and other education-related resources.

Site: Peterson's Education Center

URL: http://www.petersons.com

Sponsor: Peterson's

Subject Area(s): Guidance and Counseling   **Subcategory:** Locating a College

Grade Level(s): High School

Description

Find information on undergraduate colleges, graduate schools, and summer programs. Searching can be done by SAT scores, a major or a sport, or accreditation. The Financing Education section provides information and resources regarding steps that must be taken to obtain financial assistance. Also, find information on accredited private schools. Some schools provide application information; some online applications are available.

Commentary

The 14 main sections can be accessed from buttons or printed menus. This is a terrific reference for high school students, counselors, and parents. Searching by college name was fun, until the search ended with little data except information about purchasing the Peterson Guide. Most information seems available at no cost.

Site: Cyber High School

URL: http://www.webcom.com/~cyberhi/

Sponsor: Cyber High School

Subject Area(s): Guidance and Counseling   **Subcategory:** Online Coursework

Grade Level(s): High School

Description

Cyber High School is a private high school offering college prep courses via the Internet. Open to all students who meet entrance requirements and have Internet access. Cyber High School accepts full- and part-time students and offers a complete High School curriculum. Students go online to get assignments, communicate via e-mail, and conduct research. Instructors have "real time" office hours for questions/answers.

Commentary

Much of the required work is to be completed offline according to the assignment. The Frequently Asked Questions page is a valuable place to start for those interested in Cyber High School. Be sure to investigate whether credits earned through Cyber High School will transfer in your state. The Library resources cut across subject areas and could be useful to any high school student interested in using the Internet as a resource.

Section 01. Curriculum Corner

Site: Mindquest

URL: http://www.bloomington.k12.mn.us/mindquest/index.html

Sponsor: Bloomington Public Schools

Subject Area(s): Guidance and Counseling   **Subcategory:** Online Coursework

Grade Level(s): High School

Description

Mindquest, a public high school diploma program completely on the Internet, is open to adults and teens 17+ who do not have a high school diploma and to high school juniors and seniors who need extra credits. Mindquest uses the Internet, bulletin boards and e-mail to communicate with staff and students. Enrollment is available at no cost to eligible Minnesota residents and by tuition to qualified out-of-state residents.

Commentary

Persons holding a GED may also enroll in Mindquest. Interested individuals must complete and submit an application and must have completed one high school math course with a grade of C or better. The program is designed so that it may be completed by most people in one year. New courses begin every few months. It is recommended that students outside Minnesota check with their local school district.

ADOL:
Adolescence Directory On-Line

Site: Adolescence Directory Online

URL: http://education.indiana.edu/cas/adol/adol.html

Sponsor: Indiana University—Center for Adolescent Studies

Subject Area(s): Guidance and Counseling   **Subcategory:** Resources

Grade Level(s): High School

Description

Adolescence Directory Online (ADOL) is a guide to Internet sites for teens and the adults in their lives. From the main page select Conflict and Violence, Mental Health Issues, Health Issues, Counselor Resources or Teens Only to connect to pages full of links with a brief description of each.

Commentary

A "What's New" link is helpful for those who only want to see the latest additions to the site. ADOL has won several awards and supports other educational sites which are linked to this page. Share the ADOL address with teens, parents, and counselors whom you know.

No
Graphic
Found

Site: Learning Style Inventory

URL: http://www.hcc.hawaii.edu/hccinfo/facdev/lsi.html

Sponsor: Honolulu Community College

Subject Area(s): Guidance and Counseling   **Subcategory:** Resources

Grade Level(s): Middle School, High School

Description

Knowing how you learn can provide valuable information for yourself and for those with whom you work. Studying, completing projects and assignments, and working with others are all affected by your learning style. The Learning Style Inventory page provides one tool you can use to determine your own preferred style.

Commentary

Parents or teachers may use this inventory with students to help them gain a better understanding about themselves and the strategies they can use to maximize their potential. Students will enjoy self-assessing and recognizing why they may prefer to receive information in some ways more than others.

Job Bank

Site: America's Job Bank

URL: http://www.ajb.dni.us/

Sponsor: America's Job Bank

Subject Area(s): Guidance and Counseling   **Subcategory:** World of Work

Grade Level(s): High School

Description

The *Job Market Info* button links visitors to *The Occupational Outlook Handbook*, which projects information on employment in 250 occupations accounting or 7 of 8 jobs in the U.S. It also describes each occupation, what workers do on the job, required training and education, earnings, and working conditions. The State Occupational Projections feature projects growth for an occupation and allows an occupation to be compared among states.

Commentary

Parents, students, and educators seeking information about careers and projected areas for job growth will find America's Job Bank very useful. Job seekers may search for openings in the United States or specific states, using a menu, keywords, or occupational codes. Links to public and private employment services are also provided.

CAREERMagazine

Site: Career Magazine

URL: http://www.careermag.com/

Sponsor: Career Magazine

Subject Area(s): Guidance and Counseling   **Subcategory:** World of Work

Grade Level(s): High School

Description

Career Magazine has a resume bank for potential employers and job openings for individuals seeking work. In addition, there are articles about the world of work, an entrepreneur's corner, information about job fairs, consultant directories, and on-campus services.

Commentary

The current lead article is entitled "Full Time Jobs: Will They Exist in the Year 2000?" It will be very thought-provoking to high school students and counselors as the author presents evidence that most companies in the early 2000's will provide full-time jobs to only about 30% of their employees. The Career Forum provides guidelines for resume writing and interviewing.

Site: Career Mosaic

URL: http://www.careermosaic.com

Sponsor: Career Mosaic

Subject Area(s): Guidance and Counseling   **Subcategory:** World of Work

Grade Level(s): High School

Description

Career Mosaic offers a searchable jobs database by job title, company name, city, and/or country. There are online job fairs and listings of employers who support this site. The Employment Library provides a collection of employment-related resources and links to many more.

Commentary

As might be expected, online databases are heavily weighted with technology-related jobs. Job seekers are encouraged to look for their dream job in order to get a view of what is actually available. The Career Resource Center provides tips on job-hunting, resume writing, wage and salary information, and more.

Site: CareerPath.com

URL: http://www.careerpath.com/

Sponsor: CareerPath.com

Subject Area(s): Guidance and Counseling   **Subcategory:** World of Work

Grade Level(s): Middle School, High School

Description

CareerPath.com claims that it posts nearly 500,000 new jobs on the Internet every month and is updated daily by newspapers across the U.S. Jobs may be searched for by newspaper, job category, and keyword. Use the Employer Profiles link to read about some of the top employers in the United States along with links to their sites.

Commentary

The Employers Profiles provides a brief description of the company, types of jobs held, benefits, contact information and more. Some of the acronyms may hinder those outside the company in understanding all of the information; however, there is still much that is valuable for interested individuals.

Site: CAREERscape

URL: http://www-personal.ksu.edu/~dangle/icia/

Sponsor: Kansas State University

Subject Area(s): Guidance and Counseling   **Subcategory:** World of Work

Grade Level(s): Middle School, High School

Description

Twelve career areas are listed for exploration: artistic, scientific, plants and animals, protective, mechanical, industrial, business, selling, accommodating, humanitarian, leading, and physical performing. As an alternative, 246 occupations are listed for exploration with the related codes from the Dictionary of Occupational Titles.

Commentary

Stick with the 12 broad groupings of career areas. The arrangement of information about each career is complete and easy to follow. Some occupations are obviously listed under two career areas; for example, physical therapist is included under both scientific and humanitarian areas. You may find the use of split screens, which scroll through 12 lines at a time, somewhat annoying.

Site: CareerWeb

URL: http://www.careerweb.com/

Sponsor: CareerWeb Corporation

Subject Area(s): Guidance and Counseling   **Subcategory:** World of Work

Grade Level(s): Middle School, High School

Description

CareerWeb hosts a jobs database with over 13,000 listings from over 240 companies, and it is searchable by job category, state, city, and (optional) keywords. Applicants can upload their resumes and employers can list job openings. There is a special section for international jobs, and a variety of other products and services are available, including career-related books, a "Career Doctor" help section, and a Career Inventory exercise.

Commentary

One interesting exercise would be to have students imagine they are employers and have them search the resume bank for qualified applicants. Are the right keywords in the students' resumes so that the potential employers can find them? How do they stack up against other applicants located by that same search? How can they edit their resumes to improve their chances of getting interviewed?

Site: FutureScan Magazine

URL: http://www.FutureScan.com/

Sponsor: United Multimedia, Inc.

Subject Area(s): Guidance and Counseling   **Subcategory:** World of Work

Grade Level(s): Middle School, High School

Description
Teens will find this career guidance magazine valuable in exploring interests and directions for their life pathways. FutureScan is published monthly featuring questions and answers, interviews, and practical information about the world of work. The "Books" button links to a reading list about careers and related topics while "Gurus" provides leading experts' answers to e-mail sent to the FutureScan site.

Commentary
The FutureScan magazine reaches kids through their interests and approaches the world of work at their level. Publishers invite reader input through a survey.

Site: JobBank USA

URL: http://www.jobbankusa.com/

Sponsor: JobBank USA

Subject Area(s): Guidance and Counseling   **Subcategory:** World of Work

Grade Level(s): High School

Description
Acquiring skills for finding a job is valuable for students' career and vocational development. The JobBank USA site assists visitors in building a resume using the provided format and searches the World Wide Web's job databases. The results of each job search are provided in a table for review and include salary, geographical location and experience required.

Commentary
The JobBank USA Web site can be used as a teaching tool for students in developing use of the Internet for career exploration and job location.

Site: JobSmart: Career Guides

URL: http://jobsmart.org/tools/career/spec-car.html

Sponsor: Northern California Library Services

Subject Area(s): Guidance and Counseling   **Subcategory:** World of Work

Grade Level(s): Middle School, High School

Description
Although developed as a California Job Search Guide, the Career Guide section is generic and will apply to every state. A list of sites is provided by occupational groupings such as accounting, business, engineering, health, retail, science, trades, and more. Information given at the site includes type of education needed, earning capacity, kind of environment, employment outlook, and sometimes personal stories.

Commentary
This site is well organized, so it is easy to explore several careers as well as get information about writing resumes and cover letters. They have an interesting section on electronic job hunting which is definitely to the point.

Section 01. Curriculum Corner

Site: O*NET

URL: http://www.doleta.gov/programs/onet/

Sponsor: U.S. Department of Labor's Employment and Training Administration

Subject Area(s): Guidance and Counseling   **Subcategory:** World of Work

Grade Level(s): Middle School, High School

Description
What do you need to know about the career in which you are interested? O*NET, a comprehensive database, can provide insight into the workplace. Job requirements, worker requirements, worker characteristics, and experience requirements are a few of the descriptors found in the O*NET database.

Commentary
The information found in the O*NET database and guidelines will assist in School-to-Work curricula, counseling, and student career exploration. Terminology used in the databank are defined. The Web site assists interested individuals in tracking the progress of this project to its completion between 1997-1999.

Site: Occupational Outlook Handbook

URL: http://stats.bls.gov/ocohome.html

Sponsor: Bureau of Labor Statistics

Subject Area(s): Guidance and Counseling   **Subcategory:** World of Work

Grade Level(s): High School

Description
For over 50 years, the Bureau of Labor Statistics has produced this document which provides statistics regarding present occupations and the outlook for specific occupations in the future. Both well-known and little-known occupations are included in the database with information regarding methods used to collect the data.

Commentary
If this is your first time using the *Occupational Outlook Handbook* in hardcopy or online format, you may want to start with the Guide to the Handbook. Particularly useful are the sections on tomorrow's jobs, sources of career information, and finding and evaluating a job offer.

Site: Online Career Center

URL: http://occ.com

Sponsor: Online Career Center

Subject Area(s): Guidance and Counseling   **Subcategory:** World of Work

Grade Level(s): High School

Description
This commercial site is sponsored by a large number of recruiting firms. Job seekers can search by location and/or job titles. One can also sign up with a search firm for additional help. The program has "job seeker agents" who will continue to search the database on a daily basis and provide updates to the job seeker.

Commentary
Most jobs listed appear to be high level, requiring quite a bit of training. The best use of this database might be with high school students as a motivation to seek further education. Try having them search any location under the keywords "entry level."

Section 01. Curriculum Corner

Site: Achoo

URL: http://www.achoo.com/

Sponsor: MNI Systems Corporation

Subject Area(s): Health   **Subcategory:** Miscellaneous

Grade Level(s): Middle School, High School

Description

This is an excellent online source of information about human health topics. It is divided into three sections: Human Health and Disease, which discusses human health, health problems and how they are treated; Health Administration, which contains a hotlist of links to topics in health administration; and the Business of Health, which contains a hotlist of links to specialized topics in the business of healthcare.

Commentary

The first section will be of primary interest to students of health; the second and third sections will be useful to both practicing as well as aspiring health professionals doing research about the profession. There is also a link to a Web site delivering online education to health professionals on an experimental basis, sponsored by the same organization.

Site: Food Safety and Nutrition

URL: http://ificinfo.health.org

Sponsor: International Food Information Council

Subject Area(s): Health   **Subcategory:** Miscellaneous

Grade Level(s): Middle School, High School

Description

The purpose of the International Food Information Council is to provide sound, scientific information on food safety and nutrition to both professionals and consumers. Some examples of the broad topics are child/adolescent nutrition, food labeling, food additives, food allergy, sweeteners, and more. Each section has a brochure—an easy-to-read summary of the main issue—and it is followed by many research articles.

Commentary

Students in health and home economics will find this site useful in understanding current thinking on nutrition. The food biotechnology section is particularly interesting. The section on lifestyle choices and physical activity will benefit everyone.

Site: Global Health Network

URL: http://info.pitt.edu/HOME/GHNet/GHNet.html

Sponsor: University of Pittsburgh

Subject Area(s): Health   **Subcategory:** Miscellaneous

Grade Level(s): High School

Description

The Global Health Network is an alliance of health experts who are developing an information structure for the prevention of disease in the 21st century. The developers are looking for feedback from individuals regarding the information presented in four formats: lay, scientific, editor, and hypertext comic versions. Information can be found on health organizations and publications.

Commentary

Since the network is available in Japanese, Portuguese, Spanish, and German, it might be of additional interest to language students. The hypertext comic book unfortunately downloads between pages so is a little too slow for all but the most dedicated readers.

Section 01. Curriculum Corner

Site: Go Ask Alice!

URL: http://www.columbia.edu/cu/healthwise/alice.html

Sponsor: Healthwise, Columbia University

Subject Area(s): Health   **Subcategory:** Miscellaneous

Grade Level(s): Middle School, High School

Description

"Go Ask Alice" is an interactive question and answer service from the Health Education division of Columbia University Health Services. Alice will answer questions each week about health, including sexuality, sexual health, relationships, general health, fitness and nutrition, emotional well-being, and alcohol and drugs.

Commentary

Under each category, dozen of questions are listed with answers from the health professionals. You can scroll through the categories or search by keyword. Some questions are funny, but most were obviously asked by other teens who seemed to need the information. And you can write a question yourself for an answer online.

Site: Health Explorer

URL: http://dpalm2.med.uth.tmc.edu/ptnt/tocptnt.html

Sponsor: University of Texas at Houston Medical School

Subject Area(s): Health   **Subcategory:** Miscellaneous

Grade Level(s): Middle School, High School

Description

This forum is designed to assist the nonmedical individual in understanding health and a healthy lifestyle. There are sections on exercise, anemia, asthma, cancer, chicken pox, heart disease, and more. Articles range from simple summaries to detailed research.

Commentary

One can eventually get to a database with all major illnesses linked to other references. In a random selection, it was discovered that many of the links were closed. The reader may save time and frustration by staying on the first page of new articles and research.

Site: HealthAtoZ

URL: http://www.healthatoz.com/

Sponsor: Medical Network, Inc.

Subject Area(s): Health   **Subcategory:** Miscellaneous

Grade Level(s): Middle School, High School

Description

This is a consumer-oriented Web site with lots of timely information about health-related issues that have been covered in both professional and general print publications. Its database has been cataloged by medical professionals.

Commentary

Students looking for a health-related research topic can start looking here, not only to pick a topic, but also to research both popular and professionally published articles on the chosen subject. For health researchers, there is a link to "Medline," an authoritative archive of published medical research papers.

Site: HealthLinks

URL: http://healthlinks.washington.edu.

Sponsor: University of Washington

Subject Area(s): Health   **Subcategory:** Miscellaneous

Grade Level(s): High School

Description

The Health Sciences Department brings together knowledge resources for students and the greater community. There are featured sites, general topics, references, breaking news, and the ability to do searches. Most journal searches are restricted to University of Washington faculty and students.

Commentary

Students doing papers on personal health will find dozens of diseases and issues covered in the Personal Health Information section of this site. Some of the references are intended for medical professionals, but most can be understood by the layperson.

Site: Mimi's Cyberkitchen

URL: http://www.cyber-kitchen.com/

Sponsor: Empire Kosher

Subject Area(s): Health   **Subcategory:** Miscellaneous

Grade Level(s): High School

Description

Described as the most comprehensive food site on the Web, there are links to thousands of food-related sites, organized into 26 categories, and some of Mimi's recipes. The categories include foods, such as cheese, chocolate, fruit, seafood, and others, but you will also find sections on lowfat eating, holidays, food humor, and restaurants.

Commentary

Did you know that there has actually been a nutritional analysis of PEZ candies—unfortunately, they have no nutrients. And there is a site devoted to Ron's Doughnut of the Week. This may be a stretch for finding educational information, but it is a fun site for students to explore and examine nutritional values of some of the foods they like...and those they don't.

Site: OncoLink, the Cancer Center Resource

URL: http://cancer.med.upenn.edu

Sponsor: University of Pennsylvania

Subject Area(s): Health   **Subcategory:** Miscellaneous

Grade Level(s): High School

Description

Winner of numerous Internet awards, this site is devoted to the dissemination of a wide variety of cancer information for patients and families. There are statistics, cancer news, journals, and an art exhibition by people whose lives have been touched by cancer. The site is user-friendly for the individual who likes to scroll through menus and it also has full search capabilities.

Commentary

Updated weekly, this is a valuable resource to teachers, parents and students. It is difficult to imagine an area that has not been covered. Particularly touching is the Children's Calendar and Art Gallery. There should be a resource similar to this for other major diseases.

Section 01. Curriculum Corner

Site: The AIDS Handbook

URL: http://www.westnet.com/~rickd/AIDS/AIDS1.html

Sponsor: Eastchester Middle School

Subject Area(s): Health   **Subcategory:** Miscellaneous

Grade Level(s): Middle School

Description
Written by middle school kids for middle school kids, this handbook contains information about AIDS prevention, transmission, symptoms, treatment, and the immune system working to fight the disease. There are also AIDS-related links included.

Commentary
The language is straightforward and accurate, and each section can be read fairly quickly. The illustrations help explain the text. You may want to share this site with younger or older brothers and sisters.

Site: The Virtual Hospital

URL: http://indy.radiology.uiowa.edu

Sponsor: The University of Iowa

Subject Area(s): Health   **Subcategory:** Miscellaneous

Grade Level(s): High School

Description
Designed primarily for practicing physicians and other healthcare professionals, this continuously updated database is to be used to answer patient care questions. *The Iowa Health Book* is written for laypeople and can be searched by disease.

Commentary
This might be useful for students doing reports on various types of diseases. Search capabilities are by keywords and quite easy to accomplish. The result of the search yields the keywords in a sentence in the document, which is a very handy way to determine relevance.

Site: World Health Organization

URL: http://www.who.ch/

Sponsor: World Health Organization

Subject Area(s): Health   **Subcategory:** Miscellaneous

Grade Level(s): High School

Description
The World Health Organization came into being in 1948, when the United Nations ratified its Constitution. This is the policy-making body of WHO and meets in annual session. The objective of WHO is the attainment by all peoples of the highest possible level of health. Health, as defined in the WHO Constitution, is a state of complete physical, mental, and social well-being and not merely the absence of disease or infirmity.

Commentary
Search for information by keyword, or access current news, information, and resources worldwide on health topics such as drugs, tobacco, and others. Statistics are provided here, and you can review worldwide interest and cooperative efforts to solve specific health-related diseases and addictions.

Section 01. Curriculum Corner

Site: Your Health Daily

URL: http://yourhealthdaily.com/

Sponsor: New York Times Information Services

Subject Area(s): Health   **Subcategory:** Miscellaneous

Grade Level(s): Middle School, High School

Description

This Web site features timely, in-depth discussions on health- and medical-related topics written for the general public. It is updated daily.

Commentary

There is some advertising on the site and links to sponsors. Some topics (AIDS programs, for example) may not be suitable for all audiences.

Site: 19th Century American Writers

URL: http://www.tiac.net/users/eldred/nh/nhow.html

Sponsor: Eric Eldred

Subject Area(s): Language Arts   **Subcategory:** Literature

Grade Level(s): Middle School, High School

Description

This listing of 19th Century American writers is ordered by birth with links to references about each one. There is a glossary of words which might be unfamiliar to readers of these works. Since all links are external files, the information varies by author.

Commentary

Different authors seem to be featured from time to time. The logo pictured is from *The Old Manse* by Nathaniel Hawthorne. There is extensive material about his life and works, including several portraits.

A Literary Index

Site: A Literary Index: Internet Resources in Literature

URL: http://www.vanderbilt.edu/AnS/english/flackcj/LitIndex.html

Sponsor: Chris Flack

Subject Area(s): Language Arts   **Subcategory:** Literature

Grade Level(s): High School

Description

This Web site offers an overview and a review of collections of Internet literary resources. Contents include Literature Indices; Doing Literary Research; English Departments and Literary Institutes; Archives of Electronic Texts; Books and Presses; Composition, Rhetoric, and Writing; and The Teaching of Literature.

Commentary

There are many excellent resources included here. Teachers will appreciate The Teaching of Literature section, and teachers and students alike will certainly find some resources of particular interest in the Composition, Rhetoric, and Writing section—possibilities include links to Teaching with Excellence, World-Wide Web Resources for Rhetoric and Composition, and others.

Section 01. Curriculum Corner

Site: Aesop's Fables Online Exhibit

URL: http://www.pacificnet.net/~johnr/aesop/

Sponsor: John R. Long, STAR SYSTEMS

Subject Area(s): Language Arts   **Subcategory:** Literature

Grade Level(s): Elementary, Middle School, High School

Description

Come read and, in some cases, hear the fables of Aesop, both those you have heard time and again as well as perhaps some that will be new. The online exhibit includes over 600 fables, some with Real Audio narrations and images, some random fables, and a search engine; more is promised.

Commentary

"One good turn deserves another." "A man is known by the company he keeps." "An ounce of prevention is worth a pound of cure." As students of Aesop know, each fable has a moral. Lessons abound here, whether you are studying or reading for enjoyment. The site is frequently updated, so return often to hear stories and things to think about from the master storyteller.

No Graphic Found

Site: Alex: A Catalog of Electronic Texts on the Internet

URL: http://www.lib.ncsu.edu/staff/morgan/alex/alex-index.html

Sponsor: Eric Lease Morgan

Subject Area(s): Language Arts   **Subcategory:** Literature

Grade Level(s): High School

Description

Alex, which was initiated in 1993-1994, was an informal research project to explore the possibilities of creating catalogs of Internet-based electronic texts. You can browse the contents of the catalog (searching by author, date, host, language, subject, or title), or you can conduct a search using Boolean operators (information is provided for those not familiar with Boolean searching). Either method is fairly straightforward.

Commentary

Maintenance of the Alex Catalog has currently been suspended until adequate funding and/or a systematic method for collecting electronic texts can be obtained, but you may well find the existing links useful for research, as much work was done on this catalog, and there are an extensive number of links. Just be aware you may find some not current.

No Graphic Found

Site: Alice's Adventures in Wonderland

URL: http://www.cs.indiana.edu/metastuff/wonder/wonderdir.html

Sponsor: Project Gutenberg

Subject Area(s): Language Arts   **Subcategory:** Literature

Grade Level(s): Middle School, High School

Description

Here you can read online the unabridged twelve chapters of *Alice in Wonderland*, by Lewis Carroll.

Commentary

Project Gutenberg made arrangements for this electronic version of the classic to be available online as shareware. This is a text-based resource so perhaps not as enjoyable as the book but an easy-to-access resource for students.

Section 01. Curriculum Corner

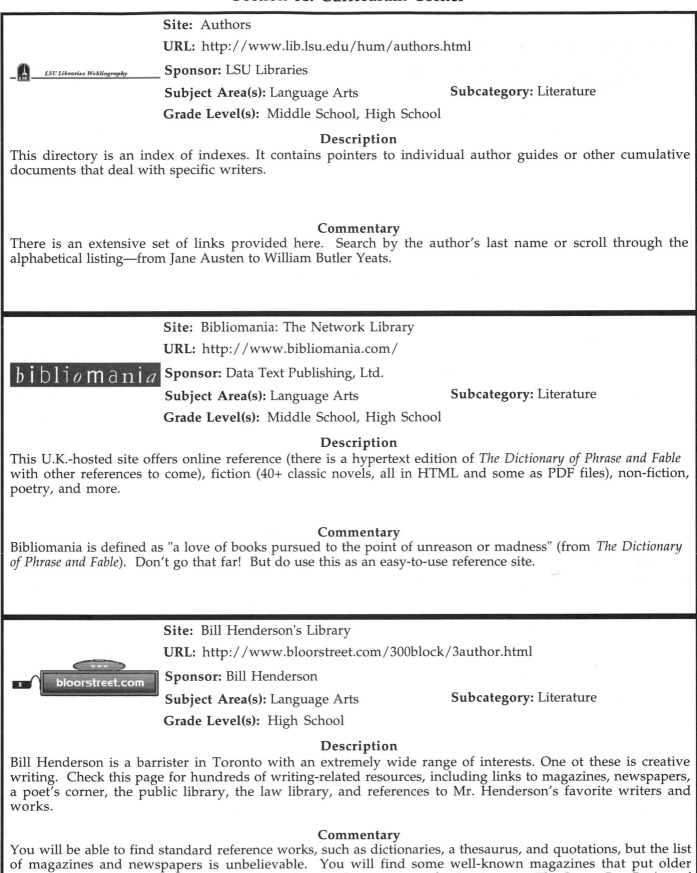

Site: Authors

URL: http://www.lib.lsu.edu/hum/authors.html

Sponsor: LSU Libraries

Subject Area(s): Language Arts   **Subcategory:** Literature

Grade Level(s): Middle School, High School

Description

This directory is an index of indexes. It contains pointers to individual author guides or other cumulative documents that deal with specific writers.

Commentary

There is an extensive set of links provided here. Search by the author's last name or scroll through the alphabetical listing—from Jane Austen to William Butler Yeats.

Site: Bibliomania: The Network Library

URL: http://www.bibliomania.com/

Sponsor: Data Text Publishing, Ltd.

Subject Area(s): Language Arts   **Subcategory:** Literature

Grade Level(s): Middle School, High School

Description

This U.K.-hosted site offers online reference (there is a hypertext edition of *The Dictionary of Phrase and Fable* with other references to come), fiction (40+ classic novels, all in HTML and some as PDF files), non-fiction, poetry, and more.

Commentary

Bibliomania is defined as "a love of books pursued to the point of unreason or madness" (from *The Dictionary of Phrase and Fable*). Don't go that far! But do use this as an easy-to-use reference site.

Site: Bill Henderson's Library

URL: http://www.bloorstreet.com/300block/3author.html

Sponsor: Bill Henderson

Subject Area(s): Language Arts   **Subcategory:** Literature

Grade Level(s): High School

Description

Bill Henderson is a barrister in Toronto with an extremely wide range of interests. One ot these is creative writing. Check this page for hundreds of writing-related resources, including links to magazines, newspapers, a poet's corner, the public library, the law library, and references to Mr. Henderson's favorite writers and works.

Commentary

You will be able to find standard reference works, such as dictionaries, a thesaurus, and quotations, but the list of magazines and newspapers is unbelievable. You will find some well-known magazines that put older issues online. Many of the titles may be unknown, but some are fascinating...try *The Oyster Boy Review* of underated and ignored poetry and fiction!

Section 01. Curriculum Corner

Site: Concertina

URL: http://www.digimark.net/iatech/books/intro.html

Sponsor: Concertina Publishers

Subject Area(s): Language Arts   **Subcategory:** Literature

Grade Level(s): Preschool, Elementary

Description

Concertina is a new Canadian children's publisher, committed to bring books simultaneously to print and to the Internet. At present, four books are on this site, with color illustrations and some sounds. Readers are encouraged to purchase hard copies of the books in order to show support for the site.

Commentary

Waking in Jerusalem, by Sharon Katz, is a charming book with nice illustrations and animal sounds. This technology is not as smooth as reading books on CD-ROM, but it is a promising alternative. Preschool children will need a reader with them, but they can click on "listen" to hear the sounds by themselves.

Site: Electronic Bookshelf

URL: http://ofcn.org/cyber.serv/resource/bookshelf/

Sponsor: Organization For Community Networks

Subject Area(s): Language Arts   **Subcategory:** Literature

Grade Level(s): Middle School, High School

Description

There are dozens of American and English classics available for reading at this site. A sampling of the authors includes Mary Wollstonecraft, Mark Twain, Robert Louis Stevenson, Lucy Maud Montgomery, Thomas Hardy, Edgar Rice Burroughs, and Jane Austen.

Commentary

These are straight copies of texts for reading online. While this may not present a very exciting prospect, it may be that some of these books are out of print or at least difficult to locate, so that this site makes available some otherwise not easily available novels.

Site: Encyclopedia Mythica

URL: http://www.pantheon.org/mythica/

Sponsor: M.F. Lindemans

Subject Area(s): Language Arts   **Subcategory:** Literature

Grade Level(s): Middle School, High School

Description

Visit this online encyclopedia on mythology, folklore, and legend that contains over 4,000 definitions of gods and goddesses, supernatural beings, and legendary creatures and monsters from around the world. Browse through one or more categories of mythology, such as Chinese, Greek, Latvian, Norse, Roman, or others. Or use the search engine to locate articles of interest.

Commentary

The pronunciation guide provided is a most helpful tool. Don't miss the Image Gallery of nearly 200 images, and be sure to look also at the list of ancient feast days. Almost any day was a cause for celebration!

Section 01. Curriculum Corner

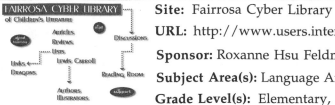

Site: Fairrosa Cyber Library

URL: http://www.users.interport.net/~fairrosa/

Sponsor: Roxanne Hsu Feldman

Subject Area(s): Language Arts   **Subcategory:** Literature

Grade Level(s): Elementary, Middle School

Description

At this Web site, you can find articles and literature reviews, online discussions, a reading room of online classics, information on authors and illustrators, a special section devoted to Lewis Carroll, and a nice set of links to other sites for general information, online libraries, special interests, and publishers and booksellers.

Commentary

There are many resources that will be of special interest to teachers and parents, and students may use a number of them as well. Elementary students will likely not use this site independently, but middle and even high school students will find information here or in the other links provided to include in research of writers and their works.

Site: LitLinks

URL: http://www.ualberta.ca/~amactavi/litlinks.html

Sponsor: Andrew Mactavish

Subject Area(s): Language Arts   **Subcategory:** Literature

Grade Level(s): High School

Description

These are literary links on the World Wide Web. Included are an extensive list of links to authors, e-text archives, literary cyberplaces, libraries and reference, theories, humanities, computing, gender issues, journals and e-zines, general humanities, and more.

Commentary

This site looks as though it has not been updated in a while, but it still provides a useful list to resources and other lists.

Site: Luminarium

URL: http://www.luminarium.org/lumina.html

Sponsor: Anniina Jokinen

Subject Area(s): Language Arts   **Subcategory:** Literature

Grade Level(s): Middle School, High School

Description

Browse through categories of English Literature—Medieval, 16th Century Renaissance, or 17th Century—and read text and listen to music accompanying information about the life and works of English writers. Or use the search capability to search the entire anthology.

Commentary

This is a lovely site—rich with information. It provides a multimedia experience designed by the editor of the site to allow visitors to view artwork and hear music of the period. It also enhances the experience of learning about the writers and works of a given period. This is a handy research site but also very enjoyable for leisurely browsing.

Section 01. Curriculum Corner

Site: Mark Twain

URL: http://marktwain.miningco.com/

Sponsor: Jim Zwick, The Mining Company

Subject Area(s): Language Arts   **Subcategory:** Literature

Grade Level(s): Middle School, High School

Description

This is described as "the definitive Twain site." The Webmaster has collected a variety of Web sites under the broad categories of best of the Net, resource list, new features, and previous features. All may be easily searched.

Commentary

There appears to be a new feature posted here every week, and it is possible to retrieve previous features as well. You might enjoy reading the debates on banning *Huckleberry Finn* as well as several articles involving the quotes (and non-quotes) attributed to Mark Twain.

Site: Online Mystery Database

URL: http://www.aetv.com/mystery/

Sponsor: A&E Television Networks

Subject Area(s): Language Arts   **Subcategory:** Literature

Grade Level(s): Middle School, High School

Description

The Online Mystery Database allows you to quickly search for a favorite mystery writer, character, novel, film, or TV show. Enter your keyword and click "Search." Try searching for John le Carre to learn about how he chose his pseudonym—or choose a mystery writer you have interest in.

Commentary

Teachers, be sure to click on the Classroom button at the bottom of the page to learn about resources designed specifically for your use—guides for classroom discussions and research projects, information for obtaining the magazine, "The Idea Book for Educators" (lesson plans and a 6-month classroom calendar), and more.

Site: Pooh Home Page

URL: http://www.lehigh.edu/~jbh6/jbh6.html

Sponsor: Jamie, Lehigh University

Subject Area(s): Language Arts   **Subcategory:** Literature

Grade Level(s): Elementary, Middle School

Description

Here they are...pictures of Pooh and the gang with links to other home pages which feature the Pooh Corner characters. The author of the page is creating a Web ring so that all Pooh sites can be more easily accessed from any of the individual Web pages.

Commentary

Send your Mom (or someone else) a Pooh greeting card. Look at the collectors' stamps or even complete a Pooh puzzle. If you happen to be a college student, as are most of the creators of these links, you may want to read about the history and re-interpretation of Pooh.

NO GRAPHIC FOUND

Site: Project Bartleby Archive

URL: http://www.columbia.edu/acis/bartleby/index.html

Sponsor: Steven van Leeuwen, Editor

Subject Area(s): Language Arts   **Subcategory:** Literature

Grade Level(s): Middle School, High School

Description

This archive offers visitors the text of many original works and reference materials popular in today's classrooms. Included in the collection are *Bartlett's Familiar Quotations*; *The Odysseys of Homer*; poems by Emily Dickinson, T.S. Eliot, and others; Thomas Paine's *Common Sense*; *The Elements of Style*; Whitman's *Leaves of Grass*; and many more.

Commentary

You can click on a writer to view the work or search the site by keyword. This is a handy online reference for research or general browsing.

Site: Scholastics Place: Books and Book Clubs

URL: http://scholastic.com/

Sponsor: Scholastic, Inc.

Subject Area(s): Language Arts   **Subcategory:** Literature

Grade Level(s): Elementary

Description

Some popular series published by Scholastic include *Animorphs, Babysitters Club, Goosebumps,* and *The Magic School Bus.* Students may get more information about these books as well as TV and video related to them.

Commentary

Head straight for *Goosebumps* if you dare—there you will find scary sounds, pictures, a fun house, and more information about the books and TV show. Other people might want to visit *The Magic School Bus* first and join Ms. Frizzle who takes her class on magical field trips.

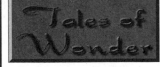

Site: Tales of Wonder: Folk & Fairy Tales from Around the World

URL: http://itpubs.ucdavis.edu/richard/tales/

Sponsor: Richard Darsie

Subject Area(s): Language Arts   **Subcategory:** Literature

Grade Level(s): Elementary, Middle School, High School

Description

Enjoy this archive of folk and fairy tales. Read tales from Africa, Central Asia, Central Europe, China, England, India, Ireland, Japan, the Middle East, Native America, Russia, Scandinavia, Scotland, and Siberia. You will also find links to other fairy tale and folk tale sites.

Commentary

Storytelling is a means of passing on history and tales of wonder, as the site suggests. This site hosts a beautiful collection of tales to enjoy and share.

Section 01. Curriculum Corner

Site: The Complete Works of William Shakespeare

URL: http://the-tech.mit.edu/Shakespeare/works.html

Sponsor: Corporation for National Research Initiatives

Subject Area(s): Language Arts   **Subcategory:** Literature

Grade Level(s): High School

Description
Shakespeare's plays are arranged in three categories: tragedy, comedy, or history. There is a separate category for poetry. In addition to complete texts of all the works, the reader will find Shakespeare resources, a chronological listing of works, and Shakespearean quotations. Some words in the texts are linked to a glossary.

Commentary
Even someone with casual interest in Shakespeare will find much of interest at this site. There is an Internet Movie Guide, for Shakespeare, naturally. And did you know that the original title of the play was *The Most Excellent and Lamentable Tragedy of Romeo and Juliet?*

Site: The Dickens Project

URL: http://humwww.ucsc.edu/dickens/index.html

Sponsor: University of California

Subject Area(s): Language Arts   **Subcategory:** Literature

Grade Level(s): High School

Description
The Dickens Project is a scholarly consortium devoted to promoting the study and enjoyment of the times and work of Charles Dickens. Often viewed as the first modern novelist, Dickens' concern with social and environmental issues makes him a writer for present day times as well as his own.

Commentary
There are resources for reading, studying, and teaching about Charles Dickens and his era. Many of his books are reproduced online. Perhaps most charming are the extensive resources surrounding *A Christmas Carol*, which provide great insight into this period in England.

Site: The English Server

URL: http://english-server.hss.cmu.edu/

The English Server **Sponsor:** Geoffrey Sauer, Carnegie Mellon

Subject Area(s): Language Arts   **Subcategory:** Literature

Grade Level(s): Middle School, High School

Description
The English Server is a cooperative which has published 18,000+ works online covering categories including 18th Century, Art and Architecture, Books, Cultronix (a journal of contemporary art and cultural theory), Cultural Theory, Cyber (a collection dedicated to the links between technology and culture), Drama, Feminism, Fiction, Government, Literacy and Education, Multimedia, Race, Reference, Rhetoric, and more.

Commentary
Choose one of the options of categories or locate specific information by entering a keyword to search the site.

Section 01. Curriculum Corner

Site: The English Server Fiction Collection

URL: http://eng.hss.cmu.edu/fiction/

Sponsor: Martha Cheng and Geoff Sauer

Subject Area(s): Language Arts   **Subcategory:** Literature

Grade Level(s): Middle School, High School

Description

This is a quick way to find works of and about fiction collected by English server members, contributing authors worldwide, and public domain texts. Find categories of Short Fiction, Novels, Magazines of and about contemporary fiction and criticism, other Internet sites publishing fiction, literary criticism, organizations which present awards for excellent fiction, Drama (plays, screenplays, and dramatic criticism), and Poetry.

Commentary

Browse through the categories of works or use the full-text search engine of the site to locate literature of interest.

Site: The Newbery and Caldecott Medals

URL: http://ils.unc.edu//award/nhome.html

Sponsor: American Library Association

Subject Area(s): Language Arts   **Subcategory:** Literature

Grade Level(s): Elementary, Middle School

Description

The Newbery Award was the first children's book award in the world and has been awarded every year beginning with 1922 for the most distinguished American children's book published the previous year. In 1937 the Caldecott Medal was created to honor the most distinguished American picture book for children published in the previous year. This site contains extensive information about both awards.

Commentary

There are pictures and summaries of the books that have won the medal each year in each category as well as the honor books. This is an excellent place to find new books to read and enjoy.

Site: The Works of the Bard

URL: http://www.gh.cs.usyd.edu.au/~matty/Shakespeare/

The works of the Bard   **Sponsor:** Matty Farrow

Subject Area(s): Language Arts   **Subcategory:** Literature

Grade Level(s): High School

Description

Shakespeare's works are categorized as Histories, Tragedies, Comedies, or Other—each providing links to the text of the work requested. Also find links to about a dozen other Shakespeare sites. Search options are varied, allowing you to execute straight links or do more sophisticated, Boolean searches.

Commentary

While the Web author claims not to be an expert on Shakespeare, he has provided a rich source of links to the works of the Bard as well as to other Internet sites on Shakespeare.

Site: Web Travel Review

URL: http://www-swiss.ai.mit.edu:80/webtravel

Sponsor: Phillip Greenspun

Subject Area(s): Language Arts   **Subcategory:** Literature

Grade Level(s): Middle School, High School

Description

"To travel is to live. To live is to travel." With over 600 pages of text and 2,000 photographs, these pages are a stimulus to both traveling and writing. Writings include pieces about North America, Europe, Central America, the Caribbean, Asia, and some links to travel book reviews.

Commentary

"Travels with Samantha" was the award-winning piece that started this site. It involves a 3.5 month trip from Boston to Alaska and back...and you will have to figure out who Samantha is. The writing and the photography are both wonderful!

Site: Welcome to the Shakespeare Web

URL: http://www.shakespeare.com/

Sponsor: dna productions

Subject Area(s): Language Arts   **Subcategory:** Literature

Grade Level(s): High School

Description

Come to this site to engage in interactive, hypermedia discussion and information about Shakespeare. Find Today in Shakespeare History and current information regarding Shakespearean festivals and productions. There's even a Java-based game called Poetry Panel that you might enjoy!

Commentary

What would the Bard think of being so accessible via the Web? In addition to the resources here, follow conversation threads among serious and not-so-serious students of Shakespeare helping one another with greater understanding of the meaning behind some of his works.

Site: Young Adult Reading

URL: http://www.spruceridge.com/reading

Young Adult Reading **Sponsor:** Murray Whitehead

Subject Area(s): Language Arts   **Subcategory:** Literature

Grade Level(s): Middle School, High School

Description

Reading materials suitable for teenagers are featured on this site. All books on the lists have been used in middle school language arts classes. Some books are marked with an asterisk due to contents of a graphic nature. Also find feature stories about some authors.

Commentary

There isn't a great deal of information about any of the books except those in the featured section. The lists for the past four years are posted in addition to the current year's list. Search either by topic or by author if you have a particular interest.

Site: English/Language Arts Department

URL: http://www.ecnet.net/users/gdlevin/engdept.html

English/Language Arts Department

Sponsor: David Levin

Subject Area(s): Language Arts   **Subcategory:** Miscellaneous

Grade Level(s): High School

Description

Find an extensive alphabetical list of Web sites here related to English/Language Arts—from "A+ Research & Writing for High School and College Students Home Page" and "A.Word.A.Day Home Page" to "Writing Argumentative Essays" and "Word Play." A graphic of a hot pepper next to a given Web site indicates that impressive and substantial information is available there. A "cool" graphic indicates a cool site.

Commentary

This site was designed for high school educators, but students will enjoy it as well and find a lot of informative and enjoyable sites to visit.

Site: Internet Connections: Language Arts

URL: http://www.mcrel.org/connect/language.html

Sponsor: McREL

Subject Area(s): Language Arts   **Subcategory:** Miscellaneous

Grade Level(s): Middle School, High School

Description

This is a hotlist of Language Arts sites on the Net. The links are organized into categories of Reading, Reference, and Writing.

Commentary

There are over 100 links here that will provide resource materials for teachers and students at varying grade levels. The Reference section, for example, includes the American Sign Language Dictionary, Citing Internet Addresses, Educational Standards and Curriculum Frameworks, The Grammar Lady, Roget's Thesaurus, the Writer's Guide—Planning, Organizing, and Presenting Essays, and others.

Site: American Verse Project

URL: http://www.hti.umich.edu/english/amverse/

Sponsor: University of Michigan

Subject Area(s): Language Arts   **Subcategory:** Poetry

Grade Level(s): Middle School, High School

Description

The American Verse Project is a collaborative project between the University of Michigan Humanities Text Initiative (HTI) and the University of Michigan Press. Find an electronic collection of American poetry prior to 1920.

Commentary

Use a variety of simple to more sophisticated search options or just browse the online works. Just for fun, click on "About the American Verse Project" and then click to generate a random poem from all the lines in the collection.

Section 01. Curriculum Corner

Site: British Poetry

URL: http://etext.lib.virginia.edu/britpo.html

Sponsor: University of Virginia

Subject Area(s): Language Arts   **Subcategory:** Poetry

Grade Level(s): High School

Description

The British Poetry Archive covers the years 1780-1910. Complete manuscripts as well as some original illustrations are included in the Electronic Text Center. Some search capabilities are possible within documents.

Commentary

This site contains a valuable link to the Modern English Collection with hundreds of additional works of British and American literature. Language arts students will find related American poetry for comparison.

Site: The CMU Poetry Index of Canonical Verse

URL: http://eng.hss.cmu.edu/poetry/

Sponsor: English Server

Subject Area(s): Language Arts   **Subcategory:** Poetry

Grade Level(s): Middle School, High School

Description

Find links to works from an alphabetical listing of poets ranging from Maya Angelou to William Wordsworth. You will also find some selected links to Essays and Humor and to assorted Web sites such as The Atlantic Monthly's Poetry Page, The Internet Poetry Archive, and others.

Commentary

Browse through the poets' works provided or search the site for poems based on a specific title, author, or keyword.

Site: Virtual Presentation Assistant

URL: http://www.ukans.edu/cwis/units/coms2/vpa/vpa.html

Sponsor: Communication Studies Department, University of Kansas

Subject Area(s): Language Arts   **Subcategory:** Speaking

Grade Level(s): Middle School, High School

Description

The Virtual Presentation Assistant is an online tutorial to guide you in planning presentations and improving public speaking skills. Contents include: (1) Determining your purpose, (2) Selecting your topic, (3) Researching your topic, (4) Analyzing your audience, (5) Supporting your points, (6) Outlining your points, (7) Using visual aids, (8) Presenting your speech, and (9) Public Speaking Links to other Web sites.

Commentary

This is a valuable resource for students and adults and a well-designed site. Educators may be particularly interested in the Visual Aids section to find a sub-section focused on computer presentation technology. You will find much current information on topics such as multimedia projectors, electronic whiteboards, presentation software and how to best use it, and more.

Site: A Word A Day

URL: http://www.wordsmith.org/awad/index.html

Sponsor: Anu Garg

Subject Area(s): Language Arts   **Subcategory:** Vocabulary

Grade Level(s): Middle School, High School

Description

This is the Web page for "A Word A Day" which mails out a vocabulary word and its definition to the subscribers—free every day. The words are often organized into a theme for the week, and there is usually additional commentary. Online each day, today's and yesterday's word can be checked out by the reader.

Commentary

There are over 100,000 subscribers to A Word a Day in more than 130 countries—it is fun to look at the breakdown of the subscribers by country. Real vocabulary addicts can look at the complete archive of words used since this service began in March of 1994. It is also possible to send a gift subscription to a friend.

Site: Syndicate

URL: http://syndicate.com

Sponsor: Carey Cook, aka "Rich Encounter"

Subject Area(s): Language Arts   **Subcategory:** Vocabulary

Grade Level(s): Elementary, Middle School, High School

Description

Find all kinds of vocabulary and word puzzles and games that can be completed online or printed to work on later. A grade-level test helps assess whether a student's vocabulary is appropriate for his or her grade level. You can compete for prizes in monthly word puzzle contests and find grade-specific puzzles, comic strips (with Dick Shinary and other characters), word games, and many other ways to sharpen vocabulary skills.

Commentary

Who would have thought learning vocabulary could be so much fun! The more you see and work with words, the easier it is to learn and use them, and these teacher-endorsed activities are a fun way to drill for vocabulary and just to learn words to expand vocabulary. Quizzes can be used to prepare for the SAT, SSAT, GRE, or LSAT tests.

Site: Digital Education Network : The Writing DEN

URL: http://www.actden.com/

Sponsor: ACT Laboratory

Subject Area(s): Language Arts   **Subcategory:** Writing

Grade Level(s): Middle School, High School

Description

The Writing DEN aims to teach students how to write effectively through new methods of interaction and stimulating materials. Each week there is a featured topic. Students can read about the topic, receive a word of the day, and respond to information. There are helps provided for writing sentences, paragraphs, and essays.

Commentary

There is a host of topics to choose from spanning the fields of history, nature, science, Canada, and lifestyles. Most topics provide pictures, narrative, and audio as a way of learning about the topic before one begins to write. Pick a topic which interests you, use the tutorials, and see if your writing really does improve.

Site: Inkspot for Young Writers

URL: http://www.inkspot.com/young/

Sponsor: Debbie Ridpath Ohi

Subject Area(s): Language Arts   **Subcategory:** Writing

Grade Level(s): Middle School, High School

Description

Inkspot offers useful writing-related resources, content, and networking opportunities on the Internet, and this particular page and links are directed towards young writers. The Feature Articles section points to advice, articles, and interviews useful to young writers. Market Info suggests markets for young writers' works. Look in the Useful Sites section for links to other helpful resources for getting started and networking with peers.

Commentary

Everything on Inkspot is free. Newcomers may want to check out the Site Map for a detailed overview on what Inkspot has to offer, but this page is well organized and easy to navigate. Student writers may want to subscribe to Inklings, a free newsletter for writers, or participate in the Forum, a discussion area, with other young writers.

Language
a r t s   p a g e

Site: Language Arts Page

URL: http://splavc.spjc.cc.fl.us/project5.html

Sponsor: David Hartmann, St. Petersburg Junior College

Subject Area(s): Language Arts   **Subcategory:** Writing

Grade Level(s): Middle School, High School

Description

The Language Arts Page is a collection of articles and links to electronic texts, copyright laws, libraries, dictionaries, other reference resources, and publications. The author, an instructor at St. Petersburg Junior College, introduces the site by writing that he takes a broad view of what might be called "language arts."

Commentary

The link to *The Language Arts Gazette* is actually a connection to a list of varied publications, most of which are news or sports. Many of the resources can be found on other lists, but there is a fine compilation of materials to help the writer.

Paradigm
Online Writing Assistant

Site: Paradigm Online Writing Assistant

URL: http://www.spaceland.org/paradigm/

Sponsor: Chuck Guilford

Subject Area(s): Language Arts   **Subcategory:** Writing

Grade Level(s): Middle School, High School

Description

The Paradigm Online Writing Assistant is an interactive, menu-driven, online writer's guide and handbook distributed for free on the Web. It is intended for both inexperienced and advanced writers. Choose a topic: Discovering What to Write, Revising, Thesis/Support Essays, Informal Essays, Documenting Sources, Organizing, Editing, Exploratory Essays, Argumentative Essays, and then proceed from the submenus provided.

Commentary

Although there is a vast amount of information located here, hyperlinks are used throughout to make navigation simple. A suggested method for students is to select and copy an activity and then paste it into a word processor to use. It could then be easily saved and printed when complete. This is a real find for students looking for assistance with writing assignments.

Section 01. Curriculum Corner

Site: Researchpaper.com

URL: http://www.researchpaper.com/

Researchpaper.com

Sponsor: Infonautics Corporation

Subject Area(s): Language Arts   **Subcategory:** Writing

Grade Level(s): Middle School, High School

Description

Researchpaper.com provides you with an online collection of topics, ideas, and assistance in conducting research projects. Click on Idea Directory to browse through 4,000+ research topics across over 100 categories or search for a topic by keyword. Consult the Writing Center for assistance with the style, organization, and presentation of your reports. What a timesaver!

Commentary

Are you stumped for a idea for your term paper or needing help pulling the research together? Check out this site. If you need the help, the Writing Center offers writing tips and techniques as well as answers to frequently asked spelling and grammar questions. Students will also likely enjoy Research Central, where you can post questions, meet up with people working on similar projects, and more.

Site: The Biography Maker

URL: http://www.bham.wednet.edu/bio/biomaker.html

Sponsor: Bellingham Schools (WA)

Subject Area(s): Language Arts   **Subcategory:** Writing

Grade Level(s): Elementary, Middle School, High School

Description

The Biography Maker guides you into taking the facts you know about someone and turning them into an engaging perspective about what you know. The goal is to make your writing more interesting and make your reader want to know even more about the subject of your writing. Four steps are to be followed: (1) Questioning, (2) Learning, (3) Synthesis, (4) Story-Telling. Also offered are the Six Traits of Effective Writing.

Commentary

This is a delightful site that guides students, inexperienced or more advanced writers, into creating an interesting biography and assessing their work. It is handy for an independent tool or might be assigned by teachers for students needing assistance with certain steps in the process of writing.

Site: The Purdue Online Writing Lab (OWL)

URL: http://owl.english.purdue.edu/

Sponsor: Purdue University

Subject Area(s): Language Arts   **Subcategory:** Writing

Grade Level(s): High School

Description

The Purdue Online Writing Lab (OWL) offers a variety of resources and direct assistance for any writer in need of help in writing matters. The handouts and resources are available to everyone; during busy time, Purdue students will receive priority in direct assistance. There are a number of pointers to search tools and directories on the Internet.

Commentary

There are wonderful ESL resources for students who want to polish up their English, i.e. use idioms correctly, deal with difficult verbs in certain tenses, and similar topics. Some of the handouts are helpful in explaining some of the more difficult aspects of writing.

Section 01. Curriculum Corner

Site: A Functional Housing Market

URL: http://www.cs.rice.edu/~sboone/Lessons/Titles/lphouse.html

Sponsor: Susan Boone, Saint Agnes Academy

Subject Area(s): Mathematics   **Subcategory:** Miscellaneous

Grade Level(s): High School

Description

In this online activity, students use the Internet to search for housing prices in Houston, Texas (the location can be changed) and compare the prices to the number of square feet found in the living area of a house. Using information from the graph of the data and the equations of the function, students answer questions about housing prices.

Commentary

The exercise is designed for mathematics students enrolled in Algebra I and studying linear equations. An Internet search is combined with off-line activities to answer questions on average cost per square foot and land values and to predict the cost of various sized homes.

NO GRAPHIC FOUND

Site: About Today's Date

URL: http://acorn.educ.nottingham.ac.uk/cgi-bin/daynum

Sponsor: Shell Centre for Mathematics Education

Subject Area(s): Mathematics   **Subcategory:** Miscellaneous

Grade Level(s): Elementary, Middle School

Description

The numbers of the day are posted at this site, and selecting one leads to a fascinating list of facts related to the selected number. The information included cuts across content areas and is valuable as a springboard to numerous topics of research, discussion, and experimentation.

Commentary

The information at this site comes from the book *Numbers: Facts, Figures and Fiction*, and a link to ordering information is included.

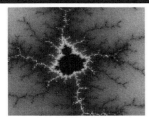

Site: Fractal Pictures & Animations

URL: http://www.cnam.fr/fractals.html

Sponsor: Frank Roussel, Rennes University

Subject Area(s): Mathematics   **Subcategory:** Miscellaneous

Grade Level(s): Middle School, High School

Description

The archives at this site contain a collection of fractal pictures (some animated) to present the idea of mathematics as art. The table of contents provides both authors and categories, so some searching is involved in finding the groupings desired.

Commentary

These pictures are all somewhat slow to load, but the Webmaster hopes to have an American mirror site up soon, which should speed things up considerably. The statistics for use show an astonishingly large number of hits, so this site must be popular with many groups of people.

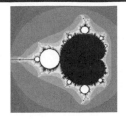

Site: Fractals

URL: http://cml.rice.edu:80/~lanius/frac/

Sponsor: The Rice School

Subject Area(s): Mathematics   **Subcategory:** Miscellaneous

Grade Level(s): Elementary, Middle School

Description

Fractals are a special kind of geometric figure, with special kinds of properties. There is a lot of information on the Web about fractals, but much of it is either just pretty pictures or very high-level mathematics. So this fractals site is a good one for kids and will help them understand what the pretty pictures are all about, that it's math—and that it's fun!

Commentary

Print materials for classroom use with the Fractals projects can be downloaded from the site, which was developed at The Rice School, in Houston, Texas, as part of GirlTECH, a teacher training program sponsored in part by the National Science Foundation. There are links from this site to the GirlTECH and other related sites.

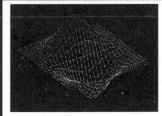

Site: Frequently Asked Questions in Mathematics

URL: http://daisy.uwaterloo.ca/~alopez-o/math-faq/math-faq.html

Sponsor: Alex Lopez-Ortiz, University of Waterloo

Subject Area(s): Mathematics   **Subcategory:** Miscellaneous

Grade Level(s): High School

Description

This is a compilation of Frequently Asked Questions and their answers concerning the topic of mathematics. Topics range from trivia, such as the Monty Hall problem, to more advanced subjects, such as Wiles recent proof of Fermat's Last Theorem.

Commentary

Changes and updates are continually being introduced. The site author describes the Frequently Asked Questions list as a compilation of knowledge of interest to most professional and amateur mathematicians. Do you know why there is no Nobel Prize in mathematics?

Site: Glenbrook South High School Math

URL: http://www.glenbrook.k12.il.us/gbsmat/gbsmat.html

Sponsor: Glenbrook South High School

Subject Area(s): Mathematics   **Subcategory:** Miscellaneous

Grade Level(s): High School

Description

The students at Glenbrook South High School have won awards in the First in the World Consortium Study. This math site contains student assignments and projects in algebra, geometry, precalculus, and statistics.

Commentary

In addition to the projects, you may want to look at the math Internet resources and projects. There is information about the math department and the type of curriculum provided for students at Glenbrook. This is a wonderful site for teachers and students.

Site: Internet Center for Math Problems

URL: http://www.mathpro.com/math/mathCenter.html

Sponsor: Internet Center for Mathematics Problems

Subject Area(s): Mathematics   **Subcategory:** Miscellaneous

Grade Level(s): High School

Description

This is a very plain site that has exactly one purpose, to host a hotlist of links to interesting mathematics problem sites on the Internet. And it does a great job! There are links to online versions of Problem Columns from both paper-based and electronic mathematics journals, newsgroups, and problem-solving projects that utilize electronic mail.

Commentary

Teachers and/or students looking for mathematics projects or research topics should start out by checking out this site and its associated links. The links to mathematics puzzle sites will be of particular interest.

Site: Introduction to Descriptive Statistics

URL: http://www.mste.uiuc.edu/hill/dstat/dstat.html

Sponsor: University of Illinois at Urbana-Champaign

Subject Area(s): Mathematics   **Subcategory:** Miscellaneous

Grade Level(s): High School

Description

After making a good case for the need for descriptive statistics in everyday life, the author then presents lessons on several types of statistics, including mode, median, mean, central tendency, variation, range, variance, and standard deviation.

Commentary

Parts of this lesson could have been done with a blackboard or software, but then the author shows that he understands the dynamics of the Internet. In teaching the median, he links to ESPN and the student can choose men's or women's basketball for the numbers to use in this lesson. 100% score on political correctness and at least a 90 on the lesson!

Site: MacTutor History of Mathematics archive

URL: http://www-groups.dcs.st-and.ac.uk:80/~history/

Sponsor: University of St. Andrews, Scotland

Subject Area(s): Mathematics   **Subcategory:** Miscellaneous

Grade Level(s): High School

Description

The archive contains the biographies of more than 1100 mathematicians. There are articles on the development of mathematical ideas, famous curves, and the Mathematician of the day. It is possible to search the archives.

Commentary

Even non-mathematicians might find interesting the story about the development of the marine chronometer or "How the English Solved the Problem of Longitude." The site is current, but you still may not know of any of the mathematicians who were born (or died) on this day.

Section 01. Curriculum Corner

Site: Math Problem Center

URL: http://www.mathpro.com/math/MathPro.html

Sponsor: MathPro Press

Subject Area(s): Mathematics

Subcategory: Miscellaneous

Grade Level(s): High School

Description

MathPro Press specializes in the publication of compendiums and indexes of mathematics problems. This section of its site links you to a host of math problems on the Internet: problem columns from math journals, math problems on the Web, online book reviews of problem books, newsgroups for math problems, and more.

Commentary

As if math problem solving wasn't tough enough for some, here you can easily find problems to solve in German and Russian, too. This site is for the student and adult who really enjoys this type of challenge. There are a number of interesting problems to access here, but you may find a few dead ends.

Site: MATHCOUNTS

URL: http://thechalkboard.com/MC/

Sponsor: GTE Foundation

Subject Area(s): Mathematics

Subcategory: Miscellaneous

Grade Level(s): Middle School

Description

MATHCOUNTS is the national math coaching and competition program for 7th and 8th grade students. In addition to information about the program, there are many activities to help students acquire problem solving skills.

Commentary

There are warm-ups and workouts, problems of the week, problem solving strategies, extended activities, and algebraic reasoning. Even if you don't plan to participate in this contest, you will enjoy this site if you enjoy math.

Site: MathMania

URL: http://csr.uvic.ca/~mmania/

Sponsor: Mathmania

Subject Area(s): Mathematics

Subcategory: Miscellaneous

Grade Level(s): Middle School, High School

Description

This Canadian site has sections on graphing theory, knots, sorting networks, and finite state machines. There are puzzles, tutorials, exercises, lesson plans, and links to related Web sites. The site is dedicated to helping young students and others explore some topics in higher mathematics. Start with the 10-minute site tour to get acquainted with the resources and activities you will find.

Commentary

The graphing and knots sections are excellent for middle school students, and the remaining topics are probably best left to students in high school. For teachers, as you choose activities best suited to your students, refer to the curriculum materials available.

Section 01. Curriculum Corner

Site: MathMol Home Page

URL: http://www.nyu.edu/pages/mathmol/

Sponsor: NYU/ACF Scientific Visualization Laboratory

Subject Area(s): Mathematics **Subcategory:** Miscellaneous

Grade Level(s): Elementary, Middle School, High School

Description
MathMol stands for Mathematics and Molecules. This site is designed to serve as a starting point for studying the field of molecular modeling. Activities, resources, simulations, hypermedia textbooks, and graphic images are included for K-12 students and teachers. Find out about molecular modeling and why it is important.

Commentary
Middle and high school students might explore the water module to calculate the density of water and ice as they review concepts in mass, volume, and density. Elementary students might take advantage of the hypermedia text for grades 3-5. The tutorials found at this site are appropriate for the math or science classroom.

Site: MegaMath

URL: http://www.c3.lanl.gov/mega-math/welcome.html

Sponsor: Los Alamos National Laboratory

Subject Area(s): Mathematics **Subcategory:** Miscellaneous

Grade Level(s): Elementary, Middle School

Description
MegaMath is for students, teachers, and mathematicians. You will find seven mathematical topics, each of which provides a variety of activities at many different levels. The topics have evaluation devices and are all related to NCTM standards.

Commentary
"The Most Colorful Math of All" is a great place to start; the activities are fun and actually related to math. The authors of this site hope that your visit here will help you discover that mathematics can be exciting and a place to use your imagination.

Site: Pi Mathematics

URL: http://www.ncsa.uiuc.edu/edu/RSE/RSEorange/buttons.html

Sponsor: National Center for Supercomputing Applications

Subject Area(s): Mathematics **Subcategory:** Miscellaneous

Grade Level(s): High School

Description
The concept of Pi, an irrational number, has been calculated and explored throughout history from Biblical time to the present. Many mathematicians have made it their life's work, and computers have made it possible to calculate Pi to over six billion decimal places. This site explores the concept with activities to promote better understanding.

Commentary
Some may find the history of Pi to be most interesting, as they consider a timeline through the ages. Others may want to head directly for the activities and applications. There are two videos for downloading and viewing.

Section 01. Curriculum Corner

Site: Plane Math

URL: http://www.planemath.com/planemathhome.html

Sponsor: InfoUse/NASA

Subject Area(s): Mathematics   **Subcategory:** Miscellaneous

Grade Level(s): Elementary, Middle School

Description
Plane Math is designed to help students learn cool things about math and aeronautics on the Internet. The site contains nine activities for students, all of which involve aviation in some way. The activities have a lot of pictures and include an explanation of terms. Just in case it is needed, there is also material for parents and teachers.

Commentary
These activities are so much fun! You can learn how a helicopter flies, how plane capacity is determined, and even fly buffalo and rock stars around. There are group activities, but each lesson can be done alone, if you wish.

Site: The Math Forum

URL: http://forum.swarthmore.edu

Sponsor: Swarthmore College

Subject Area(s): Mathematics   **Subcategory:** Miscellaneous

Grade Level(s): Elementary, Middle School, High School

Description
This site, funded by the National Science Foundation, is a virtual center for math education on the Internet. Although the original focus was on geometry, the site has been expanded to include other areas of math as well. Find an organized list of Internet Math Resources—other main areas include Key Issues in Math, Math Education, Resources by Subject, Parents & Citizens, Research, Student Center, and Teacher's Place.

Commentary
In the Student Center, ask your geometry questions of Dr. Math, check out the problem of the week, download examples, find teaching suggestions, and more. Come to this website for help with math problems and assignments. Students and teachers will both find some terrific resources here.

Site: The Mathematics of Cartography

URL: http://cml.rice.edu:80/~lanius/pres/map/

Sponsor: Cynthia Lanius, The Rice School

Subject Area(s): Mathematics   **Subcategory:** Miscellaneous

Grade Level(s): Elementary, Middle School

Description
Cartography is the art and science of mapmaking, and this Web site introduces students to its principles in lively and interesting ways. There are problem-solving exercises, online resources, lists of off-line resources, and lesson plans for teachers. There is also a section that discusses careers in cartography.

Commentary
This site is a project from The Rice School, in Houston, Texas, affiliated with Rice University. Information at the bottom of the page describes the broader GirlTECH program and links to its sponsors.

Section 01. Curriculum Corner

Site: Truly Great Real-Life Math Lessons

URL: http://www.sjen.org/esuhsd/curix/team18/math612.html

Sponsor: San Jose Education Network

Subject Area(s): Mathematics   **Subcategory:** Miscellaneous

Grade Level(s): Middle School, High School

Description

These two lessons are the work of eight teachers attending the San Jose Education Network Institute. Both lessons have multiple skills represented and are therefore adjustable to many grade levels but roughly to grades 6-12. Each lesson lists objectives, any materials needed, and instructional activities.

Commentary

The City Park Project is especially interesting. Designed to last about two weeks, the students submit a bid for a new neighborhood park after calculating cost, make an oral presentation, and build a model of the playground. The lesson developers invite you to contact them by e-mail for feedback and/or assistance.

Site: U.S. Shirts Problem

URL: http://sands.psy.cmu.edu/ACT/awpt/us-shirts.html

Sponsor: Carnegie Mellon University

Subject Area(s): Mathematics   **Subcategory:** Miscellaneous

Grade Level(s): High School

Description

This is an elaborate three-step problem written by Bill Hadley as a part of a larger algebra project. The student group assumes the role of manager in calculating the cost of various orders in a shirt factory. There are graphs to be constructed and class discussion about the problem.

Commentary

This is an interesting problem and certainly would be more fun when done as a group. A part of the objective of the lesson is to talk about mathematics and see how algebra could actually be useful in a business situation.

No Graphic Found

Site: Dance Library: Type

URL: http://www.artswire.org/Artswire/www/dance/type.html

Sponsor: Arts Wire and DanceUSA

Subject Area(s): Music & Drama   **Subcategory:** Dance

Grade Level(s): Middle School, High School

Description

Find a hotlist of types of dance, each linking to a site or resource under a specific category. Categories are extensive, including Ballet, Ballroom, Break Dancing, Contemporary/Modern Dance, Country, Dancers, Choreographers, Flamengo, Indian, Irish, Jazz/Tap, Middle Eastern, Scottish, Tango, World Dance, and others.

Commentary

What a terrific resource for students of dance! Simple and straightforward, this is a good starting place to browse or research various types of dance.

Section 01. Curriculum Corner

Site: Sapphire Swan Dance Directory

URL: http://www.SapphireSwan.com/dance/

Sponsor: Sapphire Swan, Inc.

Subject Area(s): Music & Drama   **Subcategory:** Dance

Grade Level(s): High School

Description

The dance directory is divided into three main sections: ballet links, other dance links, and dance styles. Included in all categories are both American and international companies, many with their schedules of performances. Several links include dancewear supplies and brief histories of each dance style.

Commentary

The link to Dance Pages is especially rich, although it is slow in loading, partially due to the vast number of pictures. The extensive lists of dance companies, dancers, and choreographers provide reference materials for teachers and advanced dance students. Especially welcomed are the links to modern dance companies such as Merce Cunningham (shown in the graphic).

No Graphic Found

Site: Western Square Dancing

URL: http://www.dosado.com/

Sponsor: Western Square Dancing

Subject Area(s): Music & Drama   **Subcategory:** Dance

Grade Level(s): Middle School, High School

Description

Find all types of information here related to square dancing: clubs, callers, caller schools, history, choreography, teaching, software dance simulators, and much more plus links for the non-dancer or newer dancer. Use the search function to easily search the site for information desired or merely browse through the various sections.

Commentary

This is an interesting site for those interested in square dancing. In the history section, find articles on the background of this American folk custom, a history of square and round dancing, the development of call leadership, and more. Be sure to check out F. Wm. Chickering's "Guide to Excruciatingly Correct Square Dance Behavior".

Site: Medieval Drama Links

URL: http://www.leeds.ac.uk/theatre/emd/links.html

Sponsor: Sydney Higgins

Subject Area(s): Music & Drama   **Subcategory:** Drama

Grade Level(s): Middle School, High School

Description

The 200+ links at this site are divided into categories and presented on four pages: (1) Texts; articles; books, bibliographies, and publications; news and discussion groups; performance and set design; and props and make-up; (2) Medieval costumes and illustrated material; (3) Medieval music; Medieval musical instruments; Medieval dance and other lists of Medieval drama links; and (4) Other theatre links and other useful links.

Commentary

This site of resources grew from the organizer's frustration over hours wasted spent searching for links that either no longer existed or provided little value. Anyone accessing the Web soon realizes it is difficult to keep current on sites, but Sydney Higgins has gathered and offered this list of ones she has found to be useful.

Section 01. Curriculum Corner

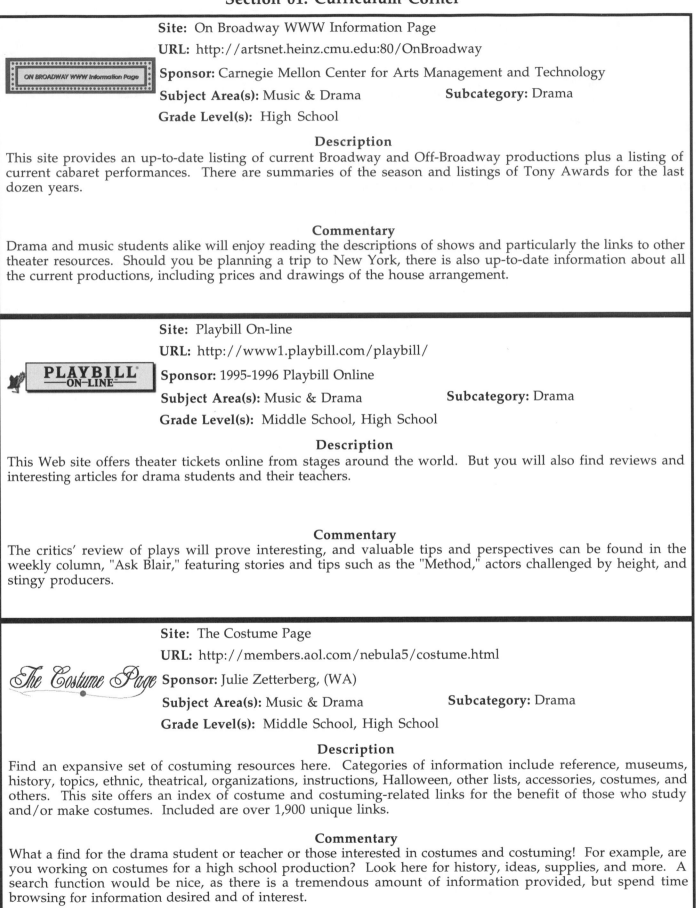

Site: On Broadway WWW Information Page

URL: http://artsnet.heinz.cmu.edu:80/OnBroadway

Sponsor: Carnegie Mellon Center for Arts Management and Technology

Subject Area(s): Music & Drama   **Subcategory:** Drama

Grade Level(s): High School

Description

This site provides an up-to-date listing of current Broadway and Off-Broadway productions plus a listing of current cabaret performances. There are summaries of the season and listings of Tony Awards for the last dozen years.

Commentary

Drama and music students alike will enjoy reading the descriptions of shows and particularly the links to other theater resources. Should you be planning a trip to New York, there is also up-to-date information about all the current productions, including prices and drawings of the house arrangement.

Site: Playbill On-line

URL: http://www1.playbill.com/playbill/

Sponsor: 1995-1996 Playbill Online

Subject Area(s): Music & Drama   **Subcategory:** Drama

Grade Level(s): Middle School, High School

Description

This Web site offers theater tickets online from stages around the world. But you will also find reviews and interesting articles for drama students and their teachers.

Commentary

The critics' review of plays will prove interesting, and valuable tips and perspectives can be found in the weekly column, "Ask Blair," featuring stories and tips such as the "Method," actors challenged by height, and stingy producers.

Site: The Costume Page

URL: http://members.aol.com/nebula5/costume.html

Sponsor: Julie Zetterberg, (WA)

Subject Area(s): Music & Drama   **Subcategory:** Drama

Grade Level(s): Middle School, High School

Description

Find an expansive set of costuming resources here. Categories of information include reference, museums, history, topics, ethnic, theatrical, organizations, instructions, Halloween, other lists, accessories, costumes, and others. This site offers an index of costume and costuming-related links for the benefit of those who study and/or make costumes. Included are over 1,900 unique links.

Commentary

What a find for the drama student or teacher or those interested in costumes and costuming! For example, are you working on costumes for a high school production? Look here for history, ideas, supplies, and more. A search function would be nice, as there is a tremendous amount of information provided, but spend time browsing for information desired and of interest.

Section 01. Curriculum Corner

Site: The Puppetry Home Page

URL: http://www-leland.stanford.edu/~rosesage/puppetry/puppetry.html

Sponsor: Rose Sage

Subject Area(s): Music & Drama   **Subcategory:** Drama

Grade Level(s): Middle School, High School

Description

Find information here about the art form of puppetry: puppetry organizations, puppetry festivals, puppet theaters, puppetry definitions, puppetry traditions around the world, puppetry exhibits and museums, puppet building, and more.

Commentary

This is a delightful site for research or browsing to see the extensive number of resources and other sites devoted to this unique art form.

Site: Theatricopia

URL: http://www.saintmarys.edu/~jhobgood/Jill/theatre.html

Sponsor: Jill Hobgood

Subject Area(s): Music & Drama   **Subcategory:** Drama

Grade Level(s): High School

Description

This Web site offers the organizer's collection of musicals sites as well as some general theatre sites. Information is organized into sections on awards, books, composers, games, general sites, lyrics, magazines, mailing lists, multimedia, performers, shows, and shops.

Commentary

The information on shows, performers, and lyricists may be of interest for general browsing by students of any age.

Site: Welcome to the Dramatic Exchange

URL: http://www.dramex.org/

Sponsor: Rob Knop and Mike Dederian

Subject Area(s): Music & Drama   **Subcategory:** Drama

Grade Level(s): Middle School, High School

Description

The Dramatic Exchange is a Web site dedicated to archiving and distributing scripts. Playwrights are encouraged to "publish" their plays here, and producers can find new plays that they might want to produce. For others, the site offers a place for anyone interested in drama to browse. Play listings include summary information, synopses, and information about contacting the playwrights.

Commentary

Be sure to check out the links to other theater-related Web sites suggested. This is a great place to review scripts of plays, and you may choose to submit one of your own for posting. Plays are indexed by author and by a number of different categories. You will want to read carefully the information included regarding appropriate use of the scripts found at this site.

Site: A Guide to Medieval and Renaissance Instruments

URL: http://www.s-hamilton.k12.ia.us/antiqua/instrumt.html

Sponsor: Musica Antiqua, Ensemble Members, Iowa State University.

Subject Area(s): Music & Drama   **Subcategory:** Music

Grade Level(s): Elementary, Middle School, High School

Description

Click on the name of an instrument to see its picture, read about it, and hear how it sounds. Some of the instruments included are the bagpipe, cornamuse, dulcian, dulcimer, harp, harpsichord, hurdy-gurdy, lizard, lute, psaltery, rackett, schalmei, shawm, viol, and zink.

Commentary

What a terrific site for exploring a variety of instruments! The text may be a little challenging for some elementary school students, but information is comprehensive about the instrument and its history, and it is fun to hear how each sounds.

Site: Catalogue of Classical Composers

URL: http://thanatos.uoregon.edu/~lincicum/complst.html

Sponsor: Jon Michael Lincicum

Subject Area(s): Music & Drama   **Subcategory:** Music

Grade Level(s): Middle School, High School

Description

This site offers a reference to the history of classical music through biographies of the composers that wrote it. Find a different Weekly Focus on a composer each week. The three main features of the site are an index of the names and dates for a number of composers, an online music dictionary to assist those knowledgeable or not so knowledgeable about music, and biographies of the composers.

Commentary

The host of the site encourages the visitors to e-mail him regarding any composer they would like to see featured. You will not currently find musical excerpts or repertoire lists for composers, but they may be added in the future. This is a handy reference site with composer biographies nicely organized into Medieval, Renaissance, Baroque, Preclassical, Classical, Early Romantic, Late Romantic, and Early 20th Century periods.

Site: Electronic Music Interactive

URL: http://nmc.uoregon.edu/emi/

Sponsor: University of Oregon—New Media Center

Subject Area(s): Music & Drama   **Subcategory:** Music

Grade Level(s): Middle School, High School

Description

This is an electronic music site at the University of Oregon that uses Shockwave. It includes 80 diagrams, 50 interactive animations with sound, and 150 interactive glossary terms explaining content across 38 topic modules.

Commentary

Visitors can interactively explore the relationships between wave forms and sounds at this site.

Site: Gilbert & Sullivan Archive

URL: http://diamond.idbsu.edu/gas/GaS.html

Sponsor: Jim Farron, Archive Curator

Subject Area(s): Music & Drama   **Subcategory:** Music

Grade Level(s): Middle School, High School

Description
This online archive is devoted to the operas and other works of Gilbert and Sullivan. Find a variety of clip art, librettos, plot summaries, pictures of the original Gilbert and Sullivan stars, song scores, MIDI and MPEG audio files (these allow you to listen to the music online), and newsletter articles. Options lead you to What's Hot, What's New, Opera Index, and Gilbert and Sullivan Files (biographies, glossaries, and more).

Commentary
This site is frequently updated, and you can link from it to other Gilbert and Sullivan sites as well as to sites pertaining to opera and the arts. Utility files are available for downloading if needed. This is a wonderful site for students and teachers.

Site: Music Education at WWW. GSYPO.COM

URL: http://www.gspyo.com/education/index.html

Sponsor: Garden State Pops Youth Orchestra

Subject Area(s): Music & Drama   **Subcategory:** Music

Grade Level(s): Elementary, Middle School, High School

Description
Visit this Web site to explore some parts of music with online tutorials and guides provided by the Garden State Pops Youth Orchestra. Categories allow you to learn and hear about different instruments, learn to read music, review information on various musical genres, read about today's date in music history, and link to other music education sites on the Web.

Commentary
Students will enjoy learning about the different families and different types of instruments. Just click on any instrument to hear it. Choose from strings, woodwinds, brass, and percussion instruments. The tutorials offered are easy to read and understand, allowing students of different age groups to each review information at a comfortable pace.

Site: The Mudcat Café

URL: http://www.deltablues.com/folksearch.html

Sponsor: The Mudcat Café

Subject Area(s): Music & Drama   **Subcategory:** Music

Grade Level(s): Middle School, High School

Description
This is an online magazine dedicated to blues and folk music. You will find a searchable index of the Digital Tradition Folk Song Database (April 1997 version), containing the words and/or music to over 6,500 folk songs plus a host of pictures and articles of interest. Joining as a member, which is free, additionally allows you to track discussion threads, control links, and privately communicate with other members.

Commentary
Enjoy browsing through the pictures and articles about some of the great blues musicians or search the Digital Tradition Folk Song Database for specific information—search by entering a keyword of your own, by choosing from an alphabetical list of keywords, or by entering a specific song title.

Site: WorldBand

URL: http://co-nect.bbn.com/WorldBand/CoNECTMusic.html

Sponsor: Department of Defense Dependent Schools

Subject Area(s): Music & Drama   **Subcategory:** Music

Grade Level(s): Elementary, Middle School

Description

World Band is an exciting music project in which each school has an electronic music studio with a midi synthesizer and computer sequencing software. Using the Internet, the students collaborate studying music composition, sequencing, and creating their own sounds.

Commentary

There are sound files that most will be able to download such as the Japanese songs...these are great. Midi files are also available for those with that type of equipment. All the schools involved are middle or high schools, but most everyone will enjoy visiting this site.

NO GRAPHIC FOUND

Site: Worldwide Internet Music Resources

URL: http://www.music.indiana.edu/music_resources/

Sponsor: William and Gayle Cook Music Library, Indiana University School of Music

Subject Area(s): Music & Drama   **Subcategory:** Music

Grade Level(s): Middle School, High School

Description

Find here a resource list of links organized by individual musicians (all genres) and popular groups, groups and ensembles (except popular), other sites related to performance, composers and composition, genres and types of music, research and study, the commercial world of music, journals and magazines, and general and miscellaneous.

Commentary

Students will enjoy researching classical composers as well as finding information on popular musicians, both individuals and groups, of today.

Site: Apollo 11

URL: http://www.gsfc.nasa.gov/hqpao/apollo_11.html

Sponsor: National Aeronautics and Space Administration

Subject Area(s): Science   **Subcategory:** Astronomy and Space

Grade Level(s): Elementary, Middle School

Description

Apollo 11 mission information includes an overview of the mission, astronauts' recollections, remarks by the President, and a bibliography.   NASA's rich history from its beginning in 1915 until today is included.

Commentary

Enjoy the collection of mission patches or take a trip to the many sites of NASA. Movies, images, audio files, and a poster are included. Be advised...the movie "One Small Step" takes 26 minutes to download. Individual images are, of course, much faster, and the quality is remarkable.

Section 01. Curriculum Corner

Site: Automated Telescope Facility

URL: http://inferno.physics.uiowa.edu/

Sponsor: University of Iowa

Subject Area(s): Science   **Subcategory:** Astronomy and Space

Grade Level(s): High School

Description

This Web site describes how an automated telescope works. The Automated Telescope is a 7" Astrophysics refracting telescope, equipped with an HPC-1 CCD camera, and is located on the roof of Van Allen Hall in Iowa City. The device is operated remotely using a PC running custom software. Technical descriptions are provided along with a database of images and links to other automated telescopes on the Web.

Commentary

This is an excellent resource for astronomy students and teachers. The project is supported by undergraduate students, graduate students, and faculty of the University of Iowa as well as by grants from the National Science Foundation and The Iowa Space Grant Consortium. Various student lab exercises and research projects for use with the facility are described. Find links to other automated telescope sites on the Web.

Site: EarthRISE

URL: http://earthrise.sdsc.edu/

Sponsor: San Diego Supercomputer Center

Subject Area(s): Science   **Subcategory:** Astronomy and Space

Grade Level(s): Middle School, High School

Description

EarthRise is a graphical database of photos of the Earth from space. These photos by astronauts were taken out the windows of the Space Shuttle over the past 15 years. Students can click on a continent and then a country for thousands of images of places in that country. The site appears to be updated on almost a daily basis.

Commentary

You will be impressed with this site if you are at all interested in space. The photography is incredible, and the ability to search the pictures in various ways is amazing. Teachers will like the additional features explaining notations about locations. Photographers will sometimes find further information about the lens and film used to capture the picture.

Site: Exploration in Education: Space

URL: http://marvel.stsci.edu/exined-html/exined-home.html

Sponsor: Space Telescope Science Institute

Subject Area(s): Science   **Subcategory:** Astronomy and Space

Grade Level(s): Elementary, Middle School

Description

The Exploration in Education program was established to explore new ways to derive social benefit from our space program by communicating its ideas and results. At this site are electronic reports, electronic tutorials, and electronic picture books. These can be retrieved in Macintosh or Windows format for later use.

Commentary

The space art by kids is a great part of this site. Almost everything can be downloaded as a screenshot, for use on Macs with Hypercard Player 2.1 and for use on Windows with WinPlusRuntime. Of course, this may take a while, but it is well worth it if you enjoy space.

Section 01. Curriculum Corner

Site: HST's (Hubble Space Telescope) Greatest Hits 1990-1995

URL: http://www.stsci.edu/pubinfo/BestOfHST95.html

Sponsor: NASA

Subject Area(s): Science   **Subcategory:** Astronomy and Space

Grade Level(s): Middle School, High School

Description

This is a photo gallery site of some of the most spectacular images photographed by the Hubble Space Telescope from 1990-1995. Background information is provided for each.

Commentary

This is an excellent resource for research project information with beautiful images and good information.

Site: International Space Station

URL: http://station.nasa.gov/

Sponsor: NASA

Subject Area(s): Science   **Subcategory:** Astronomy and Space

Grade Level(s): Middle School, High School

Description

The Space Station is designed to create a permanent orbiting science institute in space, capable of performing long-duration research in a nearly gravity-free environment. This site is updated weekly with new information. Find information in the fact book, interviews, articles, pictures, and in press releases.

Commentary

There are some great artists' concept images of the Space Station as it will look when assembly is complete. Also find information about the space shuttle, astronauts who have already been selected, and the type of preparation training they are engaged in.

Site: Jet Propulsion Lab Imaging Radar

URL: http://southport.jpl.nasa.gov/

Sponsor: National Atmospheric and Space Administration

Subject Area(s): Science   **Subcategory:** Astronomy and Space

Grade Level(s): Middle School, High School

Description

This site houses a library of radar images from the Jet Propulsion Lab in Pasadena, California. There is a virtual classroom, complete with teacher and student materials. Information about individual radar projects is available as well.

Commentary

The site opens with a multiple-choice question about a radar image. The image is selected at random, so you will get a different quiz question each time you visit this site.

Section 01. Curriculum Corner

Site: Jet Propulsion Laboratory

URL: http://www.jpl.nasa.gov/

Sponsor: NASA and the California Institute of Technology

Subject Area(s): Science   **Subcategory:** Astronomy and Space

Grade Level(s): Middle School, High School

Description

This site offers a large number of images of planets, asteroids, and other celestial objects, including educational background information pertaining to them in the Image & Information Archive. Look in Special Features for fun and interesting things, such as flying your name on the Cassini Spacecraft, learning about women at JPL and their careers and perspectives on science and technology jobs, or take a guided tour of the solar system.

Commentary

The images here are spectacular and can be downloaded. The site is very informative and varied in topics and provides a glossary of terms students can access. This site is valuable for research as well as for recreational exploration.

Site: MUFON, the Mutual UFO Network

URL: http://www.rutgers.edu/~mcgrew/mufon/index.html

Sponsor: Mutual UFO Network

Subject Area(s): Science   **Subcategory:** Astronomy and Space

Grade Level(s): Middle School, High School

Description

The Mutual UFO Network was founded in 1969 as a multidisciplinary, grass roots approach to resolving the UFO mystery. Those involved now number more than 5,000 members, field investigators, consultants, and research specialists worldwide.

Commentary

There are excerpts of articles and information from recent as well as older journals on file here. Of particular interest is the bibliography of UFO literature and the commentaries related to the variety of movie and television productions which involve aliens.

Site: NASA Home Page

URL: http://www.nasa.gov/

Sponsor: NASA

Subject Area(s): Science   **Subcategory:** Astronomy and Space

Grade Level(s): Elementary, Middle School, High School

Description

Included is historic as well as current information; recent pictures from the Hubble telescope; in the Gallery, video, audio clips and still images that can be downloaded; and more. Check out activity at the agency's field centers and see what lies ahead in NASA's planetary exploration in Space Science. Mission to Planet Earth provides information to help understand how the Earth is changing and how humans influence those changes.

Commentary

Learn all about NASA at the NASA home page. The Gallery has fascinating clips of interest and for use in research, and when there is current activity from NASA that you want to follow, Today@NASA provides links to details about the breaking news.

Section 01. Curriculum Corner

Site: Nine Planets—A Multimedia Tour of the Solar System

URL: http://seds.lpl.arizona.edu/nineplanets/nineplanets/

Sponsor: William Arnett

Subject Area(s): Science   **Subcategory:** Astronomy and Space

Grade Level(s): Middle School, High School

Description
This overview of the nine planets covers the history, mythology, and current scientific knowledge of each of the planets and moons in our solar system. Each page has text and images; sometimes there are sounds, movies, and references for related information.

Commentary
Did you know that Earth is the only planet whose English name does not derive from Greek mythology? There is significant information about each planet. Some of it is quite technical, and most is fascinating and easily understood. This is a great reference for reports!

Site: Regional Planetary Image Facility

URL: http://ceps.nasm.edu:2020/rpif.html

Sponsor: Smithsonian Institution and NASA

Subject Area(s): Science   **Subcategory:** Astronomy and Space

Grade Level(s): Middle School, High School

Description
This virtual library contains over 300,000 images of the planets and their satellites, including some earth-looking images from early space satellite missions. The images are organized by planet and can easily be accessed by students. In addition, there are links to the Web sites for other facilities with similar information.

Commentary
This site would be an excellent source of images to illustrate a research paper or multimedia presentation on any planet in the solar system.

Site: Sharing NASA

URL: http://quest.arc.nasa.gov/interactive.html

Sponsor: NASA

Subject Area(s): Science   **Subcategory:** Astronomy and Space

Grade Level(s): Elementary, Middle School

Description
The NASA K-12 Internet Initiative is making it a priority to develop a program which will help students share in the excitement of authentic scientific and engineering pursuits. Current projects include the Shuttle Team Online and Live from Mars. Other projects are planned for the next school year—look for past projects in the archives.

Commentary
In the projects currently underway, there is actual interaction between the scientists and students. Although that is no longer possible when a project is complete, the reports and pictures that can be reviewed are still fascinating.

Section 01. Curriculum Corner

Site: Students for the Exploration and Development of Space (SEDS)

URL: http://seds.lpl.arizona.edu/

Sponsor: University of Arizona Chapter at the Lunar and Planetary Laboratory

Subject Area(s): Science   **Subcategory:** Astronomy and Space

Grade Level(s): Middle School, High School

Description
This site includes resources on astronomy, space exploration, comets, space telescopes, space stations, and related topics. The planets are included with information, multimedia, and links to more sites. You can talk to astronomers and print or download images. The Mars Exploration Page is full of images, articles, and links to other sites pertaining to the planet, its exploration, and Mars missions.

Commentary
This is the Web site for the Arizona chapter of SEDS. Links are provided to the other chapters' sites, most of which have similar resources. Much of the information would be too challenging for students younger than middle school, unless someone older was working with them.

Site: The NASA Shuttle Web

URL: http://shuttle.nasa.gov/index.html/

Sponsor: National Atmospheric and Space Administration

Subject Area(s): Science   **Subcategory:** Astronomy and Space

Grade Level(s): Middle School, High School

Description
When a launch is in progress, view the countdown here or just log in to check the launch status. Information on past launches is also available, along with technical drawings and specifications as well as biographies of the crews, interviews, and audio and video clips. There is a link to the RealAudio web site for downloading a free version of the RealAudio plug-in.

Commentary
This is a "must see" site for all students, parents, and teachers interested in space flight!

Site: Welcome to the Planets

URL: http://pds.jpl.nasa.gov/planets/

Sponsor: California Institute of Technology

Subject Area(s): Science   **Subcategory:** Astronomy and Space

Grade Level(s): Middle School, High School

Description
This Web site provides a collection of some of the best images from NASA's planetary exploration program. The collection has been extracted from the interactive program "Welcome to the Planets" which was distributed in a CD-ROM version in 1995.

Commentary
You will find a series of 17 small, labeled pictures which then lead to other pictures, with a detailed description of the photos included. There is a lot of technical material here but also plenty of general, readable information for middle and high school students.

Section 01. Curriculum Corner

Site: Animal Resources

URL: http://www.bev.net/education/SeaWorld/infobook.html

Sponsor: Sea World, Inc. at Busch Gardens

Subject Area(s): Science   **Subcategory:** Biology

Grade Level(s): Elementary, Middle School

Description

The aim of Sea World is to instill an appreciation for science and especially for the ocean and its inhabitants by providing an accurate but stimulating environment for students of all ages. There is detailed information available at this site on dozens of animals and plants living in the ocean, with pictures and additional information useful for teachers.

Commentary

Animal Bytes provides quick, fun facts about a large variety of land and sea animals. You can explore the topic of ocean animals in more detail and find out about zoological park careers. Additionally find links to other sites for the animal lover.

Site: Australian National Botanic Gardens

URL: http://osprey.erin.gov.au

Sponsor: Department of Environment, Sport, and Territories

Subject Area(s): Science   **Subcategory:** Biology

Grade Level(s): High School

Description

Since 1933 the Australian National Botanic Gardens has maintained a scientific collection of native plants from all parts of the country. The plants are displayed for the enjoyment and education of visitors and are used for research into plant classification and biology.

Commentary

This site can be enjoyed at many levels since there are certainly beautiful pictures of flowers which can be appreciated by all ages. In general, however, the site will appeal to the serious botanist with discussions of threatened plants, horticultural research, and lists of botanical organizations.

USDA

Site: Bee Research Center

URL: http://gears.tucson.ars.ag.gov

Sponsor: Carl Hayden Bee Research Center

Subject Area(s): Science   **Subcategory:** Biology

Grade Level(s): High School

Description

The Carl Hayden Bee Research Center is maintained by the United States Department of Agriculture in conjunction with the University of Arizona. Their research goals are to improve crop pollination and honey bee colony productivity through studies of honey bee behavior, physiology, and diseases.

Commentary

The Amazing Beecam is well named; it features a zoom camera to operate as you move through the hive. There are a variety of research articles posted, many dealing with pollination. And who can resist visiting the Road Kill Cafe?

Section 01. Curriculum Corner

Site: Biodiversity and Biological Collections Web Server

URL: http://muse.bio.cornell.edu

Sponsor: Cornell University and others

Subject Area(s): Science   **Subcategory:** Biology

Grade Level(s): High School

Description

This collection of resources is drawn together from dozens of major universities in order to create a bibliography and a searchable database. It appears to be under constant updating and revision. Some of the categories are botany, herpetology, invertebrates, entomology, ichthyology, mammalogy, and many more.

Commentary

Articles are quite sophisticated and specific...this is a wonderful resource for the serious student of biology. Even less serious students will be impressed with the huge number of links to museums. The New York Botanical Garden is one of many glorious sites.

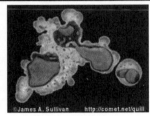

Site: Cells Alive!

URL: http://www.cellsalive.com/

Sponsor: James A. Sullivan, Quill Digital and Photo-Graphics

Subject Area(s): Science   **Subcategory:** Biology

Grade Level(s): Elementary, Middle, High School

Description

This is a very visual site with animated graphics of real cells—watch as they move around the screen. You might find bacteria dividing; white blood cells going after bacteria; relative sizes of various viruses, bacteria, and red blood cells; how living cells "keep in shape"; or how immune cells become involved when you get a splinter or a scratch.

Commentary

There are animated GIFs and QuickTime videos. The graphics load fairly quickly. Movies may take a little bit of time, but they are worth it. The downloadable videos and animations require QuickTime for Macintosh or Windows and Movie Player (Macintosh) or SmartVid (Windows) or VidVue (Windows) to be able to view them.

Site: Cincinnati Zoo and Botanical Gardens

URL: http://www.cincyzoo.org/

Sponsor: Cincinnati Zoo and Botanical Gardens

Subject Area(s): Science   **Subcategory:** Biology

Grade Level(s): Elementary, Middle School

Description

No longer simple menageries, today's zoological parks are centers for conservation. This site provides a host of information on wildlife education, conservation tips, a weekly animal guessing game, and current events and news from the zoo.

Commentary

Look through the list of births and hatchings which are very interesting—you will probably want some pictures, too. The Cat Ambassador Program, which teaches students about endangered cat species, is but one of many educational programs which goes to schools.

Section 01. Curriculum Corner

Site: Dinosaurs!

URL: http://www.hcc.hawaii.edu/dinos/dinos.1.html

Sponsor: Honolulu Community College

Subject Area(s): Science   **Subcategory:** Biology

Grade Level(s): Elementary, Middle School, High School

Description
This is a free and permanent online exhibit of dinosaur fossils. The "fossils" are replicas from the originals at the American Museum of Natural History in New York City. Find images of Triceratops, Tyrannosaurus Rex, Stegosaurus, Hypselosaurus, and Iguanadon/Deiononychus. In addition to the images, you will find in-depth information describing the dinosaurs and narrated audio by an expert on the subject.

Commentary
Students of all grade levels will love this web site showing images of and describing the dinosaurs that they most want to learn about. Clicking on a speaker icon allows you to take a narrated tour of the exhibit with Rick Ziegler, a history teacher who is one of the exhibit's founders.

Site: Entomology

URL: http://www.ColoState.edu/Depts/Entomology/ent.html

Sponsor: Colorado State University

Subject Area(s): Science   **Subcategory:** Biology

Grade Level(s): Middle School, High School

Description
Described as the first Entomology site in the world, it seems to cover every possible facet of the field. There are announcements of upcoming events, positions available, and a variety of articles and publications. A major strength of this site is the variety of links available to other sites, servers, and programs around the world.

Commentary
You'll love the images of insects and their relatives...most of which load quite quickly. The Purplish Copper butterfly is breathtaking! Even if you are not a serious student of entomology, you will be almost ready to participate in the Colorado State University Insect Lunchtime Discussion Group!

Site: Fish FAQ

URL: http://www.wh.whoi.edu/homepage/faq.html

Sponsor: Northeast Fisheries Science Center (Massachusetts)

Subject Area(s): Science   **Subcategory:** Biology

Grade Level(s): Elementary, Middle School

Description
A blue ocean with bubbles provides the background for dozens of frequently asked questions about fish. The Northeast Fisheries Science Center at Woods Hole provides the expertise based on the questions asked by the many visitors to the center.

Commentary
You might as well start scrolling through the answers to all the questions since you won't be able to resist looking at them eventually. The pictures are great, and the explanations are simple but accurate. For example, fish don't really sleep since to humans that means closing the eyelids and being still (two things that fish can't do), but they do rest...and maybe daydream.

No Graphic Found

Site: Human Body Image Browser

URL: http://www.vis.colostate.edu/cgi-bin/gva/gvaview

Sponsor: Colorado State University

Subject Area(s): Science   **Subcategory:** Biology

Grade Level(s): Elementary, Middle School

Description
This site contains 27 still images and animation of different parts of the human body. The reader can examine the skeleton with and without cartilage. It is also possible to look at the heart, lungs, veins, bronchi, ribs, and even the skin.

Commentary
One especially nice feature is the ability to zoom in on images. Each image is quite clear, though annotation or description would be a nice addition.

Site: Missouri Botanical Garden

URL: http://www.mobot.org/welcome.html

Sponsor: Missouri Botanical Garden

Subject Area(s): Science   **Subcategory:** Biology

Grade Level(s): Middle School, High School

Description
In addition to information about this museum, there are extensive links to research about the flowering plants around the world. There is both education and horticulture information, as well as a reading room and image galleries.

Commentary
This site uses a very clever legend map so that you can see the entire table of contents at one time. Head straight for the "Plants in Bloom" section where you will find one or more beautiful photos with a general description or pages of botanical names.

Site: Nanoworld

URL: http://www.uq.oz.au:80/nanoworld/nanohome.html

Sponsor: The University of Queensland

Subject Area(s): Science   **Subcategory:** Biology

Grade Level(s): High School

Description
The Centre for Microscopy and Microanalysis is an interdisciplinary research and service facility dedicated to an understanding of the structure and composition of materials of biological and non-biological origin. With its high-tech equipment, it has been able to capture images and perform microanalysis which go beyond the typical laboratory.

Commentary
There is an incredible section entitled "HHMI Holiday Lectures on Science"; it is packed with animation and other resources to help both students and teachers visualize the life-and-death struggle between antigens and antibodies. Don't bother with this site without a highspeed modem.

Section 01. Curriculum Corner

Site: Sea World/Busch Garden

URL: http://www.bev.net/education/SeaWorld/

Sponsor: Sea World, Inc. and Busch Entertainment Corp.

Subject Area(s): Science   **Subcategory:** Biology

Grade Level(s): Middle School, High School

Description

Search the Sea World/Busch Gardens Animal Information Database to find information and photos of the many animals. Included are career information, educational resources for teachers, and more. Test yourself with a fun quiz or review the most popular questions asked about animals.

Commentary

Sea World is loved by young and old and is a fascinating place to explore animal behavior and the environment. Take a virtual tour here at this easy-to-navigate site. You'll have fun exploring!

Site: Tele-Garden Project

URL: http://www.usc.edu/dept/garden

Sponsor: Arts Electronic Center

Subject Area(s): Science   **Subcategory:** Biology

Grade Level(s): Middle School, High School

Description

The tele-robotic installation allows WWW users to view and interact with a remote garden filled with living plants. Members can plant, water, and monitor the progress of seedlings via the tender movements of an industrial robot arm. The project will soon move back to the U.S. and include a chat line for American visitors to the site.

Commentary

Register as a guest, and you will be permitted a guided tour of the garden and an explanation of how the robot works. Only members can actually participate, but the tour is still quite interesting—an unusual take on gardening.

Site: The Electronic Zoo

URL: http://netvet.wustl.edu/e-zoo.html

Sponsor: Dr. Ken Boschert, Washington University, St. Louis, MO

Subject Area(s): Science   **Subcategory:** Biology

Grade Level(s): Elementary, Middle School, High School

Description

This colorful site is for animal lovers and those interested in finding a wealth of information about animals. Find everything from how to care for pets to information pertaining to veterinary medicine. Clever icons point you to new information, easy searching, publications and organizations of interest, and more. World Wide Web searching and links take you to still more information about animals.

Commentary

This is an extremely rich site, but because of the abundance of information, even with animal icons in places, it may prove overwhelming and too much text for younger students to navigate on their own. Some of the information is somewhat technical, but most students will be able to browse for information and use data they find for reports and general interest.

Section 01. Curriculum Corner

Site: The Froggy Page

URL: http://frog.simplenet.com/froggy/

Sponsor: Sandra Loosemore

Subject Area(s): Science   **Subcategory:** Biology

Grade Level(s): Elementary, Middle School, High School

Description

This Web site provides links to "froggy" resources and sites across the Internet. The Scientific Amphibian section offer links to resources categorized as anatomy and dissection, declining amphibian populations, deformed frogs, species information, information about frogs kept in captivity, herpetological resources, embryology, or miscellaneous.

Commentary

Find pictures and/or listen to sounds of frogs from all over the world. Find stories and tales of frogs by Aesop, Grimm, Twain, and others. Students (and adults!) will find this site both educational and entertaining to visit. Don't miss the Famous Frogs section. Ribbit!

Site: The Geonome Database

URL: http://gdbwww.gdb.org

Sponsor: John Hopkins University School of Medicine

Subject Area(s): Science   **Subcategory:** Biology

Grade Level(s): High School

Description

Find a variety of resources at this site, including links to chromosome-specific servers, maps of individual chromosomes, model databases, and links to universities that are collaborating on this Human Geonome Project. Search for genomic segments, all biological data, people, or citations by name/ID or by keyword.

Commentary

Though this site has valuable information for clinicians, genetic counselors, research scientists and others, teachers and students will also find information of use.

Site: The Heart: An Online Exploration

URL: http://sln2.fi.edu/biosci/

Sponsor: The Franklin Institute Science Museum, support from Unisys Corporation

Subject Area(s): Science   **Subcategory:** Biology

Grade Level(s): Elementary, Middle School, High School

Description

Explore heart development and structure, follow blood through vessels, check out body systems, learn how to have a healthy heart, and study heart science. "Preview Gallery" information is in categories: do (such as hearing heartbeats), see (such as observing open heart surgery), learn (find a glossary or information on exercise), go (where they can link to other sites), and hear (such as listening to a heart murmur).

Commentary

Take an online tour of the heart and find a variety of interesting and fun topics related to the human heart. Students will especially like the "beating" buttons and great graphics. They will have fun with and learn from this site.

Section 01. Curriculum Corner

Site: The Interactive Frog Dissection

URL: http://curry.edschool.Virginia.EDU/go/frog

Sponsor: Mable Kinzie, University of Virginia

Subject Area(s): Science   **Subcategory:** Biology

Grade Level(s): Elementary, Middle School

Description

The virtual frog dissection program includes sections providing an introduction, preparation, skin incisions, muscle incisions, and internal organs. The purpose of the lab activity is to learn the anatomy of a frog along with a better understanding of the anatomy of vertebrate animals in general. The basic teaching technique used is demonstration with a movie, followed by practice on screen.

Commentary

This program has been around for several years on the Web. It is now updated, including the addition of research articles and pictures of students using the tool in their classroom. This material is interesting and clearly outlined, with well-constructed visuals and helpful practice.

Site: The San Diego Zoo

URL: http://www.sandiegozoo.org/

Sponsor: The San Diego Zoo

Subject Area(s): Science   **Subcategory:** Biology

Grade Level(s): Middle School, High School

Description

At this San Diego Zoo site, look for information about the zoo, its history, new exhibits, pictures of the animals, games, and more. Links take you to information about many of the animals and the plants in the zoo. Send a digital postcard with an animal picture to someone or play an online game, such as Baby Talk about animal babies. You can learn a lot about animals on your virtual tour!

Commentary

You will find a lot of text information here, and navigation is not very straightforward. Go into some of the categories from the main page to links to get to some of the most interesting information. One of the best links can be found by clicking on Education Programs and then on InternQuest. The high school interns at the zoo have created a site with beautiful pictures, journal entries, and more.

Site: UT Science Bytes

URL: http://loki.ur.utk.edu/ut2kids/

Sponsor: University of Tennessee

Subject Area(s): Science   **Subcategory:** Biology

Grade Level(s): Elementary, Middle School, High School

Description

Science Bytes is designed for students of all ages and their teachers. Each installment describes the work being done by scientists at the University of Tennessee; the writers are looking for feedback and new topics. It is a very professionally done, safe site with a variety of topics and few links.

Commentary

The developers of this site used beautiful pictures of animals, clever graphics, and a great sense of humor. The Knoxville Zoo is the inspiration behind several articles which students will enjoy as they read and find much new information.

Section 01. Curriculum Corner

Site: Virtual Frog Dissection Kit

URL: http://george.lbl.gov/ITG.hm.pg.docs/dissect/info.html

Sponsor: Lawrence Berkely National Laboratory

Subject Area(s): Science   **Subcategory:** Biology

Grade Level(s): Middle School, High School

Description
The "Whole Frog" project is intended to introduce the concepts of modern, computer-based 3D visualization, and at the same time to demonstrate the power of whole body and 3D imaging of anatomy as a curriculum tool. Students will be able to explore the anatomy of a frog by using data from high resolution MRI imaging.

Commentary
Students can perform an interactive dissection of a frog and make movies from various angles. The graphics are magnificent; one can really see the organs better than in real life. Instruction is available in eight languages. Frogs all over the world will be happy about this one!

Site: Welcome to the Bug Club

URL: http://www.ex.ac.uk/bugclub

Sponsor: Committee of Students, University of Exeter Biology Department

Subject Area(s): Science   **Subcategory:** Biology

Grade Level(s): Elementary, Middle School, High School

Description
This site provides information on entomology, the study of bugs, for children or the young at heart. Students can find out about the bug club members, become a member themselves, read the bug club newsletter (containing articles and fun things to do and make), learn how to care for bugs and insects, search the glossary for insect terms, find reviews of entomology books, and find a pen pal. Links to other bug sites are included.

Commentary
Some pages are still under construction. There are over 1,000,000 known species of insects in the world, and you can begin to learn about all of these "creepy-crawlies" here! The Pen Pal Page includes insect lovers of all ages from all over the world.

Site: Zoo Atlanta

URL: http://www.zooatlanta.org/

Sponsor: Zoo Atlanta

Subject Area(s): Science   **Subcategory:** Biology

Grade Level(s): Elementary, Middle School

Description
The home page opens with animal sounds and a selection menu. This is one of the oldest zoos in America, yet one of the most modern with natural habitat for animals, an innovative educational program, and this virtual zoo. Features include What's New, Kid's Habitat, Conservation, A Learning Corner, and Visitor Information.

Commentary
Star animals are presented with both pictures and sound; the quality is excellent, but they are very slow to load. Educational activities are classified according to grade level, but most of the site will be of interest to all ages. There is lots of conservation and natural habitat information at the still-expanding site.

Site: ZooNet

URL: http://www.mindspring.com/~zoonet/

Sponsor: Jim Henley, ZooNet

Subject Area(s): Science   **Subcategory:** Biology

Grade Level(s): Middle School, High School

Description

Do you want to visit some zoos? Use the index of zoos on this site to link to a variety of zoos across the United States and all over the world. Find information about zoo animals—a different animal is featured every week.

Commentary

Don't miss the link to the ZooNet Image Archive where you will find hundreds of pictures to look at or use in projects. You'll see them as thumbnails, smaller versions of the actual picture, but they can be quickly downloaded and then viewed at full size.

Site: Web Elements

URL: http://www.cchem.berkeley.edu:80/Table/index.html

Sponsor: University of Sheffield, England

Subject Area(s): Science   **Subcategory:** Chemistry

Grade Level(s): Middle School, High School

Description

This is an interactive periodic table that serves as a main menu to a database of information about the elements. Click on an element to learn its atomic weight, valence shells, bonds, properties, and more. There is also a link to other periodic tables on the Internet.

Commentary

This is a handy tool to illustrate for teachers and students the properties of all of the recognized elements. It also illustrates some of those that scientific communities cannot agree on.

Site: Earthquake Information: Reducing Earthquake Hazards

URL: http://quake.wr.usgs.gov/

Sponsor: United States Geological Survey

Subject Area(s): Science   **Subcategory:** Earth Science

Grade Level(s): Middle School, High School

Description

This site contains information about recent earthquakes, hazards and preparedness, and other resources for studying earthquakes. Find out how the Earth is moving today. The page also contains a link to a list of recent earthquakes in the United States and around the world, with color maps of them—in both GIF and HTML formats.

Commentary

The regional earthquake maps can be downloaded and printed. The date of the earthquake and also the size of the download file is shown for each entry. This list is updated every half hour.

Section 01. Curriculum Corner

Site: Learning Through Collaborative Visualization

URL: http://www.covis.nwu.edu

Sponsor: Learning Sciences Program, Northwestern University

Subject Area(s): Science   **Subcategory:** Earth Science

Grade Level(s): Middle School, High School

Description

The CoVis project is made up of thousands of students, over a hundred teachers, and many researchers and scientists working together to improve science education in middle and high schools. While various science topics are dealt with, there appears to be an emphasis on earth science.

Commentary

Find a significant volume of software to download here (although most of it is audio/video programs available and useable in other sites). Check out the What's New section for continuing directions of this project and new links to other science sites.

Site: Learning Web

URL: http://www.usgs.gov/education/

Sponsor: United States Geological Survey

Subject Area(s): Science   **Subcategory:** Earth Science

Grade Level(s): Elementary, Middle School, High School

Description

The Learning Web has resources for students and teachers, focused on earth science and including topics such as global change and working with maps. The main sections are: Teaching in the Learning Web; educational resources to teach earth science concepts; and Living in the Learning Web, where you can learn more about topics that affect us daily, such as "Where does your household water come from?"

Commentary

The Learning Web is the K-12 Education section of the USGS web site. The "Other USGS Educational Resources" page has links to sites such as Ask-A-Geologist, volcanoes, earthquakes, marine research, and water quality. In addition to The Learning Web, there is considerable other information available by browsing the main USGS site at <http://www.usgs.gov/>

Site: National Mapping Information

URL: http://mapping.usgs.gov

Sponsor: United States Geological Survey

Subject Area(s): Science   **Subcategory:** Earth Science

Grade Level(s): Middle School, High School

Description

As the nation's largest earth science research and information agency, the USGS provides a permanent Federal agency to "conduct the systematic and scientific classification of the public lands and examination of the geological structure, mineral resources, and products of the national domain." This section of the Web site provides up-to-date cartographic data for the United States.

Commentary

The Education section has some wonderful materials for teachers and students. You will enjoy tracking snow geese on the Net; individuals or classes can pick out a favorite goose, learn about migration, follow it on a map, and send in their prediction of the next stop-over point. Earthshots contains satellite images of environmental changes. And there is lots more!

Section 01. Curriculum Corner

Site: SeaWiFS Project Home Page

URL: http://seawifs.gsfc.nasa.gov

Sponsor: National Aeronautic and Space Administration

Subject Area(s): Science   **Subcategory:** Earth Science

Grade Level(s): Middle School, High School

Description

This page provides access into the background, status, and documentation for NASA's global color monitoring mission called SeaWiFS (Sea-viewing Wide Field-of-view Sensor). Subtle changes in ocean color signify various types and quantities of marine plants, the knowledge of which has both scientific and practical applications.

Commentary

The Project Flipbook is a great place to begin the exploration of this site. There are descriptions of the equipment used, the data capture facility, a glossary, and much more. As you might expect, there are many pictures and animation sequences, as well as simulated daily coverage. The orbiting sensor views every kilometer of cloud-free ocean every 48 hours.

Site: The Cave Page

URL: http://rschp2.anu.edu.au:8080/cave/cave.html

Sponsor: Sherry Mayo

Subject Area(s): Science   **Subcategory:** Earth Science

Grade Level(s): Middle School, High School

Description

Find a number of caving articles which report on expeditions from around the world. There is also technical information provided about such things as knot tying and cave rescuing. Europe, Australia, and New Zealand are featured in a search for the best caving areas.

Commentary

Information at this site is painfully slow to load—but worth it! You'll appreciate the way the world is divided into "International" and "Australia." A section called "Odds and Sods" features photos of wonderful places like Hinkle Horn Honking Holes! There are songs, recipes, and links to caving newsgroups.

Site: Volcano World

URL: http://volcano.und.nodak.edu/

Sponsor: NASA

Subject Area(s): Science   **Subcategory:** Earth Science

Grade Level(s): Elementary, Middle School

Description

Surely the definitive site on volcanoes, it contains listings and pictures of the volcanoes of the world and volcanic parks. There are teaching and learning activities designed for both teachers and students. A volcanologist is available for questions...and career counseling.

Commentary

The graphics are wonderful on this site. It is possible to find out what volcanoes are currently erupting and to see video clips of eruptions; be patient since these movies take a long time to download. Kid's Door provides online and printed activities plus some virtual field trips.

Section 01. Curriculum Corner

Site: Good Green Fun! Music and Rainforest Ecology for Children of All Ages

URL: http://www.efn.org/~dharmika/

Sponsor: Dharmika J. Henshel

Subject Area(s): Science   **Subcategory:** Environment & Ecology

Grade Level(s): Elementary, Middle School

Description

This site takes you to the forests of the world and lets you listen to music samples and learn songs, such as Strangler Fig, Tropical Twilight, Rainforest Ants, Symphony in Green, and Forest Lullaby, about tropical and temperate rainforests. Included is information about forest ecology and links to other ecology-oriented sites. There is also an "Adopt-a-Song" project, a curriculum project for sharing ideas and activities among classrooms.

Commentary

Dharmika J. Henshel is the author of the forest songs and of this site. With each song, you can hear a sound sample; read the lyrics; do activities with your classroom, family, or friends; find answers to questions about plants, animals, and ecosystems. Various sections direct you to student resources, teacher resources, ecology projects, other children's sites, environmental education resources, and more.

Site: Journey North

URL: http://www.learner.org/k12/jnorth

Sponsor: Annenberg/CPB Math and Science Project

Subject Area(s): Science   **Subcategory:** Environment & Ecology

Grade Level(s): Elementary, Middle School

Description

With an emphasis on the Northern Hemisphere, this site tracks the migration of the seasons as evidenced by animals and flowers. Students can read about the wildlife migration, report on sightings in their own neighborhood, and/or ask questions of experts.

Commentary

What a bargain! Using the site as a Level I News Reporter is free. If a class decides to move to Level II as an Internet Field Team, there is a charge of $39 for printed materials and access to further experts. The photographs are lovely, and the site is easy to read and use. Different sections of the site are updated with field information from kids and experts on a weekly basis.

Site: Naural Resources of Canada

URL: http://www.nofc.forestry.ca

Natural Resources Canada   Ressources naturelles Canada

Sponsor: Canadian Forest Service

Subject Area(s): Science   **Subcategory:** Environment & Ecology

Grade Level(s): Middle School, High School

Description

Available in English and French, this Web page from the Canadian Forest Service is offered to help everyone understand forests. The goal of the Forest Service is to promote the sustainable management of Canada's forests for all users, both now and in the future. This site seeks to explain the research programs and support services that are available.

Commentary

Did you know that Canada has more than 10% of the total forest area of the entire Earth within its borders? It is therefore not surprising that these research programs are extensive and that each year National Forest Week is recognized.

Site: Netspedition Amazon

URL: http://sunsite.doc.ic.ac.uk/netspedition

Sponsor: Imperial College of Science, Technology and Medicine

Subject Area(s): Science **Subcategory:** Environment & Ecology

Grade Level(s): Elementary, Middle School

Description
Netspedition was an interactive scientific expedition to the Amazon rainforest, and it was conducted entirely on the Internet via this Web site. Now young explorers can relive this adventure through the pictures and records that are maintained here.

Commentary
The expedition team studied butterflies and the water conditions of two rivers, and you will likely find what they learned about each pretty interesting. But you may choose not to go near the bug collection without a friend! You can browse aimlessly through the sections or use the clickable route map.

Site: NRDC Online

URL: http://www.nrdc.org

Sponsor: National Resources Defense Council

Subject Area(s): Science **Subcategory:** Environment & Ecology

Grade Level(s): Middle School, High School

Description
Many valuable resources on the study of the environment can be found here, including daily dispatches from the Global Warming Summit, general news and information, an online journal, technical resources, the Green Guide, and even eco-friendly gift-giving tips.

Commentary
Students can take the "Health and Safety Poll" to find out what aspects of their personal environments might pose risks to them. The Search Tools page makes searching for research materials simple to accomplish, and there is a "Web Picks" section with links to sites of current interest—this section is updated weekly.

Site: The Environment Page from the WWW Virtual Library

URL: http://ecosys.drdr.virginia.edu/Environment.html

Sponsor: Shay Mitchell, University of Virginia

Subject Area(s): Science **Subcategory:** Environment & Ecology

Grade Level(s): Middle School, High School

Description
This list of Internet links can be browsed by topic, or the reader can jump to a specific letter, which may be the keyword of interest. There are hundreds of links which would seem to cover most topics of interest in the broad area of science.

Commentary
On the plus side, the author states that he updates the links frequently and reviews to see if they are still open, which must be quite a job since there are so many. On the down side, it is somewhat laborious and time-consuming to move from one link to another.

Site: U.S. Department of the Interior

URL: http://www.doi.gov/

Sponsor: U.S. Department of the Interior

Subject Area(s): Science   **Subcategory:** Environment & Ecology

Grade Level(s): Elementary, Middle School

Description

The mission of the Department of the Interior is to protect and provide access to the nation's natural and cultural heritage and to honor the trust responsibilities to Indian tribes. Topics change frequently as does hot news, but there is always the capacity to search the site.

Commentary

Visit a new part of this site called "Kids on the Web." It has hundreds of animal pictures and some animated drawings of animals. Check out the Kid's Corner in Alaska. The butterfly link is a rich one with beautiful photos, animation, and good information describing raising a caterpillar to the butterfly stage.

Site: U.S. Environmental Protection Agency

URL: http://www.epa.gov

Sponsor: U.S. Environmental Protection Agency

Subject Area(s): Science   **Subcategory:** Environment & Ecology

Grade Level(s): Elementary, Middle School, High School

Description

The mission of the Environmental Protection Agency is to protect public health and to safeguard and improve the natural environment—air, water, and land. The site provides copies of regulations, publications, programs, and initiatives which are sponsored or related to this mission. Find special information for students and teachers and links to other related sites.

Commentary

There are articles about the environment, and students are encouraged to get involved in knowing and caring about the environment in order to protect it for the future. Materials range from very technical to fun and informative (see Bloopers) and from games to simple activities for studying the world around us. Teachers will appreciate the teaching aids and facts about the environment.

Site: Wildlife Conservation Society

URL: http://www.wcs.org

Sponsor: Bronx Zoo

Subject Area(s): Science   **Subcategory:** Environment & Ecology

Grade Level(s): Elementary, Middle School, High School

Description

The Wildlife Conservation Society was founded in 1895 and continues its purpose of encouraging and advancing the study of zoology. The world's first animal hospital was built by the Society at the Bronx Zoo in 1916. The mission has spread to include wildlife, aquariums, and many educational and research services.

Commentary

Pablo Python leads kids through an adventure with animals involving sounds—and what a friendly looking snake he is! (This adventure is available as a free book from the Society, in either English or Spanish, along with some tips for your parents on wildlife conservation.) Catch up with special events if you live in the New York City vicinity.

Section 01. Curriculum Corner

Site: Kinetic City Super Crew

URL: http://www.aaas.org/ehr/kcsuper.html

Sponsor: American Association for the Advancement of Science and NSF

Subject Area(s): Science   **Subcategory:** Miscellaneous

Grade Level(s): Middle School, High School

Description

The Kinetic City Super Crew is a team of young people who solve science mysteries, using ALEC, their quirky computer and the Kinetic City Express, a railroad train that transports them around the world. Schools can form their own Super Crews and participate in experiments.

Commentary

The crew's adventures are heard on radio stations across the United States or can be downloaded from this site. RealAudio is used here, and a 28.8 KBPS or better connection is strongly recommended for those portions of the site. This is a lot of fun, and a lot of learning is taking place!

Site: The Cornell Theory Center Math and Science Gateway

URL: http://www.tc.cornell.edu/Edu/MathSciGateway/

Sponsor: The Cornell Theory Center

Subject Area(s): Science   **Subcategory:** Miscellaneous

Grade Level(s): Middle School, High School

Description

This site includes information, labs, and resources on astronomy; biology; chemistry; computers; the earth, ocean, and environment; engineering; health and medicine; mathematics; meteorology; and physics. Special features include a variety of "Ask An Expert" links—to a geologist, astronomer, volcanologist, bird expert, cardiologist, museum curator, and others. Scientific field trip links are available for online viewing.

Commentary

There are nice resources to encourage young women, minorities, and all children to pursue math, science, and technology studies, such as the Women of NASA link (which allows students to chat with women working at the NASA Ames Research Center) and the African-Americans in the Sciences link. Invention Dimension highlights a different American inventor every week.

Site: The Why Files

URL: http://whyfiles.news.wisc.edu/index.html

Sponsor: National Science Foundation

Subject Area(s): Science   **Subcategory:** Miscellaneous

Grade Level(s): Middle School, High School

Description

The subtitle of this site is "Science Behind the News," which appropriately describes the purpose. There are new features posted every few weeks which usually do relate to a current event and to science. In addition, there are the continuing features of cool science images, sports, forums, and the archives of "Why" files.

Commentary

"Two basketballs, one inflated and the other flat, are dropped from the top of the backboard. Which one hits the floor first? Why?" If this type of question intrigues you, then you will definitely enjoy this site. The site does not, however, dodge the difficult questions such as cloning for human spare parts. Check this Web page often.

Site: Thinking Fountain

URL: http://www.sci.mus.mn.us/sln/tf/nav/thinkingfountain.html

Sponsor: Science Museum of Minnesota

Subject Area(s): Science   **Subcategory:** Miscellaneous

Grade Level(s): Elementary

Description

The Thinking Fountain is a living card file which offers ideas and activities grouped into clusters around topics related to science. Each card highlights an interesting resource/activity related to science and refers you to extensions of the learning process, often in other curricular areas.   The mind maps connect related topics and identify the types of resources, such as a book or Internet site.

Commentary

The cards for creating inexpensive science discovery tools and those which use recyclable materials from around the house will make this site especially enticing to home-grown scientists. Teachers and students may submit cards to the Thinking Fountain by completing the template found at the Make a Card link.

Site: Albert Einstein: Image and Impact

URL: http://www.aip.org/history/einstein/einstein.html

Sponsor: American Institute of Physics

Subject Area(s): Science   **Subcategory:** Physics

Grade Level(s): High School

Description

This is a quite extensive collection of visual and written records and insights into the life of Albert Einstein. Find categories of various eras: Formative Years, The Great Works, E=mc2, World Fame, Public Concerns, Quantum and Cosmos, The Nuclear Age, Science and Philosophy, and An Essay: The World As I See It.

Commentary

Learn via pictures, voice, and reproductions of Einstein's written work. Clicking on Einstein in Brief will take you to a quick sketch of high points of Einstein's life, including some pictures and quotes. Go through the Main Exhibit to find over 100 pages of text and pictures.   What a mind...what a valuable site.

Site: CERN: European Laboratory for Particle Physics

URL: http://www.cern.ch

Sponsor: CERN

Subject Area(s): Science   **Subcategory:** Physics

Grade Level(s): High School

Description

The CERN laboratory provides a variety of services to the scientific community including databases, news, presentations, conferences, and publications. There are reports included here of ongoing projects in physics and related sciences. They maintain a high profile in Internet activities.

Commentary

The scientists included here offer some interesting documentation for having been the founders of the Internet. There is a history of their involvement beginning in the 1970s, with further information regarding how the Web developed in Europe.

Section 01. Curriculum Corner

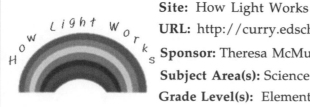

Site: How Light Works

URL: http://curry.edschool.Virginia.EDU/murray/Light/How_Light_Works.html

Sponsor: Theresa McMundo and Jason Mitchell, University of Virginia

Subject Area(s): Science   **Subcategory:** Physics

Grade Level(s): Elementary

Description

This Web site is designed for fourth and fifth grade students to assist them in acquiring a basic understanding of important concepts related to light and its various properties. In addition to the online version, it is also possible to download a HyperCard version for a hands-on, interactive experiment.

Commentary

The pictures are nice, but they need additional explanation and examples. The experiment, online or off-line, would be valuable for this age learner.

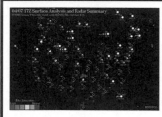

Site: Current U.S. Weather

URL: http://www.mit.edu/usa.html

Sponsor: Massachusetts Institute of Technology

Subject Area(s): Science   **Subcategory:** Weather

Grade Level(s): Middle School, High School

Description

This site is a graphical map of current weather conditions across the United States. It shows the latest radar image from an orbiting weather satellite. Clicking on any specific location on the map provides a current forecast for that location. A link is provided to the University of Illinois, Department of Atmospheric Sciences site with additional weather and climate-related resources and links.

Commentary

This is a straightforward, simple-to-use and fun site for up-to-the-minute weather conditions.

Unix Computing Group

Site: Current Weather Maps/Movies

URL: http://clunix.cl.msu.edu/weather/

Sponsor: Michigan State University Unix Computing Group

Subject Area(s): Science   **Subcategory:** Weather

Grade Level(s): Middle School, High School

Description

This site contains still images as well as video clips of satellite weather information for the world. Information includes temperature, dewpoint, pressure, wind direction, wind speed, and moisture convergence. The Interactive Weather Browser lets you click on a map or input three-letter abbreviations (usually airport designators like DFW, STL, or JFK) to find out the current weather for any location in the U.S., Canada, Mexico, or Cuba.

Commentary

The weather maps are in color and can be printed locally or saved to disk. Maps are updated every hour. Downloading video at less than 28.8 KBPS might prove frustrating.

Section 01. Curriculum Corner

Site: El Niño Theme Page

URL: http://www.pmel.noaa.gov/toga-tao/el-nino/home.html

Sponsor: National Oceanographic and Atmospheric Administration

Subject Area(s): Science   **Subcategory:** Weather

Grade Level(s): Middle School, High School

Description

An El Niño condition is a disruptive type of weather phenomenon in the tropical Pacific Ocean that results in consequences for weather around the globe. Among these consequences have been increased rainfall across the southern tier of the U.S. and in Peru, and drought in the west Pacific, and fires in Australia. This Web site tracks historical and current El Niño conditions and provides graphical information as well as data.

Commentary

El Niño means "The Little One" in Spanish. This name was used for the tendency of an El Niño condition to occur around Christmas. Student research on the topic should begin by browsing this Web site, and it is fascinating study for anyone, as this phenomenon is having an impact on our weather now.

Site: The Weather Processor

URL: http://wxp.atms.purdue.edu/

Sponsor: Purdue University

Subject Area(s): Science   **Subcategory:** Weather

Grade Level(s): High School

Description

WXP is a software package developed as a general purpose weather visualization tool for current, forecasted, and archived meteorological data. Clicking on a United States surface map will provide local data and weather forecast.

Commentary

You will find it helpful to start on the page for the first time user of WXP. There is a great deal more here than a simple printout of current weather. Information is updated hourly and loaded quickly on a weekend (in spite of the warning about slowdowns at the site).

Site: The Weather Underground

URL: http://cirrus.sprl.umich.edu/Weather_Underground.html

Sponsor: University of Michigan

Subject Area(s): Science   **Subcategory:** Weather

Grade Level(s): Elementary, Middle School

Description

Find the weather for any city, township, state, or zip code in the United States. Weather conditions in the rest of the world are also available, but the number of cities included is more limited. Teachers may want to check out the project, "One Sky, Many Voices," designed for students in grades 4–8.

Commentary

Go immediately to Shocking Weather for a talking forecast—once will probably be enough, but you will enjoy it and find that most states are now available. You may want to look up your hometown to compare the national data with what is actually happening outside.

Section 01. Curriculum Corner

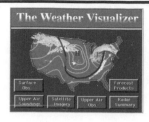

Site: The Weather Visualizer

URL: http://covis.atmos.uiuc.edu/covis/visualizer/

Sponsor: University of Illinois at Urbana-Champagne

Subject Area(s): Science   **Subcategory:** Weather

Grade Level(s): Middle School, High School

Description

Create your own customized weather maps here, using a variety of radar and satellite images. Then take a look at a variety of weather forecasting methods. When you have finished with those tours, link to the Weather World 2010 project for Online Guides and Case Studies and to tour the Archives.

Commentary

This is a wonderful resource for students to use on their own or for teachers to use for teaching about weather mapping and forecasting. Text-only pages are also provided for users with low-speed connections to the Internet.

Site: Indigenous Peoples of Mexico, Central, and South America

URL: http://www.maxwell.syr.edu/nativeweb/abyayala/

Sponsor: South and Meso American Indian Rights Center

Subject Area(s): Social Studies   **Subcategory:** Anthropology

Grade Level(s): High School

Description

The South and Meso American Indian Rights Center publishes a quarterly journal to provide news and analysis relating to indigenous issues in Meso and South America; some of this material is found at this site. The individual countries can be researched under the broad headings of South America, the Meso American Region, and Mexico.

Commentary

While most sites are in English, there are a few in Spanish only. The Webmaster indicates that there are plans to have the entire site in Spanish and other indigenous languages, which will add to interest of students of foreign languages. The material from Guatemala is especially rich, including an interview with Nobel Prize winner, Rigoberta Menchu.

Site: Judaism and Jewish Resources

URL: http://shamash.org/trb/judaism.html

Sponsor: Andrew Tannenbaum

Subject Area(s): Social Studies   **Subcategory:** Anthropology

Grade Level(s): Middle School, High School

Description

A partial listing of the table of contents includes sections devoted to Hebrew, arts, books, calendar, Kashrut, the state of Israel, Yiddish, museums, archeology, Jewish studies, travel, the Holocaust, and much more. Each section is briefly annotated.

Commentary

There are thousands of resources here, and it is a little challenging to find specific things, even with a table of contents. You will enjoy a Scavenger Hunt, which is fun and designed to encourage you to do a little searching. There are also links to a wide number of individual Web pages.

Site: Archaeological Fieldwork Opportunities

URL: http://durendal.cit.cornell.edu/TestPit.html

Sponsor: Ken Stuart, Archaeological Fieldwork Server

Subject Area(s): Social Studies   **Subcategory:** Archaeology

Grade Level(s): High School

Description

The archaeological community posts opportunities for volunteers to work as fieldworkers. A map is provided for general information about locating positions, and there are a number of links to publications and programs for the student interested in further study.

Commentary

Easter Island sounded rather interesting for further exploration. We found openings for teams and the share of cost per team member, which for fall of 1997 was $2,195. Try the link to Earthwatch—it provides some opportunities for those who can't leave home.

Site: Archaeology Online - The DigSite

URL: http://www.scriptorium.org/TheDigSite/

Sponsor: Scriptorium Center for Christian Antiquities

Subject Area(s): Social Studies   **Subcategory:** Archaeology

Grade Level(s): Elementary, Middle School, High School

Description

The Scriptorium is a nonsectarian research center which sponsors various academic initiatives reflecting a commitment to public education and scholarly research. This Web site documents an archaeological dig in Wadi Natrun, Egypt. The excavation was on the site of a Coptic monastery dating from 385 AD, and the 10-week curriculum included e-mails from a Coptic monk who lives as a hermit in a cave near the site.

Commentary

The centerpiece of this site is the Odyssey in Egypt which documents the Wadi Natrun dig. Although completed, it is still fascinating to imagine experiencing the excavation on a week-by-week basis—wonderful material is presented each week. You will also find a movie and numerous pictures to enjoy.

Site: Institute of Egyptian Art and Archaeology

URL: http://www.memphis.edu/egypt/main.html

Sponsor: The University of Memphis (Tennessee)

Subject Area(s): Social Studies   **Subcategory:** Archaeology

Grade Level(s): Middle School, High School

Description

The Institute is dedicated to the study of the art and culture of ancient Egypt through teaching, research, exhibition, and community education. The Institute owns over 150 objects ranging in date from 3500 B.C.E. to 700 C.E. There are mummies, religious items, jewelry, and objects from everyday life.

Commentary

The Tour of Egypt is especially fascinating, with the pleasant option of choosing a city to visit or browsing with a clickable map. Throughout the site, the pictures are amply annotated and can be enlarged to page size. As a bonus, there is extensive information about modern day Egypt.

Site: The Ancient City of Athens

URL: http://www.indiana.edu/~kglowack/Athens/Athens.html

Sponsor: Indiana University

Subject Area(s): Social Studies   **Subcategory:** Archaeology

Grade Level(s): High School

Description

The Ancient City of Athens is a photographic archive of the archaeological and architectural remains of ancient Athens, Greece. In addition to providing a "virtual tour" of the chief excavated regions, the site is intended to be useful to all who have an interest in archaeological exploration and preservation of the past.

Commentary

Students are invited to use the images for personal presentations and papers. Most of the pictures are high quality and download fairly quickly; some are annotated so that you can examine certain parts of the photography more closely.

Site: World Wide Web Archaeology

URL: http://www.usd.edu/anth/midarch/midarch.html

Sponsor: University of South Dakota

Subject Area(s): Social Studies   **Subcategory:** Archaeology

Grade Level(s): Middle School

Description

Archaeology is the scientific study of peoples of the past. Archaeological sites are a nonrenewable resource since, once they are destroyed, the information they contain is lost forever. While this is a serious science, it is possible for people of all ages to participate in digs and to help preserve history for future learning.

Commentary

This site provides answers to questions like: What is archaeology? What do archaeologists do? How are sites found? What can we learn from artifacts? After reviewing and augmenting your basic knowledge, you might want to visit some of the archaeological sites.

Site: African-American Mosaic

URL: http://lcweb.loc.gov/exhibits/african/intro.html

Sponsor: The Library of Congress

Subject Area(s): Social Studies   **Subcategory:** Black History

Grade Level(s): Middle School, High School

Description

The African-American Mosaic is an exhibit of selected material which has been featured in the publication *The African-American Mosaic: A Library of Congress Resource Guide for the Study of Black History and Culture*—a Library-wide guide to the Library of Congress' African-American holdings. The featured items have been carefully selected to illustrate the extent of the Library's holdings.

Commentary

The included articles have accompanying images from the Library's resources and cite the location of each item to assist in further research.

Site: African-American Resources

URL: http://www.chs.chico.k12.ca.us/libr/webres/afri.html

Chico High School Library, 901 The Esplanade, Chico CA 95926 916-891-3026

Sponsor: Chico High School Library, Chico, California

Subject Area(s): Social Studies   **Subcategory:** Black History

Grade Level(s): Middle School, High School

Description

This extensive, annotated index links visitors to sites containing African-American information and images. African art, individuals who have contributed to the advancement of science and engineering, authors, films, women's perspectives, political issues, and sites which also list African-American links are some of the resources visitors may access.

Commentary

Linking from this site back to the Chico High School "Helpful Bookmarks" page will bring up a menu of many other topics of interest to high school students.

Site: Black History

URL: http://www.ai.mit.edu/~isbell/HFh/black/bhist.html

Sponsor: Charles L. Isbell/Michael Bower

Subject Area(s): Social Studies   **Subcategory:** Black History

Grade Level(s): Elementary, Middle School

Description

There are two primary parts to this Black History Database. There is a section titled "This Week in Black History," which is updated weekly. There you can look at some interesting facts which occurred during a particular week in history. It is also possible to search the database by name, month, or year.

Commentary

This is an emerging site, and the authors request both submissions and suggestions.

Site: Black History: Exploring African-American Issues On the Web

URL: http://www.kn.pacbell.com/wired/BHM/AfroAm.html

Sponsor: Education First Fellows

Subject Area(s): Social Studies   **Subcategory:** Black History

Grade Level(s): Middle School, High School

Description

Individuals or classrooms may utilize the Subject Sampler activities which allow learners choices about aspects of African-American issues they wish to explore while emphasizing the addition of personal responses and perspectives. The Black History Treasure Hunt requires students to answer a set of questions by exploring related Internet links to discover the answers.

Commentary

There is a wonderful synthesis of information imbedded in the activities here—how is Bob Marley's modern "Dreadlock Rasta" similar to the Buffalo Soldiers of the Civil War?

Site: Black to the Future Online

URL: http://www.netnoir.com/spotlight/bhm97/

Sponsor: Netnoir, Inc.

Subject Area(s): Social Studies   **Subcategory:** Black History

Grade Level(s): Middle School, High School

Description

This site is dedicated to celebration of Black History Month each February and the recognition of achievements and contributions of African-Americans. Among the resources you will find are a daily feature on groundbreaking people and events plus special areas focused on the Harlem Renaissance, Black athletes, rhythm & blues, Black spirituality, African-American protest Movements and more.

Commentary

A Black History celebration was initially proposed by author and educator Carter G. Woodson in February of 1926, and the event lasted one week; since 1976, it has been a month-long celebration. Though February is the prime time for current activities and events, resources of interest are available throughout the year.

Site: Martin Luther King Jr.

URL: http://www.seattletimes.com/mlk/index.html

Sponsor: The Seattle Times

Subject Area(s): Social Studies   **Subcategory:** Black History

Grade Level(s): Elementary, Middle School

Description

Because of the impact of Dr. Martin Luther King Jr. on the American consciousness, this newspaper wishes to reach across the country with an electronic dialogue. At this site, it is possible to visit the scenes of the civil rights past and hear the voices of some of those contemplating the future. Specific sections include The Man, The Movement, The Legacy, The Holiday, Electronic Classroom, and Talking About It.

Commentary

This site is made especially interesting by the use of sound clips and pictures, many of them in color. You can read (and hear) the words of Dr. King as well as words written about him. In the Electronic Classroom, you can read the opinions of other students, post your thoughts, and/or take a quiz.

Site: The Museum of African Slavery

URL: http://squash.la.psu.edu/~plarson/smuseum/homepage.html

Sponsor: Pier M. Larson, The Pennsylvania State University

Subject Area(s): Social Studies   **Subcategory:** Black History

Grade Level(s): Middle School, High School

Description

Visit this online museum designed to provide accurate, engaging, and provocative information about the history of slavery in the Atlantic Ocean. There are 14 rooms with emphasis on slavery in the Americas and in the Africas. In the "To Ponder" sections, find a lengthy but interesting essay asking the question, "Who Owns History? Some Thoughts on the Slave Trade and Related Issues."

Commentary

This site is under construction but there is already much content of value here. Teachers will find useful the list of books with slavery themes and other teaching resources. Though the site suggests it is for elementary and secondary students and teachers, the goal is narrative information, and without visuals, elementary students may find the text-only too challenging.

Site: The Universal Black Pages

URL: http://www.ubp.com/

Sponsor: Georgia Tech Black Graduate Students Association

Subject Area(s): Social Studies   **Subcategory:** Black History

Grade Level(s): Middle School, High School

Description

A few of the main menu items are mostly specific to the campus, like the "Event Calendar," "Fraternities, Sororities and Living Groups," and the "Educational Opportunities/Activities" listings. But all the other items are of general interest to students of black history everywhere.

Commentary

This Web site was created to serve the needs of Black students at Georgia Institute of Technology, but it also provides a fascinating look at the opportunities and resources available to Black students on college campuses in the U.S. today.

Site: Security APL 500 Index

URL: http://www.secapl.com/secapl/quoteserver/djia.html

Sponsor: CheckFree Investment Services

Subject Area(s): Social Studies   **Subcategory:** Economics

Grade Level(s): Middle School, High School

Description

The main focus of this site is the graphing of the stock market index for the present day, the last year, the last five years, and for the last ten years. You will also find a financial network which features integrated portfolio accounting, securities and market research tools, and online trading.

Commentary

Track the market for the week, month, year, or longer. Get stock quotes and compare these with the newspaper. However, since there were at least five misspelled words found in the Web site, you may want to double check the numbers!

Site: United Nations Development Programme

URL: http://www.undp.org/

Sponsor: United Nations

Subject Area(s): Social Studies   **Subcategory:** Economics

Grade Level(s): High School

Description

This program in the United Nations is committed to the principle that development is inseparable from the quest for peace and human security. The 1997 Human Development Report is now online with the accompanying press releases, Human Development Index, and rankings.

Commentary

The Poverty Clock was created to illustrate how quickly poverty grows. A digital clock ticks off the increase in the number of people who are living on less than a dollar a day around the world. The World Bank estimates that this number is increasing by nearly 25 million a year!

Site: American and British History Resources on the Internet

NO GRAPHIC FOUND

URL: http://www.libraries.rutgers.edu/rulib/socsci/hist/amhist.html

Sponsor: Rutgers University

Subject Area(s): Social Studies   **Subcategory:** Miscellaneous

Grade Level(s): High School

Description

Find a hotlist of links organized by General Information, with sub-pages for some subjects (Afro-American History and Civil War Resources); Rutgers Online Catalogs; Access to Online Catalogs; Indexes to Articles and Other Publications; Electronic Archives, Texts and Journals; Electronic Texts by Historical Period; and Guides to other Internet resources, such as history listservs, associations, societies, and directories.

Commentary

There's nothing fancy here—just an extensive list of links to Internet-accessible resources related to American and British history.

Site: Vose Social Studies Resource Links

URL: http://www.teleport.com/~vincer/social.html

Sponsor: Vose School, Beaverton, OR

Subject Area(s): Social Studies   **Subcategory:** Miscellaneous

Grade Level(s): Elementary, Middle School, High School

Description

This Web page is actually a hotlist with links to a variety of resources of interest to students and teachers. It is organized topically under headings such as United Nations, Christopher Columbus, Benjamin Franklin, Governmental Agencies, Historical Documents, Lesson Plans, United States Congress, The American Civil War, Maps, Social Studies and Government Directories, U.S. Presidents, The Holocaust, and others.

Commentary

This is an excellent site, easy to navigate, which was created by teachers as a resource to others. As such, there is much here not only for teachers but also for students researching topics in various grades.

Site: A Brief Guide to State Facts

URL: http://phoenix.ans.se/freeweb/holly/state.html

Sponsor: Holly Sittel

Subject Area(s): Social Studies   **Subcategory:** U.S. Geography

Grade Level(s): Elementary, Middle School

Description

This is indeed a brief guide—but handy. Listed are all 50 states with an icon plus information about the capital, nicknames, motto, flower, bird, tree, song, date entered the union, and the order in which the state entered the union. The list is in alphabetical order for easy access.

Commentary

Some states provide links to further home pages about their capital city or additional state facts. The pictures of state flowers and birds are particularly attractive, such as Delaware's Blue Hen chicken shown in the photograph. These are game birds used in cockfights during the Revolutionary War and are said to have fought so bravely that the Delaware fighting men used them for inspiration.

Site: A Color Landform Atlas of United States.

URL: http://fermi.jhuapl.edu/states/states.html

Sponsor: Ray Sterner

Subject Area(s): Social Studies   **Subcategory:** U.S. Geography

Grade Level(s): Elementary, Middle School

Description

The key feature of this site is the access to color landform maps of each of the 50 states. There is information about the maps and an elevation key. Only the smallest of states will fit on the screen without scrolling, but longitude and latitude are provided and the state outline is easy to discern. The visitor to the site can also get a county map of each state.

Commentary

A very enticing part of this site are the three links to USYahoo, City Net, and Virtual Tourist so that a student could conduct extensive research about every state. Students may find it interesting to examine the county formation patterns of the original 13 colonies and compare them with the newer states, such as Texas and Oklahoma.

Site: Aloha from Hawaii

URL: http://www.hawaii.net

Sponsor: State of Hawaii

Subject Area(s): Social Studies   **Subcategory:** U.S. Geography

Grade Level(s): High School

Description

The site consists of six categories for selection: business, education, government, media, organizations, and visitor center. Each category is a list of 30 to over one hundred other links on the islands which provide further information for the potential visitor to Hawaii or others with interest in this state.

Commentary

The Web surfing motif is certainly appropriate for Hawaii. The information at this site is a little difficult to sift through, even though a keyword search is provided.

Site: Capitals of the United States

URL: http://www.awl.com/sf-aw/sfaw/resources/statescapitals/

Sponsor: Scott Foresman/Addison Wesley

Subject Area(s): Social Studies   **Subcategory:** U.S. Geography

Grade Level(s): Elementary

Description

From a map of the United States, the student selects a state. An outline map of the state appears with a multiple choice question about the state capital. A correct answer elicits some additional facts about the state, and the capital is marked on the map. A wrong answer receives a good hint for the next selection.

Commentary

This is a colorful, straightforward game that can be used to review the capitals of all the states in the United States. To access a few more games, click on the word "Resources" on the right side of the page.

Section 01. Curriculum Corner

Site: Color Shaded Relief Map of the United States

URL: http://www.zilker.net/

 **Sponsor:** Zilker Internet Park

Subject Area(s): Social Studies   **Subcategory:** U.S. Geography

Grade Level(s): Elementary

Description

This directory contains color-shaded relief maps of the United States. Two versions of the map are available. The original map shows coastlines, boundaries, and rivers with elevation shown by color bands. The newer version uses continuous color shading and has more subdued colors. Each map consists of 60 GIF images.

Commentary

This is the high-tech version of the relief maps many of us made in elementary school. Viewers are invited to add to the descriptions of each grid.

Site: Taking the Long View: Panoramic Photographs, 1851-1991

URL: http://lcweb2.loc.gov/ammem/pnhtml/pnhome.html

Sponsor: Library of Congress

Subject Area(s): Social Studies   **Subcategory:** U.S. Geography

Grade Level(s): Middle School, High School

Description

Taking the Long View contains approximately 4,000 images featuring American cityscapes, landscapes, and group portraits. Especially strong representations may be found in subject areas of agricultural life; beauty contests; disasters; engineering work, such as bridges, canals, and dams; fairs and expositions; military and naval activities; the oil industry; and schools and college campuses, sports, and transportation.

Commentary

Images depict scenes from all 50 states and the District of Columbia plus 20+ foreign countries and a few U.S. territories. These panoramas offer an overview of the nation, its enterprises, and its interests, with a focus on the start of the 20th century. The panoramas average between 28" and 6' in length, with an average width of 10". What a spectacular look at America!

Site: The Challenge: Where Are We?

URL: http://wacky.ccit.arizona.edu/~susd/chall1.html

Sponsor: Desert View High School, Tucson, Arizona

Subject Area(s): Social Studies   **Subcategory:** U.S. Geography

Grade Level(s): Middle School, High School

Description

Here is the challenge: read a set of clues and then determine the location of the city being described. Or submit a set of clues for a place and have others guess your location. An incomplete list of responses is available, so if you can answer one of the ones not yet known, submit the answer to be added to the list. This is a fun way to test your geography knowledge, and it is OK to use atlases and other resources to help out.

Commentary

Try your hand at the challenge. Work on your own or with some friends or classmates. See if you can find the answer before your teacher does. Students and teachers alike will find this a fun and challenging site for identifying locations around the U.S.—and beyond!

Hi! I'm Orbit! Welcome to the GeoNet Game! Pick the Northeast, the South, or the entire United States to start the game! Click on your choice below!

Site: The GeoNet Game: United States

URL: http://www.hmco.com/school/geo/indexhi.html

Sponsor: Houghton Mifflin

Subject Area(s): Social Studies   **Subcategory:** U.S. Geography

Grade Level(s): Elementary, Middle School

Description

The GeoNet Game is designed to help children think geographically and help them build a global context for the information they learn. The participant can choose to focus on the Northeast, the South, or the entire United States. The game is attractive and directions are easy to follow.

Commentary

The Grundargh, a group of aliens traveling through our Solar System, have discovered Earth and want to take over. They claim that humans don't know enough about their own planet to run it well. If you can answer questions related to physical systems, human culture, the environment, and more, you can become a defender of the Earth.

USA CITYLINK®

Site: USA CityLink

URL: http://usacitylink.com//

Sponsor: Neosoft

Subject Area(s): Social Studies   **Subcategory:** U.S. Geography

Grade Level(s): Middle School, High School

Description

The USA CityLink Project is a city's interface with the world. The reader begins by selecting a state from the list presented, and then a city from the next list. Information by cities varies but almost always includes a guide, a map, classified ads, real estate, events, dining out suggestions, and schools. Many of these locations permit further searches and/or the ability to reply.

Commentary

This project attracts travelers and individuals about to relocate. It is also a valuable tool for the classroom, since large amounts of information are available about American cities. Navigation is very smooth and quick.

Viva New Mexico!!
America's Land of Enchantment

Site: Viva New Mexico

URL: http://www.viva.com/nm/nmhome.html

Sponsor: viva.com, Inc.

Subject Area(s): Social Studies   **Subcategory:** U.S. Geography

Grade Level(s): Middle School, High School

Description

The purpose of this site is to provide interesting information about New Mexico—things to do and see, places to eat, purchasing Indian jewelry or pottery, historical and natural facts, and much more. Each month there are featured sites on the page.

Commentary

The cultural events page features links to a number of museums in the state. The Museum of International Folk Art in Santa Fe and the Pueblo Culture Center in Albuquerque are worth a look on this Web page and in person.

Site: Xerox PARC Map Viewer

URL: http://pubweb.parc.xerox.com/map

Sponsor: Xerox Palo Alto Research Center

Subject Area(s): Social Studies   **Subcategory:** U.S. Geography

Grade Level(s): Middle School, High School

Description

Start with a world map on your screen and click on any desired location to zoom in on it. A detailed outline map will be quickly drawn. Or, if you provide the latitude and longitude coordinates, it will draw a map at that location.

Commentary

This site contains a link to the U.S. Census Bureau's "U.S. Gazeteer," which will retrieve detailed maps based on city name or zip codes. These maps are also zoomable. Interactive mapmaking should prove fascinating for students and adults alike!

Site: All Politics

URL: http://allpolitics.com/

Sponsor: CNN Time

Subject Area(s): Social Studies   **Subcategory:** U.S. Government

Grade Level(s): Middle School, High School

Description

Today's news, analysis, and counterpoint are presented in this site. For the lighter side of politics, there is a link to the Capitol Steps, a comedy team that has been spoofing Washington for the last 16 years.

Commentary

Head straight for Capitol Steps to hear great songs such as "Boris Alive," "Don't Cry for Me, Judge Scalia," and many more. It is possible to receive this site as a newsletter each Monday in your e-mail, and it is free.

Site: American Studies Web

URL: http://www.georgetown.edu/crossroads/asw/

Sponsor: David Phillips at Georgetown University

Subject Area(s): Social Studies   **Subcategory:** U.S. Government

Grade Level(s): High School

Description

This extremely large database is designed for research and reference into the field of American Studies. It contains information about economy and politics, race and ethnicity, gender and sexuality, literature and hypertext, philosophy and religion, art and material culture, performance and broadcasting, sociology and demography, region and environment, historical and archival resources, and current events.

Commentary

Although the site does not appear to be updated on a regular basis, there is still a great deal of material here. Curriculum and technology materials are aimed at the college instructor, so stick to the American Studies Resources on the Web which can be accessed from the menu or by searching.

Site: Central Intelligence Agency

URL: http://www.odci.gov/cia/ciahome.html

Sponsor: Central Intelligence Agency

Subject Area(s): Social Studies   **Subcategory:** U.S. Government

Grade Level(s): Middle School, High School

Description
The home page for the Central Intelligence Agency contains a welcome from the director, information about the agency, a list of publications, press releases, and links to some other intelligence communities. There is a virtual tour of the agency provided and also a short video.

Commentary
The CIA is justly famous for the quality of the World Factbook produced each year containing data and maps about all of the countries in the world. While you are here, check out the links to other intelligence sources and the employment opportunities they offer.

Site: Congress.Org

URL: http://www.congress.org/

Sponsor: Capitol Advantage

Subject Area(s): Social Studies   **Subcategory:** U.S. Government

Grade Level(s): Middle School, High School

Description
In addition to providing a complete Congressional directory, this site contains information about today's schedule in the House, the Senate, and committee hearings. There are tips provided for visiting Capitol Hill as well as for writing letters to Congressmen or Congresswomen.

Commentary
The congressional directory is very easy to use. You can search by state or scroll through an alphabetical list of names, in case you aren't sure about the spelling. It is also possible to search by committee. Once a member is located, there is a picture plus other essential and/or interesting information provided.

Site: FedWorld

URL: http://www.fedworld.gov

Sponsor: National Technical Information Service

Subject Area(s): Social Studies   **Subcategory:** U.S. Government

Grade Level(s): High School

Description
The National Technical Information Service is a part of the U.S. Department of Commerce. FedWorld was created to provide the general public with a user-friendly, central resource for government information in electronic formats. Browsing can be done from a catalog, but keyword searches are encouraged.

Commentary
It helps to be familiar with the different branches of government in order to use this site effectively. The site designers have obviously sought to make the site user-friendly. Here, the Internal Revenue Service puts out a daily paper with cartoons plus news about current tax initiatives.

Section 01. Curriculum Corner

Site: Legal Information Institute

URL: http://www.law.cornell.edu/supct

Sponsor: Legal Information Institute, Cornell University

Subject Area(s): Social Studies   **Subcategory:** U.S. Government

Grade Level(s): High School

Description

The Legal Information Institute offers Supreme Court decisions using the Court's electronic dissemination project, Hermes. The archive contains all opinions of the Court issued since May of 1990 plus a collection of the 300 most important historical decisions of the Court. There is also a current calendar for the Court accompanied by pictures and biographies.

Commentary

This is relatively dry material to review but critical to a complete understanding of the ways in which government works. If you do nothing else, scroll through the list of historic Supreme Court decisions by topic. The site provides a free current awareness service via e-mail which is distributed within hours of each Supreme Court decision.

Site: Library of Congress

URL: http://marvel.loc.gov/

Sponsor: The Library of Congress

Subject Area(s): Social Studies   **Subcategory:** U.S. Government

Grade Level(s): Middle School, High School

Description

The American Memory section of the library provides documents, photographs, movies, and sound recordings that tell America's story. It is possible to search both the site and the catalogs of the library. The exhibitions and new features are a constantly changing aspect. Librarians, information professionals, and researchers can find searchable resources in Library Services or use Research Tools.

Commentary

American Treasures are fun to look at...although the Library considers more than 110 million items to be treasures. This section contains everything from the handwritten draft of the Declaration of Independence to the earliest known baseball cards. The Top Treasure exhibit is changed on a monthly basis.

Site: President

URL: http://sunsite.unc.edu/lia/president

Sponsor: Presidential Library System and the University of North Carolina

Subject Area(s): Social Studies   **Subcategory:** U.S. Government

Grade Level(s): Elementary, Middle School, High School

Description

The major portion of this site is the directory of links to resources about all past (and present) Presidents. From a page with portraits of our 12 most recent Presidents, the reader can select a picture and move to that Presidential Library with the related resources. There is additional information about four First Ladies.

Commentary

The George Bush Presidential Library was not yet online at the time of this review, but there is information on the directory page, and the other libraries seemed to be working correctly. This is a great site for team research, since there is an attempt to provide some comparable information about each of the Presidents.

Site: The American President

URL: http://AmericanPresident.com

Sponsor: Castle Rock Entertainment

Subject Area(s): Social Studies   **Subcategory:** U.S. Government

Grade Level(s): Middle School, High School

Description

After seeing the opening view of the White House, enter its lobby. Then take a virtual walk through each of six rooms for further information: press room, private office, war room, living quarters, situation room, and the Oval Office. Learn about the types of activities that might be going on in the various rooms.

Commentary

This is an informative and entertaining site from the producers of the movie, "The American President." Find an online poll, a virtual press conference, a crossword puzzle, and a Constitution quiz to test your knowledge. Test your approval rating as you pretend to be President and respond to questions from the press. It is easy to navigate from one room to another—and you will find a surprise that we won't reveal here.

The National Budget Simulation

Site: The National Budget Simulation

URL: http://garnet.berkeley.edu:3333/budget/budget.html

Sponsor: Center for Community Economic Research, UC-Berkeley

Subject Area(s): Social Studies   **Subcategory:** U.S. Government

Grade Level(s): High School

Description

How would you like to become the President? One of your challenges would be to balance the national budget. This budget simulator, which is an online game, lets you try to accomplish that. You are asked to cut the 1995 fiscal deficit in order to achieve a balanced budget. All cuts must be made in one year, and you may want to increase spending in areas you consider being shortchanged under present budget priorities.

Commentary

This appealing game will help students better understand the kinds of trade-offs which citizens and policy makers will need to make to balance the budget. You will also find links to a variety of sources of information on the federal budget.

Site: The White House for Kids

URL: http://www.whitehouse.gov/WH/kids/html/home.html

Sponsor: The White House

Subject Area(s): Social Studies   **Subcategory:** U.S. Government

Grade Level(s): Elementary

Description

This is a delightful source of information for elementary students on the White House. Learn about the location of the building, its history, and information about President Clinton, Vice President Gore, and their wives. See pictures and learn about kids and pets who have lived in the White House. You can even write a letter to the President.

Commentary

Your tour guide is Socks, President Clinton's cat and resident at the White House. Navigation is easy, and the pictures and easy-to-read text make this a great source of learning about the history behind the President's home. Children will likely enjoy knowing about the kids and animals that have also lived there.

Section 01. Curriculum Corner

Site: Thomas Web

URL: http://thomas.loc.gov/

Sponsor: U.S. Congress

Subject Area(s): Social Studies   **Subcategory:** U.S. Government

Grade Level(s): Middle School, High School

Description

See what is happening on the floors of the House and Senate this week. Review the full text of recent House and Senate bills, scan summaries of legislation that is pending, view daily updates to the *Congressional Record*, find e-mail addresses for House and Senate members and committees, and locate C-SPAN transcripts and broadcast schedules.

Commentary

What a valuable site for teachers and students! If you are studying or teaching about the legislative process or U.S. government in general, visit this site for a rich set of resources and information. Be sure to read the article, "How Our Laws Are Made."

Site: U.S. House of Representatives

URL: http://www.house.gov

Sponsor: U.S. House of Representatives

Subject Area(s): Social Studies   **Subcategory:** U.S. Government

Grade Level(s): High School

Description

Government students and others can visit this site to learn about the members of Congress and obtain contact information for each of them (or contact them online). Link to Representative's Web sites, review information pertaining to new laws and bills in progress, and find full text government documents and other valuable resource information.

Commentary

Be sure and check out the Educational Links at the bottom of the home page to find excellent resources, such as an explanation of the legislative process; a description of how laws are made; full text documents of The Declaration of Independence, the U.S. Constitution, and others; historical information; and more.

Site: Vote America On-Line

URL: http://www.virtent.com/vote

Sponsor: Virtual Entertainment

Subject Area(s): Social Studies   **Subcategory:** U.S. Government

Grade Level(s): Middle School, High School

Description

This site was created for campaign coverage in the 1996 Presidential election, but most of the information continues to be relevant. In addition to a 30-question Political IQ Test, the site offers a number of links to other political information. A wealth of information can be found on the legislative process and the Constitution.

Commentary

The Political IQ Test is quick and fun and a great way to realize how much one doesn't know about the political process—will your score show you to be a "Political Insider" or a "Political Guru"? Great photography of Washington takes several minutes to load, but there is a text version if you must speed up the process.

Site: Welcome to the White House

URL: http://www.whitehouse.gov

Sponsor: White House

Subject Area(s): Social Studies   **Subcategory:** U.S. Government

Grade Level(s): Elementary, Middle School

Description

There are some standard, always available resources here which include information about the President and Vice President, White House history and tours, and the ability to search White House documents. A very popular section is the White House for Kids, featuring a tour by the "First Cat" and a newsletter for young people.

Commentary

No matter how old you are, the White House for Kids is not to be missed. It is fun, fascinating, educational, and more. An important part of this site is the listing of current happenings and daily briefings.

Site: Yahoo List on U.S. Government Organizations

URL: http://www.yahoo.com/Government/States

Sponsor: Yahoo! Inc.

Subject Area(s): Social Studies   **Subcategory:** U.S. Government

Grade Level(s): High School

Description

This site provides information on federal organizations, such as the Council of State Governments, and others. Also find government resources available in each of the states.

Commentary

This is a quick path to state governmental agencies. Check the index, click on the state of interest, and go directly to the list of resources.

Site: 1492: An Ongoing Voyage

URL: http://sunsite.unc.edu/expo/1492.exhibit/Intro.html

Sponsor: Library of Congress

Subject Area(s): Social Studies   **Subcategory:** U.S. History

Grade Level(s): High School

Description

This exhibit examines the rich mixture of societies coexisting in five areas of this hemisphere before European arrival. The exhibition examines the first sustained contacts between American people and European explorers, conquerors, and settlers from 1492 until 1600.

Commentary

Did you know that in 1492 millions of people were already living in the Americas in an area about five times the size of Europe? It is believed that for most of the thousands (or tens of thousands) of years before 1492, these people had little contact with each other or with other parts of the world. Additional pictures would be beneficial.

Section 01. Curriculum Corner

Site: A Walking Tour of Plimoth Plantation

URL: http://spirit.lib.uconn.edu/ArchNet/Topical/Historic/Plimoth/Plimoth.html

Sponsor: Society for American Archaeology

Subject Area(s): Social Studies   **Subcategory:** U.S. History

Grade Level(s): Elementary, Middle School

Description
Plimoth (Plymouth) Plantation was the first permanent European settlement in southern New England, founded around AD 1620. Today this area is the site of a living museum, dedicated to recreating 17th century life in the New World. People in historic period costumes carry out the daily tasks which would have been conducted at that time.

Commentary
This is a great place to visit if you are ever near the Boston area. All of the interpretive guides answer your questions as though the entire group was really back in the early colonial historical period. This site really captures the flavor of the outdoor living museum.

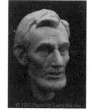

Site: Abraham Lincoln Online

URL: http://www.netins.net/showcase/creative/lincoln.html

Sponsor: Abraham Lincoln Online

Subject Area(s): Social Studies   **Subcategory:** U.S. History

Grade Level(s): Middle School, High School

Description
This site contains Lincoln's speeches and writings, but of particular interest are the comments on Lincoln's thinking. There are resources, historical sites, a bookshelf, index to links, news and events, and a weekly listing of what Lincoln was doing during this week in history.

Commentary
The Lincoln Mailbag contains a great deal of recent mail, and much of it is quite interesting. One piece, for example, describes connections between Timothy McVeigh's t-shirt and the quotes of Lincoln. The section on Lincoln's thinking is made more interesting by personal comments on his sense of humor and how his thinking ability developed.

Site: American Immigration Home Page

URL: http://www.bergen.gov/AAST/Projects/Immigration/index.html

Sponsor: Academy for the Advancement of Science and Technology

Subject Area(s): Social Studies   **Subcategory:** U.S. History

Grade Level(s): High School

Description
This page was started as a part of a school project for a 10th grade American History class. The intent is to provide information regarding why immigrants decided to come to America and how they were treated once they arrived here. The site is loosely organized by brackets of years with subtopics.

Commentary
The information about immigration in recent years is very brief, but some is included. It is useful, when navigating the site, to follow one concept—for example, the reasons for immigration—through the several waves of immigration to see if it varies.

Site: American Thanksgiving on the Internet

URL: http://www.night.net/thanksgiving/

Sponsor: Internet@Night

Subject Area(s): Social Studies   **Subcategory:** U.S. History

Grade Level(s): Elementary

Description

In the United States, Thanksgiving is celebrated on the fourth Thursday in November. There are three major sections here with links under each one: The First Thanksgiving, Thanksgiving Fun, and Thanksgiving Food. The site also has links to other holidays.

Commentary

The site opens with a Thanksgiving hymn, and there is an abundance of music and pictures to enjoy. Don't forget to find out why turkeys always go "gobble, gobble". There is even free software about Thanksgiving you may download.

Site: Betsy Ross Homepage

URL: http://libertynet.org/iha/betsy/

Sponsor: Independence Hall Association

Subject Area(s): Social Studies   **Subcategory:** U.S. History

Grade Level(s): Elementary, Middle School

Description

The Betsy Ross Homepage contains a history of the flag and includes an American Flag Picture Gallery and flag trivia. There is information about Betsy's life with quotes and notes she wrote. Tour her house and add your name to the guest book.

Commentary

Scroll through the flag timeline to see when your state became a part of the union and how it changed the appearance of the flag. The Frequently Asked Questions are things you may not know and will undoubtedly find interesting. This page is constantly improved and updated, and you will likely want to revisit it from time to time.

Site: Buffalo Bill Historical Center

URL: http://www.truewest.com/BBHC/

Sponsor: Buffalo Bill Historical Center

Subject Area(s): Social Studies   **Subcategory:** U.S. History

Grade Level(s): Elementary, Middle School

Description

The Buffalo Bill Historical Center is widely regarded as America's finest western museum. The Center actually features four museums under one roof: the Whitney Gallery of Western Art, the Buffalo Bill Museum, the Plains Indian Museum, and the Cody Firearms Museum. You will also find the Harold McCracken Research Library. Take the guided tour of the site or click to enter individual areas as you choose.

Commentary

In the late 19th century, western figures were known far and wide for their exploits on the frontier. William Frederick Cody, Buffalo Bill, was one of the most famous, as he brought his Wild West Show to all parts of the United States and Europe. You will enjoy the posters and cowboy artifacts...and trying to separate truth from fiction.

Site: California History

URL: http://www.community.net/~stevensn/4thgrade.html

Sponsor: James Stevenson Publishers

Subject Area(s): Social Studies   **Subcategory:** U.S. History

Grade Level(s): Elementary

Description

The *Oh, California* fourth grade history text is supported at this site with exploration and interactive activities. Still under development, this site currently presents information on the California missions, Mexican California, the westward movement, and the Bear Flag Revolt.

Commentary

Even if you don't live in California, you will enjoy this site. You may already know that the original 22 California missions were laid out so that they were within one day of walking distance from one another. Now some students are taking bike trips between the missions, somewhat like the original walkers. The missions are interesting both because of their history and pictures.

Site: Ellis Island—Through America's Gateway

URL: http://www.i-channel.com/ellis/

Sponsor: The International Channel

Subject Area(s): Social Studies   **Subcategory:** U.S. History

Grade Level(s): Middle School, High School

Description

This site provides an historical overview of the buildings at Ellis Island. There are detailed photographs as well as portrait icons which are linked to audio clips of stories told by some of the people who were actually processed through Ellis Island. You'll even find a cookbook listing favorite recipes from some of the immigrants to America.

Commentary

This is a fascinating site for history students. From the time Ellis Island opened in New York Harbor near the Statue of Liberty in 1892 to the time it closed in 1954, over 12 million immigrants saw it as their first look at America. An estimated 40% of all American citizens can trace their ancestry to the immigrants who came through Ellis Island. It is interesting to hear some of these immigrants tell their own stories.

Site: From Revolution to Reconstruction

URL: http://odur.let.rug.nl/~welling/usa/usa.html

Sponsor: University of Groningen

Subject Area(s): Social Studies   **Subcategory:** U.S. History

Grade Level(s): Middle School, High School

Description

This site is the result of a project by a group of German university students majoring in American studies. They started with the book, *An Outline of American History*, distributed by the United States Information Agency. There are ten chapters beginning with Early America and ending with two chapters on modern America. Chapters can be read as hypertext, following the text sequentially or navigating via links provided.

Commentary

Students have added original essays to the essays and bibliographies found in many sections. One, "Was the American Revolution Really a Revolution?", is particularly interesting. Check out the list of available source transcripts—reprints of documents critical to U. S. history. A keyword search can be made of the entire database.

Section 01. Curriculum Corner

Site: George Washington's Mount Vernon Estate and Gardens

URL: http://www.mountvernon.org/

Sponsor: Mount Vernon Ladies' Association

Subject Area(s): Social Studies   **Subcategory:** U.S. History

Grade Level(s): Elementary, Middle School

Description

The Mount Vernon tour includes pictures and explanations of the rooms in the house as well as the garden. The visitor's guide provides details about visiting the grounds. The library, collections, and archaeology describe how artifacts are used and displayed in the house. Some lesson information is included in the educational resources.

Commentary

Before the garbage man made weekly visits, trash was discarded about the yard. One of these shallow depressions was recently excavated and yielded over 75,000 artifacts dating from the time of the American Revolution. These items are used to provide information about the diet and daily life of the Washington family.

Site: History Happens

URL: http://www.ushistory.com/

Sponsor: Electron Farm Publications

Subject Area(s): Social Studies   **Subcategory:** U.S. History

Grade Level(s): Elementary, Middle School

Description

The stories from American history found at this site are on music video with pictures and sound clips. The creators looked for events that are indicative of the spirit of the American experience. Collaborators were secured to provide film and original music. The music videos and teacher's guides are available for the classroom, with CD-ROM under development.

Commentary

Make sure that you download RealAudio Player first. These are 2-3 minute sound clips of quite good quality. These will appeal to you if you like folk music and/or good stories. There is also a history mystery to enjoy.

Site: Letters from an Iowa Soldier in the Civil War

URL: http://www.ucsc.edu/civil-war-letters/home.html

Sponsor: William Scott Proudfoot, West Valley College

Subject Area(s): Social Studies   **Subcategory:** U.S. History

Grade Level(s): Middle School, High School

Description

These letters are part of a collection written by Newton Robert Scott, a private with the Iowa Volunteers. Most of the letters are written over a three-year period to a neighborhood friend, Hannah Cone, who later became his wife. There are 15 letters, unchanged from the original way in which they were written by the 21-year-old soldier.

Commentary

"If we had our choices of course we would be at home for we are not in the army for fun nor money and furthermore we wish never to fill a cowards grave...." With these letters, you are truly there—on the battlefield, in the camp, suffering with this young man and his friends. A memorable experience!!

Section 01. Curriculum Corner

Site: Monticello: The Home of Thomas Jefferson

URL: http://www.monticello.org/

Sponsor: The Thomas Jefferson Memorial Foundation

Subject Area(s): Social Studies   **Subcategory:** U.S. History

Grade Level(s): Middle School, High School

Description
Thomas Jefferson, the third President, retired to his home at Monticello, Virginia. There are facts about daily life at Monticello, some quotations, information about his interests, people who knew him, and information about slave life and plantation industries. There is also extensive information for prospective visitors to the area.

Commentary
If every historical character was blessed with this type of site, there might be a new appreciation of history in this country. Start your visit by participating in a day in the life of Thomas Jefferson for insight into the way a plantation was run. But don't miss the letters written by students asking all types of questions and answered by "Thomas" in an authenic style.

Site: National Civil War Association

URL: http://ncwa.org

Sponsor: The National Civil War Association

Subject Area(s): Social Studies   **Subcategory:** U.S. History

Grade Level(s): Middle School, High School

Description
This site provides a variety of information about the National Civil War Association as well as links to other sites with educational information, historical data, and photos regarding the Civil War.

Commentary
The NCWA is a northern California nonprofit organization committed to education regarding the Civil War. For residents of the area it presents living history in a variety of forms, such as military encampments, battles, and lectures. These events are held several times each year. For others outside the area, explore some of the other Civil War and Living History Web Sites suggested as links.

Site: Native American Indian

URL: http://indy4.fdl.cc.mn.us/~isk/

Sponsor: Paula Giese

Subject Area(s): Social Studies   **Subcategory:** U.S. History

Grade Level(s): Elementary, Middle School

Description
The author describes this site as containing information regarding the art, culture, education, history, and science of the native American Indian. There are maps, stories, herbal medicine, games, entertainment, and much more available through a variety of links.

Commentary
There are charming animated icons throughout the document, apparently all done by the author. You might find the Indian viewpoints on the movie *Pocahontas* worth reading. The huge collection of art is especially important to examine.

Site: New Deal Network

URL: http://newdeal.feri.org

Sponsor: Franklin and Eleanor Roosevelt Institute

Subject Area(s): Social Studies   **Subcategory:** U.S. History

Grade Level(s): Middle School, High School

Description

This is an online resource for students studying the Depression and New Deal eras in U.S. History. New "Feature" sections are added from time to time, and these link to "Curriculum Kits" which teachers can use in planning lessons on related topics. Old Features are archived on the site and can be accessed as well.

Commentary

NDN includes a large online database of photographs, political cartoons, and texts (speeches, letters, and other historic documents from the New Deal period). Currently there are over 3,000 items in this database, many of them previously accessible only to scholars.

Site: Old Sturbridge Village

URL: http://www.osv.org/

Sponsor: Old Sturbridge, Inc.

Subject Area(s): Social Studies   **Subcategory:** U.S. History

Grade Level(s): Elementary, Middle School

Description

Old Sturbridge Village is located in Massachusetts and is the largest history museum in the Northeast. The museum re-creates the daily work activities and community celebrations of a rural 19th century town in authentic, living history fashion. One can explore the village, ask questions of one of the villagers, link to related sites, and find information for a real-life visit.

Commentary

On the opening screen, the entire village changes colors to match the seasons. Attractive, diverse, and constantly updated, this is a site worth revisiting from time to time. Be sure to visit the Christmas in New England site and the clock factory...but you may want to avoid the music.

Site: Slave Voices

URL: http://scriptorium.lib.duke.edu/slavery/

Sponsor: Duke University

Subject Area(s): Social Studies   **Subcategory:** U.S. History

Grade Level(s): Middle School, High School

Description

The exhibit is entitled "Third Person, First Person: Slave Voices from the Special Collection Library." Its goals are to emphasize the importance of collecting records of African Americans. These records are intended to illuminate issues in the history of slavery as well as tell memorable and engaging stories.

Commentary

These records are written documents, both legal (as in the sale of slaves) and types of diaries. The collection shows parallels between the type of documents used for the sale of slaves with those for the sale of horses. The historical and legal language might prove difficult to handle.

Site: Speeches of the U.S. Presidents

URL: http://www.ocean.ic.net/rafiles/pres/thelist.html

Sponsor: Ocean Real Audio

Subject Area(s): Social Studies   **Subcategory:** U.S. History

Grade Level(s): Elementary, Middle School

Description

With Presidents listed in alphabetical order, it is possible to listen to a 20-second sound bite from each President from Bush back to Wilson. For some Presidents, you will find more than one listing. For example, you can hear a second clip for President Nixon, from his farewell speech.

Commentary

Before using this site, it is necessary to download the Real Audio Player. Calling these sound bites "speeches" is a great exaggeration, but it is fun to hear the real voice of a President. There is a link back to the main library of sounds.

Site: The American Civil War, 1861-1865

URL: http://www.access.digex.net/~bdboyle/cw.html

Sponsor: Bryan Boyle

Subject Area(s): Social Studies   **Subcategory:** U.S. History

Grade Level(s): Middle School, High School

Description

This site presents a link to Civil War documents, books, poetry, and much other information. There is current information for people interested in reenactment and living history. Lists of documents must be scrolled in order to locate materials; there is limited search capacity.

Commentary

Some sections are beautifully written, such as "Christmas in the Confederate White House," where this period of history comes alive. The poetry and music section is superb in helping us "understand the thoughts and emotions of the men who faced each other across the battlefield and those who waited for them at home."

No GRAPHIC FOUND

Site: The Emancipation Proclamation

URL: http://www.cs.indiana.edu/statecraft/emancipation.html

Sponsor: Cleveland Free-Net; National Public Telecomputing Network (NPTN)

Subject Area(s): Social Studies   **Subcategory:** U.S. History

Grade Level(s): Middle School, High School

Description

This site provides the reader with the original text of The Emancipation Proclamation, dated September 22, 1862. You will also find a commentary by Douglas T. Miller and a bibliography.

Commentary

This is a text-only site with a focused topic of information but a ready access for those researching this document from United States history.

Site: The Gettysburg Address by Abraham Lincoln

URL: http://www.cs.indiana.edu/statecraft/gettysburg.html

NO
GRAPHIC
FOUND

Sponsor: Cleveland Free-Net; National Public Telecomputing Network (NPTN)

Subject Area(s): Social Studies   **Subcategory:** U.S. History

Grade Level(s): Middle School, High School

Description

The text of Lincoln's original speech is provided here.

Commentary

The Gettysburg Address might prove useful for a classroom report or a history discussion. You can also reflect on Lincoln's speaking style.

Site: Those Were the Days

URL: http://www.440int.com/twtd/today.html

Sponsor: 440 International

Subject Area(s): Social Studies   **Subcategory:** U.S. History

Grade Level(s): Middle School, High School

Description

Today and tomorrow are included as this site presents an annotated listing of events which happened on this day in history, people born on this day, and chartbusters. The site is heavily weighed toward the entertainment industry but does list a variety of events for the history review.

Commentary

This is the type of site that some people bookmark to examine every day. There does not appear to be any way to go backward or forward in time. For trivia lovers, there are links to many other sites plus an automatic Yahoo search.

Site: U.S. Census Bureau

URL: http://www.census.gov/

Sponsor: U.S. Department of Commerce, Bureau of the Census

Subject Area(s): Social Studies   **Subcategory:** U.S. History

Grade Level(s): Middle School, High School

Description

This site provides complete census tables for anywhere in the U.S., including maps, statistical briefs, and economic indicators. Find social, demographic, and economic information, such as the current U.S. population count. The Just for Fun section provides you with a hands-on opportunity to use data and geographic information that is available while you learn about statistical information and the tools used to process them.

Commentary

The site is very well organized and has an incredible amount of information. Search by word, place, or location or go to the alphabetical listing of subjects available. You can additionally use some customized search tools to assist in your information gathering.

Site: World War II - Keeping the Memory Alive

URL: http://www.pagesz.net/~jbdavis/

Sponsor: John B. Davis

Subject Area(s): Social Studies   **Subcategory:** U.S. History

Grade Level(s): Middle School, High School

Description
The archives included at this site provide a number of World War II related files, including a collection of photographs. The archivist indicates that the site specializes in first person accounts and personal narratives of people who actually lived during the war. There are hundreds of documents to access as well as site links to other places of interest.

Commentary
The archivist does us a favor by starting the page with what he considers to be new or noteworthy. Most of the stories are quite lengthy. One of medium length you might want to read is "The War in My Backyard," which was written by a French youth.

No Graphic Found

Site: Birthdate Calendar Index

URL: http://www.wic.org/cal/idex_cal.html

Sponsor: Women's International Center

Subject Area(s): Social Studies   **Subcategory:** Women's Studies

Grade Level(s): Elementary, Middle School, High School

Description
Which aspiring woman was born on your birthday? Visit the Birthdate Calendar Index to find out. Included are sports figures, scientists, politicians, performers, authors, and historical figures, to list a few.

Commentary
The information contained at this site serves as a natural springboard into research about the women listed. The information could also be used as a daily calendar of famous female figures.

Site: Brave Girls

URL: http://members.aol.com/brvgirls

Sponsor: Jyotsna Sreenivasan in association with Amazon.com Bookstore

Subject Area(s): Social Studies   **Subcategory:** Women's Studies

Grade Level(s): Elementary, Middle School, High School

Description
Educators and parents interested in youth's literature with strong female characters will delight in the Brave Girls Web page. A list of over 40 titles is available for youths ages 2-17 years. In addition, a book list for adults concerned with girls' self-esteem is provided. Adults and youths will be interested in the interviews with authors of some of these books.

Commentary
The books identified here were selected for their positive messages and courageous young female characters who are not afraid to stand up for their beliefs. The site recommends that boys be encouraged to read these books to experience strong girls and women in action.

Site: Distinguished Women of Past and Present

URL: http://www.netsrq.com/~dbois/

Sponsor: Danuta Bois

Subject Area(s): Social Studies   **Subcategory:** Women's Studies

Grade Level(s): Middle School, High School

Description
This site has biographies of women who contributed to our culture in many different ways. The database includes writers, educators, scientists, heads of state, politicians, civil rights crusaders, artists, entertainers, and others. Searches can be made by field of activity or by name. There are additional links to related sites.

Commentary
One of the earliest Nobel Prizes was awarded to a woman, Marie Curie, in 1903. There continue to be many women of distinction in all fields of endeavor. This is an evolving site, and the author invites contributions of other women of distinction.

Site: Encyclopedia of Women's History

URL: http://www.teleport.com/~megaines/women.html

Sponsor: Portland Jewish Academy

Subject Area(s): Social Studies   **Subcategory:** Women's Studies

Grade Level(s): Elementary, Middle School, High School

Description
From Joan of Arc and Harriet Tubman to Madonna and Oprah Winfrey, information about women who have influenced history has been submitted by students in grades 1-12 and posted on this page. Connect to the links in *Other Sites* to further research women who have distinguished themselves throughout history and to review the current United Stated Census Statistics on Women.

Commentary
Students may submit an entry to be posted to this site by following the instructions and guidelines found under *Instructions*.

Site: Feminist Science Fiction, Fantasy & Utopia

URL: http://www.uic.edu/~lauramd/sf/

Sponsor: Laura Quilter

Subject Area(s): Social Studies   **Subcategory:** Women's Studies

Grade Level(s): Middle School, High School

Description
Science fiction and fantasy authored by women (and some men) are represented in bibliographies organized for readers, researchers, and writers seeking information. There is a page for children and young adult readers and tips for subject headings and literature searches in this field.

Commentary
The *Recommended Reading List* page includes a link to the list of books awarded the James Tiptree, Jr. Award which is given to the work of science fiction or fantasy published in one year which best explores or expands gender roles.

Section 01. Curriculum Corner

Site: Women's Archives

URL: http://scriptorium.lib.duke.edu/women/index.html

Sponsor: Duke University Libraries

Subject Area(s): Social Studies

Subcategory: Women's Studies

Grade Level(s): High School

Description
This is a general listing of bibliographies, guides, and periodicals available for research on women and gender. A subsection deals with Women's Studies Resources on the Web. Included are history links, archives and collections, organizations, and other assorted resources.

Commentary
Some of this material is quite old and therefore fascinating. There are materials for the study of women in the ancient world and somewhat more contemporary materials on women's suffrage. Not to be missed is the History of Bound Feet. Can you believe that a bound foot was only three inches long!

Site: Women's Studies Resources

URL: http://www.inform.umd.edu:8080/EdRes/Topic/WomensStudies

Sponsor: University of Maryland

Subject Area(s): Social Studies

Subcategory: Women's Studies

Grade Level(s): High School

Description
This comprehensive database contains collections of conference announcements, calls for papers, and employment opportunities, as well as a picture gallery, a significant number of government documents, and much more.

Commentary
The Collection of Syllabi and Program Development and Support links could prove very useful to individuals involved in developing and supporting a women's studies program.

Site: African Studies at Penn

URL: http://www.sas.upenn.edu/African_Studies/AS.html

Sponsor: University of Pennsylvania

Subject Area(s): Social Studies

Subcategory: World Geography

Grade Level(s): Middle School, High School

Description
The African Studies program at the University of Pennsylvania sponsors this site in order to provide country-specific information to its students and also to other interested parties. In addition to extensive information and maps provided for each country, there is a link to the CIA Factbook for further resources about specific countries.

Commentary
Updated weekly, this site is a great place to find out what is happening in a specific country, even though it might not be making world news. Students will find this a valuable place to conduct research for reports about anything related to Africa. And many will be interested also in the other Black/African Internet resources identified here.

Section 01. Curriculum Corner

Site: Arctic Circle

URL: http://www.lib.uconn.edu/ArcticCircle/

Sponsor: University of Connecticut

Subject Area(s): Social Studies   **Subcategory:** World Geography

Grade Level(s): Middle School, High School

Description

The overall goal of Arctic Circle is to stimulate among viewers a greater interest in the peoples and environment of the Arctic and Subarctic region. This award-winning site uses a range of textual and photographic materials in its presentations. There are three interrelated themes: natural resources, history and culture, and social equity and environmental justice.

Commentary

There is so much to learn at this site. Did you know that the Arctic Circle is the 66th parallel—a geographic ring crowning the globe? The authors of this site ask us to look beyond the Arctic as an exploitable frontier for economic growth and begin to understand the northern people and their habitat. Be sure to take a look at the Arctic Image Gallery.

ASIAN STUDIES WWW VIRTUAL LIBRARY

Site: Asian Studies WWW Virtual Library

URL: http://coombs.anu.edu.au/WWWVL-AsianStudies.html

Sponsor: Australian National University

Subject Area(s): Social Studies   **Subcategory:** World Geography

Grade Level(s): Middle School, High School

Description

This information service is divided into global, regional, and country resources. Over 60 Asian countries are included. Information for each country varies but will usually include news, culture, art, government, education, business, and travel.

Commentary

Many of the countries included here might be more appropriately classified as Mid-Eastern—and there is a link to Pacific studies. There are also art, music, and foreign language links included for most countries.

City.Net TRAVEL

Site: City.Net

URL: http://www.city.net

Sponsor: Excite, Inc.

Subject Area(s): Social Studies   **Subcategory:** World Geography

Grade Level(s): Middle School, High School

Description

Excite, one of the premier search engine companies, operates this site. It permits the user to obtain an exact map of almost any location in any city of the world. After creating the map, it is possible to move outward from the street gradually to locate this address within a larger context.

Commentary

Almost everyone lists this as one of their favorite sites! By simply typing in a home address, you can have the computer generate a map of your neighborhood with a pointer for your house. Classroom teachers may want to locate their school on a map and then zoom out by degrees so that students can obtain a larger view of geography. All maps can be printed.

Section 01. Curriculum Corner

Site: GORP—Great Outdoor Recreation Pages

URL: http://www.GORP.com

Sponsor: GORP

Subject Area(s): Social Studies   **Subcategory:** World Geography

Grade Level(s): Middle School, High School

Description
This Web site offers trips to Blue Ridge Parkway, Kenya Parks and Preserves, and other locations. Take tours and find information on international parks, waterways, forests, wilderness areas, monuments, wildlife areas, historic sites, archeology/cultural sites, and more. You can download maps for many locations and, in some cases, order things you might need to travel. Try your luck at a contest, too.

Commentary
If you are an outdoor fanatic—or want to be—this is the site for you. Find out about activities that interest you—biking, backpacking, walking, hiking, fishing, canoeing, kayaking, rafting, birding, climbing, horseback riding, windsurfing, boating, snorkling, hang gliding—there's more! Also look for humor, games and puzzles, recipes and cooking gear, tips for staying healthy while you travel, and jobs in the outdoors.

Site: Hellas Home Page

URL: http://www.Greece.org/hellas/root.html

Sponsor: Thanos Vourdouris and others

Subject Area(s): Social Studies   **Subcategory:** World Geography

Grade Level(s): Middle School, High School

Description
The Hellas Home Page deals with everything Greek and has mirror sites and contributors in the United States and the United Kingdom. There is news about the government, sports, music, publications, and more.

Commentary
Listen to the national anthem in Greek as well as in English. Then visit old Greece during the Middle Ages, including Macedonia and Constantinoupolis. And be sure to check out the Greek cheese page where there is much more than feta cheese.

Site: Map Machine

URL: http://www.nationalgeographic.com/resources/ngo/maps

Sponsor: National Geographic magazine

Subject Area(s): Social Studies   **Subcategory:** World Geography

Grade Level(s): Middle School, High School

Description
Find a Map Machine Atlas with country maps, facts, flags, and profiles—click to select a continent you would like to explore or use the Index to go to a specific country, territory, or state. Map Resources points you to information on cartography, geographic names databases, government agencies, and map libraries.

Commentary
Choose "A View From Above" and look at a view of the world from space—zoom in to a map of a specific continent or country, or choose between political or physical maps to study. National Geographic is known for its maps, and this site is a wonderful resource.

Section 01. Curriculum Corner

No Graphic Found

Site: Nice Geography Sites

URL: http://www.frw.ruu.nl/nicegeo.html

Sponsor: Faculty of Geographical Sciences, Utrecht University, The Netherlands

Subject Area(s): Social Studies   **Subcategory:** World Geography

Grade Level(s): High School

Description

Here you will find a hotlist of geography servers from around the world. New sites are noted, and a couple of links indicate they are nearly real-time.

Commentary

High school students might find this of interest for research, though they may have to spend considerable time exploring to find specific information they are seeking.

Site: Perry-Castañeda Library Map Collection

URL: http://www.lib.utexas.edu/Libs/PCL/Map_collection/Map_collection.html

Sponsor: University of Texas Library

Subject Area(s): Social Studies   **Subcategory:** World Geography

Grade Level(s): Middle School, High School

Description

This Web site offers a collection of color maps that you can download to your computer. Special and general interest maps are organized by continent and country, such as The World, Africa, The Americas, Asia, Bosnia, Iraq, and more. Find more than 300 maps of the United States as well as historical maps of the continents and links to other map-related sites.

Commentary

You will find an expansive variety of maps for reports, instruction, or mere interest. As this site is housed at the University of Texas, you can find a number of maps for Texas and its counties, too.

Site: Project GeoSim

URL: http://geosim.cs.vt.edu

Sponsor: Departments of Computer Science & Geography, Virginia Polytechnic Inst.

Subject Area(s): Social Studies   **Subcategory:** World Geography

Grade Level(s): High School

Description

Project GeoSim is a research project founded for the purpose of creating education modules for introductory geography courses. The modules have two parts: a tutorial program to introduce the vocabulary and concepts of the module and a simulation program for lab exercises. The modules may be done online, or software can be downloaded for classroom use.

Commentary

The population change simulation program is really interesting. With data from many countries, students can manipulate the variables of Birth Rate, Life Expectancy, and Migration Rate to see how population growth is affected.

Site: The United Kingdom Travel Guide

URL: http://www.uktravel.com/

Sponsor: University College, London

Subject Area(s): Social Studies   **Subcategory:** World Geography

Grade Level(s): High School

Description

There are three main sections in this travel guide, and there is an active map with pictures and points to other Web sites. The London Guide provides information about top attractions, entertainment, and more. The third section is a general collection of information about the Royal Family, money, and much more.

Commentary

The map organization is clever: click on green dots for pictures and blue dots for information. The site is being redone, so you may experience some empty links, but the ongoing work is apparent. More tourist information than history information is to be found at this site.

Site: The Webfoot's Travel Guides

URL: http://www.webfoot.com/travel/guides/

Sponsor: Kaitlin Duck Sherwood

Subject Area(s): Social Studies   **Subcategory:** World Geography

Grade Level(s): Middle School, High School

Description

This basic site is no longer being updated but is left on the Web because of the many links to other sites with valuable information. Find information about the following countries: Austria, British Virgin Islands, France, Germany, Italy, Spain, Vatican City, and Hawaii.

Commentary

The CIA Factbook information is somewhat out of date, but most other sections still make sense. There are lots of maps, history, and cultural details in these links.

Site: Virtual Tourist Guide to Ireland

URL: http://www.bess.tcd.ie/ireland.html

Sponsor: Paddy Waldron

Subject Area(s): Social Studies   **Subcategory:** World Geography

Grade Level(s): Elementary, Middle School

Description

In addition to the map of Ireland found here, there is information about the provinces, the universities, food, language, literature, theater, music, the economy, politics, and current affairs. Dublin, Ireland's capital city, receives special attention.

Commentary

There are literally thousands of links from this guide, so be prepared to do a lot of browsing. The organization is casual, which is generally helpful in allowing you to discover some new information. Irish music is a fun topic with links to Web pages for current performers.

Section 01. Curriculum Corner

CCTA Government Information Service

What's new on the GIS | G7 Information society
Organisational index | Help
Functional index | Feedback
Search facility | Server usage statistics
Public services directory | Other GIS services

Site: CCTA Government Information Service (UK)

URL: http://www.open.gov.uk

Sponsor: CCTA

Subject Area(s): Social Studies   **Subcategory:** World Government

Grade Level(s): High School

Description

Find information at this site regarding the government and services provided in England, Scotland, and Wales. There are several methods of searching by index and by keyword.

Commentary

There are government resources and other interesting resources on the UK at this site as well as links to various other types of information that may prove useful. A valuable link is to the Virtual Library of Museums, identifying exhibits and museums worldwide.

中国新闻电脑网络

China News Digest

The SyberSpace Info Center for Chinese and Friends Worldwide

About CND | China News | 华夏文摘 | InfoBase | Search

Site: China News Digest

URL: http://www.cnd.org

Sponsor: Asian American Network

Subject Area(s): Social Studies   **Subcategory:** World Government

Grade Level(s): Middle School, High School

Description

The China News Digest site is run by a nonprofit organization of volunteers. Its goal is to provide an objective and non-biased source of current news and information about China. Find China's current news stories, articles, pictures, and more.

Commentary

Most of the information located here is in English; however, you will find some in Chinese. This site is a great place to begin doing research on China, especially on current news and cultural events. It is also interesting for mere browsing.

[civnet]
journal for a civil society

Site: Civnet

URL: http://civnet.org/index.html

Sponsor: Syracuse University and the U. S. Information Agency

Subject Area(s): Social Studies   **Subcategory:** World Government

Grade Level(s): High School

Description

The Journal for a Civil Society is an online monthly publication. The term "civil society" refers to voluntary social activity which lies outside the institutions of the political order and legal duty. Each week a theme is chosen, and links are provided for that theme, such as "Responding to Racism and Bias" or "School-to-School links." Past articles, essays, reviews, and reports can be found in the Archive.

Commentary

Articles are written about countries around the world that are struggling with the implementation of democracy. The articles are serious but often interesting. Teachers may wish to read the article by Albert Shanker in which he defends his viewpoint that democracy can be taught. Look too for the calendar of events, civics resource library, and list of civics-related organizations.

Site: Israel Ministry of Foreign Affairs

URL: http://www.israel.org

Sponsor: The Israel Ministry of Foreign Affairs

Subject Area(s): Social Studies   **Subcategory:** World Government

Grade Level(s): Middle School, High School

Description

This Web site is maintained by the Information Division of the Israel Ministry of Foreign Affairs and is designed to provide basic information about the ministry, recent developments in Israel, and background about Israeli government and life. The section on facts about Israel is additionally available in French and Spanish.

Commentary

To have the opportunity to read about the Peace Process written from the perspective of the people in the Middle East demonstrates a real strength of the Internet. The facts about Israel are beautifully presented. There are information and photographs about the land, people, history, culture, economy, education, and more.

Site: Middle World—Information from Iceland

URL: http://www.centrum.is/english/

middle world **Sponsor:** Centrum

Subject Area(s): Social Studies   **Subcategory:** World Government

Grade Level(s): Middle School, High School

Description

You can visit this site to find out about current news, cultural information, commerce, and a number of interesting facts about Iceland.

Commentary

Information is provided in English, and though the site is not particularly interesting from a visual standpoint, there are a number of fascinating links to explore. Be sure to look at Craters on the Moon, a description of a previously held event where top talents in the Icelandic culture were gathered together to produce words with images—find the pictures, poems, music, lights, technology, and videos.

Site: New Zealand Government Online

URL: http://www.govt.nz

Sponsor: New Zealand Government

Subject Area(s): Social Studies   **Subcategory:** World Government

Grade Level(s): High School

Description

Find a variety of pictures, maps, and text-based information about New Zealand—its geography, people, history, and economy. Look at A Citizen's Guide to the Government or the Parliament or the Cabinet. Or check out the information about New Zealand, such as its statistics, information about immigration, business, and more.

Commentary

The site has a nice design with a place to search for information by keyword, areas organized for review by topic, and links to current articles and proposals before the government.

Site: Postcards from Moscow

URL: http://lawlib.wuacc.edu/czars/postcards/introslide.html

Sponsor: Amy Kunhardt, Topeka Capital-Journal

Subject Area(s): Social Studies   **Subcategory:** World Government

Grade Level(s): High School

Description

The photographer spent three weeks in Moscow with a Russian studies program. She has combined 15 black-and-white photographs into a slide show with brief annotations depicting a view of life in Russia. There is also a description of Moscow as it is today.

Commentary

The slides can be set to advance manually or automatically at timed intervals. Follow the directions: turn off the tool and location bars. Advancing at 20 seconds per slide provides adequate time for the slide to load...but you may prefer 40 seconds. The pictures and annotation are very nicely done.

Site: The Bucknell Russian Program

URL: http://www.bucknell.edu/departments/russian/index.html

Sponsor: Bucknell University

Subject Area(s): Social Studies   **Subcategory:** World Government

Grade Level(s): Elementary, Middle School

Description

The Russian Studies program presents this site for the prospective student, for teachers seeking research materials, or for individuals merely curious about Russia. Information to be found includes the areas of art, business, cities, grammar, history, language, literature, politics, religion, and a great deal more.

Commentary

Opening with the flag flying and the national anthem playing, this site is both educational and delightful for people of all ages. Some areas of the site are a little slow to load because of the quality of the artwork, but every page seems worth examining. A very nice site to visit!

Site: United Nations

URL: http://www.un.org/

Sponsor: United Nations

Subject Area(s): Social Studies   **Subcategory:** World Government

Grade Level(s): Middle School, High School

Description

Available in English, Spanish, and French, the United Nations site describes the main goals of this organization: peace and security, international law, economic and social development, human rights, and humanitarian affairs. General keyword searches can be conducted or the reader can browse through each content area from an alphabetical list of terms.

Commentary

The coverage of daily events is outstanding, with daily highlights, the UN Journal, briefing room, and press releases. This is primarily a text-only site with a few maps thrown in, but interesting material may be found on human rights and some other subjects.

Section 01. Curriculum Corner

Site: Virtual Canadian Law Library

URL: http://www.droit.umontreal.ca/doc/biblio/en/index.html

Sponsor: Daniel Poulin, University of Montreal

Subject Area(s): Social Studies   **Subcategory:** World Government

Grade Level(s): High School

Description

The Virtual Canadian Law Library provides you with an easy way to search for legal and government documents from the federal and provincial governments of Canada. Resources are categorized into topics such as Legislation and Regulation, Governmental Departments and Statutory Bodies, Municipalities, Judicial Decisions, and others.

Commentary

Much of the information is provided in both French and English, but you may find under the English menu listings some documents available only in French.

Site: Welcome to the Prime Minister's Office (Hungary)

URL: http://www.meh.hu

Sponsor: Prime Minister's Office, Hungary

Subject Area(s): Social Studies   **Subcategory:** World Government

Grade Level(s): High School

Description

The Web site here provides information about the government, pictures, speeches, and even some interviews with government officials in Hungary. Follow the Table of Contents to explore history and organization of the various offices, such as that of the Ministry of the Interior. Or try using the search option to go directly to information of interest.

Commentary

Much of the information here is in English, while some is in Hungarian. Click on the country flag from the home page to see all information in Hungarian. Don't miss A Virtual Tour of the Parliament near the bottom of the Table of Contents. The information is fascinating, and the pictures are beautiful.

Site: World Flags

URL: http://www.adfa.oz.au/CS/flags/

Sponsor: Christopher J. S. Vance

Subject Area(s): Social Studies   **Subcategory:** World Government

Grade Level(s): Elementary, Middle School

Description

This collection of world flag images is maintained by an individual who attempts to update the information and avoid political disputes about the flags. They are classified by ISO two-letter codes and CIA diagraphs (which are roughly alphabetical).

Commentary

The flags are displayed in full color and can be enlarged to page size. It is also possible to access an updated database with information about each country. You will probably find some countries that you didn't even know existed.

Site: ABZU

URL: http://www-oi.uchicago.edu:80/OI/DEPT/RA/ABZU/ABZU.HTML

Sponsor: University of Chicago

Subject Area(s): Social Studies   **Subcategory:** World History

Grade Level(s): Middle School, High School

Description

Abzu is an experimental guide to the data relevant to the study and public presentation of the Ancient Near East via the Internet. There are primary and secondary indexes which provide a point of entry for study of this area and period in history. Included in the indexes are directories, journals, library collections, and publishers.

Commentary

Interested readers can add their names to the e-mail list to be notified when this site adds new material...which seems to be quite frequently. There is a wealth of scientific information as well as fun facts. Did you know that both men and women in Egypt shaved their entire bodies? And that, in addition to a varied diet of vegetables and meats, they had more than 40 kinds of bread?

Site: Ancient Civilizations

URL: http://www.taisei.co.jp/cg_e/ancient_world/ancient.html

Sponsor: Taisei Corporation

Subject Area(s): Social Studies   **Subcategory:** World History

Grade Level(s): Middle School, High School

Description

From a world map of ancient civilizations, the reader can move to Central and South America, Europe, Egypt/Orient, and China. Each site contains pictures which can be viewed as small icons or enlarged for easier appreciation.

Commentary

The individual sites are mostly from Egypt, Italy, and China. There is a brief introduction to each ancient site; then each picture can be enlarged to include a brief description below it. Most of the pictures are sepia in tone, with only a few color photographs.

Site: Animated Oxford Tour

URL: http://www.etrc.ox.ac.uk/personal/tour.html

Sponsor: Peter Robinson

Subject Area(s): Social Studies   **Subcategory:** World History

Grade Level(s): Middle School, High School

Description

Welcome to a virtual tour of old Oxford, England. Spin around the Clarendon Building quadrangle and walk through the doorway to see the famous Radcliffe Camera library, or enter the Christopher Wren's Sheldonian Theatre and be taken to the splendid rooftop view. Maps and a lot of animation enable viewers to feel as if they are experiencing a walk through Oxford.

Commentary

Using this site requires software programs called Shockwave and Quick Time Movies, both available free from the Internet, with links from this site. The software is slow to download, but the site runs fairly quickly after that. The effects are spectacular! Students creating web pages will be interested in examining the layouts of these pages.

Section 01. Curriculum Corner

Site: Britain and Ireland

URL: http://www.georgetown.edu/labyrinth/subjects/british_isles.html

Sponsor: Georgetown University

Subject Area(s): Social Studies   **Subcategory:** World History

Grade Level(s): Middle School, High School

Description

Part of the much larger Medieval Studies site at Georgetown University, this section has enough information and substance to stand on its own. Two sections, Anglo-Saxon culture and 14th-Century England, were available at the time of evaluation. The Irish and Celtic language and cultures were still under construction.

Commentary

The manuscripts at this site are fascinating. The Beowulf Project takes the ancient story and provides digital restoration of the original manuscript. Be sure to examine the Book of Kells; it still resides in Dublin but is unavailable to everyone but scholars—except on the Internet.

Site: China: History in General

URL: http://darkwing.uoregon.edu/~felsing/cstuff/history.html

Sponsor: University of Oregon

Subject Area(s): Social Studies   **Subcategory:** World History

Grade Level(s): High School

Description

The Council on East Asian Libraries has provided both general and specific tools for studying Chinese history. There are links to numerous journals, reference tools, and bibliographies. The site is maintained weekly and contains features of interest, such as the history of Chinese science and women in Chinese history.

Commentary

The History Timeline is wonderful...the database starts in 2000 BC and extends to the present. Each dynasty is listed in English and Chinese, with links to further information. This site has few search capabilities but is tightly organized.

Site: Demography and Population Studies

URL: http://coombs.anu.edu.au/ResFacilities/DemographyPage.html

Sponsor: Australian National University

Subject Area(s): Social Studies   **Subcategory:** World History

Grade Level(s): Middle School, High School

Description

This document keeps track of leading information facilities of value and/or significance to researchers in the field of demography. The Webmaster requests information from the field about new resources as well as an evaluation of sites which are not good enough to be included.

Commentary

The links are arranged by categories but can be resorted alphabetically. An individual inexperienced with demography will need some time to become familiar with this type of information but there is a resource of interest to everyone. There are links to WWW sites, but most links are to gopher sites.

Site: E-HAWK

URL: http://www.e-hawk.com/

Sponsor: Harcourt Brace Publications

Subject Area(s): Social Studies   **Subcategory:** World History

Grade Level(s): High School

Description

E-HAWK is dedicated to the assembly and promotion of military history, but general history resources have now been included and are available for searching. There is an interactive, multimedia journal; subscription is necessary for some areas, but students can examine a sample. The extensive database is searchable by keywords.

Commentary

Articles of interest are posted on a rotating basis in the Education Center. The Medieval Military History section can be read either as articles or as an online course. The graphics are well done, but more would be nice.

Site: Exploring Ancient World Cultures

URL: http://cedar.evansville.edu/~wcweb/wc101/

Sponsor: University of Evansville

Subject Area(s): Social Studies   **Subcategory:** World History

Grade Level(s): High School

Description

Visit one or more of the eight ancient cultures covered by this site: the Near East, India, Egypt, China, Greece, Rome, Islam, and Europe. There is an anthology of basic texts from each of these civilizations. Search capacity is available via Argos, a peer-reviewed, limited area search engine (LASE) designed at the University of Evansville to cover the ancient and medieval worlds.

Commentary

This site is still under construction but already contains a great deal of material. Each of the eight major sections can be further examined for resources, maps, chronology, essays, and links. Can you find the difference between early, ancient, and medieval civilizations?

Site: Flags of Nations of the World

URL: http://www.globalserve.net/~photodsk/flags/flags.html

FLAGS OF NATIONS **Sponsor:** Photo Disk Ltd.

Subject Area(s): Social Studies   **Subcategory:** World History

Grade Level(s): Elementary, Middle School, High School

Description

Photo Disk Ltd. offers software with images of flags of the United States of America and the states, Australia, and Canadian national, provincial, territorial, and Francophone communities. Visitors may view samples and order software online with a credit card or order via mail. Up to ten national flag images are available free to visitors by linking to the *Free Images* page.

Commentary

Each country in the world has its own unique identifier and national symbols, and certainly a country's flag is one of the easily recognized of these symbols. This site tells us that flags have existed for over 3,000 years and that today, every independent and most dependent countries have a distinctive flag.

Section 01. Curriculum Corner

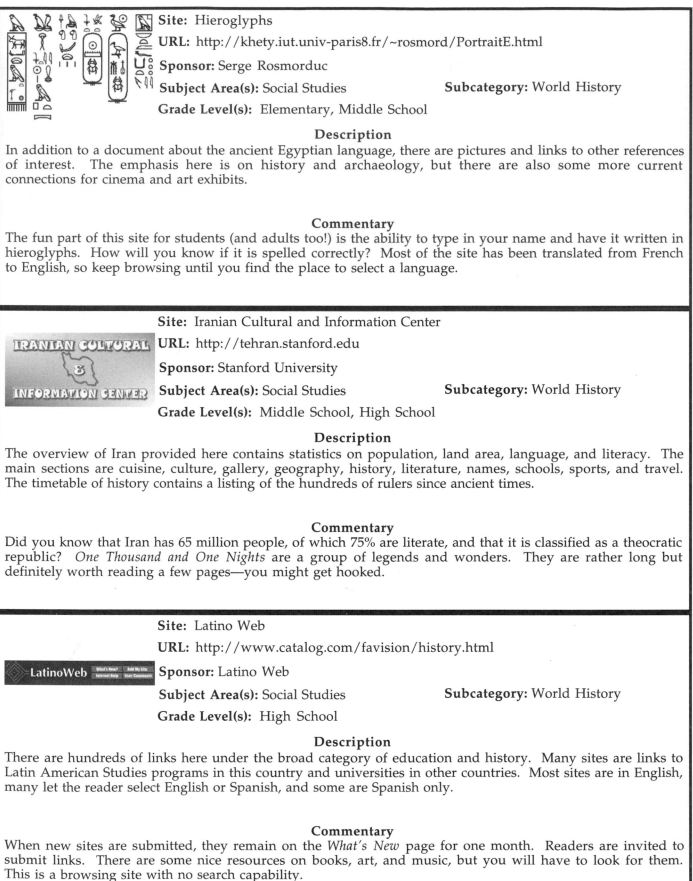

Site: Hieroglyphs

URL: http://khety.iut.univ-paris8.fr/~rosmord/PortraitE.html

Sponsor: Serge Rosmorduc

Subject Area(s): Social Studies   **Subcategory:** World History

Grade Level(s): Elementary, Middle School

Description

In addition to a document about the ancient Egyptian language, there are pictures and links to other references of interest. The emphasis here is on history and archaeology, but there are also some more current connections for cinema and art exhibits.

Commentary

The fun part of this site for students (and adults too!) is the ability to type in your name and have it written in hieroglyphs. How will you know if it is spelled correctly? Most of the site has been translated from French to English, so keep browsing until you find the place to select a language.

Site: Iranian Cultural and Information Center

URL: http://tehran.stanford.edu

Sponsor: Stanford University

Subject Area(s): Social Studies   **Subcategory:** World History

Grade Level(s): Middle School, High School

Description

The overview of Iran provided here contains statistics on population, land area, language, and literacy. The main sections are cuisine, culture, gallery, geography, history, literature, names, schools, sports, and travel. The timetable of history contains a listing of the hundreds of rulers since ancient times.

Commentary

Did you know that Iran has 65 million people, of which 75% are literate, and that it is classified as a theocratic republic? *One Thousand and One Nights* are a group of legends and wonders. They are rather long but definitely worth reading a few pages—you might get hooked.

Site: Latino Web

URL: http://www.catalog.com/favision/history.html

Sponsor: Latino Web

Subject Area(s): Social Studies   **Subcategory:** World History

Grade Level(s): High School

Description

There are hundreds of links here under the broad category of education and history. Many sites are links to Latin American Studies programs in this country and universities in other countries. Most sites are in English, many let the reader select English or Spanish, and some are Spanish only.

Commentary

When new sites are submitted, they remain on the *What's New* page for one month. Readers are invited to submit links. There are some nice resources on books, art, and music, but you will have to look for them. This is a browsing site with no search capability.

Section 01. Curriculum Corner

Site: Maya Civilization—Past & Present

URL: http://indy4.fdl.cc.mn.us/~isk/maya/maya.html

Sponsor: Paula Giese

Subject Area(s): Social Studies   **Subcategory:** World History

Grade Level(s): Middle School, High School

Description
There is a menu of Mayapages organized by topics such as culture, language, numbers, maps, curriculum, and links to other Maya Web sites. While the focus is on the ancient civilization, there is also material about present Mayan culture and problems. An interview is included with Rigoberta Menchu Tum, the Mayan refugee woman from Guatemala who won the 1992 Nobel Peace Prize.

Commentary
The graphics are beautiful, and the quality of this collection is admirable. This is a fascinating site because of the combination of information about the ancient civilization as well as the country's current political problems.

Site: Mystery of Maya

URL: http://www.cmcc.muse.digital.ca/cmc/cmceng/mminteng.html

Sponsor: Canadian Museum of Civilization Corporation

Subject Area(s): Social Studies   **Subcategory:** World History

Grade Level(s): Middle School, High School

Description
The fabled temples and palaces of the Maya have attracted many visitors to Mexico and Guatemala. This site supports the IMAX film of the same name by providing further information about the civilization, exhibits, and people of the Jaguar.

Commentary
This is a beautifully designed site (if you are interested in Web page design) and can be accessed in French or English. Be sure to look at the People of the Jaguar exhibit and the section on royal regalia. Then look at sections describing the Mayan people as they are living today. What a contrast!

Site: National Clearinghouse for U.S.–Japan Studies

URL: http://www.indiana.edu/~japan

Sponsor: Indiana University

Subject Area(s): Social Studies   **Subcategory:** World History

Grade Level(s): High School

Description
The large number of Japanese links from this site include electronic journals, government, news, research institutes, universities, geography, and more. Teachers, parents, travelers, and students will find a wealth of information about all facets of the country...constantly updated.

Commentary
You will enjoy the section on daily life in a Japanese high school, particularly the cram schools. Under teaching resources, find a Virtual Japan kit with readings, images, maps, sound bytes, and video segments.

Section 01. Curriculum Corner

Site: Peru Home Page

URL: http://www.rcp.net.pe

Sponsor: Red Científica Peruana - Internet Perú

Subject Area(s): Social Studies   **Subcategory:** World History

Grade Level(s): High School

Description

You can find a lot of information here in both picture and text-based forms about the people, culture, education, government, business, and organizations of Peru. Search on a Spanish keyword of interest.

Commentary

Students can read information in Spanish or English (click on English Version at the bottom of the home page). Be aware that even in the English version, all will not be in English as you explore deeper into the site, but Social Studies and Foreign Language students will find some useful information here.

Site: Soviet Archives

URL: http://sunsite.unc.edu:80/pjones/russian/Soviet_Archive_Introduction.html

Sponsor: Library of Congress

Subject Area(s): Social Studies   **Subcategory:** World History

Grade Level(s): High School

Description

This exhibit, which will later be shown in Moscow, is a milestone in representing a new Russia and the value of open access to information. This is the first public display of hitherto highly secret internal records of Soviet Communist rule. The exhibit illustrates both the domestic and the foreign policy of Soviet government.

Commentary

Sample pages are included from the wealth of material contained in the newly open Soviet archives. Even so, the site is for serious students of Russian history since it is text-only and most of the documents included are complicated reading.

Site: Stanford Guide to Japan Information Resources

URL: http://fuji.stanford.edu/XGUIDE/

J Guide   Stanford Guide to Japan Information Resources   **Sponsor:** U.S.–Japan Technology Management Center, Stanford University

Subject Area(s): Social Studies   **Subcategory:** World History

Grade Level(s): Middle School, High School

Description

Find a listing of newspapers that are published in Japan for current news; most are available in Japanese and English. The main table of contents includes topics such as science and technology, politics and government, education, life, and travel and culture.

Commentary

The Culture section is particularly interesting because it also includes materials about history and the language. Don't hesitate to go to some of the kid sites if you are a beginning student in Japanese, since the art work will assist in determining the meaning of unfamiliar words.

Section 01. Curriculum Corner

Site: The Bosnian Virtual Fieldtrip

URL: http://geog.gmu.edu/gess/jwc/bosnia/bosnia.html

Sponsor: George Mason University

Subject Area(s): Social Studies   **Subcategory:** World History

Grade Level(s): Middle School, High School

Description

Find a current discussion topic and the latest news from Bosnia. Information is segmented into three sections: Part I: Background, Part II: People and Places, and Part III: Dayton and After.

Commentary

There is information on people, sounds, maps, pictures, and more at this site.

Site: The History Channel Classroom

URL: http://www.historychannel.com/classroom/classroom.html

Sponsor: The History Channel

Subject Area(s): Social Studies   **Subcategory:** World History

Grade Level(s): Middle School, High School

Description

This site includes student and teacher materials pertaining to programs broadcast on The History Channel. There is information on programs teachers can videotape as well as support materials, lesson plans, and activities. The Classroom Calendar provides information on the next few months of program listings. Take a virtual tour through Exhibits—new explorations into the past are put on display each month.

Commentary

Check out the section called "This Day in History" to see what historical events occurred on the day you access the site—or enter a date to learn what historical events took place that day. Browse through the Classroom Materials to find program summaries, questions for discussion, and other valuable support materials. In Great Speeches, click to hear some of the best. Find a hotlist to even more resources.

Site: The Jerusalem Mosaic

URL: http://jeru.huji.ac.il/jerusalem.html

Sponsor: Hebrew University of Jerusalem

Subject Area(s): Social Studies   **Subcategory:** World History

Grade Level(s): Elementary, Middle School

Description

"The New Jerusalem Mosaic" provides the opportunity to travel the city through different periods, meet the people, taste the food, enjoy the costumes, and visit the sites. "The Old Jerusalem Mosaic" provides a tour of the city through portraits, old maps, landscapes, and works of arts.

Commentary

Everything about this site is beautifully constructed, so you can begin anywhere. If you start with the "New Mosaic," you will get a better sense of the history of Jerusalem. The First Temple Period begins in 1006 when David was king. Don't forget to take a tour of modern day Jerusalem.

Section 01. Curriculum Corner

Site: The Seven Wonders of the Ancient World

URL: http://pharos.bu.edu/Egypt/Wonders/

Sponsor: Alaa K. Ashmawy

Subject Area(s): Social Studies **Subcategory:** World History

Grade Level(s): Elementary, Middle School

Description

The list of the Seven Wonders of the Ancient World was originally compiled around the second century B.C. The final list was compiled during the Middle Ages to immortalize the seven most impressive monuments, only one of which has stood the test of time until this very day. The Web site lists the Wonders in chronological order, places them on a map, and provides details about each one.

Commentary

The author states that few people today can name more than a few of these Wonders. How many can you name? After looking at the Seven Wonders, you will find equally fascinating the listing of some Forgotten, Modern, and Natural Wonders.

Site: The Vietnam Veterans Home Page

URL: http://grunt.space.swri.edu

Sponsor: Bill McBride, Federal Express Corporation

Subject Area(s): Social Studies **Subcategory:** World History

Grade Level(s): Middle School, High School

Description

"The motivation in creating and publishing this WWW page is to provide a dynamic, multimedia-based chronology of the Vietnam War as seen through the eyes of veterans, their families, and their friends." This site provides an interactive forum to exchange stories, poems, songs, art, pictures, and experiences.

Commentary

The reader can scan the Wall or search for U.S. Vietnam war casualties by name or state. The Remembrances section contains stories and pictures honoring many veterans. Take time to browse another large section of resources about present day Vietnam.

Site: World War I Document Archives

URL: http://www.lib.byu.edu/~rdh/wwi/

Sponsor: World War I Military History List Volunteers

Subject Area(s): Social Studies **Subcategory:** World History

Grade Level(s): Middle School, High School

Description

These archives are international in focus and intend to present in one location primary documents concerning the Great War. There are conventions, treaties, and official papers. It is possible to search the documents by year, but there are also personal reminiscences and commentary articles.

Commentary

It is impressive that these archives are so extensive and continue to be updated and maintained by volunteers...who are looking for help, if this is a particular interest of yours. The image archives are still under construction, but the medal section is complete and contains beautiful images with explanations. This site makes the Great War come alive.

Site: Computer History

URL: http://www.si.edu/resource/tours/comphist/computer.html

Computer History **Sponsor:** National Museum of American History

Subject Area(s): Technology   **Subcategory:** Computers

Grade Level(s): Middle School, High School

Description

There is a great deal of information in varied formats at this site. Included is an Information Age Tour of the Museum's 14,000 square foot exhibition: Information Age, People, Information & Technology. Check out the oral and video histories of major figures in the history of computing and review some of the significant archived documents found here.

Commentary

Enjoy an oral or video history of major figures in computing such as Marc Andreesen, Chief Technical Officer of Netscape; J. Presper Eckert, co-inventor of the ENIAC; Larry Ellison, Chief Executive Officer of Oracle; Bill Gates, Microsoft; Steve Jobs, Apple Computer; Don Wetzel, co-patentee of the Automatic Teller Machine; and others. This is a rich resource site for research or browsing for interest.

Site: Computers: From the Past to the Present

URL: http://calypso.cs.uregina.ca/Lecture

Sponsor: University of Regina (Saskatchewan, Canada)

Subject Area(s): Technology   **Subcategory:** Computers

Grade Level(s): Middle School, High School

Description

This is the introductory lecture from a college class on Introduction to Computers for non-computer science majors. It describes the history of how computers have evolved from Stonehenge to today.

Commentary

Teachers can use a link on this site to e-mail the author, Michelle Hoyle, for a copy of this presentation to be used on a standalone computer.

Site: Generations: Through the History of Computing

URL: http://www.dg.com//about/html/generations.html

Sponsor: Data General Corporation

Subject Area(s): Technology   **Subcategory:** Computers

Grade Level(s): Middle School, High School

Description

Take a slide tour of computing from the early 1960s to today. See where the digital revolution has led us by looking at the technology as it evolved. The focus here is on the companies and computers that have made significant impact along the way.

Commentary

Students will find it interesting to review types of hardware and preferred applications from various periods in history and to see the changing costs of computing power over the years.

Site: The Computer Museum Network

URL: http://www.tcm.org

Sponsor: The Computer Museum Network

Subject Area(s): Technology   **Subcategory:** Computers

Grade Level(s): Elementary, Middle School

Description

The Computer Museum is a famous institution located in Boston, Massachusetts, and this is its Web site. Visitors can play interactive exhibits, research information on the history of computers, download educational materials, and even buy computer-related products at the Museum's Gift Shop. Visitors can personalize their session by logging on as kid, student, educator, or adult.

Commentary

Visitors can also send electronic postcards and messages to one another and discover what country other logged-in visitors are from. The Museum has a number of corporate sponsors, and there are links to the sponsors' sites as well.

2 WWW CONNECTING WITH COLLEAGUES

Section 2 identifies 55 sites where you can link up with other educators, professional organizations, and researchers in various fields. These will help you stay abreast of changes in all areas of education and educational technology, as well as help you solve problems using techniques and materials that are working for your colleagues in schools across the country.

One of the sites in this section, for example, is a virtual Teachers' Lounge where you will find interactive forums on a whole range of school-related topics, such as parental involvement and technology in education. Another site, "Technology Tutorials," helps you assess and develop your knowledge in 14 different areas. And many sites give you descriptions, curriculum information, and membership requirements for professional associations at all levels.

Section 02. Connecting with Colleagues

Site: Education, Learning, Teaching

URL: http://ifrit.web.aol.com/mld/production/mld-index-education.html

Sponsor: America Online, Inc.

Subject Area(s): Connecting with Colleagues **Subcategory:** Forums

Grade Level(s): Adult

Description
This site holds an alphabetical list of news and discussion newsgroups relating to education, with an emphasis on technology. Everything from the American Federation of Teachers to the WWW in Education Discussion list is here.

Commentary
You can link directly to any of these discussion groups from this page. AOL is a sponsor of "Give Back to the Net," and this is one of its contributions to that program.

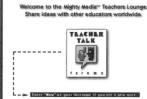

Site: Mighty Media Teachers Lounge

URL: http://www.mightymedia.com/talk/working.html

Sponsor: Mighty Media, Inc.

Subject Area(s): Connecting with Colleagues **Subcategory:** Forums

Grade Level(s): Adult

Description
Enter "new" for your user name and also use "new" for your password the first time you log on to this site. Then on the next screen you can create your account and immediately enter the virtual Teachers Lounge. You will find interactive forums on school reform, technology in the schools, parental involvement, current affairs, and other topics.

Commentary
Mighty Media, Inc. is a consortium of educators, students, and technology specialists whose stated mission is "to empower youth, teachers and organizations through the use of interactive communications technologies. Through corporate, non-profit and community partnerships, [they develop] services aimed at answering communications needs of families and educational institutions."

Site: AASA Online

URL: http://www.aasa.org

Sponsor: American Association of School Administrators

Subject Area(s): Connecting with Colleagues **Subcategory:** Professional Associations

Grade Level(s): Adult

Description
The American Association of School Administrators is the professional organization for over 16,500 educational leaders across North America and in many other countries. With the major goal of improving conditions of children and youth, this online network provides information about front burner issues, legislative alerts, conferences, publications, programs, and state groups.

Commentary
Updated weekly, there is a statistic of the day which provides serious, useful information. There are articles about contemporary topics, most of which stay posted for several months, as well as announcements of free workshops and reprints of pertinent articles from journals.

Site: American Accounting Association

URL: http://www.rutgers.edu/Accounting/raw/aaa/aaa.html

Sponsor: American Accounting Association

Subject Area(s): Connecting with Colleagues **Subcategory:** Professional Associations

Grade Level(s): Adult

Description
Organized by the American Accounting Association and located at Rutgers University, this site provides information about research, teaching, practice, the Association, and publications. There are opportunities for further study and staff development.

Commentary
This site may also be of interest to the future college business student with an interest in becoming an accountant. There are study materials for exams. Listings for the "Big 6" firms are available, as well as for other accounting firms.

Site: American Association for the Advancement of Science

URL: http://www.aaas.org

Sponsor: American Association for the Advancement of Science

Subject Area(s): Connecting with Colleagues **Subcategory:** Professional Associations

Grade Level(s): Adult

Description
Find information under the categories of Membership and Meetings, Science Online, News and Information, Science's Next Wave, ScienceNOW, International Programs, Project 2061, Science & Policy Programs, and Education & Human Resources Programs.

Commentary
This association is devoted to scientists, full-time students, postdoctorals, and residents interested in the field of science.

Site: American Association of Physics Teachers

URL: http://aapt.org

 **Sponsor:** American Association of Physics Teachers

Subject Area(s): Connecting with Colleagues **Subcategory:** Professional Associations

Grade Level(s): Adult

Description
Find information categorized as General Information, Meetings, Membership, Programs, Publications, Sections, Committees, and Others.

Commentary
There is an online membership application and the capability to search the abstract database.

Site: American Counseling Association

URL: http://www.counseling.org

Sponsor: American Counseling Association

Subject Area(s): Connecting with Colleagues   **Subcategory:** Professional Associations

Grade Level(s): Adult

Description

Find information about ACA, membership benefits, government relations, a resource catalog, latest news and developments, counseling today online, professional development, new publications, ethics and legal information, insurance information, public and community affairs, and more.

Commentary

"The American Counseling Association is an educational, scientific, and professional organization whose members are dedicated to the enhancement of human development throughout the life span." Sign up for a free e-mail newsletter for counselors and others.

Site: American Educational Research Association

URL: http://www.aera.net

Sponsor: American Educational Research Association

Subject Area(s): Connecting with Colleagues   **Subcategory:** Professional Associations

Grade Level(s): Adult

Description

In addition to providing information about the association and its meetings, this Web page provides information about each of the twelve divisions of the association and the various publications affiliated with the association. There is information for graduate students regarding grant programs and job openings.

Commentary

The major part of this site is intended for the educational researcher, either currently employed, in graduate school and/or contemplating a career change. The one section on Internet resources posed problems loading, but the remainder of the site appears to work just fine.

Site: American Federation of Teachers

URL: http://www.aft.org

Sponsor: American Federation of Teachers

Subject Area(s): Connecting with Colleagues   **Subcategory:** Professional Associations

Grade Level(s): Adult

Description

Inside AFT, the official newsletter, appears online weekly at this site. There is information about educational issues, congressional hearings, conferences, a calendar, and the organization itself. While the majority of resources are of general interest, there are also special sections for the professions: K-12 teachers, public employees, higher education, nurses and health professionals, and paraprofessionals.

Commentary

Web-related resources include state associations, government related sites, education sites, and information on labor unions. Individuals will want to be sure that they check the sections dealing with their specific profession.

Site: American Library Association

URL: http://www.ala.org

Sponsor: American Library Association

Subject Area(s): Connecting with Colleagues **Subcategory:** Professional Associations

Grade Level(s): Adult

Description

The American Library Association has been a leader in defending intellectual freedom and promoting the highest quality library and information services. It has been active in the support of access to the information superhighway. The site contains news, events, library advocacy, employment opportunities, and membership information.

Commentary

The Frequently Asked Questions are interesting. Make a guess regarding the number of libraries in the United States before you take a look at the answer.

Site: American School Counselors Association

URL: http://www.edge.net/asca/

Sponsor: American School Counselors Association

Subject Area(s): Connecting with Colleagues **Subcategory:** Professional Associations

Grade Level(s): Adult

Description

The American School Counselors Association (ASCA) is a professional organization for licensed school counselors. The ASCA Web site provides information about activities of the organization, membership, and links pertinent to counselors such as K-12 sites, college, university and career sites, mental health resources, and sites of related organizations

Commentary

Two documents—*Role Statement: The School Counselor* and *Ethical Standards for School Counselors*—are available at this site.

Site: ASCD Web

URL: http://www.ascd.org/index.html

Sponsor: Association for Supervision and Curriculum Development

Subject Area(s): Connecting with Colleagues **Subcategory:** Professional Associations

Grade Level(s): Adult

Description

The Association for Supervision and Curriculum Development provides general information for educators and the public regarding its organization, conferences, and its publications. The Web feature of the month highlights discussion of a major issue from a variety of viewpoints. Other ongoing forums permit educators to post additions to the discussion.

Commentary

In addition to a basic search field, the site also supplies a choice of keywords with the number of articles containing each one. One of the most useful parts of this site is Frank Betts' scrollable database of what seems to be just about everything related to education...it takes a significant amount of time to load but is worth it.

Section 02. Connecting with Colleagues

Site: Association for Childhood Education International

URL: http://www.udel.edu/bateman/acei

Sponsor: Association for Childhood Education International

Subject Area(s): Connecting with Colleagues **Subcategory:** Professional Associations

Grade Level(s): Adult

Description
The Association for Childhood Education International is dedicated to "the dual mission of promoting 1. the inherent rights, education and well-being of children from infancy through early adolescence, and 2. high standards of preparation and professional growth for educators." The Web page contains information about conferences, its professional journal, education resources, and various aspects of the organization.

Commentary
There are free resources, usually consisting of an article which might be duplicated for inservice education and/or for parents. The Education Resources section is especially rich and varied with the opportunity to search for resources in a variety of formats, but most are resources for sale through the organization.

Site: Association for Educational Communications and Technology

URL: http://www.aect.org

Sponsor: Association for Educational Communications and Technology

Subject Area(s): Connecting with Colleagues **Subcategory:** Professional Associations

Grade Level(s): Adult

Description
Find information about this association under the following categories: What's New, About AECT / Membership, Publications, Electronic AECT, AECT Governance, Divisions & Chapters, ECT Foundation, AECT/ECT Awards, AECT Affiliates, Employment, Professional Development, and Conventions.

Commentary
The mission of the AECT is "to provide leadership in educational communications and technology by linking professionals holding a common interest in the use of educational technology and its application to the learning process." You will find helpful resources in the Professional Development section, such as Fair Use Multimedia Guidelines, Copyright Resources, and others.

Site: AVA Online

URL: http://www.avaonline.org/index.html

Sponsor: American Vocational Association

Subject Area(s): Connecting with Colleagues **Subcategory:** Professional Associations

Grade Level(s): Adult

Description
The American Vocational Association (AVA) is a professional organization of educators and business partners. AVA is a driving force behind most legal initiatives impacting vocational education. The Web site provides information about the association, membership, publications, products, professional training and conventions, and legal updates.

Commentary
Excerpts from AVA's weekly and monthly publications are available for review as are excerpts from recent publications. Membership information is available at the Web site, but you must call AVA's membership department to join.

Site: C.U.E.

URL: http://www.cue.org

Sponsor: Computer-Using Educators (California)

Subject Area(s): Connecting with Colleagues **Subcategory:** Professional Associations

Grade Level(s): Adult

Description
CUE (or Computer-Using Educators) was founded as a California nonprofit educational corporation in 1978 and now has a membership of over 11,000 professional educators. The organization sponsors conferences and an online newsletter.

Commentary
There is continuously updated information regarding technology, education, and government in California. Educators from other states will find the listing of resources useful, with the promise of better search capabilities to come. Currently there is information about the professional organization, affiliates of CUE, and academically priced software.

Site: Children First: The Web Site of the National PTA

URL: http://www.pta.org/index.stm

Sponsor: National Parent Teacher Association

Subject Area(s): Connecting with Colleagues **Subcategory:** Professional Associations

Grade Level(s): Adult

Description
The Web page contains icons for each of the major sections at this site: PTA Membership information, Legislative Activity, Chats and Bulletin Boards, Program Areas, Online Subscriptions, Annual Convention, and Links to Child Advocacy Organizations.

Commentary
The What's New section provides ample evidence of weekly updates, but archives need to be organized in another section. Both parents and teachers will find the links to Child Advocacy groups helpful as well as the local and state resources. The majority of online publications and subscriptions carry an additional cost.

Site: Consortium for School Networking

URL: http://www.cosn.org/

Sponsor: Consortium for School Networking (CoSN)

Subject Area(s): Connecting with Colleagues **Subcategory:** Professional Associations

Grade Level(s): Adult

Description
The Consortium for School Networking is the national nonprofit voice for K-12 classroom education technology and networking of schools to the emerging national information infrastructure. The Web site features online discussion forums, articles of interest, and information about membership.

Commentary
An especially interesting link is to the Mid-continent Regional Educational Laboratory (McREL) and its Impact of Technology forum. This site contains hundreds of articles and resources useful to technology planners to use in answering the question "Does technology make a difference?"

Section 02. Connecting with Colleagues

Site: Council for Learning Disabilities

URL: http://www1.winthrop.edu/cld/

Sponsor: Council for Learning Disabilities

Subject Area(s): Connecting with Colleagues   **Subcategory:** Professional Associations

Grade Level(s): Adult

Description
Learn about the mission, the Board of Trustees, conferences, and current news on learning disabilities at the Web site of the Council for Learning Disabilities. Click on For More Information for articles and resources on the characteristics of individuals with LD, A Guide for Families, information on attention deficit disorder (ADD), the college experience for students with LD, and an infosheet on adults with LD.

Commentary
"The Council for Learning Disabilities (CLD) is an international organization of and for professionals who represent diverse disciplines and who are committed to enhance the education and lifespan development of individuals with learning disabilities."

Site: Institute for the Transfer of Technology to Education

URL: http://www.nsba.org/itte

Sponsor: National School Boards Association

Subject Area(s): Connecting with Colleagues   **Subcategory:** Professional Associations

Grade Level(s): Adult

Description
ITTE (Institute for the Transfer of Technology to Education) is a program of the National School Boards Association designed to help advance the wise use of technology in public education. Find conference information, resources for students with disabilities, education leadership tools, and hotlinks to other related sites. You can also find a directory of state school board associations and contact information.

Commentary
ITTE works actively with school districts across North America that are exploring creative ways to teach and learn with technology. Its participants include large and small districts from cities, small towns, and rural areas. Its common goal is to improve the opportunity for students and teachers to use technologies suitable for their needs.

Site: International Reading Association

URL: http://www.ira.org

Sponsor: International Reading Association

Subject Area(s): Connecting with Colleagues   **Subcategory:** Professional Associations

Grade Level(s): Adult

Description
The International Reading Association seeks to promote a high level of literacy for all by improving the quality of reading instruction. Its clearinghouse of information and resources provides a means of dissemination of research on the reading process with the intent of actively encouraging the lifetime reading habit.

Commentary
The Web site provides information about its publications, conferences, forums, research, and international projects. The site would be far more helpful if some articles about reading were posted; this might encourage teachers to join the organization and/or provide all educators with some assistance in dealing with reading problems.

Section 02. Connecting with Colleagues

Site: International Society for Technology in Education

URL: http://isteonline.uoregon.edu

Sponsor: International Society for Technology in Education (ISTE)

Subject Area(s): Connecting with Colleagues **Subcategory:** Professional Associations

Grade Level(s): Adult

Description

ISTE is a nonprofit organization dedicated to the improvement of education through computer-based technology. It is the worldwide association for education technology professionals. Information available includes educational technology news/resources, conferences, publications, ISTE affiliates, distance education courses, and a Private Sector Council that fosters partnerships among education, business, and industry.

Commentary

Many technology-using educators belong to state computer educators associations, such as Computer Using Educators in California or the Texas Computer Education Association. ISTE is the umbrella organization for a number of these state affiliates and others worldwide. ISTE publishes *Learning and Leading With Technology* (formerly *The Computing Teacher*) and is one of the sponsors of the National Education Computing Conference.

Site: Music Educators National Conference

URL: http://www.menc.org

Sponsor: Music Educators National Conference

Subject Area(s): Connecting with Colleagues **Subcategory:** Professional Associations

Grade Level(s): Adult

Description

Designed for both teachers of general music and ensemble teachers, this organization has more than 65,000 members and spearheaded the development of National Standards for Arts Education. Standard features include information about the association, a job center, online publications and teachers' guides, plus information about the organization.

Commentary

This site has nice pictures and is well organized, but wouldn't you think that it would also have some music? Nevertheless there are constantly updated new features which are available online rather than at additional cost. Don't miss "Opera: All of Music...and More!" and lesson plans with the subtitle, "Freak out your mom. Confuse your dad. Listen to opera."

Site: National Art Education Association

URL: http://www.naea-reston.org

Sponsor: National Art Education Association

Subject Area(s): Connecting with Colleagues **Subcategory:** Professional Associations

Grade Level(s): Adult

Description

This organization is intended for art educators at every level of instruction, plus anyone concerned about quality art education in schools. The Web site contains papers, publications, convention information, awards, membership information, and frequently-asked questions.

Commentary

There is little of general interest here, but it will be valuable to the art educator who is interested in exploring avenues for publishing curriculum materials and essays. There is extensive information about the Arts Education Program Standards with critique and explanation.

Site: National Association for Sport and Physical Education

URL: http://www.aahperd.org/cgi-bin/counter.pl/naspe/naspe.html

Sponsor: National Association for Sport and Physical Education

Subject Area(s): Connecting with Colleagues **Subcategory:** Professional Associations

Grade Level(s): Adult

Description

The NASPE is the professional organization of the 18,000 physical education, sport, fitness, and kinesiology educators who have teamed together to promote quality physical activity programs. The Web page contains information about publications, conferences, grants, related councils and academies, and other types of programs.

Commentary

This site contain copies of the National Standards for Physical Education and the Standards for Coaching. Membership includes affiliation with the American Alliance for Health, Physical Education, Recreation & Dance. The Web page contains a link to the parent organization with related services.

Site: National Association of Biology Teachers

URL: http://www.nabt.org/

Sponsor: National Association of Biology Teachers

Subject Area(s): Connecting with Colleagues **Subcategory:** Professional Associations

Grade Level(s): Adult

Description

You can find out information about NABT and its membership plus links to other sites of interest. They are building a component of online activities shared among members and others. Click on Send Your Best Activities To Us To Share and check out the genetic jewelry, an interesting project where students can create beautiful adornments while learning about the details of the structure of DNA.

Commentary

The NABT is the "largest national association dedicated exclusively to the concerns of biology and life science educators."

Site: National Association of Elementary School Principals

URL: http://www.naesp.org

Sponsor: National Association of Elementary School Principals

Subject Area(s): Connecting with Colleagues **Subcategory:** Professional Associations

Grade Level(s): Adult

Description

NAESP's Principal Online Web site is for elementary and middle school principals and provides information pertaining to education as well as a gathering place to exchange information, ideas, and experiences which impact education. Find an online forum, feature articles from publications, professional development programs, online research and other resources, and more.

Commentary

The National Association of Elementary School Principals is a professional association for K-8 principals and the 33 million children they serve. The organization has more than 27,000 members.

Site: National Association of Independent Schools

URL: http://www.nais-schools.org

Sponsor: National Association of Independent Schools

Subject Area(s): Connecting with Colleagues   **Subcategory:** Professional Associations

Grade Level(s): Adult

Description

At the NAIS Web site, you can find out about the association and independent education, services the association provides for families and others looking for independent schools. People who are interested in teaching in independent schools can access information about NAIS publications, programs, and member services.

Commentary

"NAIS, the National Association of Independent Schools, is a voluntary membership association for over 1,100 member schools and associations in the United States and abroad. The school community served by NAIS includes 440,000 students, 58,300 teachers, and 9,600 administrators."

Site: National Association of Secondary School Principals

URL: http://www.nassp.org/

Sponsor: National Association of Secondary School Principals

Subject Area(s): Connecting with Colleagues   **Subcategory:** Professional Associations

Grade Level(s): Adult

Description

This association serves all leaders in middle level and high school education. There is a directory of services including information about affiliated organizations, honor societies, student activities, the Universal Service Fund, and Web sites of interest to educators.

Commentary

Search capacity for this site is organized through an icon identified as EdView, which resembles any wide-range search engine with little relevant targeting. Education News was not much more helpful since very little current (i.e., the last two months') information was included. Log on to the User Survey and let them know the type of information that would be useful to you.

Site: National Business Education Association

URL: http://www.nbea.org

Sponsor: National Business Education Association

Subject Area(s): Connecting with Colleagues   **Subcategory:** Professional Associations

Grade Level(s): Adult

Description

Categories of information at this association Web site include: What's New, Membership Information, Who to Contact, Conventions/Meetings, Newest Publications, and NBEA Standards.

Commentary

"The National Business Education Association is the nation's largest professional organization devoted exclusively to serving individuals and groups engaged in instruction, administration, research, and dissemination of information for and about business." Undergraduate students majoring in business education or students pursuing initial teacher certification are eligible for a discounted membership.

Site: National Catholic Education Association

URL: http://www.ncea.org/

Sponsor: National Catholic Education Association

Subject Area(s): Connecting with Colleagues **Subcategory:** Professional Associations

Grade Level(s): Adult

Description

Find out about the association, membership, its publications, and conventions. The Resources page provides (1) non-Internet resources of interest to Catholic educators, (2) Internet-based resources, (3) Internet-based education information and grants, and (4) Internet-based general information and services.

Commentary

"NCEA has been providing leadership and service to Catholic education since 1904. The largest professional association in the world, its 200,000 members serve over 7.6 million students in preschools, elementary and secondary schools, parish catechetical/religious education programs, diocesan offices, colleges, universities, and seminaries."

Site: National Center for Montessori Education

URL: http://www.mindspring.com/~ncme/

Sponsor: National Center for Montessori Education

Subject Area(s): Connecting with Colleagues **Subcategory:** Professional Associations

Grade Level(s): Adult

Description

Find information about NCME and membership, its teacher training centers, *The National Montessori Reporter*, and their national conference.

Commentary

NCME is an independent non-profit corporation offering assistance and support to Montessorians seeking to establish Teacher Training Centers.

Site: National Communication Association

URL: http://www.scassn.org

Sponsor: National Communication Association

Subject Area(s): Connecting with Colleagues **Subcategory:** Professional Associations

Grade Level(s): Adult

Description

Review this association's Web site to learn about NCA, membership, news, its convention and conferences, publications, and more. You will find a variety of resources in the Education & Administration, Research, and Other Resources links. Of interest to many may be The Communication Education Resources Index (CERI), a compilation of published articles and documents about communication education and administration.

Commentary

"National Communication Association is a not-for-profit organization with a mission to promote study, criticism, research, teaching, and application of the artistic, humanistic, and scientific principles of communication." This association was formerly known as the Speech Communication Association.

Section 02. Connecting with Colleagues

Site: National Council of Teachers of English

URL: http://www.ncte.org

Sponsor: National Council of Teachers of English

Subject Area(s): Connecting with Colleagues   **Subcategory:** Professional Associations

Grade Level(s): Adult

Description
This site is sponsored by the professional association of educators in English studies, literacy, and language arts. The regular departments featured include conversations, affiliates, books, meetings, teaching ideas, conventions, assemblies, journals, standards, and information about membership. The site is under construction but continues to operate with regular updates.

Commentary
Literacy River is a part of the site promising a great deal of potential. Professionals are requested to submit information about books so that a framework is created for an open collection of reading resources for teachers and students at any level in K-16 education. The format is online and can be submitted instantly.

Site: National Council of Teachers of Mathematics

URL: http://www.nctm.org

Sponsor: National Council of Teachers of Mathematics

Subject Area(s): Connecting with Colleagues   **Subcategory:** Professional Associations

Grade Level(s): Adult

Description
This online service provides information about membership, a newsroom, marketplace, the organization, meetings, and getting involved. Members are requested to affiliate with a special interest group and to subscribe to the WebNews service, which is free.

Commentary
The Newsroom contains not only press releases and journal articles, but features downloadable software. The remainder of the site focuses closely on the advantages of membership in the National Council of Teachers of Mathematics, with listing of local groups for affiliation. Both national and regional meetings are held each year.

Site: National Education Association

URL: http://www.nea.org

Sponsor: National Education Association

Subject Area(s): Connecting with Colleagues   **Subcategory:** Professional Associations

Grade Level(s): Adult

Description
Standard features include tips for better schools, a What's New Section, listings of outstanding schools, resource room, public policy debate, and information about the association. The site presents listings of relevant television programs and magazine articles which focus on education issues. There is search capability, or the reader can scroll through the menus.

Commentary
Attractive, well-organized, and updated daily, this site will be useful to educators and parents. Head straight for Recess for some chuckles from the classroom...and feel free to submit your own. Then check out the cybertour of Good Schools, Good Students! Others may be interested in the article on how technology is challenging America's classrooms.

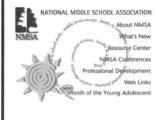

Site: National Middle School Association

URL: http://www.nmsa.org/

Sponsor: National Middle School Association

Subject Area(s): Connecting with Colleagues   **Subcategory:** Professional Associations

Grade Level(s): Adult

Description

Find out about the National Middle School Association, membership, its conferences and professional development at the association's Web site. In the Resource Center section, find articles and other resources which can be ordered online. Web Links provide hotlinks to still more sites of possible interest.

Commentary

NMSA "serves as a voice for professionals, parents, and others interested in the educational and developmental needs of young adolescents (youth 10-15 years of age)."

Site: National School Boards Association

URL: http://www.nsba.org

Sponsor: National School Boards Association

Subject Area(s): Connecting with Colleagues   **Subcategory:** Professional Associations

Grade Level(s): Adult

Description

This nationwide advocacy and outreach organization for public school governance provides information about the organization and its role before the federal government. The Web page offers search capabilities in addition to information about conferences, books, online discussion groups, court cases, and education links.

Commentary

This is one of the most complete listings of professional organizations available and located under Education Links. In addition, there is a link to all the regional labs where educators can find information on the latest in research and program information.

Site: National Science Teachers Association

URL: http://www.nsta.org/

Sponsor: National Science Teachers Association

Subject Area(s): Connecting With Colleagues   **Subcategory:** Professional Associations

Grade Level(s): Adult

Description

This site provides information on the organization and science-oriented curriculum information. You can find online forums pertaining to a variety of topics such as astronomy, medicine, and others, updated legislative information, convention information, resources such as journals and publications, and more. Look in Programs and Projects for a variety of curriculum ideas. The "Online Resources" section gives you links to other sites.

Commentary

NSTA is the largest organization in the world committed to promoting excellence and innovation in science teaching and learning for all. Its membership includes science teachers, science supervisors, administrators, scientists, business and industry representatives, and others involved in science education. An easy-to-use search tool helps you find the information you desire.

Site: NCSS Online

URL: http://www.ncss.org/online

Sponsor: National Council for the Social Studies

Subject Area(s): Connecting with Colleagues **Subcategory:** Professional Associations

Grade Level(s): Adult

Description
This site is focused on education of tomorrow's citizens and is sponsored by the largest association in the country devoted solely to social studies education. Find information about its annual conference, publications, member newsletter, awards program, membership, current news of interest, professional development opportunities, its 110 affiliated state, local, and regional councils and associated groups, upcoming meetings, and more.

Commentary
NCSS is an umbrella organization for elementary, secondary, and college teachers of history, geography, economics, political science, sociology, psychology, anthropology, and law-related education. You can become a member at the Web site or just take advantage of a vast amount of free information available to all visitors. This site has been rated among the top 5% of all sites on the Internet by Point Survey.

Site: Society for Applied Learning Technology (SALT)

URL: http://www.salt.org

Sponsor: Society for Applied Learning Technology

Subject Area(s): Connecting with Colleagues **Subcategory:** Professional Associations

Grade Level(s): Adult

Description
Find SALT online information here categorized as follows: ASTD Alliance, About the Society, Add Me to Your Mail List, Calendar, Call for Papers, Conference Information, Conference Proceedings, Glossary, Invitation to Exhibit, Online Conference, Registration, President's Letter, and Society Publications.

Commentary
Membership in SALT "is oriented to professionals whose work requires knowledge and communication in the field of instructional technology. It is a professional society, designed for individual membership participation with classes of membership keyed to the interest and experience of the individual."

Site: The Council for Exceptional Children

URL: http://www.cec.sped.org/

Sponsor: The Council for Exceptional Children

Subject Area(s): Connecting with Colleagues **Subcategory:** Professional Associations

Grade Level(s): Adult

Description
The Council for Exceptional Children is the largest international professional organization dedicated to improving education for individuals with exceptionalities, students with disabilities, and/or the gifted. The organization provides information at this Web site about professional development opportunities, journals, newsletters, special education publications, conferences, and more.

Commentary
This is a well-organized site with extensive information provided by the Council as well as links to the ERIC Clearinghouse on Disabilities and Gifted Education and other smaller clearinghouses. Teachers and administrators will find the section on public policy and legislative information helpful, and it is updated monthly.

Site: The National Association for the Education of Young Children

URL: http://www.naeyc.org

Sponsor: The National Association for the Education of Young Children

Subject Area(s): Connecting with Colleagues **Subcategory:** Professional Associations

Grade Level(s): Adult

Description

Click on Catalog (to review NAEYC resources), Conferences (to see what is coming to your area), Accreditation (for quality child care), or Membership (for information and benefits). The Public Policy page provides the latest information to strengthen public policies and public awareness, and to stimulate effective advocacy on behalf of young children. There are also separate resource areas for parents and professionals.

Commentary

"The National Association for the Education of Young Children (NAEYC) is the nation's largest organization of early childhood professionals and others dedicated to improving the quality of early childhood education programs for children birth through age eight."

Site: The National Association of Child Care Professionals

URL: http://www.naccp.org/

Sponsor: The National Association of Child Care Professionals

Subject Area(s): Connecting with Colleagues **Subcategory:** Professional Associations

Grade Level(s): Adult

Description

Find membership information—regular, student, and vendor—as well as the NACCP Child Care Yellow Pages, Training Opportunities, and information on the National Accreditation Commission.

Commentary

"NACCP is the leader among the nation's organizations for child care directors, owners and administrators. The Association's goal is to enhance and strengthen the credibility of the people who lead this industry by providing professional support services and membership benefits."

Site: United States Distance Learning Association

URL: http://www.usdla.org/

Sponsor: United States Distance Learning Association

Subject Area(s): Connecting with Colleagues **Subcategory:** Professional Associations

Grade Level(s): Adult

Description

Check out information on distance learning—what it is, a fact sheet, and research information and statistics—plus information on USDLA members, membership information, and a calendar of events. You can view discussion threads in the online forums or browse through or search for specific articles from the online version of *Education at a Distance* magazine.

Commentary

The mission of the USDLA is "to promote the development and application of distance learning for education and training." The association serves K-12, higher ed, continuing ed, corporate training, and military and government training personnel.

Section 02. Connecting with Colleagues

Site: Welcome to the National Association for Gifted Children

URL: http://www.nagc.org

Sponsor: National Association for Gifted Children

Subject Area(s): Connecting with Colleagues **Subcategory:** Professional Associations

Grade Level(s): Adult

Description
The National Association for Gifted Children is an organization of parents, educators, and other professionals who unite to address the unique needs of children and youth with demonstrated gifts and talents. The organization also provides information to assist children who may be able to develop their talent potential with appropriate educational experiences.

Commentary
The policy statements may be useful to teachers, parents, and administrators. Parents may be interested in the quarterly publication entitled *Parenting for High Potential*. Other publications and convention dates are listed.

Site: Center for Image Processing in Education

URL: http://ipt.lpl.arizona.edu/

Sponsor: The University of Arizona

Subject Area(s): Connecting with Colleagues **Subcategory:** Professional Developm.

Grade Level(s): Adult

Description
The Image Processing for Teaching (IPT) project attempts to make a new technology available as a learning tool. Students are given the tools to analyze and enhance digital imagery from the fields of mathematics, science, and technology. Educators fill out a questionnaire to become involved in the project and learn about opportunities for professional development.

Commentary
Incredible new images are posted each month with detailed descriptions of how they were achieved and enhanced. This site is a "work in progress" will be of immediate interest to people fascinated by digital imagery. It shows promise of being of instructional use to other teachers.

Center for Occupational Research and Development
Leading change in education for work

Site: Center for Occupational Research and Development

URL: http://www.cord.org/

Sponsor: Center for Occupational Research and Development (TX)

Subject Area(s): Connecting with Colleagues **Subcategory:** Professional Developm.

Grade Level(s): Adult

Description
The Center for Occupational Research and Development is a non-profit public service organization dedicated to providing educational leadership in developing a more productive workforce. This site presents some of the group's work in curriculum development efforts for contextual learners, integrating the use of instructional technology as an essential component.

Commentary
Tech Prep programs enable students to make a successful transition from school to work by balancing the school-site and worksite learning experiences. Teachers may wish to respond to the survey by expressing their ideas on the type of research and development activities needed for the future.

Section 02. Connecting with Colleagues

Site: National Center on Education and the Economy

URL: http://www.ncee.org

Sponsor: National Center on Education and the Economy

Subject Area(s): Connecting with Colleagues **Subcategory:** Standards and Reform

Grade Level(s): Adult

Description
NCEE is a not-for-profit organization dedicated to the development in the United States of a comprehensive system of education, employment, and training second to none in the world. The National Center engages in policy analysis and development, institutional design, technical assistance, and professional development. This Web site provides current information and access to publications on school reform and performance standards.

Commentary
To keep abreast of all of the discussion of school reform and performance standards for American schools, consult this site. It provides immediate access to legislative initiatives, research and reference information, news items of interest, and education community activities and progress with school reform issues.

Site: National Science Education Standards

URL: http://www.nap.edu/nap/online/nses/

Sponsor: National Academy of Sciences

Subject Area(s): Connecting with Colleagues **Subcategory:** Standards and Reform

Grade Level(s): Adult

Description
The project report documented here was approved by the Governing Board of the National Research Council, whose members are drawn from the councils of the National Academy of Sciences, the National Academy of Engineering, and the Institute of Medicine. The members of the committee responsible for the report were chosen for their special competences and with regard for appropriate balance.

Commentary
These standards represent wide agreement about what is important in science education today. The Standards are voluntary guidelines designed to ensure that all students graduate with the science knowledge and intellectual abilities they will need to make effective decisions in their everyday lives, participate in civic and cultural affairs, and become economically productive citizens.

Site: Online Activities for Standards in School (OASIS)

URL: http://www-co-cas.colorado.edu/oasis/oasis.html

Sponsor: Colorado Alliance for Science, University of Colorado at Boulder

Subject Area(s): Connecting with Colleagues **Subcategory:** Standards and Reform

Grade Level(s): Adult

Description
OASIS is a system for locating standards-based Internet science and math curriculum materials and resources. By linking these materials to the Colorado State science and math standards, the intent is to simplify the task of integrating Internet resources into the classroom. It is possible to browse the site by standards, by grade level, or by subject.

Commentary
Each link is well annotated with the grade level, the name of the developer, a summary of the site, and a rating. If you are familiar with a Web site in science, you will tend to agree with the ratings for the ones you know and therefore will likely be encouraged to explore other highly rated sites.

Section 02. Connecting with Colleagues

Site: Pathways to School Improvement: Mathematics

URL: http://www.ncrel.org/sdrs/areas/ma0cont.html

Sponsor: North Central Regional Education Laboratory

Subject Area(s): Connecting with Colleagues **Subcategory:** Standards and Reform

Grade Level(s): Adult

Description

This site includes a complete collection of the NCTM Math Standards and a wealth of other resources, including an excellent hotlist to related sites. An especially interesting topic is "Assuring Equity and Excellence in Mathematics."

Commentary

There is a section on locating, integrating, and using Internet-based mathematics materials, and a Trip Planner Inventory tool is available to help analyze your school's math curriculum.

Site: SkillsNET

URL: http://www.skillsnet.org

Sponsor: SkillsNET Corporation

Subject Area(s): Connecting with Colleagues **Subcategory:** Standards and Reform

Grade Level(s): Adult

Description

SkillsNET started as a national listserv for individuals at the grassroots level of the movement toward national occupational skill standards. SkillsNET is evolving into a site with conference rooms for those with similar interests to share documents and information about specific projects.

Commentary

A useful collection of information and links may be found in the Library. Join the SkillsNET listserv at no cost. Instructions may be found at the Listserv Services link.

Site: Standards for Education

URL: http://putwest.boces.org/Standards.html

Sponsor: Putnam Valley Schools, Putnam Valley, NY

Subject Area(s): Connecting with Colleagues **Subcategory:** Standards and Reform

Grade Level(s): Adult

Description

This site is a repository for information about educational standards and curriculum frameworks from a host of sources (national, state, local, and other). Find governmental and general resources as well as standards and framework documents. It is also possible to search for standards by state and by subject matter area. In addition there is a very complete list of Web sites for professional organizations.

Commentary

This is a well-organized site offering a one-stop place to locate a wealth of resources on education standards. It has received awards and recognition from Classroom Connect, the Eisenhower National Clearinghouse, Apple Computer, Electronic Learning, the ERIC Clearinghouse on Teaching and Teacher Education, and others.

Section 02. Connecting with Colleagues

Site: Technology Tutorials

URL: http://www.ceap.wcu.edu/Martin/index.html

Sponsor: Western Carolina University (NC)

Subject Area(s): Connecting with Colleagues **Subcategory:** Standards and Reform

Grade Level(s): Adult

Description

Test your technology competence as an educator—then brush up on any weak areas by taking the appropriate tutorials. Start by going to the Technology Competency List to become familiar with 14 different technology areas. When you click on a competency to review, you are linked to its description. Click on "Go to Tutorials" to study and prepare; then finish by clicking on Link to the Competency Assessment to test your knowledge.

Commentary

This site was designed for Western Carolina University students, future teachers, present teachers, and others interested in technology for education, but it will assist any educator in becoming skilled in technology-related areas for instruction and learning. The tutorials are designed to work with the MicroSoft Office Suite of applications but are easily adapted. Take your own online assessment.

3 WWW TEACHING IDEAS

The following section identifies 175 sites that feature innovative lesson plans and management tools in all the areas of education—from careers and technology and guidance and counseling, to language arts, music, science, social studies, and technology.

For example, "The Geometry Center," a site sponsored by the University of Minnesota, is packed with information, including lesson plans, for the geometry instructor. "Teacher's Corner—Internet Activities," sponsored by IBM, offers monthly lesson plans that make use of the Internet to explore topics such as Earth Day, Black History Month, and oceans.

Over 40 of the sites offer materials for multiple disciplines.

Site: ArtsEdge

URL: http://artsedge.kennedy-center.org/

Sponsor: The Kennedy Center and the National Endowment for the Arts

Subject Area(s): Teaching Ideas   **Subcategory:** Art

Grade Level(s): Adult

Description
With support from the National Endowment for the Arts, the Kennedy Center provides an electronic guide to the arts in this country. Its goal is to place and maintain the arts alongside science, math, and other subject areas among the vast resources and services of the National Information Infrastructure. It seeks to (1) connect people to people, (2) connect people to resources, and (3) build a base of knowledge in the arts and education.

Commentary
Find curricular resources and contributions of teachers and artist-educators who have developed arts-based, interdisciplinary programs and practices linked with new standards for excellence in education. The Web Spotlight Links for Students are extensive; browse the list alphabetically or search for a specific genre. "The Adventures of Tiger the Kitten," with its electronic illustrations and sounds, is guaranteed to bring a smile.

Site: ArtsEdNet

URL: http://www.artsednet.getty.edu/ArtsEdNet/

Sponsor: Getty Education Institute for the Arts

Subject Area(s): Teaching Ideas   **Subcategory:** Art

Grade Level(s): Adult

Description
This online service was developed to support the needs of the K-12 arts education community. It focuses on helping art educators, general classroom teachers using the arts in their curriculum, and museum educators. There are materials for professional, curriculum, and theory development.

Commentary
Discipline-Based Art Education may be a new concept for many teachers. The aim is to have students involved in art production, in art criticism, in learning about art history, and in developing an appreciation of aesthetics. The curriculum idea for teaching pluralism through multicultural art prints is particularly intriguing.

Site: ArtTeacher.com

URL: http://www.artteacher.com/

Sponsor: IconJohn.com

Subject Area(s): Teaching Ideas   **Subcategory:** Art

Grade Level(s): Adult

Description
Find research databases, a Teacher Connect section, lesson plans, CD-ROM reviews, links to other sites, public and private forums for art teachers, and more at ArtTeacher.com.

Commentary
The forums let you subscribe to various listservs and newsgroups discussing topics of interest. Go to Teacher Connect to find colleagues with whom you can set up e-mail pen pals, class-to-class e-mail pals, joint class online projects, and/or global class debates and discussions. There are only a few lesson plans currently online, but you can offer a lesson plan for co-publishing on a pay-per-view basis.

Business Education Department

Site: Business Education Department

URL: http://www.ecnet.net/users/gdlevin/bized.html

Sponsor: David Levin

Subject Area(s): Teaching Ideas   **Subcategory:** Career & Technology Ed.

Grade Level(s): Adult

Description
This Web guide is primarily intended for educators. Links are marked with different icons to indicate when they are "impressive and substantial" and when they are "a cool place that will make you smile"—some links have both icons.

Commentary
This list of links is a very valuable tool for business educators. All of the links are annotated so that you have a preview of what you will be seeing. There are numerous links, and the icon identification really helps in picking out real substance and just-for-fun links.

Site: Business Education Lesson Plans and Resources

URL: http://www.angelfire.com/ks/tonyaskinner/index.html

Sponsor: Tonya Skinner (MO)

Subject Area(s): Teaching Ideas   **Subcategory:** Career & Technology Ed.

Grade Level(s): Adult

Description
This first year teacher has shared her lesson plans but also located and organized resources in accounting, business law, computers, economics, general business, keyboarding, office technology, professional organizations, job search, and other areas—with links to each.

Commentary
The author states that this site is always under construction, but it already has a great deal of valuable materials, and everything seems to be current! Teachers who sponsor student professional organizations will be especially grateful for the collection of materials and links to Web pages of other organizations.

Site: Energy Conservation Enhancement Project

URL: http://ecep.usl.edu/ecep/ecep.html

Sponsor: University of Southwestern Louisiana

Subject Area(s): Teaching Ideas   **Subcategory:** Career & Technology Ed.

Grade Level(s): Adult

Description
The 14 Energy Curriculum Guides are provided to increase the knowledge of energy conservation/efficiency techniques of those who will work in building trades. Among the guides included are introduction to energy conservation, energy audits, energy and comfort, energy conservation in construction and design, home energy conservation, and heating/ventilation and air conditioning.

Commentary
Although aimed at the vocational-technical student, this site also has materials that teachers will find helpful. Particularly noteworthy are the developmental English activities which teach energy conservation and develop English skills at the same time.

Section 03. Teaching Ideas

Site: National Center for Research in Vocational Education

URL: http://vocserve.berkeley.edu/

Sponsor: University of California at Berkeley

Subject Area(s): Teaching Ideas   **Subcategory:** Career & Technology Ed.

Grade Level(s): Adult

Description

This research and development center in work-related education has the mission of strengthening education to prepare all individuals for lasting and rewarding employment and lifelong learning. This site contains reports of research projects, listings of publications, full-length reports, newsletters, digests, and other assorted topics related to vocational education.

Commentary

Viewers may want to look first at "Net Gain," a monthly column featuring Web sites related to the world of work. There are additional links related to vocational youth organizations as well as links to sites maintained by students in occupational programs.

Site: Sandi Goldman's Classroom Corners

URL: http://www.fcbe.edu.on.ca/~goldmans/

Sponsor: Sandi Goldman

Subject Area(s): Teaching Ideas   **Subcategory:** Career & Technology Ed.

Grade Level(s): Adult

Description

This Canadian teacher has drawn together a wide variety of Internet resources for all teachers. There are curriculum resources in careers, food preparation, health, business, computer studies, fashion and design, and technical studies. There are further listings of general interest to parents, as well as to others interested in education topics.

Commentary

The technical studies links are both challenging and fascinating. There is a great lesson plan on bridge design and an article about the construction of the Empire State Building. Fashion and design students will find links to the most up-to-date information on trends in clothing. And don't forget "CarTalk" for answers to everything about car repair.

Site: Teachers' Page

URL: http://www.plan.ml.com/family/teachers/

Sponsor: Merrill Lynch, Pierce, Fenner & Smith, Inc.

Subject Area(s): Teaching Ideas   **Subcategory:** Career & Technology Ed.

Grade Level(s): Adult

Description

The Teachers' Resource Center provides ideas for teaching students about saving and investing. Many of the materials were created in partnership with the *Wall Street Journal Classroom Edition* and Bank Street College of Education. Resources are included for elementary through high school and include links to other sites as well as materials that may be ordered.

Commentary

This beautifully organized three-page Web site provides a scrollable listing (with descriptions) of the various resources available. While the primary emphasis is on money, there are also activities for budgeting time. The section on "Saving Articles" is particularly noteworthy.

Section 03. Teaching Ideas

Site: Agora Language Marketplace

URL: http://www.agoralang.com/

Sponsor: Agora Language Marketplace

Subject Area(s): Teaching Ideas   **Subcategory:** Foreign Language

Grade Level(s): Adult

Description
The directories at this site contain publishers, distributors, bookstores, language laboratory hardware and software, services for business, language schools, study abroad, jobs, organizations, workshops, events, and other Internet resources.

Commentary
Interested individuals can subscribe to *The Agora Newsletter* which will be mailed to their e-mail address monthly during the school year. While this site is primarily for the professional language teacher, other individuals will find helpful reading material and chat rooms in various languages.

No GRAPHIC FOUND

Site: Creative French Teaching Methods

URL: http://www3.sympatico.ca/heather.zaitlin/TEACHER.HTML

Sponsor: Heather Zaitlin, Ontario Institute for Studies in Education

Subject Area(s): Teaching Ideas   **Subcategory:** Foreign Language

Grade Level(s): Adult

Description
In a page designed especially for the French teacher, the emphasis is on helping students enjoy French while meeting the needs of the students. Topics include lesson plans, class projects, teacher resources, and a discussion forum. Resources include audio and video, a dictionary, plus information about ordering publications and software.

Commentary
Intercultural E-mail Connections may be a valuable resource for the teacher, as it is designed for class-to-class correspondence. Check out the complete information on TV5, French International television broadcast around the world and customized by region.

Site: Foreign Language Teaching Forum

URL: http://www.cortland.edu/www_root/flteach/flteach.html

Sponsor: State University of New York at Cortland

Subject Area(s): Teaching Ideas   **Subcategory:** Foreign Language

Grade Level(s): Adult

Description
The Foreign Language Teaching Forum is an integrated service for foreign language teachers in all types of school settings. Materials developed by the two professors who originated this site are available along with the opportunity of becoming a member of the group.

Commentary
Possibly the most helpful part of this site are the Web resources which have been nicely organized into collections. You will find many general teaching resources as well as sites which specialize in one language. A fun link is the international collection of tongue twisters, with examples from several dozen languages.

Section 03. Teaching Ideas

Site: Foreign Language Teaching on the Internet: Resources With Teaching Activities

URL: http://www.ea.pvt.k12.pa.us/htm/programs/departments/modlang/putnam/

Sponsor: Celian B. Putnam, Episcopal Academy (PA)

Subject Area(s): Teaching Ideas   **Subcategory:** Foreign Language

Grade Level(s): Adult

Description

Ms. Putnam teaches French at the Episcopal Academy and created this Web page as a result of her frustration over searching for specific resources or topics on the Web. It contains a cluster of selected foreign language resources in French, Spanish, German, and Italian. All have specific projects, themes, and units for use in K-12 classes.

Commentary

Some projects, such as a news broadcast or an illustrated book of poetry, are described in one section but can be easily adapted to other languages. Many of these general resources have been placed in each section, but you might find it useful to browse the other language sections. Check out the food projects!

Site: Gessler Publishing

URL: http://www.gessler.com/gessler/

Sponsor: Gessler Publishing

Subject Area(s): Teaching Ideas   **Subcategory:** Foreign Language

Grade Level(s): Adult

Description

This company publishes and distributes language learning materials in French, Spanish, German, and for ESL. Catalogs and information about new releases are provided. There are teacher tips and connections to Web sites in each of the languages.

Commentary

Buen Viaje! A Journey Through Hispanic America is a nice addition to this Web site. It presents narrative and some pictures regarding the history of the area, geography, language differences, currency, and virtual trip planning. Reading is in English, so it might also be useful in a social studies classroom.

Site: Language Acquisition Center

URL: http://langlab.uta.edu/

Sponsor: University of Texas at Arlington

Subject Area(s): Teaching Ideas   **Subcategory:** Foreign Language

Grade Level(s): Adult

Description

The German Information Center features weekly newsletters in both German and English which summarize current events in Germany. They are available for about two months after publication. The German Life Magazine features articles describing culture and travel. There are also links to other publications such as the IALL Journal and the Kafka Society Journal.

Commentary

The weekly newsletters are very detailed articles primarily about the government and the economy. The German Life magazine, entirely in English, is much more readable with articles about comic strips, poverty, travel, and learning to speak German.

Section 03. Teaching Ideas

Site: NCBE

URL: http://cis.ncbe.gwu.edu/

Sponsor: The National Clearinghouse for Bilingual Education

Subject Area(s): Teaching Ideas   **Subcategory:** Foreign Language

Grade Level(s): Adult

Description

At the NCBE Web site, find an online library, technical assistance, language and education links, databases (access to over 20,000 bibliographic citations and abstracts of materials dealing with all aspects of the education of linguistically and culturally diverse students in U.S. schools), success stories, and a section called In the Classroom (comprised of lesson plans, links to schools on the Web, contributions from educators, and more).

Commentary

The National Clearinghouse for Bilingual Education (NCBE) is funded by the U.S. Department of Education's Office of Bilingual Education and Minority Languages Affairs (OBEMLA). Its purpose is to collect, analyze, and disseminate information relating to the effective education of linguistically and culturally diverse learners.

Site: RETAnet: Resources for Teaching About the Americas

URL: http://ladb.unm.edu/www/retanet

Sponsor: Lisa Falk, Latin American Database

Subject Area(s): Teaching Ideas   **Subcategory:** Foreign Language

Grade Level(s): Adult

Description

Included at this site are lesson plans, a resource materials database, an archive of photos, a contact list of teacher partners with whom to connect, contact information for embassies, and more.

Commentary

This site is the result of a project funded by the U.S. Department of Education. RETAnet works with secondary teachers, educational specialists, and scholars to make accessible resources and curriculum materials about Latin America, the Spanish Caribbean, and the U.S. Southwest. A vital component of RETAnet is communications technology using computers and the Internet.

Site: The Human Languages Page

URL: http://www.june29.com/HLP/

Sponsor: Tyler Chambers

Subject Area(s): Teaching Ideas   **Subcategory:** Foreign Language

Grade Level(s): Adult

Description

The Human Languages Page is a catalog of language-related Internet resources organized by type and by language. There are links to online language lessons, translating dictionaries, native literature, translation services, software, language schools, and organizations. Language teachers will find many resources to enhance the teaching of the more common languages.

Commentary

There will be obvious uses for the many dictionaries and translators. The site is rich in resources for teachers, students, and anyone who wants to know more about a specific language. Take time to enjoy linguistic sites such as "Greetings to the Universe in 55 languages," "I Love You in various languages," and an extensive group of magazines in languages other than English.

Section 03. Teaching Ideas

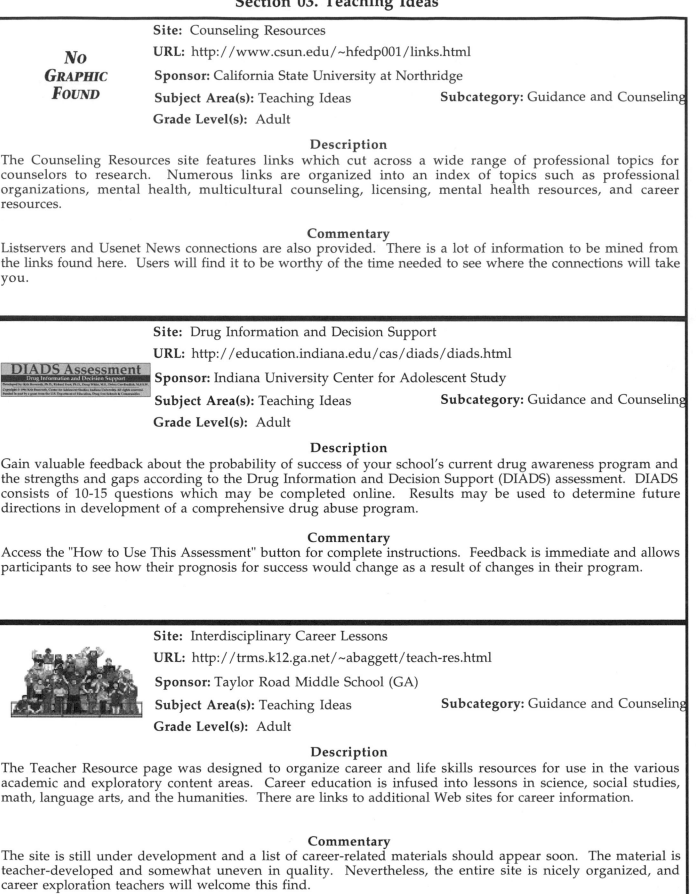

No Graphic Found

Site: Counseling Resources

URL: http://www.csun.edu/~hfedp001/links.html

Sponsor: California State University at Northridge

Subject Area(s): Teaching Ideas   **Subcategory:** Guidance and Counseling

Grade Level(s): Adult

Description

The Counseling Resources site features links which cut across a wide range of professional topics for counselors to research. Numerous links are organized into an index of topics such as professional organizations, mental health, multicultural counseling, licensing, mental health resources, and career resources.

Commentary

Listservers and Usenet News connections are also provided. There is a lot of information to be mined from the links found here. Users will find it to be worthy of the time needed to see where the connections will take you.

DIADS Assessment
Drug Information and Decision Support
Developed by: Kris Bosworth, Ph.D., Richard Yust, Ph.D., Doug White, M.S., Debra Cox-Bredlich, M.S.S.W.
Copyright © 1996 Kris Bosworth, Center for Adolescent Studies, Indiana University. All rights reserved.
Funded in part by a grant from the U.S. Department of Education, Drug free Schools & Communities

Site: Drug Information and Decision Support

URL: http://education.indiana.edu/cas/diads/diads.html

Sponsor: Indiana University Center for Adolescent Study

Subject Area(s): Teaching Ideas   **Subcategory:** Guidance and Counseling

Grade Level(s): Adult

Description

Gain valuable feedback about the probability of success of your school's current drug awareness program and the strengths and gaps according to the Drug Information and Decision Support (DIADS) assessment. DIADS consists of 10-15 questions which may be completed online. Results may be used to determine future directions in development of a comprehensive drug abuse program.

Commentary

Access the "How to Use This Assessment" button for complete instructions. Feedback is immediate and allows participants to see how their prognosis for success would change as a result of changes in their program.

Site: Interdisciplinary Career Lessons

URL: http://trms.k12.ga.net/~abaggett/teach-res.html

Sponsor: Taylor Road Middle School (GA)

Subject Area(s): Teaching Ideas   **Subcategory:** Guidance and Counseling

Grade Level(s): Adult

Description

The Teacher Resource page was designed to organize career and life skills resources for use in the various academic and exploratory content areas. Career education is infused into lessons in science, social studies, math, language arts, and the humanities. There are links to additional Web sites for career information.

Commentary

The site is still under development and a list of career-related materials should appear soon. The material is teacher-developed and somewhat uneven in quality. Nevertheless, the entire site is nicely organized, and career exploration teachers will welcome this find.

Section 03. Teaching Ideas

Site: Internet Resources for School Counselors

URL: http://www.indep.k12.mo.us/WC/wmccane.html

Sponsor: Bill McCane

Subject Area(s): Teaching Ideas   **Subcategory:** Guidance and Counseling

Grade Level(s): Adult

Description

College information, financial aid, careers, testing, family information, mental health links, substance abuse and counseling-related publications await visitors to the Internet Resources for School Counselors site.

Commentary

The links found here are comprehensive, often leading to pages with additional links on the Internet. For ideas on how to use some of these links with students, visit Mr. McCane's counseling home page at <www.indep.k12.mo.us/WC/bmccane.html>

Site: National Educational Service

URL: http://www.nes.org

Sponsor: National Educational Service

Subject Area(s): Teaching Ideas   **Subcategory:** Guidance and Counseling

Grade Level(s): Adult

Description

Explore information from the National Educational Service Journal, Teaching Kids Responsibility newsletter, How Effective Schools Get Results report, Resources & Materials, and the Community Circle of Caring Network which connects and supports families and like-minded professionals worldwide. Featured special guest schedules are published at this site.

Commentary

The interactive Community Circle Gathering provides monthly topics to encourage online discussion, interaction, and exchange of ideas for working with challenging behaviors. The National Educational Service mission is to help create places where all youth and children can succeed. This Web site is a valuable resource toward achieving its mission and will be appreciated by both educators and parents.

Welcome to NOICC on the Net — Your gateway to occupational, career, and labor market information

Site: NOICC Home Page

URL: http://www.noicc.gov/

Sponsor: National Occupational Information Coordinating Committee

Subject Area(s): Teaching Ideas   **Subcategory:** Guidance and Counseling

Grade Level(s): Adult

Description

The National Occupational Information Coordinating Committee is a network of federal and state organizations which supports individuals working directly with youth and adults in career development, employment, and workforce preparation. The Network offers products, training, systems, and programs, usually through a State Occupational Information Coordinating Committee (SOICC).

Commentary

The hierarchy of this network of networks can be overwhelming. Check the <www.soicc link> on the left side of the NOICC home page to see if your state is a member of the network. The link provides SOICC contacts and Internet home page links where available. Recent state activities are listed for review and may be helpful in locating products and services available in your state.

Section 03. Teaching Ideas

Site: SCANS/2000: The Workforce Skills Home Page

URL: http://infinia.wpmc.jhu.edu/

Sponsor: Johns Hopkins University

Subject Area(s): Teaching Ideas **Subcategory:** Guidance and Counseling

Grade Level(s): Adult

Description

The Secretary's Commission on Achieving Necessary Skills (SCANS) was appointed by the Secretary of Labor to determine the skills needed to succeed in the world of work. SCANS/2000 is the home page for a research group at the Johns Hopkins University Institute for Policy Studies (IPS). The primary focus of the group is creating a system which prepares workers to compete in the global economy.

Commentary

Information about the projects, programs, and publications of the IPS may be found at the Web site. The programs and publications pages may prove to be the most help unless you are involved in one of two projects through Johns Hopkins University. A matrix of SCANS competencies and coursework is found under publications, as are documents offered by the SCANS commission.

Site: School to Careers

URL: http://www.school-to-careers.com

School to CAREERS *.com* **Sponsor:** South Western Educational Publishing and others

Subject Area(s): Teaching Ideas **Subcategory:** Guidance and Counseling

Grade Level(s): Adult

Description

School to Careers approaches education from the belief that meaningful learning stems from application in real life and real work. To implement the School to Work Opportunities Act of 1994, each state has a system which provides school-based, work-based, and connecting activities. This site features products to assist in implementation of the School to Work initiative and a curriculum guide matrix by subject and grade level.

Commentary

Conferences and professional development opportunities are posted on the calendar page and may prove useful in locating learning opportunities in your area.

Site: School-to-Work

URL: http://stw.ed.gov/

Sponsor: The School-to-Work Learning Center

SCHOOLTO**WORK** **Subject Area(s):** Teaching Ideas **Subcategory:** Guidance and Counseling

Grade Level(s): Adult

Description

You can review the U. S. Government's Web site for the school-to-work initiative resulting from legislation signed into law in 1994. Find out what school-to-work is and how each state is addressing this critical area of education reform. Additional resources and an approved list of technical assistance providers with their profiles may also be accessed along with evaluation information, an events calendar, and a bulletin board.

Commentary

This site is well organized and easily accessed. The fact sheets found at the "What is STW" link are valuable for practitioners who need to share information with others. The Resources may be searched by subject area or key words; results provide a brief description of the tool/resource with contact information.

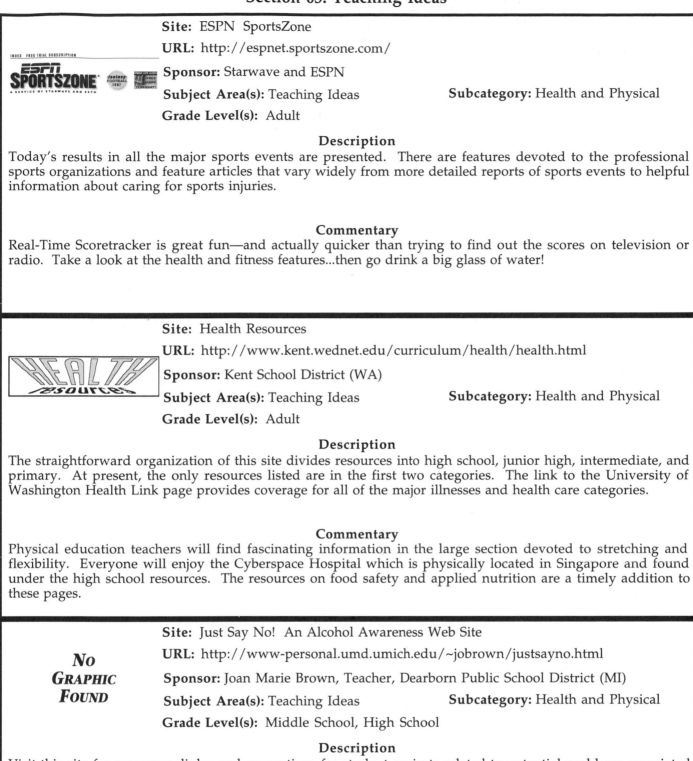

Site: ESPN SportsZone

URL: http://espnet.sportszone.com/

Sponsor: Starwave and ESPN

Subject Area(s): Teaching Ideas

Subcategory: Health and Physical

Grade Level(s): Adult

Description

Today's results in all the major sports events are presented. There are features devoted to the professional sports organizations and feature articles that vary widely from more detailed reports of sports events to helpful information about caring for sports injuries.

Commentary

Real-Time Scoretracker is great fun—and actually quicker than trying to find out the scores on television or radio. Take a look at the health and fitness features...then go drink a big glass of water!

Site: Health Resources

URL: http://www.kent.wednet.edu/curriculum/health/health.html

Sponsor: Kent School District (WA)

Subject Area(s): Teaching Ideas

Subcategory: Health and Physical

Grade Level(s): Adult

Description

The straightforward organization of this site divides resources into high school, junior high, intermediate, and primary. At present, the only resources listed are in the first two categories. The link to the University of Washington Health Link page provides coverage for all of the major illnesses and health care categories.

Commentary

Physical education teachers will find fascinating information in the large section devoted to stretching and flexibility. Everyone will enjoy the Cyberspace Hospital which is physically located in Singapore and found under the high school resources. The resources on food safety and applied nutrition are a timely addition to these pages.

No GRAPHIC FOUND

Site: Just Say No! An Alcohol Awareness Web Site

URL: http://www-personal.umd.umich.edu/~jobrown/justsayno.html

Sponsor: Joan Marie Brown, Teacher, Dearborn Public School District (MI)

Subject Area(s): Teaching Ideas

Subcategory: Health and Physical

Grade Level(s): Middle School, High School

Description

Visit this site for resources, links, and suggestions for student projects related to potential problems associated with the use of alcohol. Find project ideas such as making alcohol awareness posters, creating a bookmark of "How to Say No to Alcohol" ideas that could be presented to a library or other group or agency, writing an open letter to parents informing them about teenagers and alcohol, and many others.

Commentary

When you consider some of the statistics, such as the fact that alcohol-related car crashes are the number one killer of teenagers in the United States, it is easy to realize the importance of alcohol awareness programs. This site might be used by Social Studies, Language Arts, Health, or other teachers. The ideas are well thought out and presented for other teachers to use.

Section 03. Teaching Ideas

Site: National Center for Health Statistics

URL: http://www.cdc.gov/nchswww/nchshome.html

Sponsor: U. S. Department of Health and Human Services

Subject Area(s): Teaching Ideas   **Subcategory:** Health and Physical

Grade Level(s): Adult

Description

The mission of the National Center for Health Statistics is to provide statistical information that will guide actions and policies to improve the health of the American people. There are both monthly vital statistics reports and news releases. Information is provided about government publications and links to other sites.

Commentary

This site is likely to provide information to health teachers, school nurses, economists, and parents interested in current news. They will find some encouraging reports..."teen sex down"...and other less happy news..."number of unwed mothers up."

Site: National Clearinghouse for Alcohol and Drug Information

URL: http://www.health.org

Sponsor: U. S. Department of Health and Human Services

Subject Area(s): Teaching Ideas   **Subcategory:** Health and Physical

Grade Level(s): Adult

Description

NCADI services include culturally-diverse prevention materials tailored for use by parents, teachers, youth, and prevention professionals. It is possible to customize searches for an annotated bibliography about a specific drug. Federal grant announcements and applications, as well as personnel, are available to answer specific questions.

Commentary

New articles are posted weekly and contain interesting news items...alcohol consumption is generally down as are alcohol-related traffic deaths. Parents may wish to read the article entitled, "What Causes Children's Tobacco and Alcohol Use?" The Center estimates that the annual economic cost of alcohol, tobacco, and other drug problems is $237.5 billion!

Women's Health Hot Line
Home Page
A newsletter providing the media with information on women's health.

Site: Women's Health Hot Line

URL: http://www.libov.com/

Sponsor: Charlotte Libov and Beckwith Communications

Subject Area(s): Teaching Ideas   **Subcategory:** Health and Physical

Grade Level(s): Adult

Description

This is a newsletter published four times a year about women's health. It is written by a medical author and contains no commercial material. Past issues are also available online. A recent issue contained articles on heart disease, smoking, heart disease book awards, and women who are making a contribution to health.

Commentary

Since there are no search capabilities on this site, it is simple to read the newsletters...and go back as far in time as one wishes. There is an interesting recent article on heart disease in young women and another on the increasing prevalence of colon cancer in women.

Section 03. Teaching Ideas

Site: Booktalks—Quick and Simple

URL: http://www.concord.k12.nh.us/schools/rundlett/booktalks/

Sponsor: Nancy J. Keane, Rundlett Middle School (NH)

Subject Area(s): Teaching Ideas   **Subcategory:** Language Arts

Grade Level(s): Adult

Description

The short booktalks found at this site are designed for school library media specialists and teachers. The database currently has approximately 500 booktalks with bibliographic information included. The site is searchable by author, title, or subject.

Commentary

The organizer of the site has indicated Interest Level (IL) and Reading Level (RL) of the books, which is useful. If you check back frequently, you can click on "New" to see the updated booktalks.

Site: California Language Arts Teacher Resources

URL: http://www.sdcoe.k12.ca.us/score/frontpage.html

Sponsor: Schools of California Online Resources for Education Project (SCORE)

Subject Area(s): Teaching Ideas   **Subcategory:** Language Arts

Grade Level(s): Adult

Description

The California Online Resources for Education Project collaborates with several other state initiatives in providing the resources identified on the Web page. There is information about teaching strategies, literature, assessment, publishing, and further information about reading reform in California.

Commentary

A truly unique part of this site is the Student CyberGuides. Fourteen lessons at various grade levels (with more to come) are available. Each lesson centers around a grade-appropriate book and contains objectives, a list of materials, and many activities plus other Internet links appropriate for that book.

Site: Carol Hurst's Children's Literature Site

URL: http://www.carolhurst.com/

Sponsor: Carol Hurst's Consultants and Didax Educational Resources

Subject Area(s): Teaching Ideas   **Subcategory:** Language Arts

Grade Level(s): Adult

Description

This site offers a collection of reviews of children's books, together with ideas for using them in the classroom. There are also collections of books and activities about particular subjects, curriculum areas, themes, and professional topics. The site is searchable.

Commentary

Teachers will find lots of good ideas here and may choose to subscribe to the free newsletter offered via e-mail. Be sure to review the articles, activities, book excerpts, and Internet links on a variety of topics of interest in the area of language arts.

Section 03. Teaching Ideas

Site: Children's Literature & Language Arts Resources

URL: http://falcon.jmu.edu/~ramseyil/childlit.html

Sponsor: Inez Ramsey, James Madison University (VA)

Subject Area(s): Teaching Ideas   **Subcategory:** Language Arts

Grade Level(s): Adult

Description
Find links here to resources especially for the elementary literature and language arts student and teacher. Categories are extensive, including Book Awards, Creative Movement & Dance, Curriculum Units, Families in Children's Literature, Gifted Education Internet Resources, Holidays, Kids, Sites, Lesson Plans on the Internet, Multicultural Education Resources, Picture Books, Traditional Literature, and more.

Commentary
Get ready to spend some time browsing here or use the "Search" function to quickly locate sites of interest.

Site: Children's Literature—Resources for Teachers

URL: http://www.ucalgary.ca/~dkbrown/rteacher.html

Sponsor: David K. Brown, University of Calgary

Subject Area(s): Teaching Ideas   **Subcategory:** Language Arts

Grade Level(s): Adult

Description
This is a part of the "Children's Literature Web Guide" which is developed to assist teachers in linking to a variety of other sites, and which then contains a link back to the valuable original site. There are lesson plans, bibliographies of authors, and teaching ideas related to children's and young adults' books.

Commentary
Since the author annotates this site with icons to indicate his evaluation of the most useful links, these are worth checking out first. You will find this particularly helpful because Mr. Brown doesn't hesitate to express his frank opinion. There are also new links provided on a regular basis.

Site: Creating a Classroom Newspaper: A Teacher's Guide

URL: http://www.southam.com/calgaryherald/educa/CACNINTRO.html

Sponsor: American Newspaper Association Foundation

Subject Area(s): Teaching Ideas   **Subcategory:** Language Arts

Grade Level(s): Adult

Description
The goal of this program is to introduce educators to the use of the newspaper as a powerful and cost-effective instructional tool. The unit of instruction is organized to combine reading and writing activities, culminating with the student production of a classroom newspaper.

Commentary
There is a wealth of information pertaining to the organization and delivery of instruction at various grade levels. Sample activities are provided to accomplish each objective. The teacher selects the level of complexity of the objective, and links are provided to supporting sites.

Site: English Pavilion

URL: http://pen.k12.va.us/Anthology/Pav/LangArts/LangArts.html

Sponsor: Virginia Public Education Network

Subject Area(s): Teaching Ideas   **Subcategory:** Language Arts

Grade Level(s): Adult

Description

The English Pavilion offers educators a variety of English and Language Arts resources and is part of the Electronic Academical Village, a collection of information on academic subjects studied in schools. Find authors of children's and young adults' books, favorite book character links, lesson plans for reading and writing, a poet's corner for reading and writing tips, and more English and language arts resources.

Commentary

The lesson plan collections will prove valuable, and the English and Language Arts resources includes links to sites related to literature, children's books, book awards, publishing houses, reference material, spelling, school libraries, and professional associations—don't miss Word, Words, Words for interesting activities and ideas, and also the list on online encyclopedias, dictionaries, and similar sites.

Site: EnglishTeacher.com

URL: http://www.englishteacher.com/

Sponsor: IconJohn.com

Subject Area(s): Teaching Ideas   **Subcategory:** Language Arts

Grade Level(s): Adult

Description

Find reviews of CD-ROMs, discussion forums, research databases, links to other Web sites, and more at EnglishTeacher.com. The Research Databases page alone is worth a visit here, as it provides a significant and varied list of links and accompanying search capability for resources of value for teachers and also for students and others.

Commentary

The discussion forums let you subscribe to various listservs and newsgroups discussing topics of interest. Go to Teacher Connect to find colleagues with whom you can set up e-mail pen pals, class-to-class e-mail pals, joint class online projects, and/or global class debates and discussions. A lesson plan component is being planned—you can offer a lesson plan for co-publishing on a pay-per-view basis.

Site: It's a Great Time to Start a Reading Group

URL: http://www.penguin.com/usa/catalogs/readgroups/

Sponsor: Penguin Books

Subject Area(s): Teaching Ideas   **Subcategory:** Language Arts

Grade Level(s): Adult

Description

This Web site provides information for adults (and perhaps even young adults) who would like to start a reading group. There are reader's guides...all well-annotated...with books which range from classics such as Jane Austen to more contemporary authors such as Jamaica Kincaid and Gabriel Garcia Marquez .

Commentary

If you need further suggested reading group titles, there is a list of 500 great books by women, grouped by categories such as choices, conflicting cultures, heritage, imagined worlds, friendship, violence, and ways of knowing. Even if you don't start a reading group, you will find many titles to add to your personal reading list.

Section 03. Teaching Ideas

Site: Language Arts

URL: http://www.csun.edu/~vceed009/languagearts.html

Sponsor: Vicki and Richard Sharp, California State University at Northridge

Subject Area(s): Teaching Ideas   **Subcategory:** Language Arts

Grade Level(s): Adult

Description

Start here for links to Web sites and resources for language arts. Included are categories of Lesson Plans, References, Ideas & Activities, Literature, Publishing, and Organizations. The K-12 Web Publishing for Kids links offer a variety of resources for any teacher.

Commentary

The creators of this site, the Sharps, are professors of elementary education. The site has an extensive set of links and is very easy to navigate.

Site: Lear, Limericks, & Literature

URL: http://www.castlemoyle.com/learte.html

Sponsor: Castlemoyle Publishers

Subject Area(s): Teaching Ideas   **Subcategory:** Language Arts

Grade Level(s): Adult

Description

This is a series of five creative writing lesson plans based on the *Book of Nonsense* by Edward Lear. Mr. Lear was both an illustrator and a poet and is best known for his nonsense illustrations. The student is introduced to the limerick and other zany rhymes that he made famous. The lessons are generally intended for students from grade 5 through adult.

Commentary

There are complete explanations about limericks and information about Edward Lear for those who need it. The assignments are varied, and each could easily last more than a week. Also find additional Internet resources and a bibliography.

Site: Linguisitic Funland

URL: http://www.tesol.org

Sponsor: Kristina Pfaff-Harris

Subject Area(s): Teaching Ideas   **Subcategory:** Language Arts

Grade Level(s): Adult

Description

This Web site is the "Home of Resources for Language, Linguistics, and Language Teaching and Learning." Find Resources for TESOL (Teaching of English to Speakers of Other Languages), Resources for Teachers of Languages other than English, CGI Scripts for Educators, Computer-Mediated Communication, links to additional linguistic resources, links to online journals and working papers, and more.

Commentary

There is a tremendous amount of resource information here, so plan to spend some time browsing for those articles most meaningful to your research or teaching.

Section 03. Teaching Ideas

Site: Multicultural Book Review Homepage

URL: http://www.isomedia.com/homes/jmele/homepage.html

Sponsor: Joe Mele

Subject Area(s): Teaching Ideas   **Subcategory:** Language Arts

Grade Level(s): Adult

Description

The Multicultural Book Review Homepage is devoted to the creation of a qualitative list of multicultural literature for K-12 educators. The reviews offer opinions of the works and, in some case, suggestions on how to use them in instruction.

Commentary

Find or submit reviews of multicultural literature at this site. Check back each month to see the "Review of the Month," a featured book and its review that is considered an especially strong choice for classroom use. This is a wonderful resource for teachers, and you may want to suggest it to students as well.

Site: SCORE Language Arts

URL: http://www.sdcoe.k12.ca.us/score/cla.html

Sponsor: SCORE (Schools of California Online Resources in Education)

Subject Area(s): Teaching Ideas   **Subcategory:** Language Arts

Grade Level(s): Adult

Description

Whether you are seeking age-appropriate literature titles or instructional strategies to use with youth, the SCORE Language Arts Home Page will not disappoint you. Parents will find the *Parent Page* and *Many Stories* links particularly useful in getting started and continuing to support literacy of their children while educators will find the well-developed and organized site a rich resource for proven instructional practices.

Commentary

While this site exists to support language arts curriculum in California, it is highly useable and accessible to those outside the state. Internet technology usage is nicely integrated into learning activities found in the CyberGuides. Knowledge of current educational practices and vocabulary is helpful when accessing the *Student and Teacher Activity Banks.*

Site: Surfing for ABC's Lesson Plan

URL: http://www.siec.k12.in.us/~west/abcless.html

Loogootee Elementary West
Projects That Connect with the Internet

Sponsor: Loogootee Elementary West School, IN

Subject Area(s): Teaching Ideas   **Subcategory:** Language Arts

Grade Level(s): Adult

Description

This is the lesson plan for a project created by kindergarteners and first graders at the Loogootee Elementary West School. They used the Yahooligans search engine to find an interesting topic for each letter of the alphabet. The lesson plan includes objectives, a list of materials, and instructional procedures.

Commentary

This is very impressive! Be sure to look at the children's work first on Surfing for ABC's; a link is provided on this page. This could easily be modified for older students, and it is a perfect way to introduce young children to the wonders of the Internet—as well as to the need for considering their safety.

Section 03. Teaching Ideas

Site: Teacher's Resource Center

URL: http://www.bdd.com/teachers/

Sponsor: BDD Books for Young Readers

Subject Area(s): Teaching Ideas   **Subcategory:** Language Arts

Grade Level(s): Adult

Description

Search one of the indexes of teachers' guides provided (Title, Authors and Illustrators, Awards, Black History Month, Grade, Interdisciplinary, Newbery Award Winners, Reluctant Readers, or Thematic). Then click on a book to find a wide range of information, including an excerpt from the book, suggested classroom activities (such as pre-reading activities and thematic connections), interdisciplinary connections, and more.

Commentary

Are you looking for ideas to use in teaching award-winning books in your classroom? This is a great site to use for suggestions and helpful resources.

Site: Thoth's Place Links Page

URL: http://fox.nstn.ca/~psmith/elahome.html

Sponsor: Peter Smith

Subject Area(s): Teaching Ideas   **Subcategory:** Language Arts

Grade Level(s): Adult

Description

There are resources and ideas for teaching located here: Mainly for Teachers—links to resources and classroom ideas of interest, The Learners' Place—check out the Writer's Gallery, and Conversations and Other Stuff.

Commentary

You will likely find the most valuable information in the Mainly for Teachers section. These resources are geared toward elementary school students. Some of the information at this site is of interest especially to Canadian teachers, but all will find many of the resources useful.

Site: Writing DEN: Teacher's Guide

URL: http://www2.actden.com/writ_den/t-guide.html

Sponsor: ACT Laboratory Ltd.

Subject Area(s): Teaching Ideas   **Subcategory:** Language Arts

Grade Level(s): Adult

Description

Since students' abilities to communicate in English vary greatly, these lessons are designed to meet the needs of students who are fairly new to the English language as well as those who have been exposed to English since infancy. Instruction is provided at three levels of difficulty: words, sentences, and paragraphs.

Commentary

In addition to the Writing DEN topics, students might also wish to access the Word of the Day and writing tips. Lesson plans include classroom suggestions and adaptation for individual students. There is a discussion group available for teachers where they can share questions and views on learning and teaching English.

Section 03. Teaching Ideas

Site: Frank Potter's Science Gems: Mathematics

URL: http://www-sci.lib.uci.edu/SEP/math.html

Sponsor: Frank Potter, University of California at Irvine

Subject Area(s): Teaching Ideas   **Subcategory:** Mathematics

Grade Level(s): Adult

Description

Find a listing of the mathematics categories into which these resources have been divided. There are two sections for Grades K-12; the remainder are more advanced mathematics beginning with pre-algebra and including calculus, advanced geometry, mathematical structures, logic, and other advanced topics.

Commentary

Updated monthly, the author states that there are more than 2,000 resources contained in these Web links. First examine the mathematics categories; you can jump straight to a category, scroll the entire list, or search by keyword. The logo is from one of the links to Dr. Math.

Site: KQED/CELL Math Lessons

URL: http://www.kqed.org/Cell/math/lessons/

Sponsor: KQED (CA)

Subject Area(s): Teaching Ideas   **Subcategory:** Mathematics

Grade Level(s): Adult

Description

The KQED Center for Education and Lifelong Learning (CELL) presents a series of lessons for K-12 math classes including online and video resources. The lessons were developed by two local educators and can be explored by grade level.

Commentary

Quite impressive is the interdisciplinary lesson on youth and HIV/AIDS. There are many links to other math lessons at all grade levels, too. You might want to take a look at the "INDY 500" lesson which uses the sports event to teach mean, median, interpreting data, plus finding rates, time, and distance.

Site: Math Teacher Link: Classroom Resources for Mathematics Teachers

URL: http://www-cm.math.uiuc.edu/MathLink/resources/resources.html

Sponsor: University of Illinois, Urbana-Champaign Campus

Subject Area(s): Teaching Ideas   **Subcategory:** Mathematics

Grade Level(s): Adult

Description

Math Teacher Link is a Web site designed to deliver classroom resources to teachers of mathematics, statistics, and related subjects at the high school and lower division college levels. The resources are organized into traditional courses and extended curriculum.

Commentary

These are mostly serious, sophisticated mathematical resources for teachers of advanced subjects, although some links can be used by your students. Everyone, however, will enjoy *Today Is*, which takes the numbers involved in today's date and presents an amazing amount of information about each one.

Section 03. Teaching Ideas

Site: Math Virtual Library

URL: http://euclid.math.fsu.edu/Science/math.html

Sponsor: Florida State University

Subject Area(s): Teaching Ideas   **Subcategory:** Mathematics

Grade Level(s): Adult

Description

The Math Virtual Library provides links to highly specialized fields of mathematics, to mathematics department Web servers around the world, to newsgroups, and to journals. Search capability is by categories. For the most part, this is very sophisticated mathematics information including research.

Commentary

There is a section on math education which includes lesson plans for K-12 students. Otherwise, this is a site for the serious and advanced mathematician. The rest of us can enjoy the very attractive background paper of math equations.

Site: Mathematics Archives: K-12 Teaching Materials

URL: http://archives.math.utk.edu/K12.html

Sponsor: University of Tennessee at Knoxville and others

Subject Area(s): Teaching Ideas   **Subcategory:** Mathematics

Grade Level(s): Adult

Description

The goal of the Mathematic Archives is to provide organized Internet access to a wide variety of mathematical resources, with the emphasis on the teaching of mathematics and educational software. The instructor can search the software database by platform, subject, or name. There are listings of schools as well as lesson plans.

Commentary

This site is so expansive that it proves somewhat difficult to explore and slow to load. The subsections are organized alphabetically, and a keyword search can be done. There is a tremendous amount of material here, updated monthly.

Site: Mathematics Center

URL: http://www.hmco.com/hmco/school/math/indexlo.html

Sponsor: Houghton Mifflin Company

Subject Area(s): Teaching Ideas   **Subcategory:** Mathematics

Grade Level(s): Adult

Description

Among the resources on this site are: Math Projects Watch, a kind of matchmaking service to help classrooms at different schools work together on math projects; Activity Search, an online database of ideas for activities, searchable by grade level and curriculum area; and Math Links, a hotlist of math-related Internet sites.

Commentary

An online parent handbook for helping children understand mathematics is also available and will be of particular interest to home-schooling parents. Although the guide was created around a particular math textbook series, it can be used by all parents.

Section 03. Teaching Ideas

Site: Mathematics Lesson Database

URL: http://www.mste.uiuc.edu/mathed/queryform.html#search

Sponsor: Office for Mathematics, Science, and Technology Education (IL)

Subject Area(s): Teaching Ideas   **Subcategory:** Mathematics

Grade Level(s): Adult

Description

The Webmaster at the Office for Mathematics, Science, and Technology Education has collected a variety of exemplary lesson plans and provided the links here. The majority of the plans involve advanced mathematics, but they are all detailed and might be modified to other levels by the resourceful teacher.

Commentary

Most lesson plans involve algebra, geometry, probability, and/or statistics. All are worth looking at, but take particular note of the lessons by Susan Boone: The Internet Pizza Server, the INDY 500, and others.

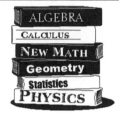

Site: MathTeacher.com

URL: http://www.mathteacher.com/

Sponsor: IconJohn.com

Subject Area(s): Teaching Ideas   **Subcategory:** Mathematics

Grade Level(s): Adult

Description

At MathTeacher.com, you can locate reviews of CD-ROMs, discussion forums, a Teacher Connect section, research databases, lesson plans, and links to other Web sites of interest to math teachers.

Commentary

Forums let you subscribe to listservs and newsgroups discussing topics of interest, and the Teacher Connect section helps you locate colleagues for setting up e-mail pen pals and online class projects. Included are several lesson plan resources, such as six lessons for secondary math teachers and 45 hyperlesson plans for K-12. Submit one of your own to be considered for co-publishing.

Site: SCORE Mathematics

URL: http://www.kings.k12.ca.us/math/

Sponsor: Kings County Office of Education (CA)

Subject Area(s): Teaching Ideas   **Subcategory:** Mathematics

Grade Level(s): Adult

Description

This subject matter Web page is designed especially for mathematics teachers and students in California since the content and links are intended to reflect the state's Mathematic Framework. Teachers from other states will find them useful as well, because the resources are organized by grade groupings: K-4, 5-8, and 9-12.

Commentary

These pages are beautifully organized so that you can work from a menu or search the entire resource database. The site is actively maintained with ongoing SCORE summer institutes, so there should be new material every year.

Section 03. Teaching Ideas

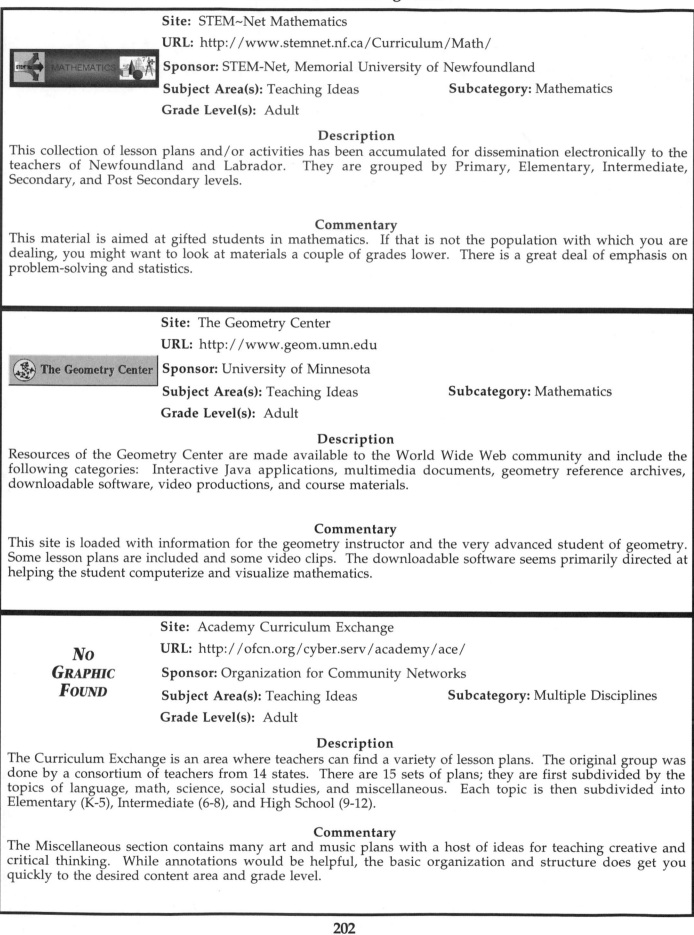

Site: STEM~Net Mathematics

URL: http://www.stemnet.nf.ca/Curriculum/Math/

Sponsor: STEM-Net, Memorial University of Newfoundland

Subject Area(s): Teaching Ideas   **Subcategory:** Mathematics

Grade Level(s): Adult

Description

This collection of lesson plans and/or activities has been accumulated for dissemination electronically to the teachers of Newfoundland and Labrador. They are grouped by Primary, Elementary, Intermediate, Secondary, and Post Secondary levels.

Commentary

This material is aimed at gifted students in mathematics. If that is not the population with which you are dealing, you might want to look at materials a couple of grades lower. There is a great deal of emphasis on problem-solving and statistics.

Site: The Geometry Center

URL: http://www.geom.umn.edu

Sponsor: University of Minnesota

Subject Area(s): Teaching Ideas   **Subcategory:** Mathematics

Grade Level(s): Adult

Description

Resources of the Geometry Center are made available to the World Wide Web community and include the following categories: Interactive Java applications, multimedia documents, geometry reference archives, downloadable software, video productions, and course materials.

Commentary

This site is loaded with information for the geometry instructor and the very advanced student of geometry. Some lesson plans are included and some video clips. The downloadable software seems primarily directed at helping the student computerize and visualize mathematics.

NO GRAPHIC FOUND

Site: Academy Curriculum Exchange

URL: http://ofcn.org/cyber.serv/academy/ace/

Sponsor: Organization for Community Networks

Subject Area(s): Teaching Ideas   **Subcategory:** Multiple Disciplines

Grade Level(s): Adult

Description

The Curriculum Exchange is an area where teachers can find a variety of lesson plans. The original group was done by a consortium of teachers from 14 states. There are 15 sets of plans; they are first subdivided by the topics of language, math, science, social studies, and miscellaneous. Each topic is then subdivided into Elementary (K-5), Intermediate (6-8), and High School (9-12).

Commentary

The Miscellaneous section contains many art and music plans with a host of ideas for teaching creative and critical thinking. While annotations would be helpful, the basic organization and structure does get you quickly to the desired content area and grade level.

Section 03. Teaching Ideas

Site: Activity Search

URL: http://www.hmco.com/hmco/school/search/activity.html

Sponsor: Houghton Mifflin

Subject Area(s): Teaching Ideas   **Subcategory:** Multiple Disciplines

Grade Level(s): Adult

Description

Teachers of students through 8th grade may search for curricular activities according to subject area and grade level. Language Arts, Math, Social Studies, Science, and Art are the curriculum areas represented. Each activity in the search results is linked to instructions which enumerate needed materials and step-by-step directions for the activity.

Commentary

More than one curricular area may be selected in the search matrix allowing teachers to locate integrated curriculum activities. The instructions are clearly written and on level. The *Teaching Options* at the end of the activity instructions allow flexibility and spark the imagination to add a bit of one's self to the activity.

Site: Blue Web 'n Applications Library

URL: http://www.kn.pacbell.com/wired/bluewebn

Sponsor: Pacific Bell

Subject Area(s): Teaching Ideas   **Subcategory:** Multiple Disciplines

Grade Level(s): Adult

Description

Learning Applications organizes, rates, and provides links to numerous lessons in art, business, English, foreign language, health & physical education, history and social studies, mathematics, science, technology, and vocational education. Once inside the lessons, there are activities, projects, resources, references, and tools. There is also a search tool for additional applications.

Commentary

There is so much material for the teacher here that quite a bit of exploration is needed. The site provides a service which will send you weekly e-mail updates...a sure sign that it will remain current. The lessons are rated by the number of stars; highly rated lessons were visually more attractive but not necessarily of more use to the teacher.

Site: Busy Teachers' Web Site K-12

URL: http://www.ceismc.gatech.edu/BusyT/

Sponsor: Carolyn Cole

Subject Area(s): Teaching Ideas   **Subcategory:** Multiple Disciplines

Grade Level(s): Adult

Description

This Web site is designed to provide educators with direct source materials, lesson plans/classroom activities with a minimum of site-to-site linking, and to provide an enjoyable and rewarding experience for the teacher who is learning to use the Internet. Click on a subject area to view links to resources for that area.

Commentary

If you are an educator with precious little time to search the Web for resources, this is a good site to bookmark for frequent visits. The site is regularly updated and a find for busy teachers. You can even request an e-mail notification when pages have been updated.

Section 03. Teaching Ideas

Site: Carrie's Sites for Educators

URL: http://www.mtjeff.com/~bodenst/page5.html

Sponsor: Carrie E. Bodensteiner

Subject Area(s): Teaching Ideas   **Subcategory:** Multiple Disciplines

Grade Level(s): Adult

Description
This site provides a hotlist of links to a number of resources. Find categories of: Search Engines, Oregon Resources, General Educational Resources, Counseling and Guidance Resources, Humanities Resources, Social Studies Resources, Science Resources, Math Resources, Internet in the Classroom, Vocational, and Technical Resources.

Commentary
Find straightforward navigation to education-related sites of resources for your classroom.

Site: CEC Lesson Plans

URL: http://www.col-ed.org/cur/

Sponsor: Columbia Education Center

Subject Area(s): Teaching Ideas   **Subcategory:** Multiple Disciplines

Grade Level(s): Adult

Description
These lesson plans were created by teachers for use in their own classrooms and are classified as language arts, mathematics, science, social studies, and miscellaneous. Within each subject matter area, the lessons are further classified into grade levels.

Commentary
The extensive Miscellaneous category contains almost 100 lesson plans with imaginative titles and activities. The Webmaster reports that some of these plans are included in the new *Encarta Lesson Collection*. You will also find links to other teacher and student resources.

Site: Cisco Educational Archive

URL: http://sunsite.unc.edu/cisco/

Sponsor: Cisco Systems

Subject Area(s): Teaching Ideas   **Subcategory:** Multiple Disciplines

Grade Level(s): Adult

Description
There are several parts to this site which centers around a Virtual Schoolhouse. The schoolhouse provides a collection of links, resources, and information of interest to students, parents, and teachers. There is information about education programs, discounts, and special offers that are available.

Commentary
This site is under continuous development. The Table of Contents of resources continues to grow with useful information under most of the categories. The Webmaster invites submissions and comments from teachers and administrators.

Section 03. Teaching Ideas

Site: Classroom Connect on the Net!

URL: http://www.classroom.com/

Sponsor: Classroom Connect

Subject Area(s): Teaching Ideas

Subcategory: Multiple Disciplines

Grade Level(s): Adult

Description
The magazine *Classroom Connect* is dedicated to the instructional use of the Internet. This site points the individual to a variety of resources. Teachers and parents might find it especially useful to examine G.R.A.D.E.S. (best K-12 Internet links) in order to bookmark sites appropriate for certain student groups and/or content areas.

Commentary
This is a totally up-to-date Web site with new information being added every day. The designers had a clear understanding of the interests of different age groups. The linked sites are fun, educational, and free of "offensive material." Some pages can be a little slow to load because they are so visual, but patience will be rewarded.

Site: Co-NECT Top Ten Educator's Guide to the Internet

URL: http://www.co-nect.com/Schools/TopTen/

Sponsor: Co-NECT

Subject Area(s): Teaching Ideas

Subcategory: Multiple Disciplines

Grade Level(s): Adult

Description
This site was created by Co-NECT Schools for use by educators who want to easily find educational Web sites of value. It is categorized by discipline with a brief description of each site. In order to be listed here, sites must (1) have valuable curriculum and project resources, (2) show comprehensive content, (3) be well-written and well-presented, and (4) be up-to-date. This site is updated frequently.

Commentary
Co-NECT is a national assistance organization dedicated to helping communities around the country use technology for comprehensive school change and improved academic results in reading, writing, mathematics, science and other core subjects. This is a quick way to the very best sites on the Net. No more than ten in any given category.

Site: Connections+

URL: http://www.mcrel.org/connect/plus/

Sponsor: Mid-Continent Regional Educational Laboratory (McRel)

Subject Area(s): Teaching Ideas

Subcategory: Multiple Disciplines

Grade Level(s): Adult

Description
These Internet resources consist of lesson plans, activities, and curriculum resources and are linked with the corresponding subject-area content standards. Most standard content areas are covered, such as the arts, economics, foreign language, geography, health, history, language arts, mathematics, multi-disciplinary, and science.

Commentary
The authors of this site state that they post a few additional resources each month in the content areas, all sites that have been recommended by teachers. There are also other links to assist teachers with using the Internet in the classroom.

Section 03. Teaching Ideas

Site: Cool Stuff — Educational Resources on the Web

URL: http://www.pacificnet.net/~mandel//EducationalResources.html

Sponsor: Dr. Scott Mandel

Subject Area(s): Teaching Ideas   **Subcategory:** Multiple Disciplines

Grade Level(s): Adult

Description

Teachers send in suggestions for helpful Internet sites—they are reviewed by Dr. Mandel, and if appropriate, he adds them to the list. There are multiple links for art and music along with other content areas. There are also extensive resources for multicultural education and special needs.

Commentary

This is a browsing site, but the resources are great—many are already mentioned in this work, but the links are too specialized to have included them all. Look for information in a desired content area and then enjoy some time getting acquainted with and exploring other fields.

Site: Core Knowledge Lesson Plans and Units

URL: http://www.coreknowledge.org/

Sponsor: Core Knowledge Foundation

Subject Area(s): Teaching Ideas   **Subcategory:** Multiple Disciplines

Grade Level(s): Adult

Description

"The Core Knowledge Sequence is a consensus-based model of specific content guidelines that, as the basis of about 50% of a school's curriculum, can provide a solid, coherent foundation of learning for students in the elementary and middle grades." Extensive units are included at the site for Kindergarten through sixth grade.

Commentary

Lesson plans are generally a unit covering several days (or sometimes weeks). They are very detailed, providing an abstract, objectives, content, activities, resources, and appendices. Titles and content are topics of obvious interest to kids.

Site: Curricular Resources and Networking Projects

URL: http://www.ed.gov/EdRes/EdCurric.html

Sponsor: U. S. Department of Education

Subject Area(s): Teaching Ideas   **Subcategory:** Multiple Disciplines

Grade Level(s): Adult

Description

The U.S. Department of Education has selected fifteen networking projects which provide curricular resources. They are each listed with a brief description of the project and a link to the main Web page for each. All are exemplary sites, although the Department of Education is careful to provide a disclaimer involving future content which might be posted.

Commentary

"World Lecture Hall" provides lecture notes, reading lists, and mini-courses on various topics and may be of use to teachers of advanced level classes in various subjects. Most of the resources are more generally aimed at the middle and high school levels. The link to Canada's SchoolNet is a significant one since all of Canada's schools are included.

Section 03. Teaching Ideas

Site: Daryl Cagle's Pro Cartoonists Index—Teacher's Guide!

URL: http://www.cagle.com/teacher

Sponsor: Peg Cagle, Teacher, Los Angeles Unified School District (CA)

Subject Area(s): Teaching Ideas   **Subcategory:** Multiple Disciplines

Grade Level(s): Adult

Description

This site provides a Teacher's Guide for using the Professional Cartoonists Index Web site in the classroom. Start with a collection of editorial cartoons available on the Web and then find lesson plans for using them in a variety of subject areas and grade levels. As cartoons are updated with the current news of the day, students can observe the ever-changing themes. Included in the lesson plans are activities, games, handouts, and more.

Commentary

This is a wonderfully creative site that is dynamic and changing with issues of the day. The teacher behind the site is married to a syndicated cartoonist—together, they have put together this resource. Start by accessing the "Teacher's Tour of the Index" or go directly to lesson plans for a specific level. You'll be back frequently!

Site: Discovery Channel School

URL: http://www.school.discovery.com

Sponsor: Discovery Communications, Inc.

Subject Area(s): Teaching Ideas   **Subcategory:** Multiple Disciplines

Grade Level(s): Adult

Description

Discovery Communications provides documentary programming for more than 100 million households in nations spread around the world. In order to bring the programming into the classroom, there are Fall and Spring schedules and features available at this site a few months in advance so that teachers can consider these programs as they plan.

Commentary

At the time of evaluation, the Discovery channel is gearing up for a large unit on Body Science, the Modern Presidency, Baby Talk, and Cultures Alive. Teacher's guides, program recording, and catalogs are free. Check to see what is happening at the site now.

Site: Education World

URL: http://www.education-world.com

Sponsor: American Fidelity Educational Services

Subject Area(s): Teaching Ideas   **Subcategory:** Multiple Disciplines

Grade Level(s): Adult

Description

Each week, the site highlights a curriculum idea and an educational article focusing on teaching; related sites are included for enrichment. Articles from previous weeks remain online. There is a searchable database of 50,000 educational sites.

Commentary

This is an attractive, well-organized site which is updated weekly. There are books, curriculum, and lesson plans with news and features for administrators on several pages. You will find that the database search feature is somewhat slow and not particularly effective—this is not one of the better features of the site.

Section 03. Teaching Ideas

Site: EdWeb

URL: http://edweb.cnidr.org/

Sponsor: Andy Carvin

Subject Area(s): Teaching Ideas   **Subcategory:** Multiple Disciplines

Grade Level(s): Adult

Description
This site explores the fields of educational reform and information technology. "With EdWeb, you can hunt down online educational resources around the world, learn about trends in education policy and information infrastructure development, examine success stories of computers in the classroom, and much more."

Commentary
Teaching ideas are primarily focused on using the Internet in the classroom, including such topics as developing Web pages and links to pages developed by kids. There are lots of quotes and essays. This is a personal site developed by an individual with broad interests in educational reform and the Internet.

Site: Houghton Mifflin Education Place

URL: http://www.eduplace.com/hmco/school/index.html

Sponsor: Houghton Mifflin

Subject Area(s): Teaching Ideas   **Subcategory:** Multiple Disciplines

Grade Level(s): Adult

Description
Education Place provides free Internet resources for teachers of grades K-8. The three areas of emphasis are the math center, the reading/language arts center, and the social studies center. There are pages for parents and students too, but the primary focus is for the teacher.

Commentary
The Online Outline maps are a useful feature, and you are encouraged to print or download ones you like for your personal use in activities, reports, or stories. Another helpful feature is the Activity Search which can be completed by either subject matter area or grade level.

Site: Imagination

URL: http://www.hmco.com/hmco/school/links/theme_10.html

Sponsor: Houghton Mifflin Company

Subject Area(s): Teaching Ideas   **Subcategory:** Multiple Disciplines

Grade Level(s): Adult

Description
This site offers a collection of seven links to other sites which share a common theme—that of imagination, with a special emphasis on inventors and inventions. You will find lesson plans from teachers on the topic of imagination and links to a variety of articles on the subject.

Commentary
"Tesseract" is the lesson plan, reports, and list of resources used in a class by Mr. Nielson; its focus is on inventors. Also look at the lesson by Christine Collins. Between these two, there are ample resources for some interesting exploration into the theme.

Site: Kathy Schrock's Guide for Educators

URL: http://www.capecod.net/schrockguide/

Sponsor: Kathy Schrock and Gradekeeper

Subject Area(s): Teaching Ideas   **Subcategory:** Multiple Disciplines

Grade Level(s): Adult

Description

This is a classified list of sites on the Internet found to be useful for enhancing curriculum and teacher professional growth. They are listed by category (search tools, subject access, and additional information). The basic list is for adults, but there are also many resources for students of all ages.

Commentary

Find a set of instruments that Kathy Schrock designed for K-12 students to use to evaluate the technical aspects and subject content of Internet resources. There are also some essays dealing with the topic of how to assess a Web page.

Site: Learning in Motion's Top Ten List

URL: http://www.learn.motion.com/lim/links/linkmain

Sponsor: Learning in Motion

Subject Area(s): Teaching Ideas   **Subcategory:** Multiple Disciplines

Grade Level(s): Adult

Description

This list of Top Ten Web sites for Education is updated monthly. In addition to the monthly top ten, there are separate (non-monthly) top ten sections for science, mathematics, social studies, language arts and elementary schools, and teacher picks. There are links to the monthly top ten as well as all other Web sites.

Commentary

While visiting this site, take time to nominate an innovative educational site you like. Then check in next month to see if that site has won a place in the top ten. While Learning in Motion is a commercial developer of K-12 software, this site will be of general interest to educators. It is also possible to link to the vendor's home page to find out more about its products.

Site: Lesson Plans and Activities

URL: http://mcrel.org/connect/lesson.html

Sponsor: McREL

Subject Area(s): Teaching Ideas   **Subcategory:** Multiple Disciplines

Grade Level(s): Adult

Description

This is a collection of hundreds of lesson plans in the arts, language arts, inter/multi-disciplinary, math, science, social studies, and technology. There is an especially broad collection of plans for interdisciplinary study, and they are developed for all ages.

Commentary

New materials are added on an ongoing basis and are flagged so that they are easy to identify. The lesson plans are organized by broad topics which are easy to scroll through. Since there are no search capabilities, an annotated list would be helpful.

Section 03. Teaching Ideas

Site: Lesson Plans and Resources for Teachers

URL: http://www.remc4.k12.mi.us/muskegon/lessons.html

Sponsor: Roger Hoekenga, Assistant Principal, Bunker Middle School (MI)

Subject Area(s): Teaching Ideas   **Subcategory:** Multiple Disciplines

Grade Level(s): Adult

Description

This site provides a collection of lesson plans, class activities, and curriculum ideas in all subject areas. Some integrate the Internet and other technology into the curriculum. There are also links to Web search engines, directories, and other Web-based resources.

Commentary

Pick up new ideas or share your own lesson plans and ideas here. There is an extensive hotlist of resources here, and they are well organized, with some including annotations describing their contents.

Site: Lesson Plans for Technology

URL: http://fcit.coedu.usf.edu/tnt/

 **Sponsor:** Florida Center for Instructional Technology

Subject Area(s): Teaching Ideas   **Subcategory:** Multiple Disciplines

Grade Level(s): Adult

Description

The database of lesson plans contains technological and subject information and detailed instructions on how to implement the lesson in the classroom. Subject areas included are social studies, business, computing, fine arts, foreign language, guidance, language arts, mathematics, and science. The database may be searched by subject area, grade level, or keyword.

Commentary

The big four are most heavily represented—anguage arts, science, social studies, and mathematics. The largest number of lesson plans is for the intermediate grades, but many plans are cross-referenced by subject and grade level.

Site: NCRTEC Search for Lesson Plan Materials

URL: http://www.ncrtec.org/tools/lessindx/plsearch.html

NCRTEC **Sponsor:** North Central Regional Technology in Education Consortium

Subject Area(s): Teaching Ideas   **Subcategory:** Multiple Disciplines

Grade Level(s): Adult

Description

This Web site helps teachers find materials on the Internet to use in creating their own lessons. Initial listings are available for lesson plan materials in Science and Mathematics, with Language Arts, Social Studies, Art, Music, and other areas to be added.

Commentary

Search by subject area, grade level, and use Boolean operators for keyword searching too. You'll also find information on making good use of these lesson plan materials, evaluating these lesson plan materials, search tips, and technical tips.

Section 03. Teaching Ideas

Site: NIE OnLine Educator

URL: http://ole.net/ole/

Sponsor: Detroit Press

Subject Area(s): Teaching Ideas   **Subcategory:** Multiple Disciplines

Grade Level(s): Adult

Description

OnLine Educator is printed monthly but new information is added every Monday. It is available free on the Internet and as an e-mail edition, but it is also possible to subscribe to a print edition. There are ready-to-use lesson plans as well as links to useful Internet resources. There is typically a featured article.

Commentary

The most useful part of the newspaper is probably the ability to search the OnLine Educator Link archive. The search may be done by grade level (one grade or clusters), by subject, and/or by a keyword search. In addition to the typical content areas, the topics also include culture, publications, references, and much more.

Site: PIGS Space: Cooperative Networking

URL: http://cspace.unb.ca/nbco/pigs/

Sponsor: New Brunswick Cooperative Networking Project

Subject Area(s): Teaching Ideas   **Subcategory:** Multiple Disciplines

Grade Level(s): Adult

Description

PIGS stands for the four components of cooperative learning: Positive interdependence, Individual accountability, Group process, and Social interaction. Lesson plans are included in the areas of language arts, mathematics, science, and social studies—all with a focus on cooperative learning.

Commentary

This is a site still under development, and the teachers involved welcome submissions from other teachers interested in cooperative learning. For those new to cooperative learning, take a look at the glossary and the resources. More experienced practitioners will want to examine the lesson plans—and perhaps submit one of their own.

Site: Puppetools

URL: http://www.puppetools.com

Sponsor: Puppetools, Inc.

Subject Area(s): Teaching Ideas   **Subcategory:** Multiple Disciplines

Grade Level(s): Adult

Description

Puppetools asserts that puppets add a powerful dimension to learning and communication, and the site provides visitors an opportunity to test this theory by accessing educational activities, resources, and products. Education Services include the Puppetools Online or Onsite Courses and an overview of the curriculum methodology. Tour the Puppetools Showcase of children's and teachers' puppets for inspiration.

Commentary

Many think of puppets as toys, but Puppetools is serious about the value of using puppets in education. "Puppetools is not about puppets. It's about using interactive, symbolic forms to facilitate higher level thinking and group dynamics. It's all about brain science and behavior," says the developer. Products, patterns, and courses have fees attached, but the free articles and resources offer a rich set of ideas.

Section 03. Teaching Ideas

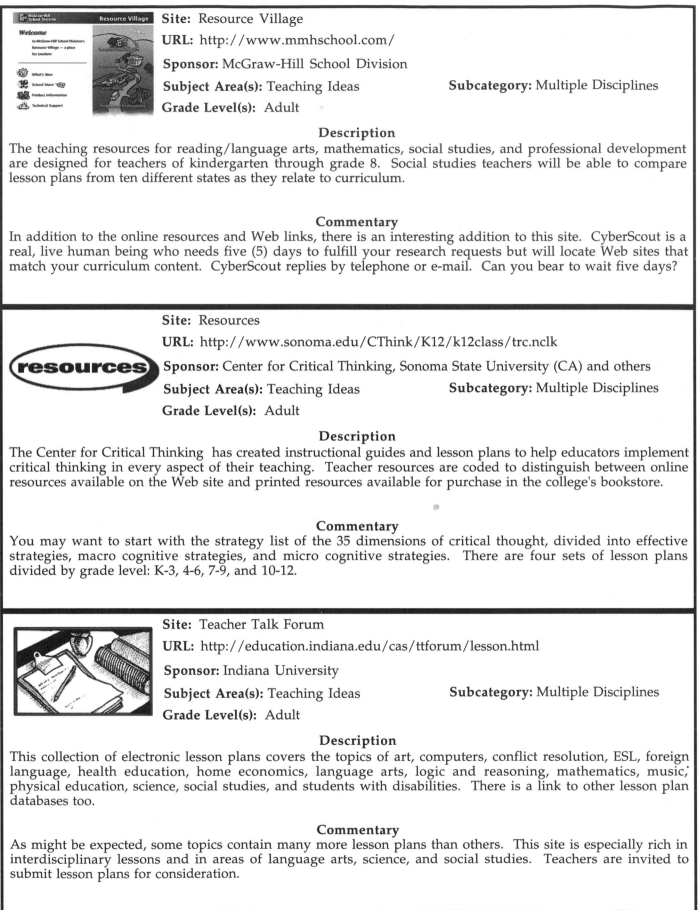

Site: Resource Village

URL: http://www.mmhschool.com/

Sponsor: McGraw-Hill School Division

Subject Area(s): Teaching Ideas   **Subcategory:** Multiple Disciplines

Grade Level(s): Adult

Description
The teaching resources for reading/language arts, mathematics, social studies, and professional development are designed for teachers of kindergarten through grade 8. Social studies teachers will be able to compare lesson plans from ten different states as they relate to curriculum.

Commentary
In addition to the online resources and Web links, there is an interesting addition to this site. CyberScout is a real, live human being who needs five (5) days to fulfill your research requests but will locate Web sites that match your curriculum content. CyberScout replies by telephone or e-mail. Can you bear to wait five days?

Site: Resources

URL: http://www.sonoma.edu/CThink/K12/k12class/trc.nclk

Sponsor: Center for Critical Thinking, Sonoma State University (CA) and others

Subject Area(s): Teaching Ideas   **Subcategory:** Multiple Disciplines

Grade Level(s): Adult

Description
The Center for Critical Thinking has created instructional guides and lesson plans to help educators implement critical thinking in every aspect of their teaching. Teacher resources are coded to distinguish between online resources available on the Web site and printed resources available for purchase in the college's bookstore.

Commentary
You may want to start with the strategy list of the 35 dimensions of critical thought, divided into effective strategies, macro cognitive strategies, and micro cognitive strategies. There are four sets of lesson plans divided by grade level: K-3, 4-6, 7-9, and 10-12.

Site: Teacher Talk Forum

URL: http://education.indiana.edu/cas/ttforum/lesson.html

Sponsor: Indiana University

Subject Area(s): Teaching Ideas   **Subcategory:** Multiple Disciplines

Grade Level(s): Adult

Description
This collection of electronic lesson plans covers the topics of art, computers, conflict resolution, ESL, foreign language, health education, home economics, language arts, logic and reasoning, mathematics, music, physical education, science, social studies, and students with disabilities. There is a link to other lesson plan databases too.

Commentary
As might be expected, some topics contain many more lesson plans than others. This site is especially rich in interdisciplinary lessons and in areas of language arts, science, and social studies. Teachers are invited to submit lesson plans for consideration.

Section 03. Teaching Ideas

Site: Teacher's Edition Online

URL: http://www.teachnet.com

Sponsor: teachnet.com

Subject Area(s): Teaching Ideas   **Subcategory:** Multiple Disciplines

Grade Level(s): Adult

Description

Use the Teacher's Edition Online site to replenish your teacher toolbox with five minute activities, lesson plans, classroom decor ideas, and classroom management tools, among others. Many of the ideas are by teachers, for teachers, who also may post questions and answers in the *Teacher-2-Teacher Webforum*. Also check the *News and Notes* column for interesting technology updates.

Commentary

This site maintains news and ideas useful to beginning and seasoned educators alike.

Site: Teachers' Corner — Internet Activities

URL: http://www.solutions.ibm.com/k12/teacher/activity.html

Sponsor: IBM Corporation

Subject Area(s): Teaching Ideas   **Subcategory:** Multiple Disciplines

Grade Level(s): Adult

Description

Every month one or two lesson plans are posted which make use of the Internet to explore interesting topics. There are teacher materials, student activities, and pointers to related sites. Activities from previous months remain on the server for three years. Some sample topics are oceans, Black History Month, Ireland, zoo animals, Earth Day, newspapers, and more.

Commentary

The range of topics is diverse at this site. Who could go wrong with the current topic of baseball! Some topics are targeted for a wide variety of grade levels, and an attempt is plainly being made to provide interdisciplinary resources and ideas.

Site: Teachers' Forum

URL: http://www.nerdworld.com/nw2633.html

Sponsor: Nerd World Media

Subject Area(s): Teaching Ideas   **Subcategory:** Multiple Disciplines

Grade Level(s): Adult

Description

This is not actually a forum, but rather links to a variety of teacher resources. The split menu also provides links to sites that specialize in conferences, exchange and study abroad, personal pages, jobs, fund-raisers, books, alternative instruction, learning disabilities, technology, museums, and assorted other categories.

Commentary

Layer after layer of Internet links are presented in various categories after searches were conducted. The organization is easy to follow so that a lot of the searching work has already been done for you. Lots of advertisements and lots of traffic, so you will need to be patient with this site—but you will likely find some new resources of value.

Section 03. Teaching Ideas

Site: Teachers Helping Teachers

URL: http://pacificnet.net/~mandel/index.html

Sponsor: Dr. Scott Mandel

Subject Area(s): Teaching Ideas   **Subcategory:** Multiple Disciplines

Grade Level(s): Adult

Description

Winner of many Internet awards, this site accomplishes a variety of things. It provides basic teaching tips to inexperienced teachers, and new ideas and teaching methodologies for all teachers. The teaching ideas and lesson plans are organized by classroom managment, language arts, math, science, social studies, the arts, and special education.

Commentary

This site is constantly being updated with poems, stress reducers, and inspiration topics of the week. A very innovative idea can be found in the Chat Room—available on Sunday evenings for new and experienced teachers to share questions and ideas.

Site: TEAMS Distance Learning

URL: http://teams.lacoe.edu/

Sponsor: Los Angeles County Office of Education

Subject Area(s): Teaching Ideas   **Subcategory:** Multiple Disciplines

Grade Level(s): Adult

Description

This is a very comprehensive site which consists primarily of clusters of links. Among the subsections are classroom projects, resources for each content area, diverse student populations, K-12 lesson plans, K-12 home pages, professional development, and parent resources.

Commentary

Both parents and educators may be interested in software that filters out unacceptable sites to keep the Internet safe for kids. There is a listing of filtering software, several programs of which offer demos—look under the parent resource pages. The classroom projects sections contain a number of ideas for curriculum applications.

Site: The Amazing Picture Machine

URL: http://www.ncrtec.org/picture.html

Sponsor: North Central Regional Technology in Education Consortium

Subject Area(s): Teaching Ideas   **Subcategory:** Multiple Disciplines

Grade Level(s): Adult

Description

This site is a wonderful index to graphical resources available on the Internet—and a real time-saver! Search by keyword to find graphics of interest. You can use Boolean operators *only, and,* and *or* on two keywords. For example, if you search by Animals *and* Africa, you find links to over 20 color photographs. Also find Lesson Ideas, Search Tips, Copyright of Pictures, and additional resource information.

Commentary

Categories of graphic resources include Aircraft, American Cities, Civil War People, Places, and Things, Dinosaurs, Famous 20th Century African-Americans, Maps of the 50 States, Paintings and Famous Works of Art, Portraits and Photographs of 19th Century Writers, Presidents of the United States, Trees and Plants, Weather and Meteorological Phenomenon, World War II, and much more.

Section 03. Teaching Ideas

Site: The Curriculum Web Resource Center

URL: http://www.curriculumweb.org/cw/rescntr/resourcecenter.html

Sponsor: Curriculum Enhancement Consultants

Subject Area(s): Teaching Ideas   **Subcategory:** Multiple Disciplines

Grade Level(s): Adult

Description
Described as the virtual classroom and beyond, the Curriculum Web Resource Center provides links to information about subject matter content, PTA, libraries, special education, schools online, projects online, government resources, and museums. The Teacher's Lounge is actually a collection of educational databases.

Commentary
The site provides a link to "Cyberhaunts for Kids," which is a wholesome, entertaining collection of art, music, literature, games, and more. Teachers are invited to contribute to this Web page in order to extend its usefulness.

Site: The Playground

URL: http://ed.info.apple.com/education/techlearn/parents/playgrd/playmenu.htm

Sponsor: Apple Computer, Inc.

Subject Area(s): Teaching Ideas   **Subcategory:** Multiple Disciplines

Grade Level(s): Adult

Description
This site could be for kids, but it has so many excellent teaching and learning ideas across varied subject matter, teachers and parents will appreciate the resource. The information is primarily designed for grades K-6 or ages 5-12. Find online field trips, stories, and parties—such as a number of acrostics and an online Arctic Adventure. There are online parties, Internet activities, and adventures with Milo, the Wonder Dog.

Commentary
Don't miss the Rainy Day Doings: Indoor Recess suggestions for teachers or parents. This is a fun site with creative ideas for activities and stories for younger children. Some will require adult assistance.

Site: TIE Web Sites for Educators

URL: http://www.tie.net/tie/resources.html#sd

Sponsor: Technology and Innovations in Education (SD)

Subject Area(s): Teaching Ideas   **Subcategory:** Multiple Disciplines

Grade Level(s): Adult

Description
Web sites are organized into groupings for humanities, social studies, math, science, and Internet. They have additional sections for general resources and South Dakota-specific educational resources. The reader can browse through a listing of links under each subsection.

Commentary
It is always more helpful when these lists are annotated; it saves a lot of time on the part of the browser. Nevertheless, this is a fairly complete list, and even experienced Internet searchers will probably find a few new links of interest.

Section 03. Teaching Ideas

Site: TRMS Teacher Developed Lessons & Curriculum Resources

URL: http://www.trms.ga.net/lessons/

Sponsor: Taylor Road Middle School

Subject Area(s): Teaching Ideas   **Subcategory:** Multiple Disciplines

Grade Level(s): Adult

Description

This site is provided by a school with a very active involvement in technology. It has lesson plans and resources in the areas of exploratory education, fine arts, foreign languages, health and physical education, language arts, math, science, and social studies.

Commentary

Career exploration lessons for every subject area will likely prove quite helpful to many teachers. Some content areas include both teacher-developed lessons and links to other Web sites. Teachers are invited to copy and use materials for any instructional purpose.

Site: USA TODAY Classline

URL: http://classline.usatoday.com/

Sponsor: USA TODAY

Subject Area(s): Teaching Ideas   **Subcategory:** Multiple Disciplines

Grade Level(s): Adult

Description

USA TODAY provides an online teacher resource center that connects news to the curriculum through daily activities linked to top news stories, at-home lessons, a question and answer area with reporters, suggestions for how teachers can use the newspaper in the classroom, and listings of free and inexpensive teacher resource materials available from national education organizations.

Commentary

Use current issues to make learning relevant to your students. One of the sections at this site, "Family Focus," provides a daily activity for students to do with their family and offers good suggestions you might send home with your students. It is interactive and encourages students to send in responses and ideas that were generated while they worked on the activity.

Site: Vose School Education Resources Page

URL: http://www.teleport.com/~vincer

Sponsor: Vose School (OR)

Subject Area(s): Teaching Ideas   **Subcategory:** Multiple Disciplines

Grade Level(s): Adult

Description

Created by teachers in one school, the resources are organized into categories of schools on the Internet: Science, math, humanities, social studies, general educational resources, and sound examples. The humanities resource links provide a grouping which is unique and applicable to several subject matter areas.

Commentary

The sound links for animals and birds are fun, but the link to the Vincent Voice Library with more than 50,000 persons is awesome. There are dozens of ways in which these resources could be used in the classroom. Find a large number of links that are well organized for browsing. The site appears to be frequently updated.

Section 03. Teaching Ideas

Site: Web Sites and Resources for Teachers

URL: http://www.csun.edu/~vceed009

Sponsor: California State University at Northridge

Subject Area(s): Teaching Ideas   **Subcategory:** Multiple Disciplines

Grade Level(s): Adult

Description

This site provides an extensive list of annotated links to school subjects, lesson plans, children's sites, and ESL/bilingual sites. It is organized into sections on Art, ESL/Bilingual, Language Arts, Math, Music, Science, and Social Studies. There is also a special section, "Just for Kids," that is listed separately.

Commentary

The creators of this site are Vicki and Richard Sharp, professors of elementary education at California State University at Northridge.

Site: Whales: A Thematic Web Unit

URL: http://curry.edschool.Virginia.EDU/go/Whales/

Sponsor: Kim Joyce, University of Virginia

Subject Area(s): Teaching Ideas   **Subcategory:** Multiple Disciplines

Grade Level(s): Adult

Description

This Web site provides a thematic unit on cooperative learning across an integrated curriculum. The table of contents features teacher resources, student activities, whale projects, and Internet resources. The variety of lesson plans included ranges from grades K-8.

Commentary

These resources are extensive and are designed to be combined in a variety of ways, at the discretion of the teacher. The emphasis is on critical thinking and discovery learning. Students will find the Internet resources especially interesting since they range from the lighthearted "Free Willy" site to more research-oriented information.

Site: K-12 Resources for Music Educators

URL: http://www.isd77.k12.mn.us/resources/staffpages/shirk/k12.music.html

Sponsor: Cynthia Shirk, Music Department, Mankato Schools (MN)

Subject Area(s): Teaching Ideas   **Subcategory:** Music

Grade Level(s): Adult

Description

This site offers a well-organized list of links to sites of interest to music educators. Find sites for band teachers, orchestra teachers, vocal/choral teachers, classroom music teachers, and valuable sites for all music educators.

Commentary

If you are a music educator, you will find this to be a rich and valuable site for access to a host of online resources and information to assist you in teaching. Students of all ages can find music-related references here by browsing the categories.

Section 03. Teaching Ideas

Site: K-8 Music

URL: http://www.u.arizona.edu/~tirwin/

Sponsor: Teresa I. Irwin, Richard B. Wilson, Jr. K-8 School (AZ)

Subject Area(s): Teaching Ideas   **Subcategory:** Music

Grade Level(s): Adult

Description

The K-8 Music home page was developed by a K-8 music teacher for her colleagues, both general music and choir teachers. Find resources: Learning Activity Packets (L.A.P.s), L.A.P. Lesson Plans, Education Resources on the Internet, Music Videos, Corporations of Interest on the WWW, Music Discussion Groups, Music Hot Spots, Cool Spots for Searching, Home Pages for Schools, and Writing Your Own School Home Page.

Commentary

L.A.P.s are music lessons, each contained in a manila envelope. Students work together to complete the lesson, typically in one class period, and work with multiple objects, e.g., scissors, stickers, CDs, instruments, etc. L.A.P.s are designed to foster independent and cooperative learning and are best used in grades 6-8, in groups of 4-5. Find lesson plans on diverse topics such as Playing C Major and G7 Chords in the Right Hand.

Site: MOTET: Music Online Telecommunications Environment for Teaching

URL: http://nsn.bbn.com/motet/CurriculumIndex.html

Sponsor: BBN Co-NECT Schools

Subject Area(s): Teaching Ideas   **Subcategory:** Music

Grade Level(s): Adult

Description

MOTET is a pilot project seeking to merge the real-life performance worlds, the online communication abilities and information worlds, and the classroom environment for learning and teaching music. Two scheduled online performances have already taken place and the curricular materials and sound files are now available on this Web site for other uses. Many related activities involve students keeping journals.

Commentary

This is a rich and interesting source for music teachers with themes and influences in music, a section on Becoming a Critic that teaches how to listen to music carefully and knowledgeably, music composition exercises, sound files related to the project, and a glossary of music terms.

Music Education Online

A Guide to Music Education for Grades K through 12

Site: Music Education Online

URL: http://www.geocities.com/Athens/2405/index.html

Sponsor: The Children's Music Workshop

Subject Area(s): Teaching Ideas   **Subcategory:** Music

Grade Level(s): Adult

Description

Music Education Online is designed to assist music educators in finding a variety of music education resources on the Internet and to provide an interactive bulletin board for posting questions and comments on music. Find links organized according to Instrumental Music, Choral, General, Music Education, Music Institutes, Music Products, and more.

Commentary

Resources are available here for K-12 instruction. Access some of the links referenced. You can also read through the comments, questions, and ideas of other music educators posted to the online bulletin board...or post one or more of your own.

Section 03. Teaching Ideas

Site: Resources for Music Educators

URL: http://www.ed.uiuc.edu/EdPsy-387/Tina-Scott/project/home.html

Sponsor: Tina Scott (Oregon State University)

Subject Area(s): Teaching Ideas   **Subcategory:** Music

Grade Level(s): Adult

Description

The purpose of this Web resource is to provide information to music teachers, particularly those who teach students ages 5-18. The site is divided into printed resources (those available at bookstores and music stores) and Web resources. The Web sites suggested include organizations, software, education resources, and other art sites.

Commentary

The online list is extensive. It would have been nice to have it annotated, but it is kept current. Some new things at the time of evaluation of this site included demos from a CD-ROM called "Experiencing Music Technology." For the classical music lover, there are plenty of links to sites for piano and opera.

Site: The Music Educator's Home Page

URL: http://www.athenet.net/~wslow

Sponsor: Fox Valley Regional Music Technology Center (WI)

Subject Area(s): Teaching Ideas   **Subcategory:** Music

Grade Level(s): Adult

Description

This Web site is an Internet resource for music educators offering music curriculum materials and links to other useful sites of potential benefit to classroom music teachers. Information is organized into categories of Colleague Corner (information, newsletters, and articles), Curriculum Resources (articles, curriculum documents, handouts, lesson plans, and more), and Net-Links to other music-related Internet sites.

Commentary

The links to other sites include music merchants, performers, topical music, as well as an assortment of other music education resources. The performer list is heavy with chamber and orchestral performers with further links to contemporary listings. Teachers are urged to submit their own original curriculum documents or musical selections.

Site: Access Excellence

URL: http://www.gene.com/ae/

Sponsor: Genentech, Inc.

Subject Area(s): Teaching Ideas   **Subcategory:** Science

Grade Level(s): Adult

Description

Communicate with teachers and scientists on topics relating to current biological issues. An activities exchange provides a vehicle for teachers to exchange biology-related lesson plans, projects, and varied resources. Look in Teaching Communities for groups of teachers developing new classroom practices and curriculum strategies for biology education. There are also online seminars, projects, and discussions, hosted by scientists and teachers.

Commentary

This is a fantastic site for biology teachers, rich with lessons, ideas, new approaches to science education, current news and interviews with scientists, and more. The site is updated frequently and has an easy-to-use search tool for finding topics of interest.

Section 03. Teaching Ideas

Site: Chemistry Teacher Resources

URL: http://rampages.onramp.net/~jaldr/

Chemistry Teacher Resources   **Sponsor:** James Aldridge, Fort Worth Day School

Subject Area(s): Teaching Ideas   **Subcategory:** Science

Grade Level(s): Adult

Description

This Web site is for chemistry teachers in grades 9 through 12; some students may find it useful. There are labs, information sheets, and other resources which teachers can access. It is assumed that users of this site are qualified chemists and therefore possess an understanding of safety precautions and proper chemical usage and disposal.

Commentary

There are outlines here for Chemistry I and AP Chemistry, plus Internet resources, bibliographies, and notes. Mr. Aldridge posts a list of other things he is looking for which would greatly enhance the existing chemistry resources.

Site: Chemistry Teaching Resources

URL: http://www.anachem.umu.se/eks/pointers.html

Sponsor: Umea University, Sweden

Subject Area(s): Teaching Ideas   **Subcategory:** Science

Grade Level(s): Adult

Description

From this site, you can link to courses, hypertexts, demonstrations, experiments, and a listing of chemistry software. Also find chemistry-related clip art and a large number of curricula and lesson plans, listings of chemistry textbooks, software for chemistry, chemical suppliers, and more.

Commentary

This is a very comprehensive listing of resources about chemistry, with an emphasis on analytical chemistry. Teachers can locate virtually anything they might need to deal with chemistry.

Site: Computer as Learning Partner

URL: http://www.clp.berkeley.edu/clp.html

Computer as Learning Partner   **Sponsor:** National Science Foundation

Subject Area(s): Teaching Ideas   **Subcategory:** Science

Grade Level(s): Adult

Description

This Web site describes the Computer as Learning Partner program, which is a ten-year-old collaboration founded for the purpose of improving the teaching of science in the middle school.

Commentary

This project has developed an integrated curriculum for teaching thermodynamics, light, and sound in the middle school. The curriculum is described in one section of the Web site.

Section 03. Teaching Ideas

Site: Earth Systems Science Education

URL: http://www.usra.edu/esse/ESSE.html

Sponsor: Universities Space Research Association (funded by NASA)

Subject Area(s): Teaching Ideas   **Subcategory:** Science

Grade Level(s): Adult

Description

This site includes curriculum information and the results of a survey of textbooks used by earth science instructors. It also has a calendar of events of interest to earth science teachers, including conferences. There is also an ESSE listserve and the site contains instructions on how to join the list.

Commentary

This site contains information about Discover Earth, a NASA-sponsored summer workshop for Educators in grades 5-12 who teach in the Northeastern United States. Information on how to apply is included.

Site: EE-Link

URL: http://nceet.snre.umich.edu

Sponsor: National Consortium for Environmental Education and Training

Subject Area(s): Teaching Ideas   **Subcategory:** Science

Grade Level(s): Adult

Description

Helping educators explore environmental education with their students is the stated mission of the site. The resource is intended for teachers, media specialists, nature center staff, and curriculum developers. In addition to information about the parent organization, there are links to references and environmental directories.

Commentary

Since this site is updated monthly, you may want to examine the "New on EE-Link" section, but note that articles stay posted for over a year. The Endangered Species page is especially interesting and useful. Since it can be searched by geographic region, it is possible to tailor materials directly for your own classroom.

Site: Environmental Education Network

URL: http://www.envirolink.org/enviroed

Sponsor: EnviroLink

Subject Area(s): Teaching Ideas   **Subcategory:** Science

Grade Level(s): Adult

Description

The Environmental Education Network is a collaborative effort to bring environmental education online and into a multimedia format. Resources for teachers and students form the larger part of the network with further links to schools in several countries and higher education. There is additional information about EnviroLink, the non-profit organization which sponsors this network, and its projects and publications.

Commentary

The resources for teachers are truly outstanding! There are curriculum materials, teacher packets, lesson plans, experiments, plus links to many sites which will be useful in the classroom. Be sure to examine the student resources (since they are not duplicates) and refer them to your students for examination. Don't miss the El Niño page for a look at this profound effect on our weather.

Section 03. Teaching Ideas

Site: Free Curriculum for Elementary Teachers

URL: http://www.plasticbag.com/education/

Sponsor: The Plastic Bag Association

Subject Area(s): Teaching Ideas   **Subcategory:** Science

Grade Level(s): Adult

Description

This site is directed toward grade 2-5 educators. It focuses on programs and information that teachers can offer to students to teach them about the environment. Included are creative teaching tips, a student essay contest, and an offer for a free teaching kit, "Don't Let a Good Thing Go to Waste."

Commentary

The five-lesson series helps students make the connection between the trash they generate and the solid waste challenges our country faces. The lesson series is ordered online and mailed to your address. Another interesting feature is the offering of creative teaching suggestions for environmental education by geographical regions.

Site: Information Technology for Science Education

URL: http://atlantis.austin.apple.com/people.pages/kmitchell/ITSE.html

Sponsor: Apple Computer, Inc.

Subject Area(s): Teaching Ideas   **Subcategory:** Science

Grade Level(s): Adult

Description

This is a support center for those seeking to integrate Apple technology into the pre-college science curriculum. Find "Solution Starter Kits" (some are still under construction) for Life Science, Earth Science, Physical Science, Biology, Chemistry, and Physics. There is also excellent information available on technology planning for science education.

Commentary

While this site is sponsored by Apple Computer, Inc., the information here will be of general interest to science educators. Elementary, middle school, and high school science teachers who are using, or who would like to begin using, technology in their classrooms will find helpful resources here.

Site: Landmarks for Schools

URL: http://www.landmark-project.com/eco-market

Sponsor: David Warlick, The Landmark Project

Subject Area(s): Teaching Ideas   **Subcategory:** Science

Grade Level(s): Adult

Description

The Eco-Marketing Project was conducted on the Internet last year with teams from around the country. There were 10 teams in each of the following categories: elementary, middle school, and high school. The purpose of the project was to use writing skills to convince and persuade other classes regarding positions on selected environmental issues.

Commentary

Mr. Warlick has plans to reformat this project into a database so that it can operate without his close monitoring. There are links to other environment sites, projects and activities, and a toolbox. Check out the Global Grocery List.

Section 03. Teaching Ideas

Site: National Education Supercomputer Program

URL: http://www.llnl.gov/sci_educ/nesp.html

Sponsor: Lawrence Livermore National Laboratory

Subject Area(s): Teaching Ideas   **Subcategory:** Science

Grade Level(s): Adult

Description

The National Education Supercomputer Program is designed to help K-12 Science teachers bridge the gap for their students between textbooks and scientific research as it is done in the real world. In addition to this Web site, the program hosts Supercomputing Workshops both in Livermore, California, and across the country. Information about the workshops is available here.

Commentary

This program is hosted on a Cray YMP-EL supercomputer, and students will be able to see what kinds of projects supercomputers are used for.

Site: Newton's Apple

URL: http://ericir.syr.edu/Projects/Newton/

Sponsor: KTCA

Subject Area(s): Teaching Ideas   **Subcategory:** Science

Grade Level(s): Adult

Description

Now in its 14th season, Newton's Apple is an award-winning national science program for kids and adults produced by KTCA-TV in Saint Paul, Minnesota. The teacher's guides for seasons 9-14 are online to accompany the television show and also for use as a stand-alone resource.

Commentary

Tapes of Newton's Apple are available from the 800 number at this site. Newer lessons are formatted to follow the National Science Education Standards with inquiry-based learning in mind. This is exceptional material—with or without the TV tapes.

Site: Science Education

URL: http://www.csun.edu/~vceed002/index.html

Sponsor: California State University at Northridge

Subject Area(s): Teaching Ideas   **Subcategory:** Science

Grade Level(s): Adult

Description

This site includes sections on Biology, Chemistry, Earth & Space Science, as well as Physics. There is an index of search engine sites, a references section with lesson plans and links to professional associations, journals, museums, and scientific supply companies.

Commentary

These pages are attractive, well-designed and well-organized. This is an excellent resource for science educators.

Section 03. Teaching Ideas

Site: Science Education Program Office

URL: http://education.lanl.gov/SEP/Education.html

Sponsor: Los Alamos Labs and the Department of Energy

Subject Area(s): Teaching Ideas   **Subcategory:** Science

Grade Level(s): Adult

Description

Los Alamos Labs conducts over 30 science education programs for teachers, students, parents, and the public on local, state, and national levels. This is their Web site. The Bradbury Science Museum (BSM) displays exhibits on the history of Los Alamos National Laboratory (LANL) and its research.

Commentary

Los Alamos National Laboratory is one of the largest multidisciplinary institutions in the world. The Laboratory is operated by the University of California for the U.S. Department of Energy. Check the Education section for programs and resources for K-12.

Site: Science Learning Network

URL: http://www.sln.org

SCIENCE LEARNING NETWORK www.sln.org **Sponsor:** National Science Foundation

Subject Area(s): Teaching Ideas   **Subcategory:** Science

Grade Level(s): Adult

Description

Developed as a model for inquiry science education, this site is an online community of educators, students, schools, museums, and other institutions. Six museum/school combinations around the United States provide a testbed for ideas for teaching science using Internet resources. The Web page provides information about inquiry science, teacher projects, the Network museums, and links to other resources.

Commentary

There are 6.5 million dollars behind this project, so one might expect it to be good—and it is. The resources developed by museums are outstanding, ready for classroom implementation in a dozen ways. Don't miss Franklin's Forecast and the other weather-related modules. As Ben said, "Some are weatherwise, some are otherwise."

Site: ScienceTeacher.com

URL: http://www.scienceteacher.com/

Sponsor: IconJohn.com

Subject Area(s): Teaching Ideas   **Subcategory:** Science

Grade Level(s): Adult

Description

At ScienceTeacher.com, you can locate reviews of CD-ROMs, discussion forums, a Teacher Connect section, research databases, lesson plans, and links to other Web sites of interest to science teachers. Forums let you subscribe to listservs and newsgroups discussing topics of interest, and the Teacher Connect section helps you locate colleagues for setting up e-mail pen pals and online class projects.

Commentary

Included are a number of lesson plans, such as Air Quality Lesson Plans and Data Lesson Plans for K-8, 100+ lesson plans for early elementary, 100+ later elementary plans, middle school and high school lesson plans, 6 aviation lesson plans, 20 lesson plans relating to outer space, and more. Visitors are invited to submit one or more of their own for co-publishing on a pay-per-view basis.

Section 03. Teaching Ideas

Site: The Daily Planet

URL: http://www.atmos.uiuc.edu

Sponsor: Department of Atmospheric Sciences, Univ. of Illinois at Urbana-Champaign

Subject Area(s): Teaching Ideas   **Subcategory:** Science

Grade Level(s): Adult

Description

The centerpiece of this site is the Weather World 2010 Project, a WWW framework for integrating current and archived weather data with multimedia instructional resources. There are teacher activity guides, classroom activities, student projects, and related resources.

Commentary

This is a site under development, with older resources in meteorology being converted to these newer guidelines. A CD-ROM is being prepared, but this is already a superb site for teachers interested in the serious study of weather.

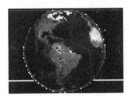

Site: The Jason Project

URL: http://seawifs.gsfc.nasa.gov/JASON/HTML/MISSION_home.html

Sponsor: Jason Foundation for Education

Subject Area(s): Teaching Ideas   **Subcategory:** Science

Grade Level(s): Adult

Description

Take your students on an electronic field trip. The Jason Foundation for Education sponsors an annual scientific expedition, which is the focus of an original curriculum developed for grades 4 through 8. Students can take part in live, interactive programs which are broadcast, using state-of-the-art technology, to a network of educational and research institutions in the United States, Mexico, Bermuda, and the United Kingdom.

Commentary

The JASON Project, founded in 1989 by Dr. Robert D. Ballard, is a result of his discovery of the wreck of the RMS Titanic and the subsequent thousands of letters from children excited by his discovery. He and his team have dedicated themselves to developing ways to assist teachers and students worldwide to take part in global explorations using advanced interactive telecommunications.

Site: The Space Educators' Handbook

URL: http://tommy.jsc.nasa.gov/~woodfill/SPACEED/SEHHTML/seh.html

Sponsor: NASA Johnson Space Center

Subject Area(s): Teaching Ideas   **Subcategory:** Science

Grade Level(s): Adult

Description

The Space Educators' Handbook contains more than 30 files available for use with HyperCard 2.1 on the Apple Macintosh or with ToolBook 1.5 on PC computers. The files are also available by sending diskettes to the address listed on the homepage. The various files deal with space memorabilia and technology, plus descriptions and pictures of many planets, satellites, and stars.

Commentary

The Space Comics might be a good place to start, although be prepared that they are line drawings exhibiting a wry sense of humor. The 19 space movies download very slowly; do not believe the amount of time listed on the screen and plan to download only once. There is even a coloring book for young space cadets.

Section 03. Teaching Ideas

Site: Calculators Online Center

URL: http://www-sci.lib.uci.edu/HSG/RefCalculators.html

Sponsor: Jim Martindale

Subject Area(s): Teaching Ideas   **Subcategory:** Science and Mathematics

Grade Level(s): Adult

Description

The Calculators Online Center contains almost 5000 calculators created by many different people. They fall loosely into the categories of mathematics, science, engineering, and general. There are applications for almost all subject matters.

Commentary

Browse through the sections for some real surprises. Of course, there are many serious scientific works here, but teachers and students will be interested in the use of calculators for fragrance making, creation of dyes, gambling calculations, international clothing size conversions, camera settings, and much, much more.

Site: Eisenhower National Clearinghouse

URL: http://enc.org/

Sponsor: Eisenhower National Clearinghouse for Mathematics and Science Education

Subject Area(s): Teaching Ideas   **Subcategory:** Science and Mathematics

Grade Level(s): Adult

Description

Each month the Clearinghouse provides the "Digital Dozen," 13 new links to Internet sites, an innovator of the month, a newsletter, and selected resources for a hot topic of interest. The Professional Development Exchange makes it possible for educators to search for workshops and conferences taking place across the country.

Commentary

The activity section presents math and science activities in isolation but also in combinations for lower and upper grades. Most are actually links to other sites...this is a good way to build a collection of bookmarks for your curriculum planning.

Site: Explorer

URL: http://explorer.scrtec.org/explorer/

Sponsor: Great Lakes Collaborative and the University of Kansas

Subject Area(s): Teaching Ideas   **Subcategory:** Science and Mathematics

Grade Level(s): Adult

Description

The Explorer is a collection of educational resources (instructional software, lab activities, lesson plans, and student created materials) for K-12 mathematics and science education. The database can be browsed or searched by key concepts. There are thousands of plans readable by Macintosh and Windows computers.

Commentary

You will find each lesson plan organized in an identical style: first by concept, then the title, resource type, physical media, grades, description, process skills, author, and availability. Lessons and software can be downloaded in a variety of formats. While all grade levels are covered, the database appears to be most extensive in high school material.

Section 03. Teaching Ideas

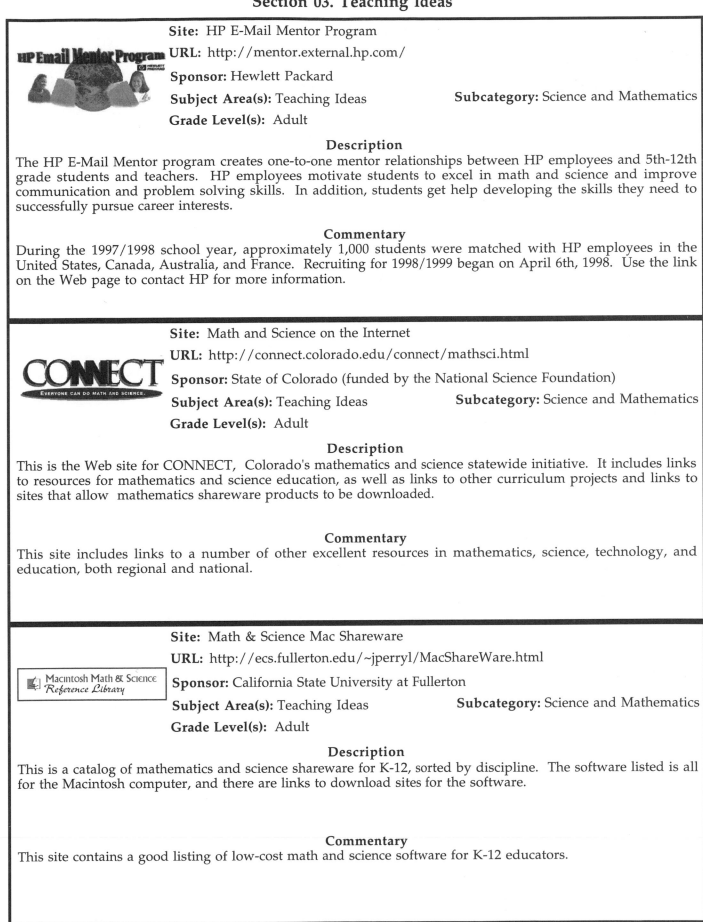

Site: HP E-Mail Mentor Program

URL: http://mentor.external.hp.com/

Sponsor: Hewlett Packard

Subject Area(s): Teaching Ideas   **Subcategory:** Science and Mathematics

Grade Level(s): Adult

Description

The HP E-Mail Mentor program creates one-to-one mentor relationships between HP employees and 5th-12th grade students and teachers. HP employees motivate students to excel in math and science and improve communication and problem solving skills. In addition, students get help developing the skills they need to successfully pursue career interests.

Commentary

During the 1997/1998 school year, approximately 1,000 students were matched with HP employees in the United States, Canada, Australia, and France. Recruiting for 1998/1999 began on April 6th, 1998. Use the link on the Web page to contact HP for more information.

Site: Math and Science on the Internet

URL: http://connect.colorado.edu/connect/mathsci.html

Sponsor: State of Colorado (funded by the National Science Foundation)

Subject Area(s): Teaching Ideas   **Subcategory:** Science and Mathematics

Grade Level(s): Adult

Description

This is the Web site for CONNECT, Colorado's mathematics and science statewide initiative. It includes links to resources for mathematics and science education, as well as links to other curriculum projects and links to sites that allow mathematics shareware products to be downloaded.

Commentary

This site includes links to a number of other excellent resources in mathematics, science, technology, and education, both regional and national.

Site: Math & Science Mac Shareware

URL: http://ecs.fullerton.edu/~jperryl/MacShareWare.html

Sponsor: California State University at Fullerton

Subject Area(s): Teaching Ideas   **Subcategory:** Science and Mathematics

Grade Level(s): Adult

Description

This is a catalog of mathematics and science shareware for K-12, sorted by discipline. The software listed is all for the Macintosh computer, and there are links to download sites for the software.

Commentary

This site contains a good listing of low-cost math and science software for K-12 educators.

Section 03. Teaching Ideas

Site: TERC Resources for Mathematics and Science

URL: http://www.terc.edu/

Sponsor: TERC

Subject Area(s): Teaching Ideas   **Subcategory:** Science and Mathematics

Grade Level(s): Adult

Description

TERC is a non-profit research and development organization committed to improving mathematics and science learning and teaching. This site contains educational materials and research papers developed by the staff and includes its publication *Hands On!*.

Commentary

Teachers will probably find the information about projects most helpful. There are more than 44 active projects included. Use the index of titles for browsing—or navigate by locating projects which are grouped by clusters. Many of the projects maintain their own Web site.

Site: The Annenberg/CPB Math and Science Project

URL: http://www.learner.org/content/k12/

 Sponsor: Corporation for Public Broadcasting

Subject Area(s): Teaching Ideas   **Subcategory:** Science and Mathematics

Grade Level(s): Adult

Description

The Annenberg/CPB Math and Science Project has funded over 40 regional and national efforts to improve math and science education in K-12 education since it was founded in 1991 with a grant from the Annenberg Foundation. These projects designed to support key groups that have a hand in changing the way math and science are taught, including parents, teachers, teacher educators, administrators, and policymakers.

Commentary

Resources on this site include Journey North, a global study of wildlife migration and seasonal change, an interactive database guide to math and science education reform, an interactive resource database for teachers on science and math initiatives, an interactive TV and web service, and a catalog.

Site: The Hub

URL: http://hub.terc.edu/

Sponsor: TERC and the U. S. Office of Education

Subject Area(s): Teaching Ideas   **Subcategory:** Science and Mathematics

Grade Level(s): Adult

Description

This is the Web site for a regional alliance in the Northeastern United States that supports educational and reform efforts in mathematics, science, and technology. It includes an archive of articles, curriculum, and project reports that can be browsed.

Commentary

Links are included that describe how the alliance's StateWide Action Teams (SWATs) collaborate. The alliance provides professional development opportunities, technical support, and other resources to schools. Information about these resources is available either on this Web site or via a link from it.

Section 03. Teaching Ideas

Site: Adventure Online

URL: http://www.adventureonline.com

Sponsor: Learning Outfitters

Subject Area(s): Teaching Ideas

Subcategory: Social Studies

Grade Level(s): Adult

Description

This site offers real-life exploration in which classrooms can participate. There is a current list of projects with links to order instructional materials. The archives feature past educational explorations, and you can locate links to other learning adventures from various groups.

Commentary

Project Central America in the archive is an example of an especially extensive project. There are links to factbooks for each Central American country, maps, activities, journey highlights, and much more. This would make a nice Internet research unit in social studies, especially with bilingual children.

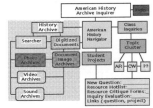

Site: American History Archive Project

URL: http://www.ilt.columbia.edu/k12/history/aha.html

Sponsor: Teachers College, Columbia University

Subject Area(s): Teaching Ideas

Subcategory: Social Studies

Grade Level(s): Adult

Description

This project, still under development, will consist of digitized archives of documents and media resources on the Web. A new type of lesson plan (the Inquirer) will use these resources with middle school and high school classes and facilitate the development of further resources by the students themselves.

Commentary

Start with *Pedagogy of History* for an essay describing how access to primary sources through networked multimedia will revolutionize the study of history. There are technical problems on several parts of this site; nevertheless, it looks promising, so keep checking back.

Site: Armadillo's WWW Resources List for the K-12 Teacher

URL: http://riceinfo.rice.edu/armadillo/Rice/Resources/geog.html

Sponsor: Houston Independent School District

Subject Area(s): Teaching Ideas

Subcategory: Social Studies

Grade Level(s): Adult

Description

This hot list provides links to geography sites around the world. Some are much like tourist sites, such as the virtual tour of Ottawa. Others offer links to Rwanda and Slovakia with information, for example, about political crises.

Commentary

Both teachers and students will enjoy and find informative many of the links contained in this resource. This is not intended to be a comprehensive bibliography but simply a listing of interesting material.

Site: EcEdWeb

URL: http://ecedweb.unomaha.edu/

Sponsor: University of Nebraska at Omaha

Subject Area(s): Teaching Ideas   **Subcategory:** Social Studies

Grade Level(s): Adult

Description

The purpose of the Economic Education Web site is to provide support for economics education in all forms and at all levels. There are categories for economic data, K-12 resources, college resources, Web teaching ideas, and information about professional organizations.

Commentary

Winner of several awards, teachers of economics, social studies, and career and technology education will find useful information here. The link to economic information is further organized into 12 categories, with the specific links described in detail. This site is easy to use and efficient for gathering large amounts of information.

---

galaxy *The professional's guide to a world of information*

Site: Einet Galaxy Education Page

URL: http://galaxy.einet.net/galaxy/Social-Sciences/Education.html

Sponsor: TradeWave Corporation

Subject Area(s): Teaching Ideas   **Subcategory:** Social Studies

Grade Level(s): Adult

Description

This is a search-engine with links to thousands of educational resources. There is a special emphasis on social science, but there are also sections for academic institutions, adult education, curriculum and instruction, financial aid, guidance and counseling, and special education.

Commentary

This site is an excellent place to initiate education research. Find links to lists of periodicals, academic organizations, educational organizations, and other types of education-related resources.

Site: Electronic Archives for Teaching the American Literatures

URL: http://www.georgetown.edu.80/tamlit/tamlit-home.html

Sponsor: Georgetown University

Subject Area(s): Teaching Ideas   **Subcategory:** Social Studies

Grade Level(s): Adult

Description

The site is one of a group of projects affiliated with the American Studies program at Georgetown University. The Electronic Archives contain essays, syllabi, bibliographies, and other resources for teaching the multiple literature of the United States.

Commentary

People interested in American Literatures will wish to examine both the section on essays on teaching and the extensive bibliography. The essays contain helpful materials for teaching ethnic materials, including early American studies.

Site: HistoryTeacher.com

URL: http://www.historyteacher.com/

Sponsor: IconJohn.com

Subject Area(s): Teaching Ideas   **Subcategory:** Social Studies

Grade Level(s): Adult

Description

Find CD-ROM Reviews, Discussion Forums, Teacher Connect, Research Databases, Tutoring Connect, Teacher Links, and more at HistoryTeacher.com. The CD-ROM reviews include links to publisher information, features, and suggestions for where they can be purchased.

Commentary

Forums let you subscribe to various listservs and newsgroups discussing topics of interest, and the Teacher Connect section helps you locate colleagues for setting up e-mail pen pals and online class projects. They are planning online lesson plans—offer one for co-publishing on a pay-per-view basis.

Site: Internet CNN Newsroom

URL: http://www.nmis.org/NewsInteractive/CNN/Newsroom/contents.html

Sponsor: CNN News

Subject Area(s): Teaching Ideas   **Subcategory:** Social Studies

Grade Level(s): Adult

Description

In addition to today's news, the site maintains newsclips for the last year which can be examined and downloaded. All newsclips are accompanied by pictures and/or video. There is also a search engine for looking at the news over the last year.

Commentary

While written primarily for teachers, the CNN Newsroom Guide has some interesting questions and vocabulary definitions that might prove fascinating for anyone to access. You will want to be sure to read directions carefully for downloading the plug-ins necessary to access different parts of this program.

Site: Labyrinth

URL: http://www.georgetown.edu.80/labyrinth/labyrinth-home.html

Sponsor: Georgetown University

Subject Area(s): Teaching Ideas   **Subcategory:** Social Studies

Grade Level(s): Adult

Description

This is a global information network providing access to electronic resources in medieval studies. Searching is done using the metaphor of Ariadne's Thread from classical mythology in which Ariadne gave her lover a thread to unwind through the labyrinth so he could find his way home again. Find pages from magnificent old manuscripts. Research a culture and find information on its history, recipes, clothing, and much more.

Commentary

Teachers of world history, world literature, art, and others will find a treasure of resources here. The Labyrinth will include a full range of new resources: an electronic library, online forums, professional directories and news, online bibliographies, an online "university" of teachers and scholars available for electronic conferencing, and an archive of pedagogical tools.

Section 03. Teaching Ideas

Site: Lesson Plans and Resources for Social Studies Teachers

URL: http://www.csun.edu/~hcedu013/index.html

Sponsor: Dr. Marty Levine, California State University at Northridge

Subject Area(s): Teaching Ideas   **Subcategory:** Social Studies

Grade Level(s): Adult

Description

Dr. Marty Levine, Professor of Secondary Education, California State University at Northridge, has gathered lesson plans and resources from the Internet which he believes social studies teachers will find useful. In addition, there are sections on teaching current events, newsgroups, educational standards, other social studies resources, and online activities.

Commentary

This site is nicely organized and annotated; at least a few links are cross-referenced when they fit more than one category. The online activities are especially interesting, drawing from a wide variety of commercial and school sources. Resources are included for K-12 students, and the large print is easy to read.

Site: Online Resources

URL: http://socialstudies.com/online.html

Sponsor: Social Studies School Service

Subject Area(s): Teaching Ideas   **Subcategory:** Social Studies

Grade Level(s): Adult

Description

Resources are organized into three large divisions: World, United States, and General—with subtopics under each division. Teachers may browse through the subtopics or search the entire site by keywords or by media category.

Commentary

This Web site is easy to navigate. All links have been screened and annotated by the author so that it is relatively easy to find appropriate material. The site does not appear to be updated frequently, since the Presidential Election of 1996 is still up, but the What's New section from the current month eliminates that criticism.

Site: Social Studies

URL: http://www.kent.wednet.edu/curriculum/soc_studies/soc_studies.html

Sponsor: Kent School District (WA)

Subject Area(s): Teaching Ideas   **Subcategory:** Social Studies

Grade Level(s): Adult

Description

Two teachers and a technology specialist are responsible for the selection and organization of this material. There is curricular material by grade level, information on district resources, and links to other cool sites.

Commentary

The site has not been updated in more than a year, so you will find some dead links. The extensive, quality listing outweighs this disadvantage. There are even rich resources for the lower grades. Don't miss the Kindergarten pages no matter what you teach. You will love the bears and farm links.

Section 03. Teaching Ideas

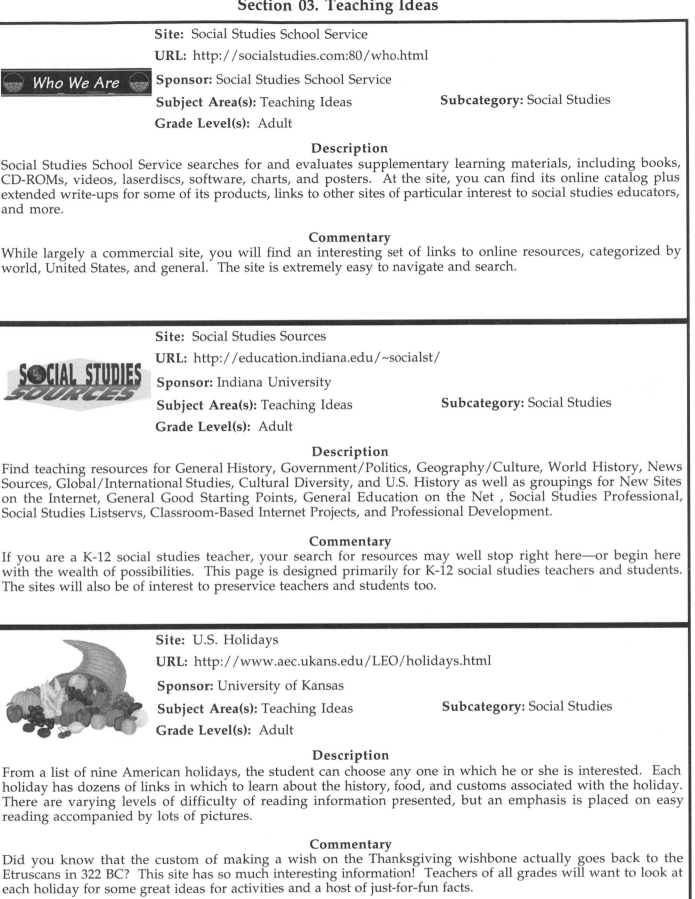

Site: Social Studies School Service

URL: http://socialstudies.com:80/who.html

Sponsor: Social Studies School Service

Subject Area(s): Teaching Ideas

Subcategory: Social Studies

Grade Level(s): Adult

Description

Social Studies School Service searches for and evaluates supplementary learning materials, including books, CD-ROMs, videos, laserdiscs, software, charts, and posters. At the site, you can find its online catalog plus extended write-ups for some of its products, links to other sites of particular interest to social studies educators, and more.

Commentary

While largely a commercial site, you will find an interesting set of links to online resources, categorized by world, United States, and general. The site is extremely easy to navigate and search.

Site: Social Studies Sources

URL: http://education.indiana.edu/~socialst/

Sponsor: Indiana University

Subject Area(s): Teaching Ideas

Subcategory: Social Studies

Grade Level(s): Adult

Description

Find teaching resources for General History, Government/Politics, Geography/Culture, World History, News Sources, Global/International Studies, Cultural Diversity, and U.S. History as well as groupings for New Sites on the Internet, General Good Starting Points, General Education on the Net , Social Studies Professional, Social Studies Listservs, Classroom-Based Internet Projects, and Professional Development.

Commentary

If you are a K-12 social studies teacher, your search for resources may well stop right here—or begin here with the wealth of possibilities. This page is designed primarily for K-12 social studies teachers and students. The sites will also be of interest to preservice teachers and students too.

Site: U.S. Holidays

URL: http://www.aec.ukans.edu/LEO/holidays.html

Sponsor: University of Kansas

Subject Area(s): Teaching Ideas

Subcategory: Social Studies

Grade Level(s): Adult

Description

From a list of nine American holidays, the student can choose any one in which he or she is interested. Each holiday has dozens of links in which to learn about the history, food, and customs associated with the holiday. There are varying levels of difficulty of reading information presented, but an emphasis is placed on easy reading accompanied by lots of pictures.

Commentary

Did you know that the custom of making a wish on the Thanksgiving wishbone actually goes back to the Etruscans in 322 BC? This site has so much interesting information! Teachers of all grades will want to look at each holiday for some great ideas for activities and a host of just-for-fun facts.

Section 03. Teaching Ideas

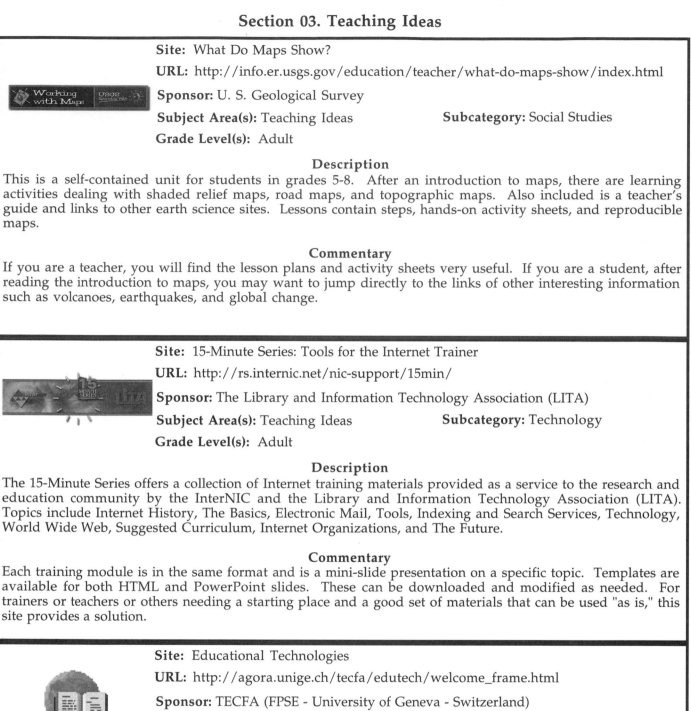

Site: What Do Maps Show?

URL: http://info.er.usgs.gov/education/teacher/what-do-maps-show/index.html

Sponsor: U. S. Geological Survey

Subject Area(s): Teaching Ideas   **Subcategory:** Social Studies

Grade Level(s): Adult

Description

This is a self-contained unit for students in grades 5-8. After an introduction to maps, there are learning activities dealing with shaded relief maps, road maps, and topographic maps. Also included is a teacher's guide and links to other earth science sites. Lessons contain steps, hands-on activity sheets, and reproducible maps.

Commentary

If you are a teacher, you will find the lesson plans and activity sheets very useful. If you are a student, after reading the introduction to maps, you may want to jump directly to the links of other interesting information such as volcanoes, earthquakes, and global change.

Site: 15-Minute Series: Tools for the Internet Trainer

URL: http://rs.internic.net/nic-support/15min/

Sponsor: The Library and Information Technology Association (LITA)

Subject Area(s): Teaching Ideas   **Subcategory:** Technology

Grade Level(s): Adult

Description

The 15-Minute Series offers a collection of Internet training materials provided as a service to the research and education community by the InterNIC and the Library and Information Technology Association (LITA). Topics include Internet History, The Basics, Electronic Mail, Tools, Indexing and Search Services, Technology, World Wide Web, Suggested Curriculum, Internet Organizations, and The Future.

Commentary

Each training module is in the same format and is a mini-slide presentation on a specific topic. Templates are available for both HTML and PowerPoint slides. These can be downloaded and modified as needed. For trainers or teachers or others needing a starting place and a good set of materials that can be used "as is," this site provides a solution.

Site: Educational Technologies

URL: http://agora.unige.ch/tecfa/edutech/welcome_frame.html

Sponsor: TECFA (FPSE - University of Geneva - Switzerland)

Subject Area(s): Teaching Ideas   **Subcategory:** Technology

Grade Level(s): Adult

Description

View a regularly updated selection of what are deemed best pages dealing with Educational Technology. You may take advantage of a guided search feature or make a specific request of the database. Selections include Virtual Reality, the 1998 Educational Technologies Conference, Commercial Science Software, Simulations for Education, Online Journals for Distance Education, and others.

Commentary

You might begin by clicking on Classification to understand how all entries have been classified according to theme, type of information, audience, level, and domain.

Section 03. Teaching Ideas

Site: Florida Center for Instructional Technology

URL: http://www.coedu.usf.edu/fcit/

Sponsor: College of Education, University of South Florida

Subject Area(s): Teaching Ideas   **Subcategory:** Technology

Grade Level(s): Adult

Description

The primary focus of the Florida Center for Instructional Technology is the development of instructional materials and databases for telecommunications. The database of lesson plans includes only plans which use technology in some form. These lesson plans may be searched by subject area, by grade level, and by keyword.

Commentary

This is a useful site for teachers who are looking for ideas on using technology in their own classrooms. The database is especially rich in ideas for the intermediate and middle grades. You may also wish to check out the products and publications that are featured.

Site: GirlTECH Lesson Plans

URL: http://www.crpc.rice.edu/CRPC/Women/GirlTECH/Lessons/

Sponsor: Center for Research on Parallel Computation, Rice University

Subject Area(s): Teaching Ideas   **Subcategory:** Technology

Grade Level(s): Adult

Description

This teacher training workshop has been sponsored by Rice University during the past two years for the purpose of providing intensive technology training and exploring innovative teaching strategies that impact gender equity in the classroom. The lesson plans would certainly not be limited to use with girls but are designed to incorporate topics of particular interest to them.

Commentary

The list of lesson plans is scrollable and organized by content topic. At first this seems like a lengthy process, but it actually turns out to be beneficial. You will end up exploring many new topics and not be quite so bound by traditional notions of grade level or content area.

Site: History/Social Studies Web Site for K-12 Teachers

URL: http://execpc.com/~dboals/boals.html

Sponsor: Dennis Boals

Subject Area(s): Teaching Ideas   **Subcategory:** Technology

Grade Level(s): Adult

Description

This site is designed to encourage use of the World Wide Web as a tool for learning and teaching and to help educators locate and use Internet resources in the classroom. Start by accessing a category (many options, including Archaeology, Diversity Sources, Genealogy, Government, K-12 Resources, Resources for Writers, Educational Resources for Parents, and more) or find, or link to, information under Special Announcements.

Commentary

This is a wonderful research site loaded with resources and links to other valuable sites. It is regularly updated and well-organized. A relatively new area at this site, Research and Critical Thinking, provides information on Concept Mapping, Web Site Evaluation, Research Skills and Tools, Search Tools and How to Use Them, and Critical Thinking and the Web—much needed resources and information.

Section 03. Teaching Ideas

Site: Integrating the Internet

URL: http://www.indirect.com/www/dhixson/index5.html

Sponsor: Susan Hixson

Subject Area(s): Teaching Ideas   **Subcategory:** Technology

Grade Level(s): Adult

Description

This is a very helpful site for locating resources, projects, a weekly newsletter, units of study, and a tutorial to help teachers plan projects and classroom homepages. Find curriculum resources, an Internet in the Classroom Tutorial, an Integrated Learning Presentation, stories relating how teachers use the Internet in their classrooms, and much more.

Commentary

Hixson, who maintains this site, is the Internet Specialist for the Tempe, Arizona, Elementary Schools. Her enthusiasm for teaching and learning and using the Internet has resulted in this collection of resources for educators.

Site: Internet for Minnesota Schools

URL: http://informns.k12.mn.us

Sponsor: University of Minnesota and others

Subject Area(s): Teaching Ideas   **Subcategory:** Technology

Grade Level(s): Adult

Description

Minnesota was one of the early states to use technology in the classroom. This informational network provides assistance to educators in utilizing the Internet to realize the instructional potential. There are subject matter sections with lessons plans, Internet projects, and links to other resources.

Commentary

This Web site is most useful for teachers of language arts, social studies, science, and mathematics; only a few resources are available in other content areas. The divided scrolling screen detracts somewhat from the readability of this resource.

Site: K-5 CyberTrail

URL: http://www.wmht.org/trail

Sponsor: WMHT Educational Telecommunications

Subject Area(s): Teaching Ideas   **Subcategory:** Technology

Grade Level(s): Adult

Description

This clever site introduces K-5 teachers to the Internet and its possibilities for education. With engaging headings such as Tenderfoot Trail (Elementary Schools on the Web), Syd's KidPicks (K-5 Student Browsing), Smoke Signals (E-Mail on the Trail), and Tips for the Trail (Using Your Browser as a CyberCompass), teachers can explore new resources, see how other teachers are using the Net, and identify new strategies to try.

Commentary

K-5 CyberTrail was designed by public broadcaster WMHT for teachers at Troy City School 14 in New York. Find models of exemplary use as well as hints, tips, and things to think about provided by Syd the CyberGuide. This effort is part of the Corporation for Public Broadcasting's larger educational technology project, the K-12 Internet Testbed.

Section 03. Teaching Ideas

Site: LiveText

URL: http://www.ilt.columbia.edu/k12/livetext

Sponsor: Teachers College, Columbia University

Subject Area(s): Teaching Ideas   **Subcategory:** Technology

Grade Level(s): Adult

Description
LiveText is a "living textbook" on how to teach with technology, designed to help teachers find what they seek and learn how to use it. It provides a comprehensive, annotated index to online resources for educators who are using network technologies for teaching and collaborating. Materials are indexed for grades 4-12. Browse the Readings area with sections on Technology Pedagogy and School Reform and Technology.

Commentary
Billed as the home page for tech-savvy teachers—if you don't consider yourself one when you start, this site will support your becoming one. With the vast amount of information available on the Web, this site provides models for considering how to best use the Internet in curriculum development and teaching—developed by experienced teachers, content developers, and coordinators of technology projects.

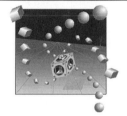

Site: NCRTEC Guiding Questions for Technology Planning

URL: http://www.ncrtec.org/capacity/guidewww/gqhome.html

Sponsor: North Central Regional Technology in Education Consortium

Subject Area(s): Teaching Ideas   **Subcategory:** Technology

Grade Level(s): Adult

Description
This site provides a set of guiding questions to help technology planners consider the most significant issues related to technology planning. The stated intent of the guiding questions is to help jump start and guide a technology planning process, develop planning criteria, refine technology planning processes, analyze technology planning models, and review technology plans developed by other school districts and organizations.

Commentary
While this site is aimed at campus or district technology planning teams and is not just a presentation of teaching ideas, it most assuredly begins with questions regarding your vision or learning and how you see technology supporting that vision. There is food for thought here for any educator and a most valuable tool for those initiating or assessing technology plans on their campus or in their district.

Site: Plugging In

URL: http://www.ncrel.org/sdrs/edtalk/toc.html

Sponsor: North Central Regional Educational Laboratory

Subject Area(s): Teaching Ideas   **Subcategory:** Technology

Grade Level(s): Adult

Description
This online document is based on the 1995 report, *Designing Learning and Technology for Educational Reform*. It discusses what is known about effective learning and effective technology and puts the two together in a planning framework for educators and education policymakers. Read the information and then follow instructions to use the framework provided to plan technology-related programs that complement learning.

Commentary
Information provided here is still timely, and educators will find the text thought-provoking for their instructional planning and will additionally find the tables (Indicators of Engaged Learning, Indicators of High Technology Performance, and The Learning and Technology Framework) to be handy online tools that can be used in planning efforts.

Section 03. Teaching Ideas

Site: Reinventing Schools: The Technology is Now

URL: http://www.nap.edu/readingroom/books/techgap/pdf.html

Sponsor: National Academy of Sciences and The National Academy of Engineering

Subject Area(s): Teaching Ideas   **Subcategory:** Technology

Grade Level(s): Adult

Description
Reinventing Schools: The Technology is Now is an online publication that was the result of a meeting in 1995 of hundreds of leaders from government, education, and the entertainment and information technology industries. At this meeting, they developed strategies for reinvigorating the K-12 educational process by integrating the school experience with the information technology that has captured children's imaginations.

Commentary
Educators will find stimulating reading here and points to use in district or other presentations regarding the importance of technology in teaching and learning. Special attention might be given to information describing the "technology gap" that exists between more technologically rich experiences many children have outside the classroom compared to the more low-tech environment found in all too many classrooms.

Site: Resources

URL: http://www.tcm.org/resources/ed-packet/epintro.html

Sponsor: The Computer Museum Network

Subject Area(s): Teaching Ideas   **Subcategory:** Technology

Grade Level(s): Adult

Description
This site has great resources for educators who are teaching about technology. The Packet contains five major themes: How Does a Computer Work? Where Did Computers Come From? Can Computers Think? How Do Computers Affect Our Lives? and What Can You Do With a Personal Computer? Each theme includes background information, classroom activities, and "museum activity circuits."

Commentary
This is the Educator's section of the Web site for The Computer Museum, located in Boston, Massachusetts. All materials can be printed from your Web browser or copied into a word processor. Be sure to credit The Computer Museum for all materials used.

Site: Software Publishers Association

URL: http://www.spa.org/project/educator.html

Sponsor: Software Publishers Association

Subject Area(s): Teaching Ideas   **Subcategory:** Technology

Grade Level(s): Adult

Description
This is an excellent centralized resource for educators about software piracy and other technology issues that are education-related. Also included is a directory of software publishers, state departments of education, lesson guides, copyright protection information, links to curriculum standards, and more.

Commentary
This site is a valuable resource in locating and effectively (and legally!) using educational software. The CyberSurfari page is an Internet-based "treasure hunt" for students. It can be quickly accessed from this page and is also listed separately.

Section 03. Teaching Ideas

**No
Graphic
Found**

Site: Student Technology Benchmarks

URL: http://ben.bcoe.butte.k12.ca.us/isd/irc/bcic/techfram.html

Sponsor: Butte County Schools (CA)

Subject Area(s): Teaching Ideas   **Subcategory:** Technology

Grade Level(s): Adult

Description

This site provides a list of benchmarks for student technology use in grades K-12, indicating when students are to be introduced to new skills and when they can continue to use previously learned skills. There are examples for each of the sixteen stated benchmarks.

Commentary

Scan a matrix indicating when skills are to be introduced, or click on a grade level to view requirements for the benchmark. For example, for students using a computer at the K level, expectation is that the student (a) can start, restart, and shut down a computer, (b) can treat disks and computer with respect, (c) demonstrates acceptable behavior at the computer and in the lab, and (d) can insert a floppy into the computer.

Site: Tammy's Technology Tips for Teachers

URL: http://www.essdack.org/tips/

Sponsor: Tammy Worcester, ESSDACK (KS)

Subject Area(s): Teaching Ideas   **Subcategory:** Technology

Grade Level(s): Adult

Description

Find terrific technology tips for teachers at this site. There are Classroom Management resources, Classroom Projects (lesson plans, student instructions, and rubrics for assessment of classroom computer projects), Nuts About the Net resources (physical setup, policies and procedures, and integration suggestions), and Electronic Portfolios resources (ideas for using HyperStudio or Claris Home Page to create electronic portfolios of student work).

Commentary

What a terrific site for teachers! So often, teachers are challenged by not just getting comfortable with the technology but also figuring out how to merge it into daily classroom activities. Check out the "Classroom Management" area for ideas for printing on sticky notes (Post-It™ Notes), making computer cleaning kits, creating business cards, personalizing name tags, creating spreadsheet skill sheets, and more.

THE COMPUTER TEACHER'S RESOURCE PAGE

Site: The Computer Teacher's Resource Page

URL: http://nimbus.temple.edu/~jallis00/

Sponsor: Jane Allison (PA)

Subject Area(s): Teaching Ideas   **Subcategory:** Technology

Grade Level(s): Adult

Description

This site provides links to educational Web sites, lesson plans, and ideas for using technology in the K-8 curriculum. The creator of the page has gathered links in the following categories: Art Education, Music Education, Language Arts, Science Education, Math Education, Social Studies, General Education Links, Kid-to-Kid Links, Software & Shareware, Resources, and Web Page Development Tools.

Commentary

While not an extensive list, the links are helpful and well-organized. There are quite a few focused on Web Page Development, which will be of interest to many teachers who are creating or whose students are creating Web pages.

Section 03. Teaching Ideas

Site: The Well Connected Educator

URL: http://www.gsh.org/wce

Sponsor: National Science Foundation, Global SchoolNet Foundation, Microsoft

Subject Area(s): Teaching Ideas   **Subcategory:** Technology

Grade Level(s): Adult

Description

This Web site offers success stories, strategies, and examples of technology integration in the classroom. Writers of the columns, articles, and features include teachers, administrators, parents, and community partners. Links to other online resources are available as well. Monthly online forums on specified topics are offered, and included are listings of Special Education and African American resources.

Commentary

This wonderful site was created by and for teachers, administrators, parents, and community partners regarding the use of technology for teaching and learning. All of the articles are reviewed by an editorial board at the International Society for Technology in Education (ISTE). This site provides a rare opportunity for K-12 educators and others to share their experiences and engage in moderated discussions.

4 WWW PLACES FOR PARENTS

This section identifies more than two dozen sites to help parents find information on a wide range of topics, including discipline, learning disabilities, booklists for children, drug prevention, family activities, homeschooling, pregnancy, single parenting, and many others. "A Guide to Internet Parenting," the very first site, includes a pamphlet entitled "Internet Parent Safety Tips," to help parents get their children off to a safe start in using the Net. And "Parenthood Web" features favorite articles for parents and parents-to-be with an opportunity to review and send comments about a specific topic.

Section 04. Places for Parents

Site: A Guide to Internet Parenting

URL: http://www.vtw.org/parents/

Sponsor: Voters Telecommunications Watch

Subject Area(s): Places for Parents   **Subcategory:** Miscellaneous

Grade Level(s): Adult

Description

Concerned about protecting your children as they explore the Internet? The Guide to Internet Parenting site offers information in its pamphlet, *Internet Parent Safety Tips*, along with a list of parental control tools and links to sites supported by other families working through similar issues.

Commentary

Seven kid-friendly links are included to get children started safely on their Net surfboards.

Site: ALA Resources for Parents & Kids

URL: http://www.ala.org/parents

Sponsor: American Library Association

Subject Area(s): Places for Parents   **Subcategory:** Miscellaneous

Grade Level(s): Adult

Description

If you have wondered just which books are the Caldecott and Newbury Medal winners, or are seeking book lists and recommended Internet site lists for kids, the Librarian's Guide to Cyberspace for Parents and Kids is the site to visit. Also find Parents Page, Library Connections for Parents, For Parents and Caregivers, Cool Sites for Kids, Notable Books for Children, KidsConnect, Internet Sites for Young Adults, and more.

Commentary

Eric Carle, Dr. Seuss, The Babysitter's Club, and dozens of other Web sites are listed under Cool Sites for Kids. The Young Adult Book Lists and Internet Sites for Young Adults can help teens locate avenues to explore a wide variety of interests. Though this site could provide a rich resource for kids and teachers too, there seems to be a special focus here for parents seeking guidance.

Site: Dear Parents

URL: http://www.dearparents.com

Sponsor: Edmark Corporation

Subject Area(s): Places for Parents   **Subcategory:** Miscellaneous

Grade Level(s): Adult

Description

This site provides information to parents regarding learning and technology. Enjoy reading the question and answer of the week or find questions and answers of particular interest sorted by category. Categories include various subject areas, thinking skills, learning styles, special needs, gifted children, homeschooling, educational software, girls and computers, kids on the Internet, and more.

Commentary

Parents will find this a rich resource for answering some of the questions they have about learning and technology—or considering some responses to questions they have not even yet considered. Pose a question of your own!

Section 04. Places for Parents

Site: Empowering People

URL: http://www.empoweringpeople.com/

Sponsor: Media Designs

Subject Area(s): Places for Parents   **Subcategory:** Miscellaneous

Grade Level(s): Adult

Description
Subscribe to a free monthly newsletter or just read articles online from an author and lecturer on topics of interest to parents and classroom teachers. In the "Ask Dr. Nelsen" section, you can browse through questions and answers to parenting and classroom issues or ask questions of your own.

Commentary
Both parents and educators will find articles and information of interest on parenting, discipline, empowerment, and more. Dr. Jane Nelsen is a licensed Marriage, Family, and Child Counselor who has appeared on Oprah, Sally Jessy Raphael, Twin Cities Live, and was the featured parent expert on the National Parent Quiz with Ben Vereen.

Site: family.com

URL: http://www.family.com

Sponsor: Disney

Subject Area(s): Places for Parents   **Subcategory:** Miscellaneous

Grade Level(s): Adult

Description
Disney's family.com site is a gold mine for parents and includes numerous articles and publications which have been organized for easy access. Visitors can elect to browse by categories such as activities, computing, food and learning, or use the FOR YOUR EYES ONLY option to customize searches according to a given category and age. Software reviews, parenting tips, and seasonal activities are a few of the resources to access.

Commentary
Use the GET YOUR HOMETOWN ANGLE link for local information and activities. Find information on activities, computing, food, learning, parenting, travel, and more. Send digital cards and interact with bulletin board and chat areas.

Site: Family Education Network

URL: http://www.familyeducation.com

Sponsor: AT&T, Microsoft, Nellie Mae

Subject Area(s): Places for Parents   **Subcategory:** Miscellaneous

Grade Level(s): Adult

Description
Vast information resources, over 8,000 pages, and weekly features will appeal to parents supporting children's education whether at school, home, or college. Each "channel" connects to a page of topical articles with a "highlights" list to more readily locate areas of interest—or use the online search capability which includes a comprehensive list of topics. This is a site you are sure to visit again and again.

Commentary
Parents of students with special needs will find "channels" specifically for learning disabilities and special needs; however, don't ignore the other channels which may link to helpful information for you and your child.

Section 04. Places for Parents

Site: Family Internet

URL: http://www.familyinternet.com

Sponsor: Family Internet

Subject Area(s): Places for Parents　　　**Subcategory:** Miscellaneous

Grade Level(s): Adult

Description

Family-friendly links to suit a variety of interests are featured at the Family Internet site. Parenting, Health, Kids, and Education are a few of the buttons for links to educational information; however, others have potential for curricular application as well.

Commentary

For those concerned with maintaining wholesome exploration of the Internet, the Family Internet site will prove helpful. Family Internet is also one of few sites which includes articles for stay-at-home dads.

Site: Family Surfboard

URL: http://www.familysurf.com/

Sponsor: Steve and Ruth Bennett

Subject Area(s): Places for Parents　　　**Subcategory:** Miscellaneous

Grade Level(s): Adult

Description

Tap into your child's creativity, curiosity, and playfulness using the Internet links for children found at the Family Surfboard Web site. Satisfy your parental concerns about raising children, education, and family issues. And find out about technology trends through the Profiles in Computing Microstats and Family Computing Survey links. These and more await you here.

Commentary

The electronic public service announcement provides interesting and practical information not necessarily related to computing, while the Parentware page presents thought-provoking views on technology.

Site: George Lucas Educational Foundation

URL: http://glef.org/

Sponsor: George Lucas Educational Foundation

Subject Area(s): Places for Parents　　　**Subcategory:** Miscellaneous

Grade Level(s): Adult

Description

The George Lucas Educational Foundation is a tax-exempt, charitable organization that disseminates the filmmaker's views regarding educational reform. There are sound clips and/or readings to describe the philosophy. A film and book have been produced to examine ways in which families can be more involved in their children's schools.

Commentary

Edutopia is a free, semiannual newsletter distributed by the Foundation to showcase effective programs and disseminate research findings. The information found here is interesting, but visually, the site is quite bland. One might expect a little more creativity in a Web site designed by those associated with Lucas.

Site: Helping Your Child Learn Science

URL: http://www.ed.gov/pubs/parents/Science/index.html

Sponsor: U.S. Department of Education

Subject Area(s): Places for Parents   **Subcategory:** Miscellaneous

Grade Level(s): Adult

Description
This short book is available completely online here or by request from the Department of Education. The two main sections included are "Activities at Home" and "Activities in the Community." All of the activities are based on the belief that science includes "observing what's happening, predicting what might happen, testing predictions, and trying to make sense of our observations."

Commentary
These are fun, hands-on activities which parents and children will enjoy doing together. Don't miss "Celery Stalks at Midnight." The best part of this book is suggestions of how to use things found in your community, such as zoos, museums, farms, libraries, and similar things, in order to develop scientific thinking skills.

NO GRAPHIC FOUND

Site: Helping Your Child Learn to Read

URL: http://www.ed.gov/pubs/parents/Reading/

Sponsor: U.S. Dept. of Education, Office of Educational Research & Improvement

Subject Area(s): Places for Parents   **Subcategory:** Miscellaneous

Grade Level(s): Adult

Description
This online book focuses primarily on what you can do to help children up to 10 years of age to lay the foundation for their becoming lifelong readers. Resources are available.

Commentary
When parents help children learn to read, they help open the door to a new world. Read to your children, and they will develop a love of stories and poems. Then they will want to read on their own, they will practice reading, and they will read for their own information or pleasure. This book is in the public domain and can be reproduced for educational purposes.

Site: Homeschooler Information Network

URL: http://www.homeschooler.com

Homeschooler Information Network **Sponsor:** Homeschooler Information Network

Subject Area(s): Places for Parents   **Subcategory:** Miscellaneous

Grade Level(s): Adult

Description
Promoted as the Internet Source for Homeschoolers, this site delivers pertinent information in a well-organized layout. Four choices simplify the welcome page into *Organizations and Resources, Fun and Games, Homeschoolers on the Internet,* and *Join the Homeschoolers Listserv.* Each page is loaded with links that are sure to tap information critical for parents who homeschool their children.

Commentary
Parents who are not homeschooling, but are interested in supporting their children's education using the Internet as a resource, will also find this site of benefit.

Section 04. Places for Parents

Site: How to Raise Drug-Free Kids

URL: http://www.drugfreekids.com

Sponsor: Reader's Digest

Subject Area(s): Places for Parents   **Subcategory:** Miscellaneous

Grade Level(s): Adult

Description

This online family guide seeks to give parents information, tools, and support to help keep their kids off drugs. Information has been divided according to children's ages, and resources are listed with links where applicable.

Commentary

The support groups (by age of child or topics, such as raising healthy boys, raising healthy girls, and talking to your kids about drugs) are only accessible to members of Parent Soup. Membership to this area is free, however, and it takes only a few seconds to join online.

Site: Jon's Homeschool Resource Page

URL: http://www.midnightbeach.com/hs/

Sponsor: Jon Shemitz

Subject Area(s): Places for Parents   **Subcategory:** Miscellaneous

Grade Level(s): Adult

Description

The Table of Contents presents the organization of the site into sections entitled What's New, Frequently Asked Questions, Online Discussion and Support Groups, Web Pages, Vendors, Offline Homeschooling Resources, and Miscellaneous. The author has homeschooled all of his children and provides both his advice and the ideas of others who wish to contribute to the home page.

Commentary

Updated frequently, this home page provides new information in a special section so that parents do not have to read through the same material. The Resources section will probably prove to be most helpful. There are reprints of articles, resources to write for, and information about curriculum for sale and exchange. Legal questions are dealt with in a separate section.

Site: Kidsource Online

URL: http://www.kidsource.com/

Sponsor: Kidsource Online, Inc.

Subject Area(s): Places for Parents   **Subcategory:** Miscellaneous

Grade Level(s): Adult

Description

Kidsource Online is a comprehensive source of information for parents of children from newborns to adolescents. The services, articles, and features are timely and include a wide variety of topical information about education, health, safety, and new products.

Commentary

The *Computing EDGE*, a free public service of KidSource OnLine, helps match needy schools with computer equipment donated by individuals and corporations. Interested educators and donors may submit information online which will remain posted for six months before resubmission is required.

Section 04. Places for Parents

Site: NCSS Online for Parents

URL: http://www.ari.net/online/parents.html

Sponsor: National Council of Social Studies

Subject Area(s): Places for Parents   **Subcategory:** Miscellaneous

Grade Level(s): Adult

Description
The National Council of Social Studies developed this Online Parents' Area to help children develop as citizens of a culturally diverse and interdependent world. There are Internet links, children's books, student news and views, and a listing of television programs that teach.

Commentary
Parents will likely find everything on this site quite interesting. The list of notable children's books in the field of social studies will be handy for trips to the library. You may be astonished at the monthly listing of worthwhile television programs.

Site: Parent Soup

URL: http://www.parentsoup.com

Sponsor: iVillage™, Inc. — The Women's Network

Subject Area(s): Places for Parents   **Subcategory:** Miscellaneous

Grade Level(s): Adult

Description
Parent Soup received a 5-star rating from Yahoo Internet Life—one of 12 such awards given each year. At Parent Soup, a community feeling is promoted through membership so that you can find others who share particular interests, hobbies, and concerns, who live nearby and enjoy the same Discussion Groups. Membership is free and takes a few seconds online.

Commentary
Much of the informational material is accessible (and valuable) to non-members; however, discussion groups are for members only.

Site: ParenthoodWeb

URL: http://www.parenthoodweb.com

Sponsor: ParenthoodWeb

Subject Area(s): Places for Parents   **Subcategory:** Miscellaneous

Grade Level(s): Adult

Description
Weekly spotlights and favorite articles await parents and parents-to-be at the ParenthoodWeb site. Articles of interest may be reviewed with the option to link to related topics and the opportunity to review and send comments about a particular topic.

Commentary
Most of the material is for the pre-birth through elementary audience. This site is a great way to gather information about the "chat," which tends to float about on topics such as whether listening to Mozart improves your child's math skills.

Section 04. Places for Parents

Site: Parenting Q&A

URL: http://www.parenting-qa.com

Sponsor: Families Plus LLC

Subject Area(s): Places for Parents   **Subcategory:** Miscellaneous

Grade Level(s): Adult

Description

For general information about parenting concerns, access the Parenting Q&A Web page. Some unique topics here include Grandparenting, Fatherhood, Religion and Spirituality, and Special Needs. Each topic is linked to an overview with selected books and resources for further reading.

Commentary

When your best friend isn't available and you just have to chat with someone about your parenting dilemma, contact the Cyber Mom Dot Com.

Site: ParentsPlace

URL: http://www.parentsplace.com

Sponsor: iVillage™, Inc. — The Women's Network

Subject Area(s): Places for Parents   **Subcategory:** Miscellaneous

Grade Level(s): Adult

Description

Parents are welcome at ParentsPlace, a site which offers articles ranging from pregnancy and birth to adolescence, fathering, single parenting, and more. Also featured are opportunities to chat with other parents and shopping at the ParentsPlace Mall. Visitors may sign up to receive a free weekly newsletter.

Commentary

Information abounds in the Children's Health Center, Pregnancy Center, Activities Center, Reading Room, and Weekly Features, all accessible (and valuable) to non-members; discussion groups are for members only. Membership is free and only takes a few minutes online.

Site: PBS Online

URL: http://www.pbs.org

Sponsor: PBS Online

Subject Area(s): Places for Parents   **Subcategory:** Miscellaneous

Grade Level(s): Adult

Description

The Public Broadcasting System is dedicated to providing quality television for families in the areas of education, culture, and citizenship. There is information provided here on the individual PBS stations and the upcoming programming. Each month you will find several feature articles tied in with selected news events and/or programs.

Commentary

There are several "neighborhoods" for visiting at this site, and some are designed to visit with your kids. PBS Kids provides a place for children to visit with their favorite characters from Sesame Street, Mister Rogers' Neighborhood, and other shows popular with them.

Site: Project OPEN

URL: http://www.isa.net/project-open/index.html

Sponsor: Online Public Education Network

Subject Area(s): Places for Parents   **Subcategory:** Miscellaneous

Grade Level(s): Adult

Description

Project OPEN is concerned with maximizing consumers' online experiences in relation to parental empowerment, intellectual property rights, consumer protection, and privacy. Informational articles and brochures may be accessed and printed from the site at no cost.

Commentary

Protecting Your Privacy When You Go Online and How to Get the Most Out of Going Online are two of the latest brochures found at this site. With a "knowledge is power" attitude, Project OPEN can arm and inform Internet surfers.

Site: The Children's Partnership

URL: http://www.childrenspartnership.org

Sponsor: The Children's Partnership

Subject Area(s): Places for Parents   **Subcategory:** Miscellaneous

Grade Level(s): Adult

Description

The Children's Partnership is a national organization which informs policymakers and the public about the needs of America's 70 million children by identifying trends and emerging issues, and providing analysis and strategies. Visit this site to review current legislation affecting children and the Partnership's view of how specific societal trends may affect children.

Commentary

Resources include a Parent's Guide to the Information Superhighway and a report regarding how the Information Superhighway affects children. Review the Next Generation Report, an informational tool reflecting current issues and strategies for leaders of children, youth, and families.

Site: The Multimedia Mom Network

URL: http://www.harbornet.com/mediamom/

Sponsor: Bonnie Scott, Director, MultiMedia Mom Network

Subject Area(s): Places for Parents   **Subcategory:** Miscellaneous

Grade Level(s): Adult

Description

This site labels itself "The Thinking Parent's Guide to Children's Software and Video." It is maintained by a group of parents and educators who work together to review and evaluate children's media. Their findings are posted monthly. Find video and software reviews, information regarding how to join, and Web site links that are "mom-approved." Bargain Bytes identifies good deals that have been found.

Commentary

This is a rich site for parents and teachers regarding appropriate software and videos for learning. One section, Too, Too Dumb, lists some of the "really dumb" things the group has found in children's media, e.g., animated crows singing rap music, creepy nightmare-producing ghosts in software made for pre-schoolers, and a child character that can be made to leap from the roof of a house to the ground without consequence.

Section 04. Places for Parents

Site: The National Parent Information Network (NPIN)

URL: http://ericps.ed.uiuc.edu/npin/npinhome.html

Sponsor: ERIC Clearinghouse

Subject Area(s): Places for Parents   **Subcategory:** Miscellaneous

Grade Level(s): Adult

Description
This is a comprehensive Internet resource for parents, with information devoted to child development, child care, education and parenting, and more. NPIN publishes an online newsletter for parents with timely information on issues of concern to them, special reports on children by age, and other reference information.

Commentary
Find high-quality information on topics relevant and meaningful to parents.

Site: Wizzywygs

URL: http://www.wizzywygs.com

Sponsor: Indelible Blue

Subject Area(s): Places for Parents   **Subcategory:** Miscellaneous

Grade Level(s): Adult

Description
Here you will find an online activity component from Wizzywygs, a catalog of software and hardware for K-12. The online component is designed to assist parents and their children in learning about computers and the World Wide Web. Find articles by parents, educators, and guest writers about issues of interest to parents as they strive to understand the best uses of technology by and for their children.

Commentary
This site is a fun and informative "newsalogue" for kids and their parents about computers. Though it is a commercial site where you can locate and order products, you can also find answers to your most basic questions and feel a little more comfortable talking to your kids about technology.

Site: WorldVillage

URL: http://www.worldvillage.com

Sponsor: InfoMedia

Subject Area(s): Places for Parents   **Subcategory:** Miscellaneous

Grade Level(s): Adult

Description
WorldVillage is a virtual community focused on family and home computing. Resources include reviews of computer software games and educational and multimedia programs. Also find a variety of interactive components, including chat, online gaming, and software that can be downloaded. Editorial content is closely screened to be sure it adheres to high standards.

Commentary
This is a helpful site for parents and also for educators. Use resources to help in your decisionmaking for purchasing software and find activities and articles of interest for you and for kids. Early childhood activities and a section just for kids are available.

5 WWW
MOSTLY FOR KIDS

Section Five identifies 61 fun-to-visit sites especially for kids, many of them featuring activities and help with homework assignments. Others focus on high-interest subjects such as sports and pets.

One of the sites in this section, "Kids Did This! Hotlist," sponsored by the Franklin Institute, presents a hotlist of student-produced sites in a variety of content areas and invites children to add to the sites listed. "Fun Things for Kids to Do," sponsored by Wangaretta Primary School, takes children on a trip to Australia. They hear the sounds of creatures such as the kookaburra, see animals like the rainbow lorikeet, make a hopping kangaroo, work on an Australian word search puzzle, and more.

Site: BONUS.COM

URL: http://www.bonus.com

Sponsor: The Bonus Network Corporation

Subject Area(s): Mostly for Kids   **Subcategory:** Activities

Grade Level(s): Elementary, Middle School

Description
Play, color, explore, inspect, imagine—the wonder of being a youngster is captured in the Bonus Web site's pages. Parents and teachers will appreciate the inherent instructional value of many of the pages. Visit the lab, the sports arena, travel back through time, and take a field trip—all without leaving the Bonus site. It will take a long time to exhaust your use of the material here.

Commentary
This site appeals to the child in all of us. Once at the site, navigation and commands may be completed within the Web site instead of the browser program. This is especially convenient when young children are surfing—the interface is arcade-like and lots of fun! Tell your parents and teachers they can find activities for the classroom or family room in a special section just for them.

Site: Carlos' Coloring Book

URL: http://www.ravenna.com/coloring/

Sponsor: Carlos

Subject Area(s): Mostly for Kids   **Subcategory:** Activities

Grade Level(s): Preschool

Description
This fun site is designed for kids who like to color. The child artist can select a picture, select some colors and a paintbrush, and that's all there is to it. The pictures can be saved.

Commentary
This is a somewhat slow process, though it may not be so apparent to young children. There are a limited number of pictures to color, and including more would be a nice feature. There is a link provided to directions for creating your own coloring book.

Site: Cyberjacques

URL: http://www.cyberjacques.com

Sponsor: ImaginEngine Corporation

Subject Area(s): Mostly for Kids   **Subcategory:** Activities

Grade Level(s): Elementary, Middle School

Description
Cyberjacques claims to be the captain of the grizzliest, silliest site on the high seas of the Internet! Find some great online versions of games: Fish!, Tangram Game, Tile Puzzle, Memory Matching Game, Connect the Dots, Plank Jumper, What's Inside?, Secret Word II, Hangman, and Simon Says.

Commentary
Linked sites are intended to be appropriate for kids but would be fun for adults as well. You need Macromedia's Shockwave plug-in to run the online games, but it can be downloaded from the site.

Site: CyberKids

URL: http://www.cyberkids.com/

Sponsor: Mountain Lake Software

Subject Area(s): Mostly for Kids   **Subcategory:** Activities

Grade Level(s): Elementary

Description

When first created by Julie and Mark Richer, CyberKids published original creative work from a writing and art contest. It has since been expanded to promote the youth community worldwide and give kids a place to express their creativity. This site has won many awards.

Commentary

Check out the art gallery and the reading room. Your favorite section might be the young composers...the selections download quite quickly, and it is fun to hear a composition and learn something about the composer. You are encouraged to submit your own music, art, and writing.

Site: Cyberteens

URL: http://www.cyberteens.com/ctmain.html

Sponsor: Mountain Lake Software

Subject Area(s): Mostly for Kids   **Subcategory:** Activities

Grade Level(s): Middle School, High School

Description

The online magazine is published four times a year and contains varying features. There are games, young composers, and an art gallery section, most of which features original work by young artists. An entire book is available online and was apparently chapter by chapter for 25 weeks, but the entire text remains for re-reading or printing.

Commentary

This attractive, friendly site encourages you to look at work done by other teens and then think of submitting your own in various contests. There is an advice columnist and new postings almost every week.

Site: Fledge

URL: http://www.fledge.com

Sponsor: McGraw-Hill Home Interactive, Oracle

Subject Area(s): Mostly for Kids   **Subcategory:** Activities

Grade Level(s): Elementary, Middle School

Description

First time visitors to the Fledge site should select the Check It Out page to see what Fledge has to offer and sign up if interested. Fledge offers Internet treasure hunts and archaeological digs, sports, pop culture and activity links, an electronic library, and a Tomorrow's News page featuring the acclaimed Tomorrow's Morning news for kids.

Commentary

When kids sign up and enter a password, they can customize Fledge. Tomorrow's Morning, a national newspaper, is available online, or teachers can order the classroom edition which includes a teacher's guide. A free trial subscription is available and may be ordered online or from the toll free number: 1-800-607-4410.

Section 05. Mostly for Kids

Site: Freezone

URL: http://www.freezone.com

Sponsor: Free Range Media, Thomson News Corporation

Subject Area(s): Mostly for Kids   **Subcategory:** Activities

Grade Level(s): Elementary, Middle School

Description
Remember pen pals? The current twist is e-pals, and Freezone has a page for kids to find one. Freezone encourages curiosity and exploration of a wide selection of articles, games, information, and activities. Follow "Mooselips" the rock band on tour, get help with homework, or become a reporter for the FZ Times, Freezone's weekly newspaper.

Commentary
Freezone is a monitored, safe site for kids with a totally monitored "Chat Box" and bulletin boards for kids only. Registration is required.

Site: Fun Things for Kids to Do

URL: http://www.ozemail.com.au/~wprimary/acts.html

Sponsor: Wangaratta Primary School

Subject Area(s): Mostly for Kids   **Subcategory:** Activities

Grade Level(s): Elementary

Description
Travel to Australia via this Web site. You can hear sounds of Australia such as the kookaburra or look at pictures of other animals such as the rainbow lorikeet. Work on an Australian word search puzzle, complete a dot-to-dot picture, make a hopping kangaroo, and more.

Commentary
The site is colorful, and the drawings are beautiful. Be aware that you will need a printer in order to participate in most of the activities. All of the activities were created by the children in this elementary school in Australia.

Site: Global Show-n-Tell Museum

URL: http://www.telenaut.com/gst/

Sponsor: Telenaut Communications

Subject Area(s): Mostly for Kids   **Subcategory:** Activities

Grade Level(s): Preschool, Elementary, Middle School

Description
The Global Show-n-Tell Museum is divided into wings by the age of the artist: The Egg Wing exhibits art from ages 0-2, Creeper Wing from ages 3-5, Parrot Wing from ages 6-8, Condor Wing from ages 9-12, and the Eagle Wing, which has art from ages 13-17. There is a brief description of each artist and sometimes a link to his/her family home page.

Commentary
The pictures are delightful! Follow the link to the home page of the artist of a picture you enjoy. You will often discover more paintings and even stories by the artist. This is a site which very young viewers can navigate with ease, but it can also be enjoyed by older students.

Site: GusTown

URL: http://www.gustown.com

Sponsor: Modern Media Ventures

Subject Area(s): Mostly for Kids   **Subcategory:** Activities

Grade Level(s): Preschool, Elementary

Description

GusTown provides children with a safe entry into the cyberworld by allowing them to send e-mail to Gus and his Cyberfriends (the inhabitants of GusTown), send artwork to the Museum for display, submit creative writing, watch movies at the Library, and more. Also there are activity ideas for grownups to do with kids inside each building, as well as related links.

Commentary

The representation of each page as a building gives younger surfers a visual image or environment which is easy to understand. Children (and their parents and teachers!) will like the activity ideas for kids found inside each building.

Site: Hands On Children's Museum

URL: http://www.wln.com/~deltapac/hocm.html

Sponsor: Hands On Children's Museum

Subject Area(s): Mostly for Kids   **Subcategory:** Activities

Grade Level(s): Elementary

Description

Hands On Children's Museum is both a nonprofit, educational institution and a virtual museum. The current exhibit theme is about the forest and the animals that live there. Games, jokes, and leaf collections combine to make this an enjoyable place for children.

Commentary

With the current theme, learn all about the forest and even pick up a few jokes...How do you catch a unique rabbit? Unique up on him...and how do you catch a tame rabbit? Tame way. Kids are invited to send their own jokes about animals into this site.

Site: Kidlink

URL: http://www.kidlink.org

Sponsor: KIDLINKS

Subject Area(s): Mostly for Kids   **Subcategory:** Activities

Grade Level(s): Elementary, Middle School

Description

KIDS-97 is a grassroots project aimed at getting as many children as possible in the age group 10-15 involved in a global dialog. There is language support for English, Norwegian, and Spanish with other groups being added as they find classrooms. While the purpose is serious, the site is full of activities which will be fun for older children.

Commentary

There are lots of interesting activities found in the calendar of events. The Multi-Cultural Calendar permits kids to share holidays and significant cultural events from around the world. A teacher and 22 middle school students in Saudi Arabia are taking others on a Sumatran Rainforest Trek.

Section 05. Mostly for Kids

Site: KidNews

URL: http://www.vsa.cape.com/~powens/Kidnews3.html

Sponsor: KidNews

Subject Area(s): Mostly for Kids   **Subcategory:** Activities

Grade Level(s): Elementary, Middle School

Description

KidNews offers a place for you to submit stories and poems you have written and read those written by others. You can also find a pen pal from around the world. In the Reviews section, read what other kids have to say about books, software, games, movies, TV shows, sports equipment, music, toys, cars, bikes, and more—or submit a review of your own. Or choose to read or write about various sports.

Commentary

This is an easy-to-use site with lots of interesting writing from kids around the globe. If you want to add your own e-mail address to receive pen pal mail from others, your parents will need to complete and mail a permission form.   And you might tell your teachers there's a section for them, too!

Site: KidPub

URL: http://www.kidpub.org/kidpub/

Sponsor: KidPub Worldwide Publishing

Subject Area(s): Mostly for Kids   **Subcategory:** Activities

Grade Level(s): Elementary, Middle School

Description

KidPub is a part of the World Wide Web where children are encouraged to publish their stories and news about their schools and towns. The stories will be reviewed (and perhaps reformatted), but they remain the property of the author. There are more than 18,000 stories online here, with Publisher's Picks for favorite stories and poems, and more stories coming every day!

Commentary

It's fun to have a story published and read by other people. Authors can send pictures with the stories, but most don't. Browsing through the list of stories takes a lot of time but can be fun. It is also possible to do a simple search, for example, for all the stories which have the keyword "mystery" or the word "horse" in them.

Site: Kids Backstage

URL: http://www.pbs.org/kids/

Sponsor: Public Broadcasting Service

Subject Area(s): Mostly for Kids   **Subcategory:** Activities

Grade Level(s): Preschool, Elementary

Description

Young children can hang out with their favorite PBS stars from Arthur, Mister Rogers' Neighborhood, Sesame Street, and others. Find a host of "knock, knock" jokes—you are invited to send in your own. Then check out the Web sites of your favorite TV shows.

Commentary

Non-readers will need some help at times from an adult, but most of the activities do not require extensive reading ability. When you get to the activities, you can decide if you are a "little Big Kid" or a "big Big Kid"...little is more fun.

Site: Kids' Corner

URL: http://kids.ot.com/

Sponsor: Oasis Telecommunications

Subject Area(s): Mostly for Kids   **Subcategory:** Activities

Grade Level(s): Elementary

Description

Kids' Corner displays artwork from children and invites them to write letters to the Corner. Other kids may reply to that letter, but it is posted on the site rather than routed to individual mailboxes. There is a puzzle, a game, and some sites for Websurfing.

Commentary

The games will likely not interest kids for long. The most useful part of this site is the set of links to other places that are fun and even educational. Almost everyone loves the yucky worms! The art is attractive and might be motivational to future artists.

Site: Kids on Campus

URL: http://www.tc.cornell.edu/Kids.on.Campus/

Sponsor: Cornell University Theory Center (NY)

Subject Area(s): Mostly for Kids   **Subcategory:** Activities

Grade Level(s): Elementary

Description

The Cornell Theory Center sponsors this program as a way to increase computer awareness and scientific interest among third to fifth grade students. Hands-on computer activities, videos, and demonstrations are designed to develop interest and excitement among kids. Find the 1996 and 1997 exhibits here online.

Commentary

Some of the activities are original at this site. Other activities are actually links to other sites. No one should miss "Cockroach World" or the link to "Bonus.com" where you will find hundreds of activities.

Site: Kids' World Online

URL: http://www.kidsworld.com

Sponsor: Kids' World Adventure Company

Subject Area(s): Mostly for Kids   **Subcategory:** Activities

Grade Level(s): Elementary

Description

There are two main characters at Kids' World: Lil' Howie and Virgil Reality. Lil' Howie offers activities in reading, language, and arithmetic. Virgil Reality provides activities in earth science, physical science, and life science. These characters and activities are related to software which is available for sale online.

Commentary

The online activity centers are fun. You may want to try an activity, so head straight for "Howie Activities" and "Virgil Activities." CD-ROMS are available for sale, if you and your parents find the activities worthwhile.

Section 05. Mostly for Kids

Site: Kidzeen

URL: http://www.cyberkids.com/issue10/

Sponsor: Mountain Lake Software

Subject Area(s): Mostly for Kids   **Subcategory:** Activities

Grade Level(s): Elementary

Description

This magazine is part of the CyberKid site. The magazine is published four times a year and features artwork plus articles, fiction, news, and activities. A large number of the features are constructed by kids and submitted in ongoing contests.

Commentary

You will find and enjoy fun activities in every issue of Kidzeen. Go back to the very first issue in January of 1995, read the article about ancient Eygpt, and try to solve the pyramid crossword puzzle. Then go to Issue #10 to try an Egyptian Word Search and a concentration game with hieroglyphs.

Site: Kite Flier's Site

URL: http://www.kfs.org/kites/

Sponsor: Andrew Beattie

Subject Area(s): Mostly for Kids   **Subcategory:** Activities

Grade Level(s): Middle School, High School

Description

Nearly anything of interest to kite enthusiasts and related recreation endeavors may be found in the extensive links listed at the Kite Flier's Site. Children of all ages who are fascinated with kites will find this site useful to locate plans and instructions for making kites of many different forms. Stories about kites are also listed under the Story Links.

Commentary

The commentary by Andrew Beattie, the person responsible for site maintenance, is useful when trying to sort through the large quantity of information contained here.

Site: Lego World Wide Web Site

URL: http://www.lego.com/

Sponsor: The Lego Group

Subject Area(s): Mostly for Kids   **Subcategory:** Activities

Grade Level(s): Elementary, Middle School

Description

Lego, a popular toy among many kids, has a Web site which includes Internet games based on popular products. Help the pirate collect treasure by navigating his boat, play Lego/Duplo (requires Shockwave Technology), or Build a Duck. Players who play "Build A Duck" and submit the duck they built are eligible to receive a Lego product awarded weekly.

Commentary

Visitors who join the Lego Surfer Club benefit from free downloads of Wallpapers, Screensavers, and Video Clips. The games are fun for kids of all ages! Younger kids will need assistance with some of the reading required in the games.

Section 05. Mostly for Kids

Site: Mister Rogers' Neighborhood

URL: http://www.pbs.org/rogers/

Sponsor: Family Communications

Subject Area(s): Mostly for Kids　　　　**Subcategory:** Activities

Grade Level(s): Preschool, Elementary

Description
This site features the cast and characters of the PBS television program, Mr. Rogers' Neighborhood. The activities featured are gentle and in keeping with the philosophy of the program. For parents, there are essays on child rearing, an extensive booklist, and the words to the TV songs.

Commentary
Almost all activities need to be printed and completed offline. Some activities are artistic (coloring and making gifts), while many involve simple materials for lessons (bubble play and talking about love). This is not an interactive site, but many children will enjoy looking at the pictures.

Site: nationalgeographic.com/kids

URL: http://www.nationalgeographic.com/kids/

Sponsor: National Geographic Society

Subject Area(s): Mostly for Kids　　　　**Subcategory:** Activities

Grade Level(s): Elementary, Middle School, High School

Description
Share your tale of terror, join "Spin" (National Geographic's global character) on a safari, play the GeoBee challenge (a daily geography quiz), or read National Geographic for Kids and National Geographic articles featured at the National Geographic web site. GeoBee Challenge players who reside in the U. S. and who answer every question correctly may become eligible to win a WebTV Internet Unit by Philips Magnavox.

Commentary
This is a great site for kids of all ages. You'll find safety tips for surfing the Web and enjoy lots of places on the Internet that are both fun and interesting.

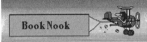

Site: The Book Nook

URL: http://i-site.on.ca/isite/education/bk_report/booknook

Sponsor: I-Site.On.Canada

Subject Area(s): Mostly for Kids　　　　**Subcategory:** Activities

Grade Level(s): Elementary, Middle School, High School

Description
This site is by kids and for kids, offering books you most want to read about and allowing you the opportunity to write about the books you read. Book reviews are grouped according to grade level or age group—K-3, 4-6, 7-9, and 10-12. You can search by title, author, publisher, or for any key word. There is also a list of books awaiting student review.

Commentary
This is a clever site that will encourage you to read new books and allow you to comment on those you have read. Books with reviews provide the author, the ISBN number, and information about the publisher. Read a review from one or more of your peers regarding what they thought about the book or add your own—including your rating of the number of thumbs up or down the book deserves.

Section 05. Mostly for Kids

Site: The Kids Web

URL: http://www.lws.com/kidsweb/links.html

Sponsor: Robert, Aaron, Derek, and Samantha

Subject Area(s): Mostly for Kids   **Subcategory:** Activities

Grade Level(s): Elementary

Description

Four kids (with their parents) have prepared this home page and maintain it. There is a large section of Christmas materials, including pictures, songs, stories, toys, and more. There are links to sites which specialize in news, art (low and high tech), history, and weather.

Commentary

The Webmasters report that the site is "seriously under construction," and that is definitely true. You may find several problems technically, such as downloading multiple, not-requested movies. Nevertheless, the site is so terrific that you will want to hang in with this group until things get smoothed out. All mail is monitored by the parents.

Site: The Yuckiest Site on the Internet

URL: http://www.nj.com/yucky

Sponsor: New Jersey Online

Subject Area(s): Mostly for Kids   **Subcategory:** Activities

Grade Level(s): Elementary, Middle School, High School

Description

Wendell, the inquiring Worm Reporter, helps you navigate this site of fun and interesting information pertaining to Science. Ask him any question you choose, even if it is a puzzling or strange, yucky or gross aspect of our world. Or click on Your Gross and Cool Body to learn about burps, spit, and more. How do you feel about bugs? Wendell can give you some amazing facts about them in Yucky Bug World.

Commentary

So you didn't think Science could be fun? Well, just check out this fun site! This is easy to navigate and interesting to read. Yes, some of it is yucky—all of it is fascinating!

Site: ThinkQuest

URL: http://io.advanced.org/thinkquest/

Sponsor: Advanced Network and Services

Subject Area(s): Mostly for Kids   **Subcategory:** Activities

Grade Level(s): Middle School, High School

Description

ThinkQuest is an annual contest that challenges students, ages 12-19, to use the Internet as a collaborative, interactive teaching and learning tool. You can find details and information for participating and also link to ThinkQuest Junior for students in grades 4-6. All the tips and strategies you need to get started are provided.

Commentary

Visit the ThinkQuest site, where the goal is to use the Internet to create Web-based educational tools and materials that make learning fun and contagious! Awards and scholarships of more than $1 million are available, and regional workshops are offered for teachers and coaches who want to learn the contest rules and support student contestants.

Section 05. Mostly for Kids

Site: Wacky Web Tales

URL: http://www.hmco.com/hmco/school/tales

Sponsor: Houghton Mifflin

Subject Area(s): Mostly for Kids   **Subcategory:** Activities

Grade Level(s): Elementary, Middle School

Description

Want to test out your knowledge of parts of speech and have some fun at the same time? Try out one of the Wacky Web Tales. Choose a tale, such as Mother Goose Gazette, What a Buy!, Lessons Aesop Never Taught, On the Track of Bigfoot, and many more. Fill in words for various parts of speech asked for and view the wacky tale that results.

Commentary

These can be completed over and over. Make your own or compare yours with one created by a friend. This is just a lot of fun! But to make the story read as it should, you do have to know those parts of speech!

Site: What's in the News

URL: http://www.cde.psu.edu/EdComm/WITNweb/witnhome.html

Sponsor: Penn State Public Broadcasting

Subject Area(s): Mostly for Kids   **Subcategory:** Activities

Grade Level(s): Elementary, Middle School

Description

What's in the News is a public broadcasting news program for kids. The aim is to present events in a clear, concise vocabulary and style so that young viewers can readily understand the important issues and events of our times. These pages contain both resources for teachers to accompany each program and also some direct activities for students.

Commentary

Each year, kids are invited to submit essays in response to certain topics; the best essays are posted on the Web site. Go to the library to find out what happened 10, 20, or 30 years ago this week, or to read more on specific topics.

Site: Writes of Passage

URL: http://www.writes.org

Sponsor: Writes of Passage USA, Inc.

Subject Area(s): Mostly for Kids   **Subcategory:** Activities

Grade Level(s): Middle School, High School

Description

Writes of Passage bills itself as the online source for teenagers. This site provides an outlet for teens who are creative, talented, and who have something to say by showcasing their work—poems and stories that reveal some of the experiences and emotions felt by teens. If you like to write, you may want to submit some of your own work. Or you may just enjoy reading the work of some of your peers.

Commentary

A subscription for your home or for a classroom has a fee attached, but check out the Teen Resources with links and information such as College Newspapers, College Web Site Database, High School Newspapers, High School Web Site Database, HTML Tools, On-line Dictionaries, On-line Foreign Word Translators, and more.

Site: ZuZu

URL: http://www.zuzu.org

Sponsor: Restless Youth Press

Subject Area(s): Mostly for Kids   **Subcategory:** Activities

Grade Level(s): Elementary, Middle School, High School

Description

Here is a place you can submit artwork, poetry, and stories you have created—or view those from other kids. The artwork section offers pictures to print and color and more. Or to submit written work, look at the Mystery Picture and write a story to solve the mystery. Speak out about your passion in Courageous Kids, tell a story about the place you live, or read stories from others about the places all over the world where they live.

Commentary

ZuZu used to be a real print newspaper that existed from the spring of 1992 to the summer of 1995. It was published by Restless Youth Press, Inc., a non-profit organization dedicated to publishing original work by young authors and artists. As of September 1996, Zuzu has resurfaced on the Web. This is a delightful site!

Site: 6th Grade Brain Bank

URL: http://www.zygomedia.com/61wc/

Sponsor: Patrick White

Subject Area(s): Mostly for Kids   **Subcategory:** Homework and Experts

Grade Level(s): Elementary, Middle School, High School

Description

Sixth-grader Patrick White's page includes links to Web information organized by category—math, science, English, and social studies. Also included are links to general homework-help sites, and you can submit your own links to add to the site. The sources offered cover grades K-12, with Math links.

Commentary

This site began as a science project by White and has become a very popular site. It is a very nice example of people assisting one another with information via the Internet.

Site: Ask an Expert Page

URL: http://njnie.dl.stevens-tech.edu/curriculum/aska.html

Sponsor: New Jersey Networking Infrastructure in Education

Subject Area(s): Mostly for Kids   **Subcategory:** Homework and Experts

Grade Level(s): Elementary, Middle School, High School

Description

This Web site gives you the opportunity to ask questions—homework or those of interest—of real experts. Link to sites where you can ask questions of professionals in an extensive list of fields. Experts are grouped into Science and Technology, Medicine and Health, Computing and the Internet, Economy and Marketing, Professionals, Personal and College Advisors, Library Reference, Literature, and Just out of Curiosity....

Commentary

Ask a question of an astronomer, a pharmacist, a banker, a guitar maker, or perhaps a movie expert. Links are included for locating people online, for colleges and universities, and other resources. Sponsors of this site include Stevens Institute of Technology, NJIN, New Jersey Department of Education, NJ/SSI, Bellcore, and PPPL. Get online and ask away! These experts are valuable for homework as well as general interest.

Section 05. Mostly for Kids

Site: Ask Dr. Math

URL: http://forum.swarthmore.edu/dr.math/

Sponsor: techweb

Subject Area(s): Mostly for Kids   **Subcategory:** Homework and Experts

Grade Level(s): Elementary, Middle School, High School

Description

Check out the Dr. Math FAQs (Frequently Asked Questions) and archives; if you still have not found the answer to your question, send your questions via e-mail. You will additionally find links to an online mathematics dictionary, a puzzle archive, and to the FAQs for the newsgroup sci.math.

Commentary

This site is the place to come for help with mathematics problems and assignments. The resources located here will be useful for both mathematics students and teachers.

Site: Homework Helper

URL: http://tristate.pgh.net/~pinch13

Sponsor: Bruce P. Pinchbeck

Subject Area(s): Mostly for Kids   **Subcategory:** Homework and Experts

Grade Level(s): Elementary, Middle School, High School

Description

This Web site has a number of strong search engines to help you successfully research topics. Links are provided to a multitude of sites, many of which are dedicated to English, math, science, history, foreign languages, or music. Links are organized by major subject areas plus current events.

Commentary

Supposedly written by a 10-year-old boy and his father, this site is primarily a long list of links organized by subject matter. Very brief annotations of each link aid in choosing something appropriate to help with homework. The "boys" say that they have won more than 25 awards—and well deserved. The scrollable list is very helpful to a student who has not yet targeted a search.

Site: Mrs. Fliegler's Homework Helper

URL: http://www.trabuco.org/

Sponsor: Trabuco Hills High School (CA)

Subject Area(s): Mostly for Kids   **Subcategory:** Homework and Experts

Grade Level(s): High School

Description

Mrs. Katie Fliegler, a science teacher at Trabuco Hills High School in Mission Viejo, California, will try to respond to e-mailed questions about science within 48 hours—though her own current and former students get priority attention!

Commentary

What a great science teacher, to put up a Web site just for helping out her own students! And then to open the door to all the science students in the world as well—what can we say? We hope including her Web site doesn't overload her server.

Site: Pitsco's Ask an Expert

URL: http://www.askanexpert.com/askanexpert/

Sponsor: Pitsco, Inc.

Subject Area(s): Mostly for Kids   **Subcategory:** Homework and Experts

Grade Level(s): Middle School, High School

Description

Ask an Expert is a directory of links to people who have volunteered their time to answer questions and Web pages that provide information. The categories are: Science/Technology, Industry, Health, Computers, Entertainment, Education/Personal Development, International, Resources, Money/Business, Fine Arts, Law, and Religion.

Commentary

The student interested in health occupation will be able to e-mail an arthritis specialist, a chiropractor, a health center worker, a disability financial planner, and many other medical specialties. Home economics students might wish to contact a nutritionist, pediatrician, vegetarian cook, or others. Scroll the list of experts or do a keyword search.

Site: Study WEB

URL: http://www.studyweb.com/

Sponsor: American Computer Resources

Subject Area(s): Mostly for Kids   **Subcategory:** Homework and Experts

Grade Level(s): Middle School, High School

Description

Study WEB bills itself as the meta-encyclopedia for student research. Search by keyword or topic or from a list of subject areas for the information you are interested in. Site listings provide a description plus an approximate grade level for which it is intended. A visual content rating indicates the presence of downloadable or printable images which may be useful for including in a school report.

Commentary

This is an extremely comprehensive site of over 47,000 URLs that are easy to use. Categories range from Agriculture, Animals & Pets, and Architecture to Teaching Resources, Transportation, and Writing & Writers. You are invited to add a link to be considered by the Study WEB staff. Students and teachers alike will find this a wonderful resource.

Site: The Author Page

URL: http://www.ipl.org/youth/AskAuthor/

Sponsor: The Internet Public Library

Subject Area(s): Mostly for Kids   **Subcategory:** Homework and Experts

Grade Level(s): Elementary, Middle School, High School

Description

Find three easy-to-access options: Ask the Author Biographies (there are photos and links to question forms for both authors and illustrators), Author Biographies (these also include photos and Frequently Asked Questions with their answers from some of the authors and illustrators), and AuthorLinks (Internet links to authors and illustrators on the Web).

Commentary

There is not a lengthy list of authors currently participating, but for those who are, you can click on a name and get a Web page with a biography, photo, and a link where you can ask a question. Some of these are well-known and some are newer authors, but it is fun to read about each and learn something about their backgrounds. Ask a question about their work and wait for the response.

Site: The Grammar Lady

URL: http://www.grammarlady.com/

Sponsor: Phoenix Business Technologies Group

Subject Area(s): Mostly for Kids   **Subcategory:** Homework and Experts

Grade Level(s): High School

Description

Go to "The Column" for selected grammar questions from the Pittsburgh Post-Gazette. The 1997 set includes examples of triple puns, e.g., "Focus Ranch"—where the sons/sun's raise/rays meat/meet. "English Grammar" offers resources such as Spelling Rules, Homophones, and others. Click on "Grammar Hotline" for the 800 number to pose a question during business hours or post your grammar question on the Web site.

Commentary

Reading through the online postings is informative. Dr. Mary Bruder is the Grammar Lady and, with assistants, provides this resource. She cites questions which are frequently asked and also notes a few that took some research, such as "Why is the first paragraph of a chapter in a book not indented?" and "Why is the name of the country (Philippines) different from the name of the people (Filipinos)?"

Site: You Can

URL: http://www.nbn.com/youcan

Sponsor: Jok Church

Subject Area(s): Mostly for Kids   **Subcategory:** Homework and Experts

Grade Level(s): Elementary, Middle School

Description

This is the official Web site for the science TV show, Beakman's World. Find answers to a variety of "kid-submitted" questions offered in a fun format, such as "Why Does My Voice Sound Different On A Tape Recorder?", "What Are Fingernails Made Out Of?", and more. Check out the interactive demos, too.

Commentary

This is a fun site for kids in grades 4-5 and older. One demo explores the question, "What is earwax ?" Learn the answer and click to view a photo showing how dust and other particles get caught in the trap of wax—gross! The Shockwave plug-in is required to run the demos, but you can download it from the site. Beakman and Jax make learning fun and interactive!

Site: Berit's Best Sites for Children

URL: http://db.cochran.com/db_HTML:theopage.db

Sponsor: Cochran Interactive

Subject Area(s): Mostly for Kids   **Subcategory:** Hotlists

Grade Level(s): Elementary, Middle School

Description

Berit, the company's on-line librarian, selects and reviews each site and gives a rating out of 5 points. The categories featured here are Just for Fun, Serious Stuff, Kids on the Net, Creatures Great and Small, and more. There are sub-topics under each division.

Commentary

Most links receive a "4" or "5", which is logical because the librarian rejected all of the sites considered to be poor. Both "Socks the White House Cat" and "Math Baseball" received a 5, and both are dynamite sites. The rating system seems to be accurate. There are plenty of sites for very young children, but the target audience should be able to read.

Site: Just For Kids!

URL: http://www.kings.k12.ca.us/kcoe/curric/just.for.kids.html

Sponsor: Kings County Office of Education (CA)

Subject Area(s): Mostly for Kids   **Subcategory:** Hotlists

Grade Level(s): Elementary, Middle School

NO GRAPHIC FOUND

Description

Subject matter experts screened many Internet resources and included these on a list which would be interesting for kids to explore. The list is very diverse, with lots of book sites but also a variety of links to projects and games.

Commentary

Be sure to visit "Welcome to the White House for Kids" so that Socks, the First Cat, can take you on a fascinating tour of the White House. You may also want to visit the "Goosebumps Forever" site if you enjoyed the book, since each character has its own room in the funhouse.

Site: Just for Kids, at Cal State Northridge

URL: http://www.csun.edu/~vceed009/justkids.html

Sponsor: California State University at Northridge

Subject Area(s): Mostly for Kids   **Subcategory:** Hotlists

Grade Level(s): Elementary, Middle School

Description

This is the "Just for Kids" section of Web Sites and Resources for Teachers. It is primarily a collection of links to other Web sites suitable for younger students. You will find it is organized into sections on Animals and Pets, Holiday Celebrations, Entertainment, Sports, Web Playground, and Homework Help.

Commentary

This is a great selection of Web sites suitable for younger students! It is the work of Vicki and Richard Sharp, professors of elementary education at California State University at Northridge.

Site: Kids Did This! Hotlist

URL: http://sln.fi.edu/tfi/hotlists/kids.html

Sponsor: Franklin Institute

Subject Area(s): Mostly for Kids   **Subcategory:** Hotlists

Grade Level(s): Elementary, Middle School

Description

This hotlist of student-produced sites includes science, art, social studies, mathematics, language arts, school newspapers, and miscellaneous. You can go into one of the categories or search by a broader set of subcategories such as Geography, Museums, Space Science, and others. Kids are invited to add to the sites listed.

Commentary

The logo for this site was done by a kindergarten student, Arash, and is of a Colorsaurus. Since the pages were mostly done by kids, the quality is somewhat inconsistent. Don't be too disappointed when you find that some of the links no longer work...most still do!

Section 05. Mostly for Kids

KiDS

Site: KIDS WEB

URL: http://www.luc.edu/schools/education/csimath/kidsweb.html

Sponsor: Chicago Schools Systematic Initiative

Subject Area(s): Mostly for Kids   **Subcategory:** Hotlists

Grade Level(s): Elementary, Middle School

Description

The Chicago Schools Systematic Initiative is funded to provide additional training and resources in science and mathematics for teachers and students. Teachers may want to explore the home page for the initiative in order to explore ways in which these activities might be used in the classroom.

Commentary

This is a series of links for Web fun in science and math. Some sites have only one game which might be quite simple, but many of the sites have multiple games. Be sure to look at some of the NASA sites and take a virtual tour of the Johnson Space Center in Houston.

Site: Surfing for ABC's

URL: http://www.siec.k12.in.us/~west/abcproj.html

Sponsor: Loogootee Elementary West

Subject Area(s): Mostly for Kids   **Subcategory:** Hotlists

Grade Level(s): Preschool, Elementary

Description

This site is the result of a project created by kindergarteners and first graders at the Loogootee Elementary West School. They used the Yahooligans search engine to find an interesting topic for each letter of the alphabet.

Commentary

Most letters will connect you to more than one site. Be sure to look at Cats, Dog House, Frogs, Raccoons—and there are pages about things other than animals. Your parents and/or teachers will find directions on how the class organized this project.

Kid Safe!

Site: The Kids on the Web

URL: http://www.zen.org/~brendan/kids.html

Sponsor: Brendan Kehoe

Subject Area(s): Mostly for Kids   **Subcategory:** Hotlists

Grade Level(s): Elementary, Middle School, High School

Description

This is an often-updated hotlist of sites that offer information for and about kids. Find activities and fun sites for kids, information for adults, and information about schools and education. Choose from among sites in the following categories: Fun Stuff, Homework Tools, Things for Adults, Safety on the Net, PenPals, Educational Sites, Children's Books and Stories, and Things for Teens.

Commentary

The sponsor of this site claims the goal is "to collect, in one place, a body of information that people can use either to let kids play with stuff on the Internet or to find the things they need for their work related to the care and education of children." That they have done. Kids, be sure to tell your teachers and parents there is some good "stuff" for them, too!

Section 05. Mostly for Kids

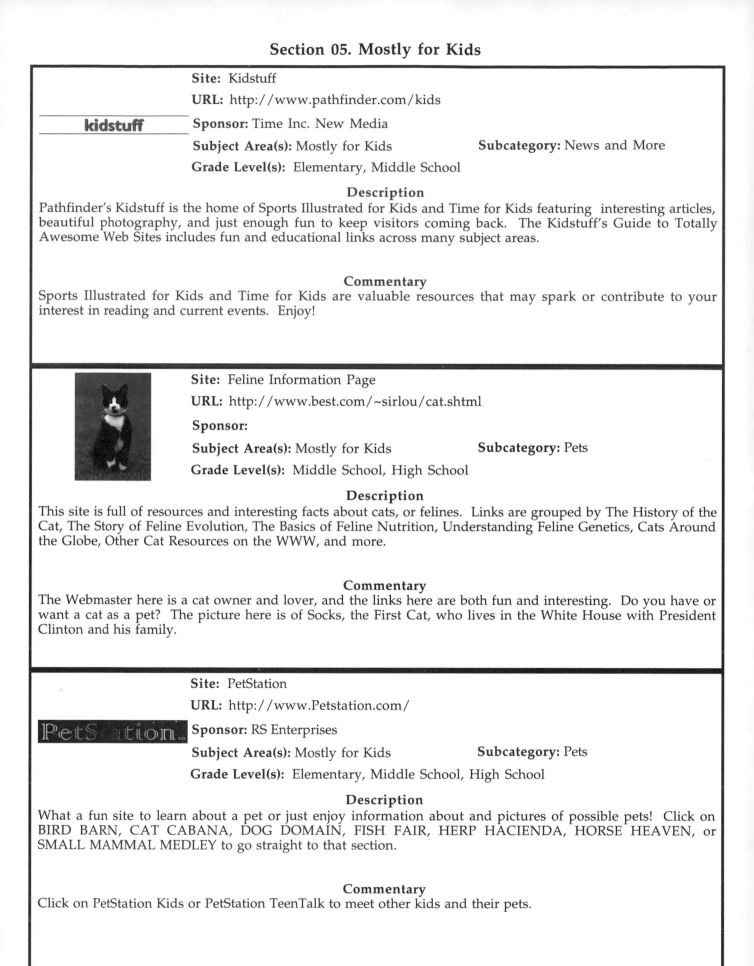

Site: Kidstuff

URL: http://www.pathfinder.com/kids

Sponsor: Time Inc. New Media

Subject Area(s): Mostly for Kids   **Subcategory:** News and More

Grade Level(s): Elementary, Middle School

Description

Pathfinder's Kidstuff is the home of Sports Illustrated for Kids and Time for Kids featuring interesting articles, beautiful photography, and just enough fun to keep visitors coming back. The Kidstuff's Guide to Totally Awesome Web Sites includes fun and educational links across many subject areas.

Commentary

Sports Illustrated for Kids and Time for Kids are valuable resources that may spark or contribute to your interest in reading and current events. Enjoy!

Site: Feline Information Page

URL: http://www.best.com/~sirlou/cat.shtml

Sponsor:

Subject Area(s): Mostly for Kids   **Subcategory:** Pets

Grade Level(s): Middle School, High School

Description

This site is full of resources and interesting facts about cats, or felines. Links are grouped by The History of the Cat, The Story of Feline Evolution, The Basics of Feline Nutrition, Understanding Feline Genetics, Cats Around the Globe, Other Cat Resources on the WWW, and more.

Commentary

The Webmaster here is a cat owner and lover, and the links here are both fun and interesting. Do you have or want a cat as a pet? The picture here is of Socks, the First Cat, who lives in the White House with President Clinton and his family.

Site: PetStation

URL: http://www.Petstation.com/

Sponsor: RS Enterprises

Subject Area(s): Mostly for Kids   **Subcategory:** Pets

Grade Level(s): Elementary, Middle School, High School

Description

What a fun site to learn about a pet or just enjoy information about and pictures of possible pets! Click on BIRD BARN, CAT CABANA, DOG DOMAIN, FISH FAIR, HERP HACIENDA, HORSE HEAVEN, or SMALL MAMMAL MEDLEY to go straight to that section.

Commentary

Click on PetStation Kids or PetStation TeenTalk to meet other kids and their pets.

Site: The American Kennel Club Online

URL: http://www.akc.org/

Sponsor: The American Kennel Club

Subject Area(s): Mostly for Kids   **Subcategory:** Pets

Grade Level(s): Elementary, Middle School

Description
This is the official site of the American Kennel Club, and you will find here a wealth of information pertaining to dogs and various dog breeds. Learn about how to care for dogs, tips for buying a dog, and more. Pictures are provided for some dog breeds.

Commentary
Wouldn't you like to have a dog? Find a variety of types of information about man's best friend at this Web site. Be sure to check out the "Dog of the Month." If you love dogs or are interested in learning more about them, you will find this site most enjoyable and useful.

Site: Welcome to Petz

URL: http://www.pfmagic.com/

Sponsor: PF. Magic, Inc.

Subject Area(s): Mostly for Kids   **Subcategory:** Pets

Grade Level(s): Middle School, High School

Description
Are you ready for this? Adopt a virtual pet at this site and then raise your computer dog or cat. These virtual pets live, play, and learn on your computer, and you have responsibility to take care of them. Be sure to also enjoy playing with them and discipline them when needed.

Commentary
Love your virtual pet and teach it tricks. Reward it for good behavior. You can even submit a story or picture of your computer companion for others to enjoy, too.

Site: AOL Net Find Kids Only

URL: http://www.aol.com/netfind/kids

Sponsor: America OnLine

Subject Area(s): Mostly for Kids   **Subcategory:** Search Engines

Grade Level(s): Elementary, Middle School

Description
Kids can use America OnLine's Net Find Kids Only for safe searching and links to Internet sites to entertain and inform. The Top Sites page lists links by category of interest, or use the search option to find kid-friendly sites on a particular topic.

Commentary
This site is a good location for finding other kid-safe sites on the Net, and searching is easy!

Site: Yahooligans!

URL: http://www.yahooligans.com

Sponsor: Yahoo! Inc.

Subject Area(s): Mostly for Kids   **Subcategory:** Search Engines

Grade Level(s): Elementary, Middle School

Description

This is a searchable, browsable index of the Internet designed for Web surfers ages 7 to 12. Search from eight categories of information appropriate for children: Around the World; Art Soup; Computers, Games and Online; Entertainment; School Bell; Science and Oddities; Sports and Recreation; and The Scoop.

Commentary

This is a great site that is frequently updated and enhanced. Find game tips, computer product reviews, computer use ideas, Internet safety issues, and more. This is a safe and easy-to-use site for kids. The index structure may be a little challenging for primary age children, but older kids will be able to successfully use the help screens.

Site: Sports Illustrated for Kids

URL: http://www.pathfinder.com/@@KqPxvQUATClhRoPb/SIFK/

Sponsor: Time, Inc.

Subject Area(s): Mostly for Kids   **Subcategory:** Sports

Grade Level(s): Middle School, High School

Description

This is the kids' version of Sports Illustrated, and the screens, sound effects, and features tell you that is so. Read the latest sports news or check out sports trivia. Click on Games to play some fun ones! Find different activities, stories, and items of interest each month.

Commentary

This is a site kids will enjoy! You will need Shockwave to run a few of the games, but directions are clear for downloading it to your computer—or you can download a stand-alone version of the games, if you don't have or can't run Shockwave.

Site: CyberSurfari

URL: http://www.spa.org/cybersurfari/lessons.html

Sponsor: Software Publishers Association

Subject Area(s): Mostly for Kids   **Subcategory:** Using the Internet

Grade Level(s): Middle School, High School

Description

CyberSurfari is an Internet treasure hunt in which students compete for cash and prizes to benefit their school's technology labs and classrooms. As each school team searches for cyber-treasures, they discover the vast educational resources, information, and opportunities available through the World Wide Web.

Commentary

This site also links to "Sites of Interest for Teachers."

Section 05. Mostly for Kids

Site: KidsCom

URL: http://www.kidscom.com

Sponsor: KidsCom

Subject Area(s): Mostly for Kids   **Subcategory:** Using the Internet

Grade Level(s): Elementary, Middle School

Description

Browse this site in English, Dutch, French, or Spanish. The motto of this site is "Learn to Play Smart, Stay Safe, and Have Fun on the Internet." In the World View section, find out about holidays around the world. In Making New Friends, find e-mail pen pals (key pals) or chat with others your age. Go to Learn and Earn to learn about computers and the Internet or Just for Fun for games and crafts—write stories and more.

Commentary

This is billed for ages 4-15, but is probably best for kids 9 or older. Bright colors and graphics make the site very engaging. Chat walls are geared towards 11 and younger and those 12-15. They are computer-monitored 24 hours a day, 7 days a week with the younger wall also monitored by staff a significant number of hours each week, as posted online. There is some advertising, but Ad Bug™ makes it clear when it occurs.

6 WWW
MUSEUMS AND EXHIBITS

Section Six steers you to 32 exciting sites sponsored by museums and corporations throughout North America, Europe, and Asia and featuring art masterworks from around the globe. The last site described in this section, "World Wide Art Resources," developed by a corporation with the same name, "provides a gateway to over 3,000 categories of arts on the Internet."

Two other sites included are "Smithsonian Photographs Online," sponsored by the Smithsonian Institute, and "Treasures of the Czars," sponsored by the Florida International Museum. The former offers a collection of photos relating to a wide range of subjects and events, many of them contemporary, such as the Million Man March. The latter highlights the Romanov Dynasty which ruled Russia from 1615 to 1917.

Site: Asian Arts

URL: http://www.webart.com/asianart/index.html

Sponsor: Various Asian Art Galleries

Subject Area(s): Museums and Exhibits   **Subcategory:** Miscellaneous

Grade Level(s):

Description

Asian Arts is an online journal for the study and exhibition of the arts of Asia. There are numerous exhibitions from around the world. The articles have an abstract but can also be read in full. This site is sponsored by a wide-ranging group of galleries which also exhibit some of their holdings.

Commentary

The Asian Arts Letter Board is a public forum for those who wish to post (and read) messages regarding the various pieces of art. Some people have artifacts for sale; others are looking for information regarding certain periods of history and/or art work. Settle in with a cup of coffee; the exhibitions take a lot of time to examine and are worth every moment to the art enthusiast.

Site: California Academy of Sciences

URL: http://www.calacademy.org/

Sponsor: California Academy of Sciences

Subject Area(s): Museums and Exhibits   **Subcategory:** Miscellaneous

Grade Level(s):

Description

The California Academy of Sciences is located in San Francisco and offers this Web site with museum exhibits and descriptions of eight scientific departments conducting research—its natural history collections are used by scientists worldwide. Find science, art, and other topics, or tour the museum. Scientists here are conducting research on systematics, the science of naming organisms and arranging them into groups.

Commentary

The online tour can be used to visit Reptiles and Amphibians, the Planetarium, or an area of your choice. Each week, the site focuses on a different scientist, organism of current study, or one of the locations where research is being done, so it is worth checking frequently. Students will love the classification of frogs in Kenya—including images, descriptions, and croaking, screeching, or guttural sounds for each.

Site: Diego RiveraWeb Museum

URL: http://www.diegorivera.com/diego_home_eng.html

Sponsor: Javier A. Rivera

Subject Area(s): Museums and Exhibits   **Subcategory:** Miscellaneous

Grade Level(s):

Description

Winner of multiple awards, this virtual museum is devoted to the works of Diego Rivera. The muralist painter was born in Mexico in 1886 and is considered one of the greatest artists of the 20th century. There is a gallery, murals, a magazine, film, biography, opinions, and links to other sites. The site may be visited in Spanish or in English.

Commentary

Since Diego Rivera is most famous for his murals, you may want to start in that section. Reproduction of the murals is excellent. Rivera captured some significant moments in Mexican history by using the earth, farmer, laborer, and appropriate costumes. A description of each mural would have been a nice addition...or use your imagination to compose your own.

Site: Discovery Begins Here

URL: http://www.sci.mus.mn.us/

Sponsor: Science Museum of Minnesota

Subject Area(s): Museums and Exhibits   **Subcategory:** Miscellaneous

Grade Level(s):

Description

The Science Museum is a real place in St. Paul, Minnesota. The Web site, however, uses parts of the museum to build six science/social studies discovery sites. While the site is designed to appeal to kids, there is also excellent teaching material here.

Commentary

Some 1st graders helped develop the site on exploring worms. It contains worm questions, answers, and experiments. Not to be missed are the worm songs and art. Don't forget to stop by the Whirligig Farm for a very special tour.

Site: Exploratorium

URL: http://www.exploratorium.edu

Sponsor: The Exploratorium

Subject Area(s): Museums and Exhibits   **Subcategory:** Miscellaneous

Grade Level(s):

Description

The Exploratorium is a museum of science, art, and human perception with over 650 interactive, hands-on exhibits. The Web site brings some of these exhibits to life so that they can be experienced by kids outside the state and provides links to sites with similar content.

Commentary

Each month the museum curator selects ten cool sites, so you may well want to start with them. Of course, that doesn't mean to ignore what is "Still Cool" or the sites of special interest such as the online activities in science. This could become one of your favorite sites on the Internet!

Site: Famous Paintings: Musee D'Orsay

URL: http://www.paris.org./Musees/Orsay/Collections/Paintings/

Sponsor: Musee D'Orsay, Paris

Subject Area(s): Museums and Exhibits   **Subcategory:** Miscellaneous

Grade Level(s):

Description

The painting in the logo is the "Ball at the Moulin de la Galette, Montmartre" by Auguste Renoir. The Web site also features the most famous paintings by Claude Monet, Edgar Degas, Honore Daumier, Georges Seurat, Edouard Manet, Henri de Toulouse-Lautrec, Vincent van Gogh, and others.

Commentary

This is a glorious site! With only 20 paintings, it is possible to enlarge each one and examine them more closely. Many first-time visitors to Paris miss this museum, which is world famous for its collection of Impressionist paintings. Even if you are not a serious art student, you likely will recognize a number of the paintings.

Section 06. Museums and Exhibits

Site: Henry Ford Museum and Greenfield Village

URL: http://hfm.umd.umich.edu

Sponsor: Henry Ford Museum and Greenfield Village

Subject Area(s): Museums and Exhibits   **Subcategory:** Miscellaneous

Grade Level(s):

Description

Take a virtual tour of the museum and historic Greenfield Village. Some of the exhibits that can be viewed are The Automobile in American Life, Made in America, and Presidential Limousines. You will find educational programs and archival information.

Commentary

This is the largest indoor/outdoor museum complex in the United States and has more than one million visitors every year. Its central theme is the process of innovation and change in American culture. Tech Trekkers is a science, technology, and adventure camp for 11-14 year olds. There are four 2-week sessions, each with a different topic. Web pages created by students at the camp can be seen here.

Site: Michael C. Carlos Museum

URL: http://www.emory.edu/CARLOS/

Sponsor: Emory University

Subject Area(s): Museums and Exhibits   **Subcategory:** Miscellaneous

Grade Level(s):

Description

Find a variety of artwork, including African, Ancient America, Egyptian, Near Eastern, and Asian works in the permanent collection, which is indexed and searchable. In the Odyssey Online section, students can explore various cultures and click on museum objects to learn more about them. They can also make their own discoveries as they work with puzzles, games, and worksheets.

Commentary

This is an excellent site with beautiful artwork and is easy to navigate for students. A 28.8 modem is needed as well as ReadAudio and QuickTime plug-ins, which can be downloaded.

Site: Museum of Science and Industry

URL: http://www.msichicago.org

Sponsor: The Museum of Science and Industry of Chicago

Subject Area(s): Museums and Exhibits   **Subcategory:** Miscellaneous

Grade Level(s):

Description

Regular features at this site include news about current exhibits, education, the Omnimax, unique gifts, collections, and general information about the museum. There is almost always an online interactive tour of a book or exhibit which is currently being featured. The emphasis at this site is to create interest in a visit, but it does provide things to see on the Internet.

Commentary

There are many sound clips and video clips at this site, and they are nicely organized in the archives after the exhibit is no longer the new item being featured. Check for current versions of plug-ins required; the technical people responsible for this site keep them updated.

Section 06. Museums and Exhibits

Site: National Gallery of Canada

URL: http://national.gallery.ca

Sponsor: National Gallery of Canada

Subject Area(s): Museums and Exhibits   **Subcategory:** Miscellaneous

Grade Level(s):

Description

Bilingual in French and English, this museum site specializes in the art of Canada in order to assist in better understanding the immigrant population, the developing land, the faces of diversity, and the cities of Montreal and Quebec. The viewer can choose a narrated virtual tour for exploration or visit the different sections of the museum as he/she chooses.

Commentary

While there is a variety of art in this museum and a lovely Renoir collection, it is certainly the collection of Canadian art which sets it apart from the rest. There is also a collection of Inuit art from the Arctic which includes both sculptures and drawings. Similar to most museums which are online, only a small part of the collection is available here.

Site: National Museum of American Art

URL: http://www.nmaa.si.edu/

Sponsor: National Museum of American Art

Subject Area(s): Museums and Exhibits   **Subcategory:** Miscellaneous

Grade Level(s):

Description

Visit the NMAA's virtual museum. Go to Research Resources to gain online access to its extensive holdings of art historical research materials. Enjoy the online exhibition tours or go to the Education section to find student and teacher guides that include videos and reproductions that can be used in classroom curriculum.

Commentary

There is an online edition of American Art with articles and commentaries. The variety of online collections can be viewed with or without audio and with selected pieces of video, some of which seem particularly slow in loading. "The White House Collection of American Crafts," now touring regional museums, is especially beautiful.

Site: National Museum of Natural History

URL: http://nmnhwww.si.edu/

Sponsor: Smithsonian Institution

Subject Area(s): Museums and Exhibits   **Subcategory:** Miscellaneous

Grade Level(s):

Description

Since the Smithsonian has a seemingly endless supply of resources, they frequently change exhibits within the museum as well as at this virtual museum. Head straight for the What's New section, since it will offer a rich selection of new exhibits in the sciences and social sciences.

Commentary

Global Warning: A Virtual Museum will keep you awake at night! Did you know that the number of cars on earth is expected to double by 2030? Find out what is happening, how broad the problem is, and what you can do about it.

Site: Natural History Museum

URL: http://www.nhm.ac.uk

Sponsor: The Natural History Museum

Subject Area(s): Museums and Exhibits   **Subcategory:** Miscellaneous

Grade Level(s):

Description

The goal of the Natural History Museum is to maintain and develop its collections and to use them to promote the understanding, responsible use, and enjoyment of the natural world. There is information available at this site regarding all of the permanent exhibits as well as some online exhibitions extracted from these main exhibits.

Commentary

The virtual Endeavour experiment is terrific! Based on a 3D replica of Captain Cook's ship, this experiment is designed to test the reactions of visitors to this type of exhibit. Download all the plug-ins, enjoy the experience, and let them know if you'd like to see more of the same in the future at this site.

Site: Natural History Museum of Los Angeles County

URL: http://www.lam.mus.ca.us/lacmnh/

Sponsor: Los Angeles County

Subject Area(s): Museums and Exhibits   **Subcategory:** Miscellaneous

Grade Level(s):

Description

Both an actual and a virtual museum, The Natural History Museum of Los Angeles County offers exhibits that focus on art, history, and science. The site is attractively organized with links to other museums in the Los Angeles area. A search can be done of the Web sites linked to this museum.

Commentary

There are many beautiful, fascinating sections in this museum. The Discovery Center and Insect Zoo are good starting places for exploration. Be sure to look at "An Inordinate Fondness for Beetles"—perhaps you already know that beetles are the most successful animal on Earth, representing a fourth of all living animals!

Site: Powersource Native American Art & Education Center

URL: http://www.powersource.com/powersource/gallery/default.html

Sponsor: Powersource

Subject Area(s): Museums and Exhibits   **Subcategory:** Miscellaneous

Grade Level(s):

Description

This award-winning site offers a "collection of Native American artistic symbols portraying powerful people, powerful places and powerful objects." Find Native American art collections, legends, historical information, information on ceremonial dances (such as the Fancy War Dance or Grass Dance), and much more.

Commentary

This is a rich and beautiful site filled with much information. You may be inspired by the Essential Blessings, links to people "who are walking the Beauty Way."

Section 06. Museums and Exhibits

Site: Scrolls from the Dead Sea

URL: http://sunsite.unc.edu/expo/deadsea.scrolls.exhibit/intro.html

Sponsor: Library of Congress

Subject Area(s): Museums and Exhibits   **Subcategory:** Miscellaneous

Grade Level(s):

Description

This hypertext museum was reorganized from the exhibition *Scrolls From the Dead Sea: The Ancient Library of Qumran and Modern Scholarship*. The exhibition describes the historical context of the scrolls and the Qumran community from whence they may have originated. It also relates the story of their discovery 2,000 years later.

Commentary

Students will be interested in the story of the discovery of the scrolls by young shepherds and the later work by archaeologists. The narrative is written in a condensed format, but there are some graphics.

Site: Smithsonian Photographs Online

URL: http://photo2.si.edu/index.html

Sponsor: Smithsonian Institution

Subject Area(s): Museums and Exhibits   **Subcategory:** Miscellaneous

Grade Level(s):

Description

The Smithsonian has used its major resources to provide this collection of photographs about a wide range of subjects and major events. Many are frankly contemporary: President Clinton's Inaugural, the Million Man March, etc. Other selections are based on exhibits such as Kayapo Indian Headdresses and Pacific Sea Snakes. It is possible to search the database by keyword.

Commentary

Many exhibits are simply beautiful, such as Washington's cherry blossoms. Especially poignant is the exhibit entitled *Personal Legacy: The Healing of a Nation;* it shows objects left at the Vietnam Veterans Memorial. More than 25,000 keepsakes have been left at the Memorial by visitors from home and abroad.

Site: The Allen Memorial Art Museum

URL: http://www.oberlin.edu/wwwmap/allen_art.html

Sponsor: Oberlin College

Subject Area(s): Museums and Exhibits   **Subcategory:** Miscellaneous

Grade Level(s):

Description

When it was founded in 1917, this was the first college museum west of the Allegheny mountains. At this Web site, you can find images of and infomation about ancient, American, Asian, European, and African art.

Commentary

These are excellent images. Current and back issues of the museum's online newsletter can also be viewed here.

Section 06. Museums and Exhibits

Site: The Dallas Museum of Art

URL: http://www.unt.edu/dfw/dma/www/dma.htm

Sponsor: Dallas Museum of Art

Subject Area(s): Museums and Exhibits **Subcategory:** Miscellaneous

Grade Level(s):

Description
Founded in 1903, the Dallas Museum of Art has major holdings in ancient American, Indonesian, and contemporary art as well as American decorative arts. The two largest galleries present works which describe the civilizations of the original Americans and the art of the pilgrims, pioneers, and other immigrants.

Commentary
Particularly attractive are the pictures of the outdoor sculpture garden. Don't miss "The Icebergs," an oil painting by Frederic Church which is considered a landmark painting by an American artist.

Site: The Field Museum

URL: http://www.fmnh.org/Home.html

Sponsor: The Field Museum of Natural History

Subject Area(s): Museums and Exhibits **Subcategory:** Miscellaneous

Grade Level(s):

Description
The Field Museum site features various ways to examine how life has developed over time, with particular emphasis on the Chicago area. At the time of evaluation, an exhibit on dinosaurs included a media page, a quick tour of the exhibit, a longer tour of the dinosaurs, movies, sound, games, and a teacher's guide too.

Commentary
One current feature, "The Man-Eaters of Tsavo," is based on a true story involving lions and the building of a railroad in East Africa in 1898. There are great photographs, an interesting story, and links to further information about this event. Look for games, animation of animals, and some mammoth bone music!

Site: The Franklin Institute Science Museum

URL: http://sln.fi.edu

Sponsor: The Franklin Institute Science Museum

Subject Area(s): Museums and Exhibits **Subcategory:** Miscellaneous

Grade Level(s):

Description
The Franklin Institute Science Museum is located in Philadelphia, Pennsylvania. It provides information about present and future exhibitions. For individuals who live too far away to visit, the aim of the site is to bring the resources and fun of a museum to the desktop. Each month, the staff of the Institute selects five favorite Web sites.

Commentary
Amy, the resident science student, walks kids through the exhibitions but also introduces them to a wide range of science topics. One current feature involves braces: the student will learn a lot about these metal discs for the teeth and can participate in a brace survey.

Section 06. Museums and Exhibits

Site: The J. Paul Getty Museum

URL: http://www.getty.edu/museum/

Sponsor: The J. Paul Getty Museum

Subject Area(s): Museums and Exhibits   **Subcategory:** Miscellaneous

Grade Level(s):

Description
Take an online tour of the J. Paul Getty Museum in Santa Monica, California, where you will be able to observe Getty's love of art. View the collections or read information about the varied exhibits, and if you are fortunate enough to be in the area, click on Visits to find information on locating and getting to the actual museum.

Commentary
The permanent collections include seven areas of art from Greek and Roman antiquities to contemporary American and European photographs. You will find a brief history of the collections and a selection of objects from each of the collection areas. Be sure to click on the picture to enlarge it for better viewing.

Site: The Museum of Modern Art, New York

URL: http://www.moma.org/

Sponsor: Museum of Modern Art

Subject Area(s): Museums and Exhibits   **Subcategory:** Miscellaneous

Grade Level(s):

Description
This is the Web site for one of the most famous museums in North America, located in New York City. Its collections include painting, sculpture, drawings, prints, architecture, photography, film, and video. In addition to information about current exhibitions, programs, and events, there are special sections for art study and research as well as other art-related resources in New York City.

Commentary
The home page for this site uses an animated object that will be slow to load over low-speed connections. To bypass that page, go directly to <http://www.moma.org/menu.html>.

Site: The Smithsonian

URL: http://www.si.edu

Sponsor: Smithsonian Institution

Subject Area(s): Museums and Exhibits   **Subcategory:** Miscellaneous

Grade Level(s):

Description
At the Smithsonian Web site, you can learn about the history of the Smithsonian, tour the many museums, and locate a multitude of resources in areas of natural history, art, science, astronomy, and others. Take specialized tours, such as A Kid's Guide to the Smithsonian, one of mammals or dinosaurs, or another topic offered.

Commentary
The Smithsonian is billed as "America's Treasure House for Learning," and it is just that! The site is rich with textual information and beautiful pictures. You can also search this vast site with a search tool asking for a range of specific criteria to help you narrow the information sources you find. Be prepared to spend a while, as there is so much to investigate and enjoy at this site.

Section 06. Museums and Exhibits

Site: Time/Life Photo Gallery

URL: http://pathfinder.com/@@D6Ch0aKJCQIAQKej/photo/gallery/home.html

Sponsor: Time/Life Corporation

Subject Area(s): Museums and Exhibits   **Subcategory:** Miscellaneous

Grade Level(s):

Description

This Photography Gallery contains seven sections. The People Gallery includes people from the arts, popular culture, sports, plus non-celebrities in various locations. Other galleries feature places, the arts, science, nature, sports, and war.

Commentary

Although most pictures are in black-and-white, it takes a little time to load each section. These are some of the best photos from *Time/Life Magazines*.

Site: Tokugawa Art Museum

URL: http://cjn.meitetsu.co.jp/tokugawa/index.html

Sponsor: Tokugawa Art Museum

Subject Area(s): Museums and Exhibits   **Subcategory:** Miscellaneous

Grade Level(s):

Description

This art museum ranks as the third oldest privately-endowed museum in Japan. It survived air-bombing during World War II and celebrated its fiftieth anniversary in 1985. The Museum showcases art and a vast array of heirloom objects and furnishings intended for the lord and his household, and includes eight designated National Treasures, fifty registered Important Cultural Properties, and forty-four Important Art Objects.

Commentary

Tour this museum to find an array of beautiful things as well as a rich collection of historic information. There is a Japanese version, if you choose.

Site: Treasures of the Czars

URL: http://www.sptimes.com/Treasures/TC.Lobby.html

Sponsor: Florida International Museum

Subject Area(s): Museums and Exhibits   **Subcategory:** Miscellaneous

Grade Level(s):

Description

The Florida International Museum opened its doors in 1995 with its premier exhibition, Treasures of the Czars. This virtual tour was created to promote the exhibition and remains with support from the Moscow Kremlin Museums. The exhibit highlights the Romanov Dynasty who ruled from 1615 to 1917.

Commentary

The Gallery of Treasures is amazing; the guided tour is quite well done. Playground of the Czars contains a variety of activities which all relate to the Romanov Dynasty. Do you know the height of Peter the Great—or how to say "yes" and "no" in Russian?

Section 06. Museums and Exhibits

Site: Treasures of the Louvre

URL: http://www.paris.org./Musees/Louvre/Treasures/

Sponsor: Musee du Louvre, Paris

Subject Area(s): Museums and Exhibits   **Subcategory:** Miscellaneous

Grade Level(s):

Description
These paintings, prints, and drawings are selected for this Web page because of their fame and/or uniqueness. There are antiques from Egypt, the Orient, Greece, and the Etruscan and Roman civilizations. Browse through the gift shop and find extensive information about traveling in Paris and visiting other museums.

Commentary
If you have ever been to the Louvre, you might find this site disappointing...or a relief from wandering around all day looking for the famous pieces. Each picture can be expanded to page size. If you are still interested in exploring the museum, return to the main site for additional art to view.

Site: United States Holocaust Memorial Museum

URL: http://www.ushmm.org:80/index.html

Sponsor: Holocaust Memorial Council

Subject Area(s): Museums and Exhibits   **Subcategory:** Miscellaneous

Grade Level(s):

Description
This is America's national institution for the documentation, study, and interpretation of Holocaust history. The exhibits encourage visitors to reflect upon the moral and spiritual questions raised by the events of the Holocaust. In addition to viewing portions of the exhibits, the reader can initiate database queries of documents about this era.

Commentary
One exhibit, Daniel's Story, was designed especially for younger visitors to become aware of life as it was growing up in Nazi Germany. Students will be interested in the story of Father Jacques who hid three young boys from the Nazis.

Site: Vatican Exhibit

URL: http://www.ncsa.uiuc.edu/SDG/Experimental/vatican.exhibit

Sponsor: Library of Congress

Subject Area(s): Museums and Exhibits   **Subcategory:** Miscellaneous

Grade Level(s):

Description
During the Renaissance when the popes and cardinals returned to Rome, they straightened streets, raised bridges, provided hospitals, and built splendid palaces and gardens. The church attracted pilgrims whose alms and living expenses made the city rich once more. In addition to the Vatican Library, there are exhibits of objects and rooms which emphasize certain themes.

Commentary
The Music Room contains beautiful copies of ancient musical scores and descriptions of the Sistine Chapel singers, but, alas, no music to hear. You will have a little bit better luck with the library and the origins of archeology. This site is probably most advantageous for the scholar who knows what he or she is looking for and not for the casual browser.

Site: World of Art

URL: http://www.bloorstreet.com/300block/8art.html

Sponsor: Bill Henderson

Subject Area(s): Museums and Exhibits   **Subcategory:** Miscellaneous

Grade Level(s):

Description

Apparently constructed by an individual art lover, this site provides hundreds of links to other art sites such as Vincent Van Gogh, the Louvre, art exhibits and galleries, art on the Web, and similar art resources.

Commentary

Although the site is not continuously updated, these links are to major museums and collections which continue to remain active. There are thousands of documents and images, so be prepared to wait quite a bit while moving from link to link. The quality of the pictures varies somewhat by site, but much of it is excellent.

Site: World Wide Arts Resources

URL: http://wwar.com/

Sponsor: World Wide Arts Resources Corporation

Subject Area(s): Museums and Exhibits   **Subcategory:** Miscellaneous

Grade Level(s):

Description

World Wide Arts Resources Corporation provides a gateway from this site to over 3,000 categories of arts on the Internet. These resources include art events, museums, and cyber galleries.   A search feature is provided that allows you to search the database of artists by keywords.

Commentary

There is information for each of the major art categories, but you will also find information about art schools, agencies, antiques, and crafts. The dance category yielded more than 40 types of other resources from African dance to tango.

7 WWW ONLINE REFERENCES

This section identifies 86 online references that are useful for teachers, parents, and in many cases, kids. These are organized for quick access into the following subcategories:

- ➤ BOOKS AND LIBRARIES
- ➤ CURRENT NEWS
- ➤ EDUCATION RESOURCES
- ➤ ENCYCLOPEDIAS
- ➤ FILES TO DOWNLOAD
- ➤ GOVERNMENT RESOURCES
- ➤ MAGAZINES AND JOURNALS
- ➤ MISCELLANEOUS
- ➤ SOFTWARE REVIEWS
- ➤ TECHNOLOGY
- ➤ WRITING RESOURCES

Several examples include the "Children's Literature Web Guide" (David K. Brown, Doucette Library of Teaching Resources, University of Calgary), an organized set of resources related to books for Children and Young Adults . . . "Encyberpedia" (Monte Cristo Information Services), an award-winning site that provides reference links to a variety of encyclopedias on the Web . . . and "Jumbo Shareware" (Jumbo, Inc.), a list of over 93,000 freeware and shareware software titles for downloading.

Section 07. Online References

Site: Books A to Z

URL: http://www.booksatoz.com

Sponsor: Books A to Z

Subject Area(s): Online References   **Subcategory:** Books and Libraries

Grade Level(s):

Description
The services provided at this site include production information, bookmaking materials, listings of publishers, new publications in French and English, and a Site of the Week. The reader can search the database and/or browse the listings, organized 1-9, and then alphabetically. These are publishers and distributors, not a listing of books.

Commentary
Be sure to look at the Site of the Week and especially the archives. You will be amazed at the variety of presses and resources available in the publishing field. You will find several links for bookmarking.

Site: BookWire

URL: http://www.bookwire.com

Sponsor: Reed Elsevier Business Information

Subject Area(s): Online References   **Subcategory:** Books and Libraries

Grade Level(s):

Description
This is a resource site for those interested in books. Find online book reviews, information on best-sellers, interviews with authors, and more. Included are specialized categories, such as the Computer Book Review and Quarterly Black Review.

Commentary
This is a useful reference for anyone. Teachers will appreciate the School Library Journal and other resources to be found here.

Site: Children's Literature Web Guide

URL: http://www.acs.ucalgary.ca/~dkbrown/index.html

Sponsor: David K. Brown, Doucette Library of Teaching Res., University of Calgary

Subject Area(s): Online References   **Subcategory:** Books and Libraries

Grade Level(s):

Description
The Children's Literature Web Guide is an organized set of resources related to books for Children and Young Adults. You will also find information about movies based on children's books. There are Features, Discussion Boards, Quick Reference sources (Children's Book Awards, Children's Best-sellers, and Teaching Ideas for Children's Books), and more. Brown hopes these resources will help guide people towards the printed works.

Commentary
This is a wonderful resource for parents, teachers, writers, and others. Check out links from this site to others organized as Authors on the Web, Stories on the Web, Journals and Book Reviews, Resources for Teachers, Resources for Parents, Resources for Storytellers, Resources for Writers and Illustrators, Internet Book Discussion Groups, Children's Publishers and Booksellers on the Internet, and others.

Site: Electric Library

URL: http://www.elibrary.com/

Sponsor: Infonautics

Subject Area(s): Online References   **Subcategory:** Books and Libraries

Grade Level(s):

Description

Here you can conduct Internet research by posing questions in plain English. The service searches over 150 full-text newspapers, hundreds of full-text magazines, 2 international newswires, 2,000 classic books, hundreds of maps, thousands of photographs, and major works of literature/art. Information is updated daily by satellite. Print, copy, or save information into a word processor with bibliographic information transferred.

Commentary

This is a subscription service, but you can sign on for 30 days free access to check it out. The service provides an incredibly easy way to accomplish extensive searching in the shortest amount of time and does not require knowledge of sometimes unfamiliar search query terms required by other search engines. Advanced searching options let you limit searches by source type, publication, date, title, and author.

Site: Gryphon House Books

URL: http://www.ghbooks.com/

Sponsor: Gryphon House

Subject Area(s): Online References   **Subcategory:** Books and Libraries

Grade Level(s):

Description

Gryphon House has a very complete bibliography of books for preschool and elementary students. Each entry contains an ISBN notation in addition to publisher, author, description, and a color photo of the cover. When an author has written more than one book, those are cited and summarized. It is possible to search by title, author, or keyword.

Commentary

This database has several nice features for teachers and parents. Many of the books are cross-referenced with activities and teaching strategies. As you browse through the library, you can drop a book you are interested in into a shopping basket. All books can be ordered by e-mail.

Site: Internet Public Library

URL: http://ipl.sils.umich.edu

Sponsor: Internet Public Library

Subject Area(s): Online References   **Subcategory:** Books and Libraries

Grade Level(s):

Description

The Internet Public Library was founded by librarians with the mission of serving the public by finding, evaluating, selecting, organizing, describing, and creating quality information sources. They have collected and cataloged 12,202 items at the time of this evaluation, with more to come daily.

Commentary

Some of the resources identified here have been organized under the two headings of "Teen" and "Youth"—this last group seems to be for elementary school kids. There is also a significant number of reference resources which can be located by browsing or with keyword searches.

Section 07. Online References

Site: Kids Web—A World Wide Web Digital Library for Schoolkids

URL: http://www.npac.syr.edu/textbook/kidsweb/

Sponsor: Syracuse University

Subject Area(s): Online References   **Subcategory:** Books and Libraries

Grade Level(s):

Description

This site is part of Syracuse University's Living School Project and is a catalog of sources on specific topics. You can link to sites in science, mathematics, social studies, and the arts, and you can also find links to schools with their own Web sites. A reference section links you to other types of useful information, such as U.S. census data, a zip code reference, a dictionary, a thesaurus, and more.

Commentary

There are great combinations of the serious and the fun. For example, in the searchable Shakespeare database, one can find a randomized list of Shakespearean Insults, such as, "Thou mammering ill-breeding maggot-pie." Because this site is linked around the world, some of the links are very slow to load or may be unavailable, but new locations are added frequently.

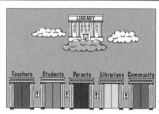

Site: Library-in-the-Sky

URL: http://www.nwrel.org/sky/

Sponsor: Northwest Regional Educational Laboratory

Subject Area(s): Online References   **Subcategory:** Books and Libraries

Grade Level(s):

Description

The Library-in-the-Sky provides an organized way to find what you need on the Web by listing links under the subheadings of teachers, parents, librarians, community, and students. Some links appear on more than one page when they are appropriate for more than one group.

Commentary

Parents may be overjoyed or overwhelmed at finding the number of resources available for them. Many are related to subject matter content areas so that they can be used to better assist children. The majority relate to family life and how it can be enhanced. There are numerous travel resources, too.

Site: The On-Line Books Page

URL: http://www.cs.cmu.edu/Web/books.html

The On-Line Books Page **Sponsor:** John Mark Ockerbloom

Subject Area(s): Online References   **Subcategory:** Books and Libraries

Grade Level(s):

Description

Updated weekly, the site provides the ability to search more than 5,000 listings by authors, titles, and subjects. It is also possible to browse several other sections devoted to new listings, women writers, banned books, foreign language books, and more. The Web site author accepts submissions and posts a list of requested books for information from readers who might have located these books.

Commentary

A wonderful section in preparation is the Prize Winning Books On-Line. These are complete texts of books which have won major literary prizes such as the Newbery, Nobel, and Pulitzer. These books are either out of copyright or are online with the permission of the copyright holder. Do take a look at *The History of Mankind*, the first Newbery winner from 1922.

Section 07. Online References

Site: 2002 Winter Olympic Games

URL: http://www.slc2002.org/

 **Sponsor:** Salt Lake City 2002 Olympic Organizing Committee

Subject Area(s): Online References   **Subcategory:** Current News

Grade Level(s):

Description

On February 8–24, 2002, Salt Lake City will host the XIX Olympic Winter Games for more than 2,000 athletes from 85 nations. This is the official site for postings of schedules, news, people, and links.

Commentary

There was not a great deal of information available at the time of evaluation, but expect the site to expand as the months go by. The schedule for different events is already posted. The links will also take you to the Nagano 1998 Winter Games and to the Sydney 2000 Summer Games.

Site: Boston Globe Online

URL: http://www.boston.com/globe/

The Boston Globe   **Sponsor:** Boston Globe

Subject Area(s): Online References   **Subcategory:** Current News

Grade Level(s):

Description

Articles at this site are updated every 30 minutes and come from the Associated Press National Wire. They feature news stories from around the United States. Breaking AP sports, business, and New England regional news is also available from the Globe Online.

Commentary

The *Boston Globe* is a cosmopolitan newspaper, carrying news from around the world as well as local and national news.

Site: CNN Interactive

URL: http://www.cnn.com

Sponsor: Cable News Network

Subject Area(s): Online References   **Subcategory:** Current News

Grade Level(s):

Description

Updated hourly, this Web site contains information on the variety of topics covered by CNN. Special features include world, U.S., and local news in combination with feature articles on sports, science, travel, health, and the environment. The rolling banner at the top of the page helps the reader select the most current stories without further searching.

Commentary

This site has good images, and they load quickly. News articles with QuickTime movies are annotated with a movie camera icon. The entire site is easy to read, attractive, and easy to navigate. If you like CNN, you'll like this Web site.

Site: Discovery Channel Online

URL: http://www.discovery.com/

Sponsor: Discovery Communications, Inc.

Subject Area(s): Online References   **Subcategory:** Current News

Grade Level(s):

Description

Online news is available daily in categories of history, technology, nature, exploration, and science. There are precise, annotated schedules provided here for both the Discovery Channel and the Learning Channel. The main categories for exploration are history, technology, nature, exploration, science, and a miscellaneous group called Live.

Commentary

Since this site changes daily, there is always a lot of new information presented in fascinating ways. The pictures from Mars appeared here the same day as did discussion of the events in Roswell, New Mexico. This site is for any with curiosity about the world around us.

Site: Electronic Telegraph

URL: http://www.telegraph.co.uk

Sponsor: Telegraph Group Limited

Subject Area(s): Online References   **Subcategory:** Current News

Grade Level(s):

Description

This Web site provides news stories from the UK and around the world from the *London Daily Telegraph* newspaper. Electronic Telegraph went online in November of 1994 and became Europe's busiest Web site within a few months of its launch. Find lots of hyperlinks from stories to previous stories and related resources.

Commentary

The design of this site is very nice, and it is especially interesting to read foreign perspectives on what is occurring in the news in the United States.

Site: Hotlinks

URL: http://www.naa.org/hotlinks/

Sponsor: Newspaper Association of America

Subject Area(s): Online References   **Subcategory:** Current News

Grade Level(s):

Description

This is the gateway to newspapers and other related media organizations' Internet sites. Newspaper links include U.S. dailies, Canadian papers, selected international papers, weeklies, business papers, and the alternative press. The reader may choose from many options including selecting a state (for the United States papers), looking at an alphabetical list, or examining one of the categories listed above.

Commentary

Newspaper readership may be down nationwide because some sections are so readily available on the Internet! Headlines, advertisements for rentals and jobs, and much more from hundreds of newspapers are now here online. You will still need to buy the newspaper for the complete story—and the comics.

Site: NewsPage

URL: http://pnp.individual.com/

Sponsor: Individual, Inc.

Subject Area(s): Online References   **Subcategory:** Current News

Grade Level(s):

Description

Easily create a personalized online newspaper. Just fill out a brief survey regarding your interests. NewsPage then searches the Internet to find current news items that match those interests. When you visit your personal newspage, you will see a table of contents on the left side of the page. Just click on a headline to read that story. To get the full text of some stories requires a fee.

Commentary

Choose a current events topic of interest for your class and let NewsPage keep you abreast of what is happening. Choose your level of service carefully. If you elect to visit your personal newspage each day, the service is free. If you want your personal newspaper e-mailed to you, there is a charge. This latter option is an example of "Push" technology.

NO GRAPHIC FOUND

Site: The Daily News—Just the Links

URL: http://www.cs.vu.nl/~gerben/news.html

Sponsor: Gerben Voss

Subject Area(s): Online References   **Subcategory:** Current News

Grade Level(s):

Description

This is a worldwide index of news sources, provided as a hotlist of links to other sites. Categories at the home page include: World, North Western Europe, South Western Europe, Eastern Europe, Africa, Asia, Oceania, U.S.A., the rest of North and South America, and other lists of news sources.

Commentary

There's nothing fancy here, but find easy access to news sources from around the world. The U.S.A. category, for example, links to dozens of sites such as ABC Hourly News, AP Wire search, CNN Newsource, US Information Agency Wireless File, Time and Time Daily, USA Today, White House Summaries, The Christian Science Monitor, and others plus online publications from numerous states.

The Nando Times

Site: The Nando Times

URL: http://www.nando.net/

Sponsor: The Nando Times

Subject Area(s): Online References   **Subcategory:** Current News

Grade Level(s):

Description

This news service provides daily—and sometimes hourly—updates in the broad categories of global news, stateside news, sports, and politics. There are links to many local news servers and to sources of information about entertainment, health, and science.

Commentary

This Web site is very nicely organized. For example, if you go to the politics section, you will find the top story plus headlines summarized with time of posting. The complete article is then easily accessed for viewing. And the sports information may be the best available!

Section 07. Online References

Site: The Wall Street Journal Interactive Edition

URL: http://update2.wsj.com/

Sponsor: The Wall Street Journal

Subject Area(s): Online References   **Subcategory:** Current News

Grade Level(s):

Description

Top stories in today's news, and quick navigation to the Front Page, Money & Investing, and other sections of topical interest are available to subscribers only. However, features available to non-subscribers include Careers.wsj.com, which provides valuable information, whether you are searching for a job or seeking career and workplace information.

Commentary

Non-subscribers can also access The Wall Street Journal Americas, which features news in Spanish and Portuguese—this may be of interest to a foreign language class—and the Mutual Funds Quarterly, Global Investing, Annual Reports Service for selected companies, and Small Business Suite with news and information for small business owners.

Site: Time Daily

URL: www.pathfinder.com/time/daily

Sponsor: Time Communication

Subject Area(s): Online References   **Subcategory:** Current News

Grade Level(s):

Description

Much of the content of the weekly *Time Magazine* is online here, though without the pictures. Stories are also available from *Time International*, which is not sold in the United States. There is daily news, and the site can be searched by keyword.

Commentary

This is probably not the best source for daily news, but the addition of the magazine plus its archives provides a great source of news. It is always interesting to read the international edition in order to get news from other local perspectives.

Site: Academe Today

URL: http://thisweek.chronicle.com/

The Chronicle of Higher Education **Sponsor:** The Chronicle of Higher Education

Subject Area(s): Online References   **Subcategory:** Education Resources

Grade Level(s):

Description

Academe Today is the online version of *The Chronicle of Higher Education*. With a long history of publication, this is often considered to be the definitive source of information about colleges and universities. There are features of general education news, an international section, interviews, and weekly columns.

Commentary

Published weekly, this is an always current source of information. There is an "Internet Resources of the Week" feature, and readers are invited to nominate their favorite sites. Once beyond the front page, readers will discover that most of the news is unavailable unless they become paid subscribers.

Section 07. Online References

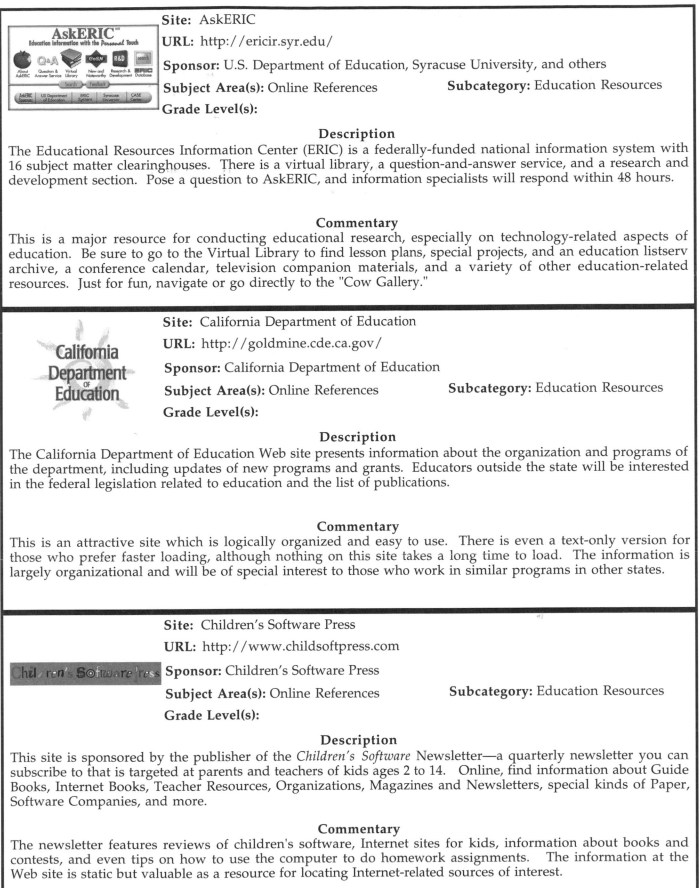

Site: AskERIC

URL: http://ericir.syr.edu/

Sponsor: U.S. Department of Education, Syracuse University, and others

Subject Area(s): Online References   **Subcategory:** Education Resources

Grade Level(s):

Description

The Educational Resources Information Center (ERIC) is a federally-funded national information system with 16 subject matter clearinghouses. There is a virtual library, a question-and-answer service, and a research and development section. Pose a question to AskERIC, and information specialists will respond within 48 hours.

Commentary

This is a major resource for conducting educational research, especially on technology-related aspects of education. Be sure to go to the Virtual Library to find lesson plans, special projects, and an education listserv archive, a conference calendar, television companion materials, and a variety of other education-related resources. Just for fun, navigate or go directly to the "Cow Gallery."

Site: California Department of Education

URL: http://goldmine.cde.ca.gov/

Sponsor: California Department of Education

Subject Area(s): Online References   **Subcategory:** Education Resources

Grade Level(s):

Description

The California Department of Education Web site presents information about the organization and programs of the department, including updates of new programs and grants. Educators outside the state will be interested in the federal legislation related to education and the list of publications.

Commentary

This is an attractive site which is logically organized and easy to use. There is even a text-only version for those who prefer faster loading, although nothing on this site takes a long time to load. The information is largely organizational and will be of special interest to those who work in similar programs in other states.

Site: Children's Software Press

URL: http://www.childsoftpress.com

Sponsor: Children's Software Press

Subject Area(s): Online References   **Subcategory:** Education Resources

Grade Level(s):

Description

This site is sponsored by the publisher of the *Children's Software* Newsletter—a quarterly newsletter you can subscribe to that is targeted at parents and teachers of kids ages 2 to 14. Online, find information about Guide Books, Internet Books, Teacher Resources, Organizations, Magazines and Newsletters, special kinds of Paper, Software Companies, and more.

Commentary

The newsletter features reviews of children's software, Internet sites for kids, information about books and contests, and even tips on how to use the computer to do homework assignments. The information at the Web site is static but valuable as a resource for locating Internet-related sources of interest.

Site: Computer Learning Foundation

URL: http://www.computerlearning.org

Sponsor: Computer Learning Foundation

Subject Area(s): Online References   **Subcategory:** Education Resources

Grade Level(s):

Description

This is the Web site for an international nonprofit education foundation dedicated to helping parents and educators use technology effectively with children at home and at school. One important section of the site deals with using the Internet responsibly, and a collection of student posters on this topic is available.

Commentary

The hotlists at this site also make it a great "jumping-off place" to link to collections of CLF-approved sites for students of all ages, family sites, home-school connection sites, and excellent Web sites for educators.

Site: Cool School Tools!

URL: http://www.bham.lib.al.us/cooltools/

Cool School Tools! **Sponsor:** Birmingham Public Library

Subject Area(s): Online References   **Subcategory:** Education Resources

Grade Level(s):

Description

Cool School Tools! is an index to the World Wide Web and other Internet resources for students in grades K-12. All of the educational resources are organized according to the Dewey Decimal System, with main categories such as philosophy and psychology, religion, social sciences, and much more. The quantity and quality of the resources provided demonstrate the involvement of professional librarians.

Commentary

This is just like browsing for information and tools for school in your public library—but maybe better. This is a wonderful resource for the home and/or the school with a limited library. The section on Languages is especially fascinating, with more than a dozen languages covered plus links to other foreign language resources.

Site: EdCentral

URL: http://www.edcentral.com/menu/

Sponsor: Creative Adventures in Education, Open Access Publishing Group, & others

Subject Area(s): Online References   **Subcategory:** Education Resources

Grade Level(s):

Description

This is a central site for access to educational resources of many types, including important events, press information, access to educational experts of various kinds, as well as grant and scholarship programs.

Commentary

The four principals in these organizations have more than 50 years' experience in developing online information services for educators.

Site: EdLinks

URL: http://webpages.marshall.edu/~jmullens/edlinks.html

Sponsor: Marshall University

Subject Area(s): Online References   **Subcategory:** Education Resources

Grade Level(s):

Description

This award-winning site exists purely to provide links to commercial sites, general public, government, libraries, networks, newsgroups, organizations, and projects. Since it is updated frequently, this is the place to check for links for which one might have an old address. Most subject matter areas are included, and the focus is on education-related Web sites.

Commentary

This site involves a lot of scrolling through long lists, and there is no search tool for quickly navigating the lists. However, once you become familar with the links, it is possible to scroll fairly quickly and link to almost anything you can imagine related to education.

Site: Georgia PeachNet

URL: http://www.peachnet.edu/

Sponsor: University System of Georgia

Subject Area(s): Online References   **Subcategory:** Education Resources

Grade Level(s):

Description

Not only do you have access to a wide list of resources within the Georgia University system, it is possible to find out other state information, browse other government servers, and explore news. One section, Other Resources, connects to search engines, education publications, libraries, newspapers and publications online, and technology.

Commentary

If you live in (or are interested in) Georgia, this is a great site. Other users will find it almost equally interesting, and it is nicely organized.   The list of newspapers which can be accessed covers the entire world. For example, *The St. Petersburg Times* (Russia) loaded quickly, is published weekly, and is printed in English.

Site: InfoWeb of the Public Schools of North Carolina

URL: http://www.dpi.state.nc.us

Sponsor: North Carolina Department of Public Instruction

Subject Area(s): Online References   **Subcategory:** Education Resources

Grade Level(s):

Description

"The Internet is very much like a used bookstore...after an earthquake." In order to assist with this problem, North Carolina educators have organized and catalogued many references of use to other educators. The Internet Library is comprehensive and up-to-date.

Commentary

Much of the news about education and schools is specific to North Carolina. However, the Classroom Resources section, and particularly the Internet Library, is outstanding. If you have had trouble locating something, this might be the place to find it.

Site: K-12 World

URL: http://www.k-12world.com

Sponsor: JDL Technologies, Inc.

Subject Area(s): Online References   **Subcategory:** Education Resources

Grade Level(s):

Description

K-12 World is built on the assumption that educators and students wish to maximize the time needed to find resources, study, or do research. This site provides access to Internet resources of value to this group and supports teacher interaction and communication among students.

Commentary

There are both commercial and professional organization sponsors for this site. The use of the right half of the screen for permanent icons is somewhat annoying when one wants to read a document such as a lesson plan. Many educators may enjoy the links to chat rooms by content areas.

Site: McREL...Making a Difference

URL: http://www.mcrel.org/

Sponsor: Mid-continent Regional Educational Laboratory

Subject Area(s): Online References   **Subcategory:** Education Resources

Grade Level(s):

Description

The Mid-continent Regional Educational Laboratory has a variety of funding sources and projects, but all have the common mission of making a difference in the quality of education. The Web site provides information about resources, products, services, programs, and projects available through this organization.

Commentary

"Educator Resources" is the most helpful part of this site. You will find links to resources for classroom use as well as a variety of reports and articles. Subcategories of links related more specifically to the Internet and technology are extensive, and the site seems to be updated every couple of weeks.

Site: North Central Regional Educational Laboratory

URL: http://www.ncrel.org

Sponsor: North Central Regional Educational Laboratory

Subject Area(s): Online References   **Subcategory:** Education Resources

Grade Level(s):

Description

This not-for-profit regional laboratory provides research-based resources and assistance to educators, policymakers, and communities in the north central part of the United States, and additionally makes some of these resources available to all educators. Information is provided about research projects, publications, and professional development activities.

Commentary

The centerpiece of the Web site is the Strategic Teaching and Reading Project designed to measurably improve student reading comprehension. This includes a School Improvement Internet Server with "best information" in a variety of categories. These categories can be examined by topics, or further searches can be conducted.

Site: Publishers Resource Group

URL: http://www.prgaustin.com

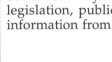

Sponsor: Publishers Resource Group

Subject Area(s): Online References   **Subcategory:** Education Resources

Grade Level(s):

Description

This site proves to be an excellent resource to check adoption schedules by state and subject, and to check the latest news and calendar of meetings and conferences. Utilize the well-organized, annotated Internet site list to research curricular and instructional issues on the following topics: Educational Publishing, Standards/Curriculum, Reference Materials, School Web Sites, Teaching Tools, PRG Fave Sites, and more.

Commentary

While this site has a decidedly Texas flavor (and assumes visitors will know Texas educational acronyms, such as TEKS) it is a useful resource for locating educational conferences and finding additional World Wide Web information.

Site: Software Publishers Association Education Market Section

URL: http://www.spa.org/project/edu_legislation/statedoes.html

Sponsor: Software Publishers Association

Subject Area(s): Online References   **Subcategory:** Education Resources

Grade Level(s):

Description

The Software Publishers Association has compiled a listing of Web site addresses for each state department of education. By linking to one's own state, it is possible to find further information about projects, staff, legislation, publications, standards, testing, and a variety of other resources. Readers may wish to compare information from a variety of states.

Commentary

In addition to the directory, the site also provides links to education market information and other education information. The Curriculum Standards section is extensive and focuses on national standards, but provides local information whenever possible.

Site: TENET (Texas Education Network)

URL: http://www.tenet.edu

Sponsor: Texas Education Agency

Subject Area(s): Online References   **Subcategory:** Education Resources

Grade Level(s):

Description

The Texas Education Network contains news and announcements, opportunities for educators, a resource center, the educators' forum, and K-12 schools on the Web. A Jumpstart section permits the reader to immediately select those resources relevant for an administrator, elementary or secondary teacher, parent, or student.

Commentary

Recently updated and improved, this is a great source of information for teachers and administrators, both inside and outside the Lone Star State. Go first to Jumpstart, select your category of occupation, and then browse the resources listed. The pages are attractive and in readable print. The links are annotated and current.

Site: The Learning Exchange

URL: http://www.peoplesoft.com/peoplepages/c/marcia_conner/

Sponsor: Marcia Conner

Subject Area(s): Online References

Subcategory: Education Resources

Grade Level(s):

Description

This site hosts a lengthy list of online learning resources for training, development and adult learning-related issues. A sampling of links includes AAHESGIT (the American Association for Higher Education's Information Technology list), ALTLEARN (a listserv for alternative approaches to learning), DEOS-L (an international discussion forum for distance learning), and ITTE (a listserv on information technology and teacher education).

Commentary

Instructions on how to subscribe to newsgroups and general netiquette are included. This site is not limited to school-related training and development issues, but also includes information for the corporate world.

Site: TIES (Technology and Information Educational Services)

URL: http://www.ties.k12.mn.us

Sponsor: Technology and Information Educational Services

Subject Area(s): Online References

Subcategory: Education Resources

Grade Level(s):

Description

TIES was organized to help educators apply technology to education and has been in operation for 28 years. It provides professional staff development, consulting, and technical support. There are annual conferences and workshops in its training center.

Commentary

While TIES was designed to provide services to Minnesota educators, most of the conferences and projects are available to other educators as well. Of special interest is the planning framework for technology-infused school transformation.

Site: WebEd K-12 Curriculum Links

URL: http://badger.state.wi.us/agencies/dpi/www/WebEd.html

Sponsor: Bob Koechley, Wisconsin Department of Public Instruction

Subject Area(s): Online References

Subcategory: Education Resources

Grade Level(s):

Description

The author is a librarian, and since 1993 he has been reviewing and modifying his list of useful resources for K-12 teachers. Directions for searching are included so that the visitor can easily do a keyword search of this database. The site contains hundreds of links in content fields and technology-related topics.

Commentary

Each month there is a list of new "must see" sites, and there is a lot of variety here. Some annotation of the sites would have been useful, but a curriculum resource search would be very targeted from this beginning point.

Section 07. Online References

Site: Encyberpedia

URL: http://www.encyberpedia.com/ency.html

Sponsor: Monte Cristo Information Services

Subject Area(s): Online References   **Subcategory:** Encyclopedias

Grade Level(s):

Description

An award-winning site, The Encyberpedia provides reference links to a variety of encyclopedias found on the Web. There is a subject index and extracts, and the list of very general and very specific reference numbers in the thousands. The section on maps and geography, for example, contains scenic information as well as detailed map references.

Commentary

You will be surprised at all of the encyclopedias devoted to very specific subjects, such as African wildlife. Both the main site and links are somewhat slow in loading because of the large amount of graphics, movies, and sounds—but there is a low-graphic alternative. Even cat owners will love "Cyberdog!"

Site: Martindale's The Reference Desk

URL: http://www-sci.lib.uci.edu:80/~martindale/Ref.html

Sponsor: Jim Martindale, UCI Library (CA)

Subject Area(s): Online References   **Subcategory:** Encyclopedias

Grade Level(s):

Description

Winner of numerous awards, this site provides links to hundreds of reference works. They include domestic and international travel schedules, dictionaries, encyclopedias, science tables and databases, health and science centers, and graduate programs.

Commentary

This is a very good place to go to locate a resource, bookmark it, and then go there directly on subsequent trips. The links are a little slow to access, probably because there are so many references here in many varied locations.

Site: C/NET shareware.com

URL: http://www.shareware.com/

Sponsor: CNET, Inc.

Subject Area(s): Online References   **Subcategory:** Files to Download

Grade Level(s):

Description

This is a one-stop shopping location for finding and downloading software for both Windows and Macintosh-based computers. Search for, browse, and download software, including freeware, shareware, demos, fixes, patches, and upgrades from a variety of Internet software vendors. There is a "Pick of the Day" for each type of computer and searchable archives by software category.

Commentary

While the sponsor works hard to make sure that only quality shareware appears on this site, users are on their own when it comes to software support, unless the author of the shareware can be contacted directly. In the unlikely event a downloaded file contains a virus, that is also the user's responsibility.

Site: Jumbo Shareware

URL: http://www.jumbo.com

Sponsor: Jumbo, Inc.

Subject Area(s): Online References   **Subcategory:** Files to Download

Grade Level(s):

Description

This site contains over 93,000 titles of freeware and shareware software for downloading. Search by platform or category to find programs of interest. The education subsection contains listings for foreign languages, SAT tutors, vocabulary builders, test makers, lesson plan makers, and classroom organizers—but only for Windows and DOS.

Commentary

Look no further—this site contains an extensive list of software for downloading. It appears that most of the titles have no solid educational value, but you will find many that do. The screensavers and games are fun. Parents and teachers may need to be extra careful in supervising the site since it is so extensive, with more programs added weekly.

UMICH MAC ARCHIVE

Site: University of Michigan Macintosh Archive

URL: http://www-personal.umich.edu/~sdamask/umich-mirrors/

Sponsor: Students at University of Michigan

Subject Area(s): Online References   **Subcategory:** Files to Download

Grade Level(s):

Description

UMich is an archive of shareware and freeware available for the Apple Macintosh and run by student volunteers. In addition to this main site, there are many mirror sites for ease in downloading.

Commentary

There are hundreds of files available for downloading but other than the filename, there is no information available about each one. Try a few to see if they are worth the trouble. There was no trouble getting into two of the mirror sites.

Site: Air Force Link

URL: http://www.af.mil/index.html

Sponsor: United States Air Force

Subject Area(s): Online References   **Subcategory:** Government Resources

Grade Level(s):

Description

There is detailed news regarding the Air Force over the past month, and archives are kept at this Web site for three years. Other sites include artwork, images, music, careers, and library resources. Each month an Air Force Web site is selected as the featured site.

Commentary

Take a look at the professional reading program for officers and enlisted men; each list is divided into basic, intermediate, and advanced categories. The career information is especially well-organized and useful to individuals inside the Air Force or those contemplating a career there.

Site: Bureau of Indian Affairs

URL: http://www.doi.gov/bureau-indian-affairs.html

Sponsor: Department of the Interior

Subject Area(s): Online References   **Subcategory:** Government Resources

Grade Level(s):

Description

The Bureau of Indian Affairs is responsible for the administration of federal programs for Indian tribes and for promoting Indian self-determination. There are approximately 1.2 million American Indians and Alaska Natives who are members of the 557 recognized Indian tribes.

Commentary

There is some interesting material on Native American Ancestry at this site and links to other American Indian Web sites. This is straight-forward statistical information of value, but could be made a great deal more interesting with pictures and some cultural insights included. Use it for the links to other sites.

Site: CIA Publications and Handbooks

URL: http://www.odci.gov/cia/publications/pubs.html

Sponsor: Central Intelligence Agency

Subject Area(s): Online References   **Subcategory:** Government Resources

Grade Level(s):

Description

Five publications are online: 1996 World Factbook, 1995 Factbook of Intelligence, CIA Maps and Publications, Chiefs of States and Cabinet Members of Foreign Governments, and Suggested Reading of Intelligence Literature. One can browse the volumes or conduct a keyword search.

Commentary

The CIA Factbook is a mind-boggling source of data! Search for any country and find maps and flags (which can be viewed in several formats). Then continue by locating information about geography, people, government, economy, transportation, communication, and defense...plus additional links under all of these topics.

Site: The Administration for Children and Families

URL: http://www.acf.dhhs.gov/

Sponsor: Department of Health and Human Services

Subject Area(s): Online References   **Subcategory:** Government Resources

Grade Level(s):

Description

The Administration for Children and Families (ACF) holds responsibility for federal programs which promote economic independence and social well-being of families, children, individuals, and communities. Programs overseen by the ACF include welfare, child adoption, foster care, protective services, runaway and homeless youth, health, and youth development.

Commentary

Use the ACF Web site to locate federal statistics, ACF programs and their Websites, fact sheets about ACF programs, information about the organizational structure and staff of the ACF, and more. This is a valuable tool for locating assistance for youth and families. Keep abreast of the latest information by using the "What's New" connections.

Site: The U. S. Army Homepage Index

URL: http://www.army.mil

Sponsor: United States Army

Subject Area(s): Online References   **Subcategory:** Government Resources

Grade Level(s):

Description

Material at this site falls into three main categories. There is leadership and organization information with names of current ranking officers. There are current news articles provided in brief as well as in detail. It is also possible to search the home page alphabetically by date or by keyword.

Commentary

The news at this site is updated every couple of days and presented in a very readable format. There is a paragraph about the story, sometimes a picture, but always the capability to access the full article if the brief is of interest.

Site: U.S. Department of Education

URL: http://www.ed.gov/

Sponsor: U.S. Department of Education

Subject Area(s): Online References   **Subcategory:** Government Resources

Grade Level(s):

Description

Find information about U.S. Department of Education policies and publications. Clicking on Money Matters leads you to grant information. Secretary's Initiatives highlights current program focus and initiatives. Look for resources available in your area and review publications and products that are offered. Many of the publications are offered in full-text form online.

Commentary

What education-related information are you looking for? Assessment? Disabilities? Magnet Schools? Technology? Find easy links to current and valuable information resources on a wide range of topics of interest to teachers and parents at this site.

Site: Welcome to the U.S. Department of Commerce

URL: http://www.doc.gov/

Sponsor: U.S. Department of Commerce

Subject Area(s): Online References   **Subcategory:** Government Resources

Grade Level(s):

Description

The U.S. Department of Commerce has responsibilities including expanding U.S. exports, developing innovative technologies, gathering and disseminating statistical data, measuring economic growth, granting patents, promoting minority entrepreneurship, predicting the weather, and monitoring stewardship. This is its Web site.

Commentary

Students, parents, and teachers can find a variety of resources at this site. Some of particular interest might include information and statistics about the country's economy or the section dealing with science and technology. Follow links to visit the White House, search for Federal job opportunities, and more.

Site: Curriculum Administrator Magazine

URL: http://www.edmediausa.com

Sponsor: Curriculum Administrator Magazine

Subject Area(s): Online References   **Subcategory:** Magazines and Journals

Grade Level(s):

Description

The main frame on this site's home page talks about this month's featured product and lists recent feature stories in the print version of this established magazine. Scan the left-side frame, which contains an extremely comprehensive list of resources for every aspect of teaching technology from A/V Equipment, to Home & School Products, to Professional Development Tools, to Testing/Assessment Topics—and more!

Commentary

The graphic image at the top of the page is an illustration from the current month's feature product and will change each month. This is a strong site for varied resources of interest to curriculum and technology administrators.

E·ZINE·LIST

Site: E-ZINE-LIST

URL: http://www.meer.net/~johnl/e-zine-list/index.html

Sponsor: John Labovitz

Subject Area(s): Online References   **Subcategory:** Magazines and Journals

Grade Level(s):

Description

E-zines are magazines published online. In May of 1997, this site contained 1,785 zines. The reader can browse in two ways: a list of keywords is provided for searching, or the reader may see the entire list of zines available.

Commentary

While parents and teachers will probably want to provide supervision when this site is used, there is actually quite a bit of worthwhile information. Some zines are written for youth by youth, with varying content. Even searches on innocent-sounding words can lead to strange sites, and some zines with somewhat titillating titles can be quite respectable.

Instructor

Site: Instructor Magazine

URL: http://www.scholastic.com/Instructor/

Sponsor: Scholastic Inc.

Subject Area(s): Online References   **Subcategory:** Magazines and Journals

Grade Level(s):

Description

Based on (but not identical to) the *Instructor Mazagine* for teachers, this Web site provides strategies for integrating the curriculum and meeting the needs of kids. There is a cover story, assessment answers, interaction, grade level focus, and professional development.

Commentary

This site is updated daily. The Integrating the Curriculum section is outstanding, offering ideas for K-6 teachers in improving reading and using technology, plus teaching spelling, math, science, social studies, and art. Check in frequently for contests and offers of reduced prices on software.

Site: Interactive Teacher

URL: http://www.interactiveteacher.com/ito/itdirect.stm

TEACHER InterActive

Sponsor: Ann E. Dotes

Subject Area(s): Online References   **Subcategory:** Magazines and Journals

Grade Level(s):

Description

Find issues of this magazine available online. There are some recurring features such as techniques, strategies, mentors, reviews, and feature articles. You will see a heavy technology focus, but the magazine covers all aspects of the teacher's job.

Commentary

The "After School" feature has included articles on calculating net worth, auto repair, road to fitness, and travel. A delightful article was found on the Dick and Jane books (with pictures). Did you know that the books were first published in 1930 and used for more than 35 years?

Site: Media & Methods

URL: http://www.media-methods.com

Sponsor: American Society of Educators

Subject Area(s): Online References   **Subcategory:** Magazines and Journals

Grade Level(s):

Description

This is the online version of an established print publication, *Media & Methods*. Of particular interest to teachers and other school personnel will be the buyers' guide which includes information about virtually every kind of technology-related product suitable for use in schools.

Commentary

You will also find a searchable archive of past articles published in the print version of the magazine and a hotlist of great sites to visit.

Site: Midlink Magazine

URL: http://longwood.cs.ucf.edu:80/~MidLink

Sponsor: North Carolina Department of Public Instruction

Subject Area(s): Online References   **Subcategory:** Magazines and Journals

Grade Level(s):

Description

Winner of many awards since its inception in 1994, this electronic magazine for kids in the middle grades is actually created by the kids. Each issue has a theme, and back issues are available online. Articles range from somewhat serious, such as the one about St. Francis of Assisi, to games and animation.

Commentary

A fun part of the site is the list of appealing home pages from other schools. Midlink staff invite you to submit your school's home page. You will find this is also a great place to get ideas for a home page you are developing or enhancing. The staff has also selected a number of engaging sites to link to which are fun and/or educational.

Site: MultiMedia Schools

URL: http://www.infotoday.com/MMSchools/

Sponsor: Information Today, Inc.

Subject Area(s): Online References   **Subcategory:** Magazines and Journals

Grade Level(s):

Description

This online version of *MultiMedia Schools Magazine* focuses on CD-ROM, multimedia, online, and Internet resources used in today's K-12 classrooms. Articles, columns, news, and product reviews are contributed by practicing educators who use these technologies. Find editorials, Internet-focused columns, product reviews, current news stories, and more.

Commentary

Find online articles of interest and take advantage of the archived issues available as well.

Site: National Geographic Online

URL: http://www.nationalgeographic.com

Sponsor: National Geographic Society

Subject Area(s): Online References   **Subcategory:** Magazines and Journals

Grade Level(s):

Description

This world-famous magazine provides parts of its resources online for kids and adults. A current feature on Cats (both domestic and wild) describes the perfect physiology of the animals. A companion piece entitled "CyberTiger" is designed for the younger reader.

Commentary

Updated daily, there is always something new of interest to read. "The Cover Game" presents the 108 years of National Geographic's coverage with a chance to match events to the year of publication for prizes—maybe Mom or Dad will help.

Site: School Planning and Management

URL: http://www.spmmag.com

Sponsor: Peter Li, Inc.

Subject Area(s): Online References   **Subcategory:** Magazines and Journals

Grade Level(s):

Description

This is the Internet home for an established print magazine for chief administrators, superintendents, business office officials, and technology managers in schools. Computer labs have a number of physical requirements, including physical space, electricity, network connectivity, and a number of other important characteristics. This is the place to keep track of what other districts and the industry are doing to address those needs.

Commentary

District technology coordinators, purchasing office staff, and others will find a number of valuable resources either on this site or via the links hotlisted here.

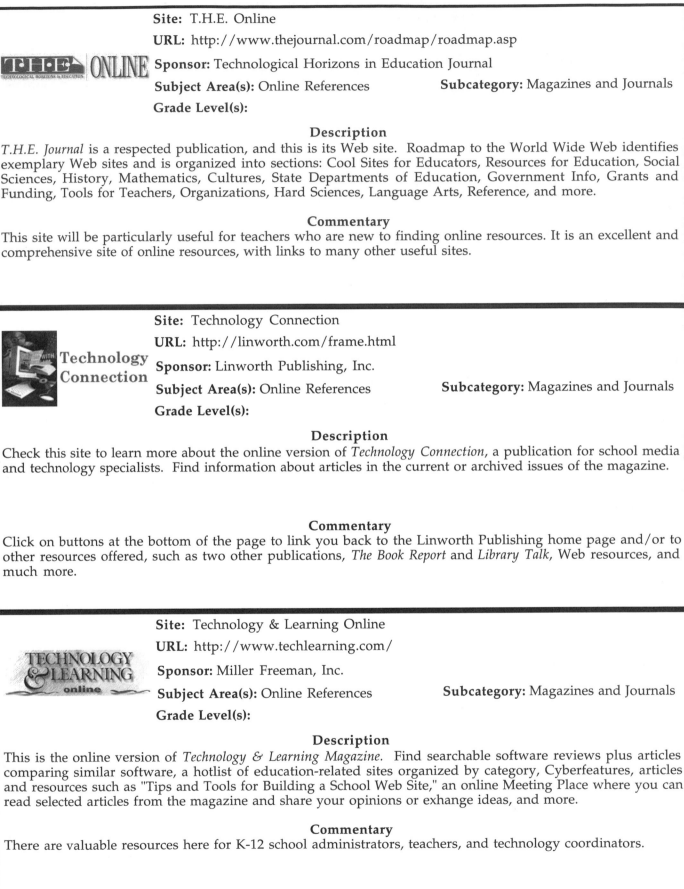

Site: T.H.E. Online

URL: http://www.thejournal.com/roadmap/roadmap.asp

Sponsor: Technological Horizons in Education Journal

Subject Area(s): Online References   **Subcategory:** Magazines and Journals

Grade Level(s):

Description
T.H.E. Journal is a respected publication, and this is its Web site. Roadmap to the World Wide Web identifies exemplary Web sites and is organized into sections: Cool Sites for Educators, Resources for Education, Social Sciences, History, Mathematics, Cultures, State Departments of Education, Government Info, Grants and Funding, Tools for Teachers, Organizations, Hard Sciences, Language Arts, Reference, and more.

Commentary
This site will be particularly useful for teachers who are new to finding online resources. It is an excellent and comprehensive site of online resources, with links to many other useful sites.

Site: Technology Connection

URL: http://linworth.com/frame.html

Sponsor: Linworth Publishing, Inc.

Subject Area(s): Online References   **Subcategory:** Magazines and Journals

Grade Level(s):

Description
Check this site to learn more about the online version of *Technology Connection*, a publication for school media and technology specialists. Find information about articles in the current or archived issues of the magazine.

Commentary
Click on buttons at the bottom of the page to link you back to the Linworth Publishing home page and/or to other resources offered, such as two other publications, *The Book Report* and *Library Talk*, Web resources, and much more.

Site: Technology & Learning Online

URL: http://www.techlearning.com/

Sponsor: Miller Freeman, Inc.

Subject Area(s): Online References   **Subcategory:** Magazines and Journals

Grade Level(s):

Description
This is the online version of *Technology & Learning Magazine*. Find searchable software reviews plus articles comparing similar software, a hotlist of education-related sites organized by category, Cyberfeatures, articles and resources such as "Tips and Tools for Building a School Web Site," an online Meeting Place where you can read selected articles from the magazine and share your opinions or exhange ideas, and more.

Commentary
There are valuable resources here for K-12 school administrators, teachers, and technology coordinators.

Site: The Electronic Newsstand

URL: http://www.enews.com

Sponsor: The Electronic Newsstand

Subject Area(s): Online References   **Subcategory:** Magazines and Journals

Grade Level(s):

Description

The Electronic Newsstand is home to more than 200 actual magazine sites, plus it provides links to 2,000 other magazine-related sites. For each magazine hosted, there is a table of contents, some cover art, sample articles, and information about a subscription.

Commentary

Because this is such a large site, there is quite a bit of loading time as you shift from page to page. A wide variety of magazines is available, though. Keyword searches can be done, but can only access the sample articles online. The main purpose of the site is to stimulate interest in a magazine in order for the reader to subscribe.

Site: The Heller Reports

URL: http://HellerReports.com

Sponsor: Nelson B. Heller & Associates

Subject Area(s): Online References   **Subcategory:** Magazines and Journals

Grade Level(s):

Description

This is the Internet home for a collection of print-based newsletters for industry executives in the educational technology business and their counterparts in school districts and state departments of education throughout the United States. You will also find information on Desktop EdNET Pro, an online version of the newsletters, as well as information regarding the EdNET Conferences, which are sponsored by The Heller Reports.

Commentary

Check out this site to find out what is happening in the world of educational technology—in the schools, in established firms, and in start-up technology-based companies—as seen by industry movers and shakers.

Site: www.PopSci.com

URL: http://www.popsci.com

Sponsor: Popular Science Magazine

Subject Area(s): Online References   **Subcategory:** Magazines and Journals

Grade Level(s):

Description

Regular features at this site are on topics related to automotive, computers, science, electronics, and home technology. Most features include both a picture and a summary. Contents of the present month's magazine are outlined with a preview of what to anticipate in future months.

Commentary

Updated daily, this site provides reports of special events and news. Some especially interesting stories remain for a while. Check out the story of President Bush's use of a virtual reality simulator before he actually took the jump and learn how this technology will soon be available for the rest of us.

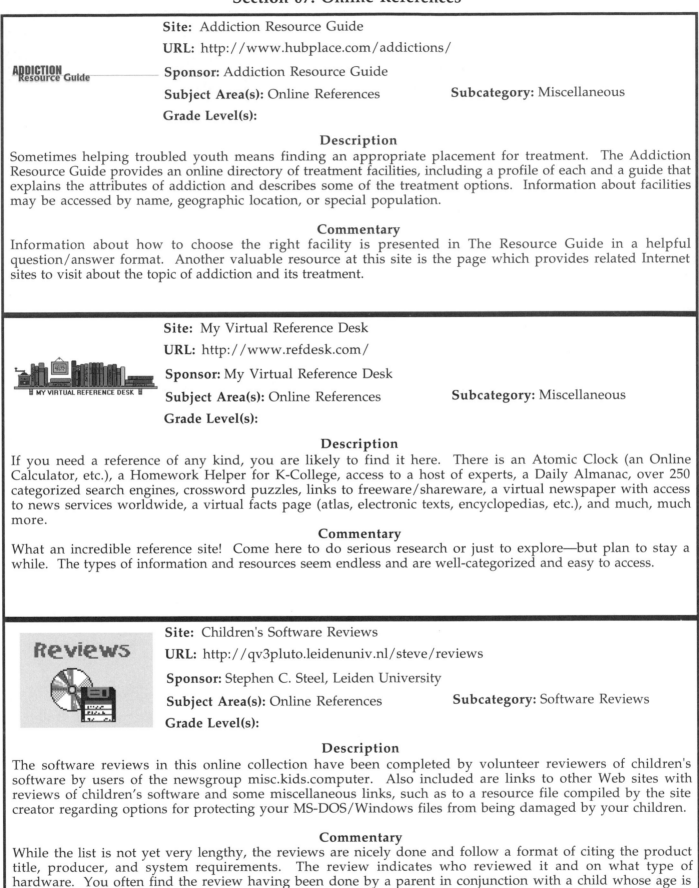

Site: Addiction Resource Guide

URL: http://www.hubplace.com/addictions/

Sponsor: Addiction Resource Guide

Subject Area(s): Online References   **Subcategory:** Miscellaneous

Grade Level(s):

Description

Sometimes helping troubled youth means finding an appropriate placement for treatment. The Addiction Resource Guide provides an online directory of treatment facilities, including a profile of each and a guide that explains the attributes of addiction and describes some of the treatment options. Information about facilities may be accessed by name, geographic location, or special population.

Commentary

Information about how to choose the right facility is presented in The Resource Guide in a helpful question/answer format. Another valuable resource at this site is the page which provides related Internet sites to visit about the topic of addiction and its treatment.

Site: My Virtual Reference Desk

URL: http://www.refdesk.com/

Sponsor: My Virtual Reference Desk

Subject Area(s): Online References   **Subcategory:** Miscellaneous

Grade Level(s):

Description

If you need a reference of any kind, you are likely to find it here. There is an Atomic Clock (an Online Calculator, etc.), a Homework Helper for K-College, access to a host of experts, a Daily Almanac, over 250 categorized search engines, crossword puzzles, links to freeware/shareware, a virtual newspaper with access to news services worldwide, a virtual facts page (atlas, electronic texts, encyclopedias, etc.), and much, much more.

Commentary

What an incredible reference site! Come here to do serious research or just to explore—but plan to stay a while. The types of information and resources seem endless and are well-categorized and easy to access.

Site: Children's Software Reviews

URL: http://qv3pluto.leidenuniv.nl/steve/reviews

Sponsor: Stephen C. Steel, Leiden University

Subject Area(s): Online References   **Subcategory:** Software Reviews

Grade Level(s):

Description

The software reviews in this online collection have been completed by volunteer reviewers of children's software by users of the newsgroup misc.kids.computer. Also included are links to other Web sites with reviews of children's software and some miscellaneous links, such as to a resource file compiled by the site creator regarding options for protecting your MS-DOS/Windows files from being damaged by your children.

Commentary

While the list is not yet very lengthy, the reviews are nicely done and follow a format of citing the product title, producer, and system requirements. The review indicates who reviewed it and on what type of hardware. You often find the review having been done by a parent in conjunction with a child whose age is noted.

Site: Children's Software Revue

URL: http://www.childrenssoftware.com

Sponsor: Children's Software Revue Newsletter

Subject Area(s): Online References   **Subcategory:** Software Reviews

Grade Level(s):

Description

This is the online version of the Software Revue Newsletter and has a database of nearly 3,000 software reviews that have been written by educators who are also parents. Reviews include feedback from families. Add a review of a product you know and have used with kids.

Commentary

Staff members at Children's Software Revue do a wonderful job! They produce a bi-monthly newsletter for parents and teachers that you may want to subscribe to. But there is a wealth of information at this Web site. Whether you are looking for ways to use your computer with kids in the classroom or at home, you know the computer is only as good as the software you select to use. This site will help you in that task.

Site: PEP Registry of Educational Software Publishers

URL: http://www.microweb.com/pepsite

Sponsor: *Children's Software Revue* and Custom Computers for Kids

Subject Area(s): Online References   **Subcategory:** Software Reviews

Grade Level(s):

Description

PEP stands for Resources for Parents, Educators, and Publishers. This site provides a comprehensive listing of educational software companies with direct links to their sites. You can also search for companies by state or by country location.

Commentary

Make a stop here periodically to quickly find out about new children's software, the latest software industry news, and more. Software reviews are provided by *Children's Software Revue* and a radio program conducted by the creator of Custom Computers for Kids.

Site: Superkids Educational Software Review

URL: http://www.superkids.com

Sponsor: Knowledge Share LLC

Subject Area(s): Online References   **Subcategory:** Software Reviews

Grade Level(s):

Description

Find reviews on a number of software programs as well as a buyer's guide to products. Reviews are organized into categories by subjects and also by interest area, such as software for girls. You will also find Feature Articles, such as "How to Prepare for the SAT: What the Experts Think," Columns such as "Computing at Home: What is the Appropriate Role for Parents?", links to other sites, contests, and more.

Commentary

Software listed at this site is reviewed by parents, teachers, and kids and can be used by each as well! However, some of the offerings in the humor section are more geared toward adults than children. The site is very easy to use and a valuable resource.

Site: The Review Zone

URL: http://www.TheReviewZone.com

Sponsor: Tina Velgos

Subject Area(s): Online References   **Subcategory:** Software Reviews

Grade Level(s):

Description

Parents and teachers can locate in-depth software reviews on kids' and family edutainment CD-ROMs, computer hardware, books, and more. CD-ROM reviews for both Macintosh computers and PCs are organized by categories, such as Creativity/Art, Early Learning, Family Edutainment/Productivity, and others. Look in the Family Computing section for articles of interest. Book reviews and hardware reviews are available as well.

Commentary

"Edutainment" is a fairly new term used to describe products that are both fun to use and educational. This site seems to be kept current and provides very helpful information for parents and educators in selecting products for children—and themselves. The Just for Girls! section provides a long list of links to some great places on the Net for young females.

Site: The Technology in the Curriculum (TIC) Evaluation Database

URL: http://tic.stan-co.k12.ca.us

Sponsor: The California Instructional Technology Clearinghouse

Subject Area(s): Online References   **Subcategory:** Software Reviews

Grade Level(s):

Description

Find a database of over 2,000 software reviews that is searchable by media, computer platform, language, and other criteria. Reviews include a description of the product, platform requirements, ideas for using the product in the curriculum, the suggested age range for use, and an indication of support material that is available.

Commentary

Included in the database are computer software programs, CD-ROMs, and instructional video programs. They recruit reviewers each year from teachers who are members of a Computer Using Educators group. The programs are also evaluated by students.

Site: Thunderbeam

URL: http://www.thunderbeam.com

Sponsor: Thunderbeam

Subject Area(s): Online References   **Subcategory:** Software Reviews

Grade Level(s):

Description

Reviews are provided in "The Trail Guide;" screen shots/downloadable demos are included. Registered members can purchase products at "The Trading Post" in the "world's largest kids' software store" online, with products shipped the same day. Parents participate in chats initiated by education/technology writers. Kids, make a "wish list" of software, play games, download shareware, and chat with peers.

Commentary

Parents and homeschoolers may find this site helpful in locating and purchasing software for their children. The theme is Western, and the site is designed for parents of children in preschool through middle school. At the time of posting, more than 2,000 software reviews were available—25 are to be added each month. Kids can buy online within pre-defined spending limits set by their parents.

Site: 3-D Dictionary

URL: http://207.136.90.76/dictionary/

Sponsor: maranGraphics

Subject Area(s): Online References   **Subcategory:** Technology

Grade Level(s):

Description

Click on the first letter of the word you choose to look up to see a list of words beginning with that letter. Then click on your choice. Each entry for identified words has an easy-to-understand definition and an accompanying graphic.

Commentary

The design of this site is very appealing and colorful. Definitions are simple for younger and more novice technology users, and the 3-D graphics are very engaging. This is a wonderful resource for home or school use.

Site: An Educator's Guide to School Networks: Solving the Networking Puzzle

URL: http://fcit.coedu.usf.edu/network/

Sponsor: Florida Center for Instructional Technology

Subject Area(s): Online References   **Subcategory:** Technology

Grade Level(s):

Description

This informative site begins with the basics of what a network is and proceeds with describing three basic kinds: Local Area Network (LAN), Metropolitan Area Network (MAN), and Wide Area Network (WAN). Other sections of explanation and diagrams include Protocol, Hardware, Cabling, Topology, Software, a Glossary, a Game, and References to articles, books, and other Web sites on the topic.

Commentary

The Florida Center for Instructional Technology has done a nice job with the design of this organized and easy-to-understand site. Educators might use this information for their own reference or as an aid in explaining networking needs to colleagues, school boards, and others.

Site: Maintaining a Healthy Computer

URL: http://pip.ehhs.cmich.edu/healthy/index.html

Sponsor: Hogg, O'Leary-Morence, Bitterling, Crawley, Central Michigan University

Subject Area(s): Online References   **Subcategory:** Technology

Grade Level(s):

Description

The subtitle for this site is "Now That I Have This Computer, What Do I Do About It?" Information is designed for the average computer user regarding how to manage one or more computers and prevent problems. Topics include Setting Up Your Computer, Managing Computer Paperwork, Common Sense Hardware Maintenance, Keeping Things Clean, Managing Software, Preventing Problems, and Troubleshooting.

Commentary

You will find that many of the suggestions are focused on the education environment and come directly from teachers' experiences, but most are applicable for other settings as well. This site will prove handy for both teachers and parents.

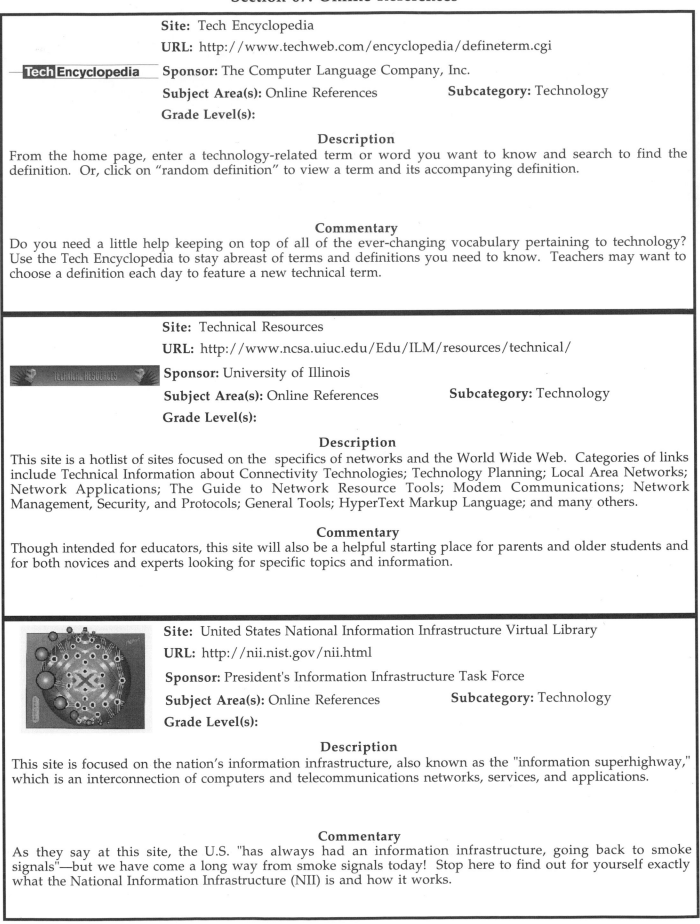

Site: Tech Encyclopedia

URL: http://www.techweb.com/encyclopedia/defineterm.cgi

Sponsor: The Computer Language Company, Inc.

Subject Area(s): Online References   **Subcategory:** Technology

Grade Level(s):

Description

From the home page, enter a technology-related term or word you want to know and search to find the definition. Or, click on "random definition" to view a term and its accompanying definition.

Commentary

Do you need a little help keeping on top of all of the ever-changing vocabulary pertaining to technology? Use the Tech Encyclopedia to stay abreast of terms and definitions you need to know. Teachers may want to choose a definition each day to feature a new technical term.

Site: Technical Resources

URL: http://www.ncsa.uiuc.edu/Edu/ILM/resources/technical/

Sponsor: University of Illinois

Subject Area(s): Online References   **Subcategory:** Technology

Grade Level(s):

Description

This site is a hotlist of sites focused on the specifics of networks and the World Wide Web. Categories of links include Technical Information about Connectivity Technologies; Technology Planning; Local Area Networks; Network Applications; The Guide to Network Resource Tools; Modem Communications; Network Management, Security, and Protocols; General Tools; HyperText Markup Language; and many others.

Commentary

Though intended for educators, this site will also be a helpful starting place for parents and older students and for both novices and experts looking for specific topics and information.

Site: United States National Information Infrastructure Virtual Library

URL: http://nii.nist.gov/nii.html

Sponsor: President's Information Infrastructure Task Force

Subject Area(s): Online References   **Subcategory:** Technology

Grade Level(s):

Description

This site is focused on the nation's information infrastructure, also known as the "information superhighway," which is an interconnection of computers and telecommunications networks, services, and applications.

Commentary

As they say at this site, the U.S. "has always had an information infrastructure, going back to smoke signals"—but we have come a long way from smoke signals today! Stop here to find out for yourself exactly what the National Information Infrastructure (NII) is and how it works.

Section 07. Online References

Site: Virtual Computer Library

URL: http://www.utexas.edu/computer/vcl/

Sponsor: Christine M. Henke, ACITS, University of Texas at Austin

Subject Area(s): Online References   **Subcategory:** Technology

Grade Level(s):

Description

The Virtual Computer Library is a collection of links to information about computers and computing. Categories of links include Academic Computing, Book Reviews, Computer Technology, Conferences, Documentation, FAQs, Internet Information, Journals, News/Press Releases, Nonprofit/Government Organizations, Online Books/Dictionaries, Publishers, User Groups/Associations, Vendors Index, and WWW Information.

Commentary

The site is well-designed and organized with subcategories under the major topic headings, and you can also use the search capabilities offered across the site, which include support for AND, OR, NOT, and operators.

Site: Bartlett's Familiar Quotations

URL: http://www.columbia.edu/acis/bartleby/bartlett/

Sponsor: Columbia University

Subject Area(s): Online References   **Subcategory:** Writing Resources

Grade Level(s):

Description

The first edition of *Familiar Quotations* was printed in 1891; revised and enlarged, it continues to be reprinted. This is an ideal vehicle for the Internet. The reader can search the database by keyword to look for quotations, or it is possible to scroll the hundreds of authors listed to examine their famous sayings.

Commentary

This is an easy-to-use site for reference or just browsing. Authors can be arranged in alphabetical order or in chronological order for certain types of searches. A search for the word "happiness" yielded 34 matches, each with a reference to the author and the word within a phrase.

NO GRAPHIC FOUND

Site: Grammar and Style Notes

URL: http://www.english.upenn.edu/~jlynch/Grammar/

Sponsor: Jack Lynch, University of Pennsylvania

Subject Area(s): Online References   **Subcategory:** Writing Resources

Grade Level(s):

Description

This professor has compiled a set of grammatical rules and explanations, comments on style, and suggestions on usage. His goal seems to be to assist others in making their writing more clear and effective. Included are specific articles on usage for quick reference and more general articles on style.

Commentary

There is nothing very fancy here, but you will find an easy-to-use guide for grammar and style. Click on a letter to quickly go to the term you wish to learn about or check.

Section 07. Online References

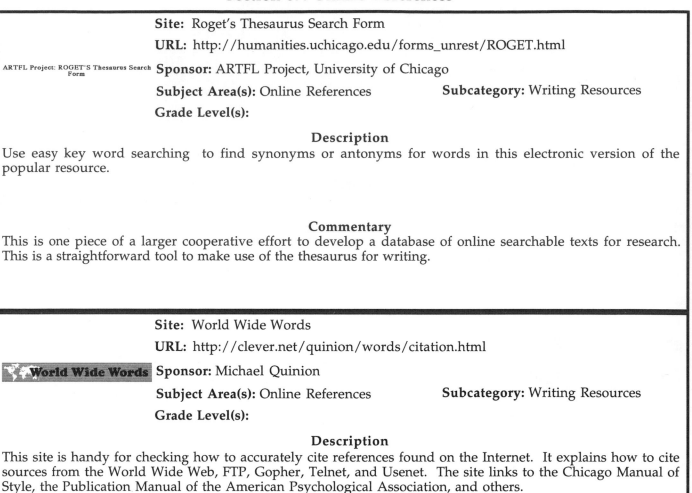

Site: Roget's Thesaurus Search Form

URL: http://humanities.uchicago.edu/forms_unrest/ROGET.html

ARTFL Project: ROGET'S Thesaurus Search Form **Sponsor:** ARTFL Project, University of Chicago

Subject Area(s): Online References   **Subcategory:** Writing Resources

Grade Level(s):

Description

Use easy key word searching to find synonyms or antonyms for words in this electronic version of the popular resource.

Commentary

This is one piece of a larger cooperative effort to develop a database of online searchable texts for research. This is a straightforward tool to make use of the thesaurus for writing.

Site: World Wide Words

URL: http://clever.net/quinion/words/citation.html

World Wide Words **Sponsor:** Michael Quinion

Subject Area(s): Online References   **Subcategory:** Writing Resources

Grade Level(s):

Description

This site is handy for checking how to accurately cite references found on the Internet. It explains how to cite sources from the World Wide Web, FTP, Gopher, Telnet, and Usenet. The site links to the Chicago Manual of Style, the Publication Manual of the American Psychological Association, and others.

Commentary

This is a very useful reference site that will come in handy when you need to know how to cite references from the Internet in a paper or project you are preparing.

8 WWW
GRANTS AND FUNDING

Section 8 identifies 22 sites with information on grants and funding, including three different sites sponsored by the U.S. Department of Education and two by the National Science Foundation. Another site, "The Foundation Center," sponsored by a non-profit organization of the same name, includes valuable links to *The Foundation Center's User-Friendly Guide to Funding Research and Resources*, "A Short Course for Proposal Writing," and several common grant application formats.

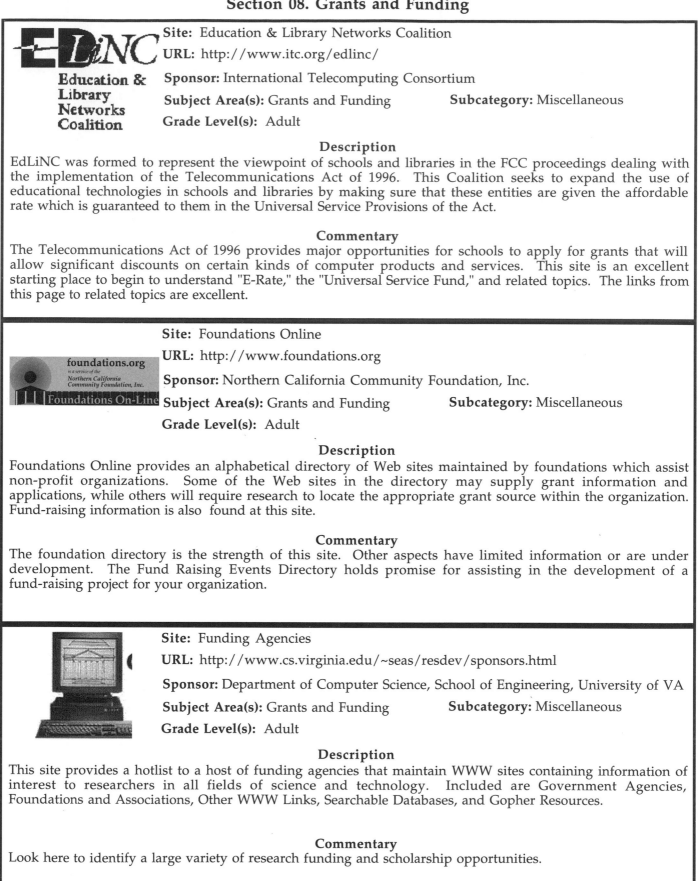

Site: Education & Library Networks Coalition

URL: http://www.itc.org/edlinc/

Sponsor: International Telecomputing Consortium

Subject Area(s): Grants and Funding   **Subcategory:** Miscellaneous

Grade Level(s): Adult

Description
EdLiNC was formed to represent the viewpoint of schools and libraries in the FCC proceedings dealing with the implementation of the Telecommunications Act of 1996. This Coalition seeks to expand the use of educational technologies in schools and libraries by making sure that these entities are given the affordable rate which is guaranteed to them in the Universal Service Provisions of the Act.

Commentary
The Telecommunications Act of 1996 provides major opportunities for schools to apply for grants that will allow significant discounts on certain kinds of computer products and services. This site is an excellent starting place to begin to understand "E-Rate," the "Universal Service Fund," and related topics. The links from this page to related topics are excellent.

Site: Foundations Online

URL: http://www.foundations.org

Sponsor: Northern California Community Foundation, Inc.

Subject Area(s): Grants and Funding   **Subcategory:** Miscellaneous

Grade Level(s): Adult

Description
Foundations Online provides an alphabetical directory of Web sites maintained by foundations which assist non-profit organizations. Some of the Web sites in the directory may supply grant information and applications, while others will require research to locate the appropriate grant source within the organization. Fund-raising information is also found at this site.

Commentary
The foundation directory is the strength of this site. Other aspects have limited information or are under development. The Fund Raising Events Directory holds promise for assisting in the development of a fund-raising project for your organization.

Site: Funding Agencies

URL: http://www.cs.virginia.edu/~seas/resdev/sponsors.html

Sponsor: Department of Computer Science, School of Engineering, University of VA

Subject Area(s): Grants and Funding   **Subcategory:** Miscellaneous

Grade Level(s): Adult

Description
This site provides a hotlist to a host of funding agencies that maintain WWW sites containing information of interest to researchers in all fields of science and technology. Included are Government Agencies, Foundations and Associations, Other WWW Links, Searchable Databases, and Gopher Resources.

Commentary
Look here to identify a large variety of research funding and scholarship opportunities.

Site: Grants and Contracts

URL: http://www.nih.gov/grants/

Sponsor: National Institutes of Health

Subject Area(s): Grants and Funding   **Subcategory:** Miscellaneous

Grade Level(s): Adult

Description

Spend time exploring this site for information about ongoing grant programs and special initiatives available through the National Institutes of Health.

Commentary

You may want to navigate from the Grants Page to Funding Opportunities to the NIH Guide for Grants and Contracts. Enter your search criteria, such as K-12, to begin to narrow the opportunities of interest to you.

U. S. Department of Education
Grants & Contracts Information

Site: Grants and Contracts Information

URL: http://gcs.ed.gov/

Sponsor: U. S. Department of Education

Subject Area(s): Grants and Funding   **Subcategory:** Miscellaneous

Grade Level(s): Adult

Description

This is the source of information on grants and other related programs of the Department of Education. Find descriptions of funded programs, such as Goals 2000, School-to-Work, and Technology. The site lists its publications and guides for teachers and researchers, and displays available programs and services by state on a map of the United States.

Commentary

Updated daily, this is the most current information from the Department and the Federal Register. You might want to link back to the home page of the Department of Education (easy to do at the bottom of the page) in order to discover other programs, services, and current news.

Site: Grants Web

URL: http://web.fie.com/cws/sra/resource.html

Sponsor: The Society of Research Administrators

Subject Area(s): Grants and Funding   **Subcategory:** Miscellaneous

Grade Level(s): Adult

Description

The Grants Web is a resource page for resource administrators which provides a comprehensive list of worldwide links to general resources, government resources, private funding sources and periodicals which provide policy and information. Four categories of information are provided: Government Resources, General Resources, Policy Info and Circulars, and Private Funding Resources.

Commentary

Each topic area is subdivided for better location of information. Visitors will have to be savvy enough to sort the educational information from funding and grant information in other fields. There are numerous links to other funding sites which could prove quite useful.

Site: Internet Nonprofit Center

URL: http://nonprofits.org/

Sponsor: Internet NonProfit Center

Subject Area(s): Grants and Funding   **Subcategory:** Miscellaneous

Grade Level(s): Adult

Description

The Internet Nonprofit Center provides information about nonprofit organizations and provides space for these organizations to post information about themselves. The Parlor features events, frequently asked questions, live chat, information about nonprofits and the World Wide Web, nonprofit news, and starting your own Web site.

Commentary

This site offers a good vehicle for networking and gaining expertise from others involved in nonprofit organizations. The Library is valuable for locating bibliographies, the top 40 charities, essays, government information on U.S. nonprofit organizations, and standards in philanthropy.

Site: Mini Grants, Information, and Freebies

URL: http://www.learner.org/sami/sami.html

Sponsor: Annenberg/CPS Math and Science Project

Subject Area(s): Grants and Funding   **Subcategory:** Miscellaneous

Grade Level(s): Adult

Description

This is a part of the Science and Math Initiative which deals most directly with small grants and projects. There are links to the ETS Policy Information Center, the Center for Applied Special Technology, and the Federal Communications Commission.

Commentary

Updated regularly, the site is a great place to find out about projects, publications, freebies, grants, and a variety of Internet resources related to science and math. The list of freebies is huge and ranges from posters to free software for Web page development. The list of available mini-grants is also extensive with links to services which provide larger grants.

Site: Money Matters

URL: http://www.ed.gov/money.html

Sponsor: U.S. Department of Education

Subject Area(s): Grants and Funding   **Subcategory:** Miscellaneous

Grade Level(s): Adult

Description

Money Matters is the U.S. government's site for information about current grants and funding assistance for education. Also included are documents to aid in understanding the processes and rules to apply for funds. "What Should I Know About ED Grants?" and "Guide to U.S. Department of Education Programs" are two documents to assist with the application process.

Commentary

This site also has a valuable section devoted to student financial assistance including the "Student Guide to Financial Aid" which provides information on Pell Grants, student and parent loans, and campus-based programs. Included is the U.S. Department of Education budget and information about the budget process.

Site: National Science Foundation

URL: http://www.nsf.gov/

Sponsor: National Science Foundation

Subject Area(s): Grants and Funding

Subcategory: Miscellaneous

Grade Level(s): Adult

Description

The National Science Foundation is an independent U.S. government agency responsible for promoting science and engineering through programs that invest over $3.3 billion per year to research and education programs. In addition to extensive information about the Foundation, the program areas are listed with research guidelines and priorities for each one.

Commentary

News Highlights provides information about research that is underway. Check out the Antarctic Research and/or the Science and Engineering of Earthquakes. There is an interesting summary of each article so that the reader is provided with a clear indication of what the article contains.

Site: Philanthropy Journal Online

URL: http://philanthropy-journal.org/

Sponsor: Cost Management Associates, Mindspring, and others

Subject Area(s): Grants and Funding

Subcategory: Miscellaneous

Grade Level(s): Middle School

Description

The Philanthropy Journal Online provides visitors a source of nonprofit news, information and links including Philanthropy Links, and the Meta-Index of Nonprofit Organizations. Philanthropy Journal Online also publishes Philanthropy Journal Alert, a free weekly newsletter providing news about grants, fundraising and corporate sponsorships, updates about current trends and issues, as well as programs and tools.

Commentary

Bookmark this site and subscribe to the Philanthropy Journal Alert to stay abreast of the latest grants and funding opportunities, as well as related legal issues.

Site: RAMS-FIE

URL: http://www.fie.com

Sponsor: Research Administration Management Systems/Federal Info. Exchange

Subject Area(s): Grants and Funding

Subcategory: Miscellaneous

Grade Level(s): Adult

Description

Two agencies have merged to form a diversified information services company providing a full range of database services, software development, and technical support for electronic research administration. The system attempts to allow institutions and organizations of every size instant access to federal agency information for research opportunities and other educational opportunities.

Commentary

You can download the grants keyword thesaurus and examine updated databases of research and education funding opportunities. FEDIX Opportunity Alert provides the reader with e-mail about research opportunities in chosen interest areas.

Site: Researchnet

URL: http://researchnet.asu.edu/funding/

Sponsor: Arizona State University

Subject Area(s): Grants and Funding   **Subcategory:** Miscellaneous

Grade Level(s): Adult

Description

The opening Web page provides subscription information in the categories of physical science, social science, arts and humanities, and engineering. The reader may select from a menu with categories of funding information, proposal toolkit, regulatory affairs, resource library, and technology collaborations.

Commentary

This site seems particularly helpful for the teacher and/or administrator living in Arizona, but it provides resources for other educators as well. The Proposal Toolkit provides several guides to proposal writing and grant-seeking and a guide to Federal Agency Programs. The Project Director Handbook is useful for both preparing and implementing a research project.

Site: Statewide Systemic Initiatives in Science, Mathematics, & Engineering

URL: http://www.ehr.nsf.gov/EHR/ESR/index.html

Sponsor: National Science Foundation

Subject Area(s): Grants and Funding   **Subcategory:** Miscellaneous

Grade Level(s): Adult

Description

This Web site showcases the National Science Foundation's Guiding Principle of Systemic Initiatives and Overview of Systemic Approach. Included is information from the portfolio of 59 systemic initiatives (statewide, urban, rural, and comprehensive partnerships for mathematics and science achievement). Find program solicitation, information, and guidelines for projects to be funded.

Commentary

Find information describing the systemic approach being used and click on locations on a U.S. map to learn more about programs in specific cities and communities.

Site: The Chronicle of Philanthropy

URL: http://www.philanthropy.com/gifts.dir/deadline.dir/gdead.html

THE CHRONICLE OF PHILANTHROPY   **Sponsor:** The Chronicle of Philanthropy

Subject Area(s): Grants and Funding   **Subcategory:** Miscellaneous

Grade Level(s): Adult

Description

This site provides a summary of the newspaper of the same name. Find deadlines in gifts and grants listed alphabetically by field with a brief summary, eligible applicant information, as well as deadline and contact information. Visitors may also browse the site by the following topics: Gifts and Grants, Fund Raising, Managing Nonprofit Groups, and Technology.

Commentary

The Chronicle's listings are extensive and not exclusive to education. There is a lot of value here, but be prepared to sift through for those related to your funding needs.

Site: The Council on Foundations

URL: http://www.cof.org

Sponsor: The Council on Foundations

Subject Area(s): Grants and Funding   **Subcategory:** Miscellaneous

Grade Level(s): Adult

Description

The Council on Foundations is a member organization for philanthropic entities which assists members in meeting their charitable goals. The frequently asked questions page offers useful information about seeking grants, corporate community involvement, and the various types of foundations. Use the map in the "About the Council on Foundations" link to locate regional, state, and local foundations in your area.

Commentary

While this site is primarily for foundations seeking to make grants, there is a good deal of valuable information for those seeking funds. The Council on Foundations site is well written in easily understood terms without acronyms which only insiders would understand.

Site: The Distance Learning Funding $ourcebook

URL: http://www.technogrants.com

Sponsor: Arlene Krebs

Subject Area(s): Grants and Funding   **Subcategory:** Miscellaneous

Grade Level(s): Adult

Description

This Web site claims to provide the latest research on funding sources for telecommunications and interactive technologies for schools, higher ed, nonprofits, arts/cultural organizations, health/social service agencies, and grassroots community organizations.

Commentary

Find information categorized by Foundations, Regional Bell and Local Telephone Companies, Corporate Giving Programs, Print and Electronic References, Federal Government and Grantwriting for Success, and Cable Television Industry. Visit this site often for updates in funding information and to find strategies for successful grantwriting.

Site: The Foundation Center

URL: http://www.fdncenter.org/

Sponsor: The Foundation Center

Subject Area(s): Grants and Funding   **Subcategory:** Miscellaneous

Grade Level(s): Adult

Description

The Foundation Center is a nonprofit organization which serves as a clearinghouse for information related to foundations and corporate giving. The Foundation Center operates five libraries throughout the United States, conducts educational opportunities, and publishes documents to assist its clients. Interested visitors may subscribe to the e-mail periodical *Philanthropy News Digest* at no cost through this site.

Commentary

The online library features a help desk with frequently asked questions, an online librarian, and links to nonprofit resources. Valuable links for those seeking funding include the orientation to grantseeking, *The Foundation Center's User-Friendly Guide to Funding Research and Resources,* A Short Course for Proposal Writing, Glossary, and several common grant application formats.

Site: The Grant Getting Page

URL: http://www.uic.edu/depts/ovcr/ors1.html

Sponsor: The University of Illinois at Chicago

Subject Area(s): Grants and Funding   **Subcategory:** Miscellaneous

Grade Level(s): Adult

Description

This Web page of links is broadly organized into Online Search Tools; Forms, Policies, and Administrative Information; Federal Home Pages; and Not-For-Profit and Commercial Funders. A few of the links are restricted to faculty at the University of Illinois, but most are links available to any Internet user.

Commentary

The site is well-organized with links to a wide variety of federal and not-for-profit organizations. Grant writers will eventually begin to find a duplicate of effort from different resources, but locating even one additional funding resource may be the key to eventual success.

Site: U.S. Department of Education Federal Register Documents

URL: http://www.ed.gov/legislation/FedRegister/

Sponsor: U.S. Department of Education

Subject Area(s): Grants and Funding   **Subcategory:** Miscellaneous

Grade Level(s): Adult

Description

This directory contains documents published in the *Federal Register* of the U.S. Department of Education. The documents are in a searchable database but may also be browsed in reverse chronological order. Proposed and final regulations are included in separate sections, along with information about meetings and research priorities.

Commentary

This site is updated weekly with past information remaining in archives. The grantseeker may find the section of Announcements of most use, since it includes grant competitions in reverse chronological order and removes them from the list after the due date.

Site: United States Government and Grant Resources

URL: http://pegasus.uthct.edu/OtherUsefulSites/Govt.html

Sponsor: University of Texas Health Center at Tyler

Subject Area(s): Grants and Funding   **Subcategory:** Miscellaneous

Grade Level(s): Adult

Description

This is a listing of resources compiled by a university professor for use in locating grant money. The links are arranged in alphabetical order, some with annotations. It is possible to search many of the links but not the database of links as presented at the site.

Commentary

This is a straightforward list with about 100 names. Some listings are government resources but not grant resources. Almost everyone will enjoy taking a look at the United States National Debt Clock, which is unfortunately updated every hour with your own personal share of this debt.

Site: Wellspring Foundation

URL: http://www.isp.net/Wellspring/index.html

Sponsor: Wellspring Foundation

Subject Area(s): Grants and Funding   **Subcategory:** Miscellaneous

Grade Level(s): Adult

Description
Organizations seeking grant funding for specific projects, organizational support, and capital improvements may submit a request to the Wellspring Foundation. Grants are made in Education, Southeast Asia, Documentary Film Production, and Environmental Conservation. Be apprised that the Wellspring Foundation does not sponsor individuals or fund endowments.

Commentary
The inquiry submission form at this site may be completed and submitted via e-mail, and a response will be returned within one week. A list of grant-related sites on the Web was under construction at the time of evaluation.

9 WWW

SPECIAL NEEDS

Section 9 identifies over three dozen sites, offering help for meeting a variety of special education needs, organized into the following subcategories:

- ➤ A.D.D.
- ➤ ADAPTIVE TECHNOLOGY
- ➤ ASSISTIVE TECHNOLOGY
- ➤ AUDITORY IMPAIRMENTS
- ➤ AUTISM
- ➤ DISABILITIES
- ➤ GIFTED AND TALENTED
- ➤ LEARNING DISABILITIES
- ➤ MENTAL RETARDATION
- ➤ VISUAL IMPAIRMENTS

For example, "Children and Adults with Attention Deficit Disorders," sponsored by the organization CH.A.D.D., provides detailed information about this disability, its treatment, related parenting issues, and more. And "LD Resources," sponsored by Richard and Anne Wanderman, features freeware and shareware for Macintosh computers that may be downloaded from the site, plus many articles on learning disabilities.

Section 09. Special Needs

Site: Children and Adults With Attention Deficit Disorders

URL: http://www.chadd.org/

Sponsor: Children and Adults With Attention Deficit Disorders

Subject Area(s): Special Needs   **Subcategory:** A.D.D.

Grade Level(s): Adult

Description

CH.A.D.D. is the nation's largest organization dedicated to attention deficit disorder. Information about this disability, treatments, parenting issues, legal rights, and many others, may be found at this Web site.

Commentary

Visitors may join CH.A.D.D. and additionally find a state chapter while online.

Site: Adaptive Technology Lab

URL: http://www.scsu.ctstateu.edu/SCSU/ATL/Index.html

Sponsor: Southern Connecticut State University

Subject Area(s): Special Needs   **Subcategory:** Adaptive Technology

Grade Level(s): Adult

Description

The Adaptive Technology Laboratory (ATL) of Southern Connecticut State University trains persons with disabilities to use adaptive technology, provides access technology for Southern Connecticut State University students, conducts individual technology evaluations of school-aged children and adults, and serves as a resource through open houses and workshops.

Commentary

Links to related sites include vendors of assistive technology hardware and software, and information about ergonomic considerations in technology use.

Site: Alliance for Technology Access

URL: http://www.ataccess.org/

Sponsor: Alliance for Technology Access

Subject Area(s): Special Needs   **Subcategory:** Assistive Technology

Grade Level(s): Adult

Description

If assistive technology is of interest to you, this site is a great place to visit. Vendors, information about assistive technology, funding, organizations for individuals with disabilities, advocacy resources, and frequently asked questions are pages you can expect to find. Technology centers in 29 states which help children and adults explore options for technology access are identified with addresses and phone numbers.

Commentary

The most interesting and unique features of this site are the stories which feature individuals with disabilities using technology solutions. Suggestions for making Web sites more readily accessible for people with disabilities serve as a valuable resource, as do suggestions for overcoming barriers met by those with physical, visual, auditory, and comprehension challenges when surfing the Internet.

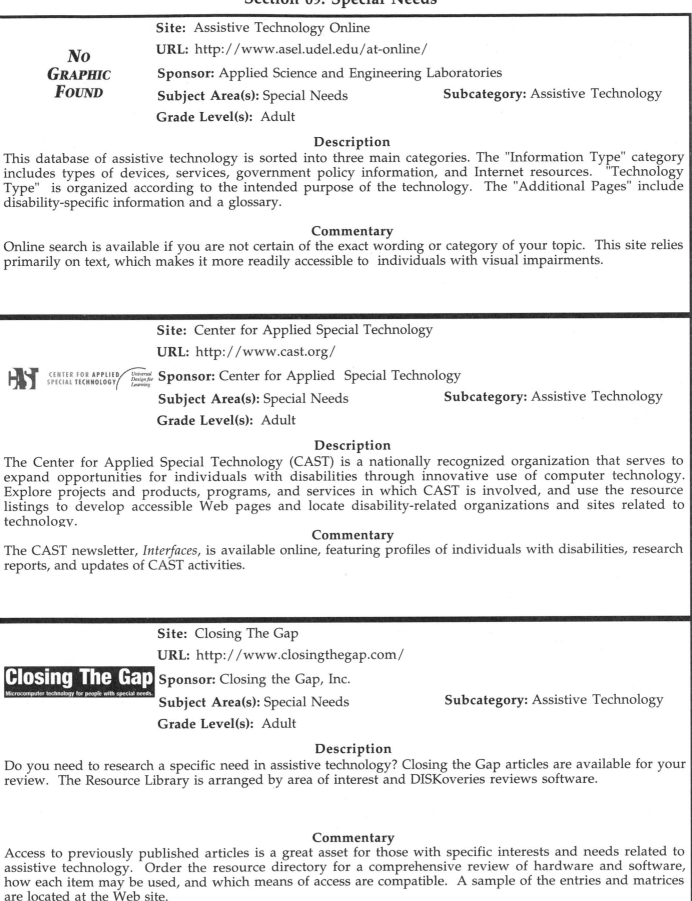

Site: Assistive Technology Online

URL: http://www.asel.udel.edu/at-online/

Sponsor: Applied Science and Engineering Laboratories

Subject Area(s): Special Needs   **Subcategory:** Assistive Technology

Grade Level(s): Adult

No Graphic Found

Description

This database of assistive technology is sorted into three main categories. The "Information Type" category includes types of devices, services, government policy information, and Internet resources. "Technology Type" is organized according to the intended purpose of the technology. The "Additional Pages" include disability-specific information and a glossary.

Commentary

Online search is available if you are not certain of the exact wording or category of your topic. This site relies primarily on text, which makes it more readily accessible to individuals with visual impairments.

Site: Center for Applied Special Technology

URL: http://www.cast.org/

Sponsor: Center for Applied Special Technology

Subject Area(s): Special Needs   **Subcategory:** Assistive Technology

Grade Level(s): Adult

Description

The Center for Applied Special Technology (CAST) is a nationally recognized organization that serves to expand opportunities for individuals with disabilities through innovative use of computer technology. Explore projects and products, programs, and services in which CAST is involved, and use the resource listings to develop accessible Web pages and locate disability-related organizations and sites related to technology.

Commentary

The CAST newsletter, *Interfaces*, is available online, featuring profiles of individuals with disabilities, research reports, and updates of CAST activities.

Site: Closing The Gap

URL: http://www.closingthegap.com/

Sponsor: Closing the Gap, Inc.

Subject Area(s): Special Needs   **Subcategory:** Assistive Technology

Grade Level(s): Adult

Description

Do you need to research a specific need in assistive technology? Closing the Gap articles are available for your review. The Resource Library is arranged by area of interest and DISKoveries reviews software.

Commentary

Access to previously published articles is a great asset for those with specific interests and needs related to assistive technology. Order the resource directory for a comprehensive review of hardware and software, how each item may be used, and which means of access are compatible. A sample of the entries and matrices are located at the Web site.

Site: Project PURSUIT

URL: http://pursuit.rehab.uiuc.edu/pursuit/homepage.html

Sponsor: University of Illinois at Urbana-Champaign

Subject Area(s): Special Needs   **Subcategory:** Assistive Technology

Grade Level(s): Adult

Description

PURSUIT is aimed at addressing the underrepresentation of people with disabilities in math, engineering, and science careers. The site makes recommendations for accommodations which may assist students, lessons regarding assistive technology and selection of an appropriate device, and links to Internet sites for math, science, computer engineering, and disability resources.

Commentary

The Career Guide is especially beneficial in providing information about various careers in math, science, and engineering fields. Each career page describes the type of work, terminology, where the work takes place, required education and coursework, and sources for additional information.

Site: Deaf Resource Library

URL: http://www.yale.edu/~nakamura/deaf.html

Sponsor: Karen Nakamura

Subject Area(s): Special Needs   **Subcategory:** Auditory Impairments

Grade Level(s): Adult

Description

Described as an online library, this site lists contents pertinent to deaf and hard-of-hearing individuals from sources as varied as universities, magazines, technology innovations, and individuals' home pages.

Commentary

Labels for new items provide quick help when reviewing the contents. The author admits bias toward deafness issues—only two listings are under resources for the hard-of-hearing.

Site: National Information Center on Deafness

URL: http://www.gallaudet.edu/~nicd

Sponsor: Gallaudet University

Subject Area(s): Special Needs   **Subcategory:** Auditory Impairments

Grade Level(s): Adult

Description

The National Information Center on Deafness lists publications available for purchase with costs and ordering information included. State agencies and contacts, as well as links to dependable sources on deafness, may be found here.

Commentary

This site is a valuable resource for information and additional resources. Check the American Sign Language dictionary online at the Deaf World Web link.

Site: Autism Network International

URL: http://www.students.uiuc.edu/~bordner/ani.html

Sponsor: James Sternberg and Jim Sinclair

Subject Area(s): Special Needs   **Subcategory:** Autism

Grade Level(s): Adult

Description

Autism Network International is an advocacy organization run by individuals with autism. This site describes the organization, how to join, descriptions of autism from members and clinical sources, and links to sights about autism and disabilities in general.

Commentary

The personal descriptions of autism are poignant and provide a rare insight into how autism has affected individuals' lives.

Autism Society of America

Serving the needs of individuals with autism and their families through advocacy, education, public awareness, and research since 1965

Site: Autism Society of America

URL: http://www.autism-society.org/

Sponsor: Autism Society of America

Subject Area(s): Special Needs   **Subcategory:** Autism

Grade Level(s): Adult

Description

For those beginning to seek information about autism and its characteristics, this site is extremely helpful. Information such as What is Autism? Getting Started (for the newly-diagnosed), and The Autism Checklist will inform visitors and provide resources and further articles for review.

Commentary

The glossary of terms and acronyms may also be found on this page—you will find this a useful resource for keeping up with terminology used in the field of special education.

No Graphic Found

Site: Center for the Study of Autism

URL: http://www.autism.org/

Sponsor: Khera Communications

Subject Area(s): Special Needs   **Subcategory:** Autism

Grade Level(s): Adult

Description

Visit this site to review the latest autism research results and intervention approaches written in laymen's terms. The articles are submitted by individuals across the continent on a wide range of topics pertinent to autism.

Commentary

Parents and professionals will find the Sibling Center valuable. It helps parents and others prepare to answer questions and find information and exercises to use with the siblings of children diagnosed with autism.

Section 09. Special Needs

Site: A Web Resource for Special Education

URL: http://curry.edschool.Virginia.EDU/go/specialed/

Sponsor: University of Virginia

Subject Area(s): Special Needs   **Subcategory:** Disabilities

Grade Level(s): Adult

Description
Although primarily designed for the special education teacher, this site also has information that will be of interest and use to parents. Categorical information is arranged by the type of disorder. There are links to information about the laws governing special education, and to publications of use by professionals in the field.

Commentary
You may find the pictures and e-mail addresses for some of the professionals in special education of great value to you as a reference. There are also discussion lists for a number of topics in special education. The *Journal of Behavioral Analysis* abstracts can be searched by keyword to find scientific information.

No Graphic Found

Site: Americans with Disabilities Act Document Center

URL: http://janweb.icdi.wvu.edu/kinder/

Sponsor: Job Accommodation Network

Subject Area(s): Special Needs   **Subcategory:** Disabilities

Grade Level(s): Adult

Description
The primary focus of this site is to distribute information about the Americans with Disabilities Act, the Job Accommodation Network, employment of people with disabilities, and accommodations on the job. It also includes an extensive listing of topic areas and links relative to special education and disabilities.

Commentary
The Americans with Disabilities Act Document Center has been cited in several periodicals and rated among the top 5% of all sites on the Internet by Point Survey.

Site: DO-IT at the University of Washington

URL: http://weber.u.washington.edu/~doit

Sponsor: DO-IT Program, University of Washington

Subject Area(s): Special Needs   **Subcategory:** Disabilities

Grade Level(s): Adult

Description
Communicate with 100 mentors and scholars, most of whom have some disability. Photos and graphics are minimal, so those with visual impairment will not be at a disadvantage. The hearing impaired will find descriptions of all sounds. This site is funded by the National Science Foundation and contributions from NEC Foundation of America, U.S. West, and the University of Washington.

Commentary
DO-IT is an acronym for the Disabilities, Opportunities, Internetworking, and Technology project based at the University of Washington. They won the education category award of the National Information Infrastructure (NII) Awards program. The mentors are high school students with disabilities from a number of states, and this site may give you helpful ideas for achieving increased accessibility for the disabled.

Site: Educational Resources Information Center

URL: http://www.cec.sped.org/ericec/ericecer.html

Sponsor: The Council for Exceptional Children

Subject Area(s): Special Needs   **Subcategory:** Disabilities

Grade Level(s): Adult

Description
Access the United States Department of Education's information database of the Educational Resources Information Center (ERIC)—sixteen subject-specific clearinghouses of education-related publications. Those who utilize ERIC will access abstracts of articles, proceedings, papers, speeches, reports, curriculum guides, and books from the database.

Commentary
The Exceptional Child Education Resources (ECER) database is available through the Council for Exceptional Children on compact disc or by subscription for Internet access. This proprietary database is devoted solely to professional literature in special education, gifted education, and related services.

E A S I
Equal Access to Software and Information

Site: Equal Access to Software and Information

URL: http://www.rit.edu/~easi

Sponsor: St. John's University

Subject Area(s): Special Needs   **Subcategory:** Disabilities

Grade Level(s): Adult

Description
The Equal Access to Software and Information (EASI) site focuses on access to higher mathematics and science for individuals with disabilities. The Electronic Journal contains information which is highly valuable to academic students who have visual and auditory impairments and the professionals who work with them.

Commentary
Math and science materials present a particular challenge to those assisting students with sensory impairments. The EASI Web site contains information not readily available in teachers' references, such as methods for assisting students with organic chemistry and calculus. Users who need a text interface can access EASI's old gopher site at: gopher://SJUVM.stjohns.edu:70/11/disabled/easi

---

Site: Facts for Families

URL: http://www.psych.med.umich.edu/web/aacap/factsFam/

Sponsor: American Academy of Child and Adolescent Psychology

Subject Area(s): Special Needs   **Subcategory:** Disabilities

Grade Level(s): Adult

Description
Facts for Families articles are published by the American Academy of Child and Adolescent Psychology to educate parents on psychiatric issues affecting children and youth. The index and articles are available in both English and Spanish and range from infant and children to adolescent topics.

Commentary
This page has been cited and recommended by a number of periodicals. Each article is concise, including pertinent, general information about the selected topic, often with a description and suggestion for how to seek professional assistance, if needed.

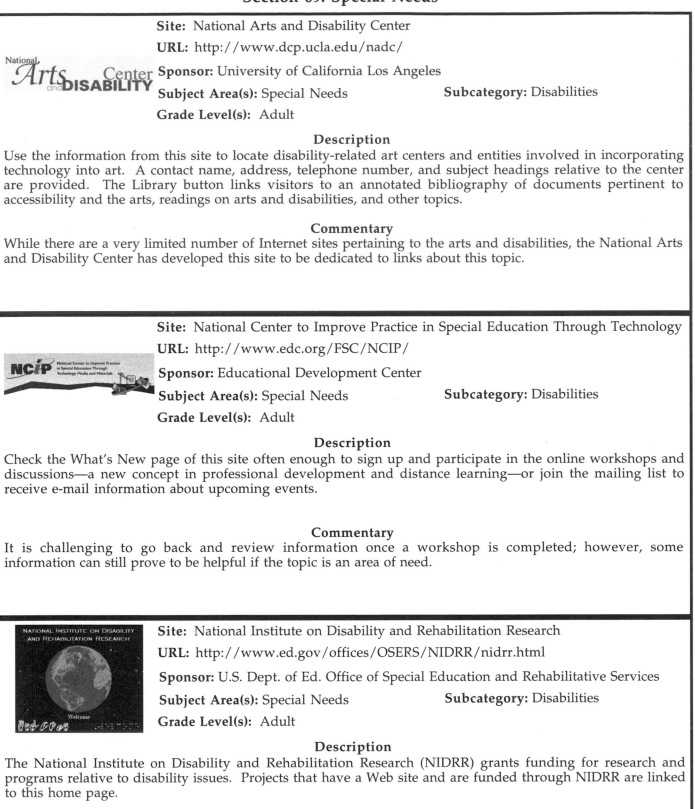

Site: National Arts and Disability Center

URL: http://www.dcp.ucla.edu/nadc/

Sponsor: University of California Los Angeles

Subject Area(s): Special Needs   **Subcategory:** Disabilities

Grade Level(s): Adult

Description
Use the information from this site to locate disability-related art centers and entities involved in incorporating technology into art. A contact name, address, telephone number, and subject headings relative to the center are provided. The Library button links visitors to an annotated bibliography of documents pertinent to accessibility and the arts, readings on arts and disabilities, and other topics.

Commentary
While there are a very limited number of Internet sites pertaining to the arts and disabilities, the National Arts and Disability Center has developed this site to be dedicated to links about this topic.

Site: National Center to Improve Practice in Special Education Through Technology

URL: http://www.edc.org/FSC/NCIP/

Sponsor: Educational Development Center

Subject Area(s): Special Needs   **Subcategory:** Disabilities

Grade Level(s): Adult

Description
Check the What's New page of this site often enough to sign up and participate in the online workshops and discussions—a new concept in professional development and distance learning—or join the mailing list to receive e-mail information about upcoming events.

Commentary
It is challenging to go back and review information once a workshop is completed; however, some information can still prove to be helpful if the topic is an area of need.

Site: National Institute on Disability and Rehabilitation Research

URL: http://www.ed.gov/offices/OSERS/NIDRR/nidrr.html

Sponsor: U.S. Dept. of Ed. Office of Special Education and Rehabilitative Services

Subject Area(s): Special Needs   **Subcategory:** Disabilities

Grade Level(s): Adult

Description
The National Institute on Disability and Rehabilitation Research (NIDRR) grants funding for research and programs relative to disability issues. Projects that have a Web site and are funded through NIDRR are linked to this home page.

Commentary
The project list may be viewed by program area or alphabetical listing for easier location of project titles. Listings include postal addresses and Internet Universal Resource Locator (URL) addresses.

Site: Office of Special Education and Rehabilitative Services

URL: http://www.ed.gov/offices/OSERS/

Sponsor: U. S. Department of Education

Subject Area(s): Special Needs   **Subcategory:** Disabilities

Grade Level(s): Adult

Description

The Office of Special Education and Rehabilitative Services Web site links visitors to the three program components under its jurisdiction—The Office of Special Education Programs, The Rehabilitative Services Administration, and the National Institute on Disability and Rehabilitation Research.

Commentary

Check the What's New in OSERS link for an update of the latest policies affecting the Office of Special Education and Rehabilitative Services.

Site: Peterson's: Special Schools

URL: http://www.petersons.com/special/

Sponsor: Peterson's

Subject Area(s): Special Needs   **Subcategory:** Disabilities

Grade Level(s): Adult

Description

At the Peterson's Education & Career Center Web site, pressing the "Special Schools" button brings visitors to this site, which has a listing of residential schools, primarily for students with learning and emotional challenges. There is a description of each program and the population served. Links to more in-depth program information are provided when available.

Commentary

The Summer Programs button allows you to search by submitting criteria including "Specialty Clientele" under which disability-specific information may be selected, if desired. Select Peterson's Open Choices button to utilize its new enrollment advisory service in which you select "message categories" and are provided information about universities seeking students for enrollment.

Site: Special Education Resources on the Internet

URL: http://www.hood.edu/seri/serihome.html

Sponsor: Hood University

Subject Area(s): Special Needs   **Subcategory:** Disabilities

Grade Level(s): Adult

Description

The main menu of this site is categorized into numerous comprehensive topic areas in special education. Links to Web sites are listed under each topic, usually with a brief description to aid in narrowing the focus of your search.

Commentary

Online searching is not available here; however, the topic list will prove helpful when you are looking for a specific area of interest.

Section 09. Special Needs

Modest

Site: Special Needs Education Network

URL: http://www.schoolnet.ca/sne/

Sponsor: SchoolNet Project

Subject Area(s): Special Needs   **Subcategory:** Disabilities

Grade Level(s): Adult

Description

This award-winning site connects visitors to multiple links through a directory which includes disability-specific categories, family support, gifted and talented, youth at-risk, and many others. Online searching of the SNE site and the World Wide Web is possible. The SNE monthly newsletter is available online, as is a listing of international conferences, user comments, and mailing lists.

Commentary

This site is a must for anyone interested in youth with special needs.

Site: The Federal Resource Center for Special Education

URL: http://www.dssc.org/frc/

Sponsor: U.S. Dept. of Ed., Office of Special Education and Rehabilitative Services

Subject Area(s): Special Needs   **Subcategory:** Disabilities

Grade Level(s): Adult

Description

The Federal Resource Center for Special Education is dedicated to benefiting children, youth, toddlers and infants with disabilities, and the families and professionals who are associated with them. The Web site of the Federal Resource Center relates the latest information and current trends in education, education Web resources, and research and technical assistance projects, among others.

Commentary

All of the sites listed in the Education Web Resources Special and General Education Links are non-commercial and not-for-profit enterprises. The annotated parent and family resource list will prove beneficial to those seeking parent support and information.

Site: CTDNet (Center for Talent Development Network)

URL: http://ctdnet.acns.nwu.edu

Sponsor: Northwestern University

Subject Area(s): Special Needs   **Subcategory:** Gifted and Talented

Grade Level(s): Adult

Description

The Center for Talent Development provides support and services for academically gifted and talented youth. There are updated articles of interest; information for parents, such as recommended reading lists and the suggested role for parents in homework; resources for teachers and counselors, such as use of the Internet; curriculum standards; and more. CTD also conducts a Midwest Talent Search for gifted students.

Commentary

CTDMOO, the CTD's virtual community, is a gathering place of bright students, a place you may want to let your child or students explore. In the gallery, they will find student writing, artwork, music, video, sound, and more. You must be a subscriber to submit work. The "Letterlinks" program allows students to take correspondence courses via postal mail, electronically utilizing multimedia course materials and e-mail.

Site: LD OnLine

URL: http://ldonline.org/

Sponsor: Corporation for Public Broadcasting

Subject Area(s): Special Needs   **Subcategory:** Learning Disabilities

Grade Level(s): Adult

Description

Learning disabilities and attention deficit disorder are addressed in depth on multiple information pages accessed from the directory. Weekly highlights, an artist and author of the week, on the home page are enticing and attractive. Don't miss the Kid Zone which displays art and writing submitted by youths, a reading list to help kids handle learning and reading differences, and articles to promote self-advocacy.

Commentary

Select Interact Up in the Kid Zone to find out which famous people had learning differences and experience reading with a learning disability. The emphasis on personal responsibility and self-advocacy is commendable.

LD Resources

Site: LD Resources

URL: http://www.ldresources.com/

Sponsor: Richard and Anne Wanderman

Subject Area(s): Special Needs   **Subcategory:** Learning Disabilities

Grade Level(s): Adult

Description

Freeware and shareware for Macintosh computers may be downloaded from this site, as well as numerous articles pertaining to learning disabilities, dyslexia, and related topics. Several of the articles were written by individuals with learning disabilities, lending a personal perspective to the information included.

Commentary

Freeware may be downloaded, copied, and shared freely at no cost. Shareware is available at no cost for trial and may be copied and shared with others; however, the developers request that you send in a registration fee if you use the shareware beyond trying it. Shareware registration costs are usually minimal ($5.00 for those from LD Resources). The articles often apply to areas beyond learning disabilities.

Site: Family Village at University of Wisconsin

URL: http://www.familyvillage.wisc.edu/

Sponsor: The Joseph P. Kennedy, Jr. Fdn.; Mitsubishi Electric America Fdn.

Subject Area(s): Special Needs   **Subcategory:** Mental Retardation

Grade Level(s): Adult

Description

This nicely-organized site is devoted to information and resources needed by family members involved in the life of a person with mental retardation. Some of the unique information found at this site includes recreation and leisure, art activities, and religious education.

Commentary

This site is more comprehensive than it appears when first looking at the home page. It is worth spending some time exploring the many pages and links included.

Site: The Arc

URL: http://TheArc.org/welcome.html

Sponsor: The Arc

Subject Area(s): Special Needs   **Subcategory:** Mental Retardation

Grade Level(s): Adult

Description
The Arc is the largest voluntary organization committed to the welfare of children and adults with mental retardation. Fact sheets found under the Q&A heading are well written and contain useful information written in understandable language. Some fact sheets are available in Spanish. Extensive Internet links about disabilities are listed in the section titled Disability-Related Sites on the World Wide Web.

Commentary
Visitors may locate home pages of state and local chapters of The Arc that are linked to this national site.

Site: Access Ability Alaska

URL: http://www.alaska.net/~ckayaker

Sponsor: Doyle E. Burnett, M. Ed.

Subject Area(s): Special Needs   **Subcategory:** Visual Impairments

Grade Level(s): Adult

Description
Access Ability Alaska provides information about access to World Wide Web pages for persons with visual impairments who use screen-reading software. Links are included to sites relative to Assistive Technology, Blind Resources, and Internet Tools and Resources.

Commentary
This site serves as a means to link to vendors and individuals who use alternative methods to access technology and communicate.

Site: American Council of the Blind

URL: http://acb.org/

Sponsor: American Council of the Blind

Subject Area(s): Special Needs   **Subcategory:** Visual Impairments

Grade Level(s): Adult

Description
Use this site for information about the purpose of the American Council of the Blind, activities in which it is involved, current and back issues of the monthly publication, a jobs list, resources for products and services, and links to related sites.

Commentary
The American Council of the Blind also includes members who are not visually impaired. Scholarship assistance to individuals who are blind or visually impaired is one of the services provided.

Site: American Foundation for the Blind

URL: http://www.igc.apc.org/afb

Sponsor: MCI Foundation

Subject Area(s): Special Needs   **Subcategory:** Visual Impairments

Grade Level(s): Adult

Description
As a leading national resource for individuals with visual impairments, the American Foundation for the Blind's Web site provides articles, bibliographies, and reports of activities involving public and political policy.

Commentary
Parents may be especially interested in the "Guide to Toys for Children Who Are Blind and Visually Impaired" and the list of jobs held by individuals with visual impairment. Some information is not available online and must be accessed by request to the American Foundation for the Blind.

Site: Blindness Resource Center at the NY Institute for Special Education

URL: http://www.nyise.org/blind.html

Sponsor: Duxbury Systems, Humanware, Raised Dot Computing, et. al.

Subject Area(s): Special Needs   **Subcategory:** Visual Impairments

Grade Level(s): Adult

Description
This site is well-designed and comprehensive within the field of visual impairments. All pages allow for text access by individuals using speech access software. One unique listing includes links to Web home pages of the blind community. The directory provides access to research information, resources, technology, Web design for people with disabilities, and audio, e-texts, books, libraries, and news/magazines on the Internet.

Commentary
"What's New on the Web" is updated monthly with new or newly-found links related to blindness and visual impairment.

Site: Braille

URL: http://world.std.com/~duxbury/braille.html

Sponsor: Duxbury Systems, Inc.

Subject Area(s): Special Needs   **Subcategory:** Visual Impairments

Grade Level(s): Adult

Description
Read about Louis Braille, who at the age of 3, while playing in his father's shop, injured his eye on a sharp tool. Blindness eventually resulted in both eyes. Learn how the basic technique of using raised dots for tactile writing and reading, known as Braille, was invented.

Commentary
Learn about the history behind Braille and the process itself. Also included at this site are links to additional resources, e.g., pamphlets, fact sheets, and similiar materials.

Site: Internet Braille Wizard

URL: http://www.access2020.com/access-cgi/braille.bin

Sponsor: Access 20/20

Subject Area(s): Special Needs   **Subcategory:** Visual Impairments

Grade Level(s): Adult

Description
Type in a word or phrase and have the Braille Wizard translate it into braille.

Commentary
The translation to braille is produced using grade 2 braille—contractions are used for certain words and letter combinations.

10 WWW
USING THE INTERNET

The last section of the *Directory* identifies 63 sites for learning about the Internet and its various uses in education organized into subcategories such as:

- ➤ ACCEPTABLE USE
- ➤ COMMUNICATION AND E-MAIL
- ➤ GUIDES TO THE INTERNET
- ➤ MISCELLANEOUS
- ➤ PROJECTS
- ➤ RESEARCH
- ➤ SEARCH ENGINES
- ➤ WEB PAGE DESIGN
- ➤ WORLD WIDE WEB INDEXES

One interesting site under Projects, for example, is "Intercultural E-mail Classroom Connections," sponsored by St. Olaf College. This site provides mailing lists so teachers and classes can link with partners in other countries and cultures. And "A Beginner's Guide to Effective E-mail," sponsored by Kaitlin D. Sherwood, offers instruction and tips for effective electronic communications.

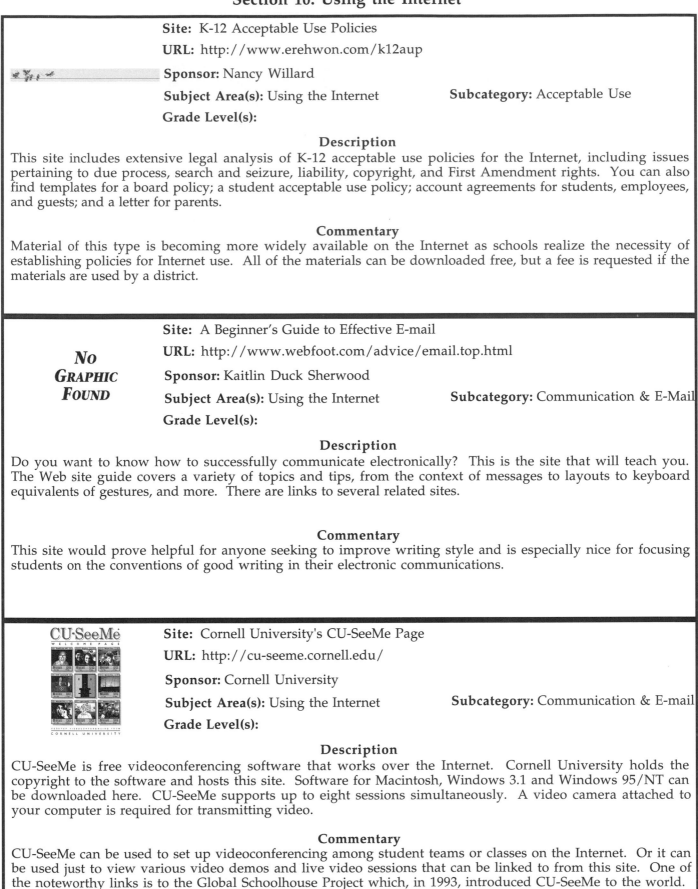

Site: K-12 Acceptable Use Policies

URL: http://www.erehwon.com/k12aup

Sponsor: Nancy Willard

Subject Area(s): Using the Internet   **Subcategory:** Acceptable Use

Grade Level(s):

Description
This site includes extensive legal analysis of K-12 acceptable use policies for the Internet, including issues pertaining to due process, search and seizure, liability, copyright, and First Amendment rights. You can also find templates for a board policy; a student acceptable use policy; account agreements for students, employees, and guests; and a letter for parents.

Commentary
Material of this type is becoming more widely available on the Internet as schools realize the necessity of establishing policies for Internet use. All of the materials can be downloaded free, but a fee is requested if the materials are used by a district.

No Graphic Found

Site: A Beginner's Guide to Effective E-mail

URL: http://www.webfoot.com/advice/email.top.html

Sponsor: Kaitlin Duck Sherwood

Subject Area(s): Using the Internet   **Subcategory:** Communication & E-Mail

Grade Level(s):

Description
Do you want to know how to successfully communicate electronically? This is the site that will teach you. The Web site guide covers a variety of topics and tips, from the context of messages to layouts to keyboard equivalents of gestures, and more. There are links to several related sites.

Commentary
This site would prove helpful for anyone seeking to improve writing style and is especially nice for focusing students on the conventions of good writing in their electronic communications.

CU-SeeMe WELCOME PAGE

CORNELL UNIVERSITY

Site: Cornell University's CU-SeeMe Page

URL: http://cu-seeme.cornell.edu/

Sponsor: Cornell University

Subject Area(s): Using the Internet   **Subcategory:** Communication & E-mail

Grade Level(s):

Description
CU-SeeMe is free videoconferencing software that works over the Internet. Cornell University holds the copyright to the software and hosts this site. Software for Macintosh, Windows 3.1 and Windows 95/NT can be downloaded here. CU-SeeMe supports up to eight sessions simultaneously. A video camera attached to your computer is required for transmitting video.

Commentary
CU-SeeMe can be used to set up videoconferencing among student teams or classes on the Internet. Or it can be used just to view various video demos and live video sessions that can be linked to from this site. One of the noteworthy links is to the Global Schoolhouse Project which, in 1993, introduced CU-SeeMe to the world.

Site: CU-SeeMe Schools

URL: http://www.gsn.org/gsn/cu/index.html

Sponsor: Global SchoolNet Foundation

Subject Area(s): Using the Internet   **Subcategory:** Communication & E-mail

Grade Level(s):

Description

This list puts the teacher in touch with other K-12 schools around the world who have the capability to do CU-SeeMe video conferencing over the Internet. There is information about exemplary sites, equipment, and resources for teleconferencing.

Commentary

It's a lot of fun to look at what some of the schools are doing with this technology and to pick up new terminology, such as "collapse the header to get more screen real-estate." This is a great place to explore implementing this technology or perhaps to improve your existing program.

Site: Highway 1

URL: http://www.highway1.org

Sponsor: Highway 1

Subject Area(s): Using the Internet   **Subcategory:** Guides to the Internet

Grade Level(s):

Description

Highway 1 is a non-partisan, nonprofit organization seeking to help the U.S. Congress and other government leaders to understand and use technology. This site provides a clearinghouse of resources, including research, program reports and Web sites of special schools, libraries, and community centers. You will find a tribute to the late Secretary of Commerce Ron Brown.

Commentary

Highway 1 is a steering committee member of the U. S. Internet Council, and its Web site can be linked to from this one.

Site: Internet Advocate

URL: http://www.monroe.lib.in.us/~lchampel/netadv.html

Sponsor: L. Champelli

Subject Area(s): Using the Internet   **Subcategory:** Guides to the Internet

Grade Level(s):

Description

Categories at this site include: Respond to Inaccurate Perceptions of Porn on the Net, Promote Positive Examples of Youth Internet Use, Develop an "Acceptable Use Policy" (AUP), Understand Software to Block Internet Sites and Related Safety/Censorship Issues, Contact Organizations Committed to Electronic Freedom of Information, and Familiarize Yourself with Additional Internet Resources for Librarians.

Commentary

This site claims to be a Web-based Resource Guide for Librarians and Educators Interested in Providing Youth Access to the Net. It is true that many who are not so informed about the Internet are fearful of stories they hear about its dangers to youth, and this site offers justification and resource information to cite in defending the Internet as a valuable tool for teaching and learning.

Section 10. Using the Internet

Site: Internet Hoaxes

URL: http://ciac.llnl.gov/ciac/CIACHoaxes.html

Sponsor: U.S. Department of Energy

Subject Area(s): Using the Internet   **Subcategory:** Guides to the Internet

Grade Level(s):

Description

There are real computer viruses and fake ones on the Internet, and this is the official and authoritative site for finding out which are real and which are not. There are a number of examples you may find quite humorous.

Commentary

This site is an excellent resource for teaching acceptable use and responsible computing. What are the ethical issues involved when computer hoaxes are created and spread on the Internet? Who gets hurt by them? What can be done to control them?

Site: InternetDEN

URL: http://www.actden.com/net_den/index.html

Sponsor: ACT Laboratory, Ltd.

Subject Area(s): Using the Internet   **Subcategory:** Guides to the Internet

Grade Level(s):

Description

Join Sputnik, your cyberspace flight instructor (and great, great, grand-puppy of the first dog in space), is online to guide you through the basics of the Internet. Lessons begin with A Brief History of Cyberspace—An Introduction to the Internet: Past and Present, and go through Beaming Up and Down—Transferring Files Using WS_FTP.

Commentary

Lessons and navigation are based on Microsoft's Internet Explorer as the chosen browser. If you are using Netscape or another browser, the lessons, 12 in all, will still have value. Lessons are written in an easy-to-understand style with screen shots and diagrams to contribute to the user's understanding. Use this as a personal reference or with students.

Site: Just for Educators: Your Own Web Guide

URL: http://place.scholastic.com/el/guide/index.html

Sponsor: Scholastic, Inc.

Subject Area(s): Using the Internet   **Subcategory:** Guides to the Internet

Grade Level(s):

Description

Electronic Learning provides getting-started tips, stories from teachers at each level from pre-K through high school, plus more than 100 favorite sites of the editors. For the novice on the Web, the "All about the Web" section includes some Web basics, starter sites, search engines, and terms that are helpful to know.

Commentary

Outstanding—an absolute must for educators! While some might view the search engine section as incomplete, it is apparent that the main focus here is on the beginning Web user. The section entitled "Making It Work for Your Grade Level" is unique among Web sites in providing concrete grade level information for teachers.

Section 10. Using the Internet

Site: KickStart

URL: http://www.benton.org/Library/KickStart/

Sponsor: Benton Foundation

Subject Area(s): Using the Internet   **Subcategory:** Guides to the Internet

Grade Level(s):

Description

KickStart, an initiative of the U.S. Advisory Council on the National Information Infrastructure, was created by President Clinton at the end of 1993 and was comprised of representatives of state and local government, community, public interest, education, labor groups and also creators and distributors of content, private industry, privacy and security advocates, and learning experts in NII-related fields.

Commentary

Gain information to help communities get onto the Information Superhighway, including reasons why stakeholders in schools, libraries, and the community should be part of advocacy groups to build the required infrastructure. Link to schools, libraries, and community centers that are models of connectivity.

Site: NetGlos: The Multilingual Glossary of Internet Terminology

URL: http://wwli.com/translation/netglos/netglos.html

NetGlos - The Multilingual Glossary of Internet Terminology **Sponsor:** WorldWide Language Institute

Subject Area(s): Using the Internet   **Subcategory:** Guides to the Internet

Grade Level(s):

Description

NetGlos is a multilingual glossary of Internet terminology currently being compiled as a voluntary project by a number of translators and other professionals. There are about a dozen languages on the site now, with others being prepared. The viewer selects a language, then reads an alphabetical list of Internet terms and the English equivalent.

Commentary

There is a large advantage for the English reader here. The English list of Internet terms provides a definition of each with the opportunity to learn that word in a variety of languages. Readers in other languages scroll through a list of terms in their own language, which then connects to the word and definition in English. Still...a great idea as the Internet increasingly globalizes.

Site: The Internet–Ideas, Activities, and Resources

URL: http://www.coedu.usf.edu/inst_tech/publications/pinkbook/

The Internet-Ideas, Activities and Resources **Sponsor:** Florida Center for Instructional Technology

Subject Area(s): Using the Internet   **Subcategory:** Guides to the Internet

Grade Level(s):

Description

This electronic book can be used directly from the Internet or reproduced for some offline activities. Find telecommunication project ideas listed by subject area. The overview of the Internet explains the concept and terminology associated with telecommunications, and there are links to some standard reference databases.

Commentary

This site is just a little bit outdated, but text-based browsers and gophers have not yet disappeared from the world. Most of the information and activities are appropriate. The Internet hunts are fun—especially "Where in the Internet is Carlos Sarasota?"

Section 10. Using the Internet

Site: The List

URL: http://thelist.internet.com/

Sponsor: Mecklermedia

Subject Area(s): Using the Internet   **Subcategory:** Guides to the Internet

Grade Level(s):

Description

This site provides lists of Internet Service Providers (ISPs) for the U.S., Canada, and the world. It is organized to be easily searched in a variety of ways, and there is also a map showing the location of area codes for the U. S. and Canada.

Commentary

Many ISPs operate in a wide geographic territory and have 800 numbers. To locate ISPs who have actual offices near your school, search by fax area code.

Site: Web66: A K-12 World Wide Web Project

URL: http://web66.coled.umn.edu

Sponsor: University of Minnesota

Subject Area(s): Using the Internet   **Subcategory:** Guides to the Internet

Grade Level(s):

Description

This site provides an international Registry of K-12 Schools on the Web, a Network Construction Set, and additional resources to help schools get connected and on the Web. Find curriculum suggestions, technical tips and resources for designing Web projects, and integrating Web activities into the curriculum. The link to the Mustang Project is valuable—a site focused on integrating use of the Internet into the K-12 classroom.

Commentary

The Web66 project has been designed to facilitate the introduction of Internet technology into K-12 schools. This is an excellent site for educators to get started with on the World Wide Web. There is a great deal of support information here for both teachers and students. At the beginning of 1996, Web66 reported nearly 2,000 K-12 Web sites; by early 1997, the number exceeded 6,000 and continues to grow.

Widener University/Wolfgram Memorial Library
Evaluating Web Resources

Site: WWW Evaluations

URL: http://www.science.widener.edu/~withers/webeval.html

Sponsor: Widener University / Wolfgram Memorial Library

Subject Area(s): Using the Internet   **Subcategory:** Guides to the Internet

Grade Level(s):

Description

Here you'll find a variety of materials to assist in the teaching of how to evaluate World Wide Web resources. The focus is on teaching critical thinking skills. Some of the resources you will find include a PowerPoint presentation, Checklists for Advocacy, Business, News, Informational and Personal Web Pages, and links to sites which can be used to illustrate evaluation concepts of Authority, Accuracy, and Objectivity.

Commentary

As students and teachers are doing more and more research on the Internet, there is an increasing need to be able to evaluate the resources that are being found. There are no graphics here—just a very informative site that offers teaching ideas, checklists, examples, and links to additional sites with Web evaluation materials.

Site: American School Directory

URL: http://www.cfe.com/asd.html

Sponsor: Computers for Education, Inc.

Subject Area(s): Using the Internet

Subcategory: Miscellaneous

Grade Level(s):

Description

The American School Directory, an Internet guide to all 106,000 K-12 schools, provides information and communication for teachers, students, and parents. Schools can be located by name, city, state, or zip code. The reader can then examine the Web site for the school, search for a student, register in the Alumni Directory, or locate classmates with the message board.

Commentary

Classmates must register at this site in order to be located, so in its early stages this may not be the most efficient way to locate friends. It is, however, a great way to examine sample Web pages—there is always a "School of the Day" featured. It also provides a means of checking out schools in a new location to which a family is contemplating a move.

Site: Learning@Web.Sites: Educational Computing Department

URL: http://www.ecnet.net/users/gdlevin/educomp.html

Educational Computing Department **Sponsor:** David Levin

Subject Area(s): Using the Internet

Subcategory: Miscellaneous

Grade Level(s):

Description

Start here for two great hotlists of links—one for Internet Topics and Tools and one for WWW Design Resources. Find Acceptable Use policies, e-mail classroom exchange information, technology planning resources, Internet newsgroups and resources, shareware, tutorials, and links to much, much more.

Commentary

Educators should be sure to review the section on The Impact of Technology. The question constantly arises, "Does technology really improve learning?" The resources offered here will help educators successfully respond to this question.

Site: NetDay 2000

URL: http://www.netday96.com

Sponsor: NetDay 2000

Subject Area(s): Using the Internet

Subcategory: Miscellaneous

Grade Level(s):

Description

This is the site of the Internet roll call. Find out how many schools are online. A map of the US shows the locations of the nearly 140,000 K-12 schools in the country. Different colors reflects no Internet connection, a single-user or a multi-user connection. Your school can communicate with the Webmaster at this site to let them know the changed status of your own school.

Commentary

For those interested in organizing a NetDay, there are strategies, handouts, and opportunities to assist in the task. A free online and satellite-distributed workshop is available as well as phone and e-mail support for questions that might arise. There is also a glossary of Internet terms that students, teachers, and parents might all find useful.

Section 10. Using the Internet

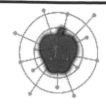

Site: NetSchool

URL: http://www.netschool.com

Sponsor: Pierian Spring Software

Subject Area(s): Using the Internet   **Subcategory:** Miscellaneous

Grade Level(s):

Description
The sponsors of this site are providing free Web site hosting for schools, students, and teachers. The emphasis is on the secondary and primary education community. Viewers may examine thousands of school-related Web pages in addition to registering their own. A showcase spotlights the best of the K-12 authored Web sites.

Commentary
Two additional features will be of interest to teachers. The first is a Web Page Workshop for individuals (separate areas for teachers and students) interested in learning how to create Web pages and access a variety of education-related images. Teacher Resources for Effective Education contains a decision tree for ease in locating resources in specific subject matter areas.

Site: California Web Project

URL: http://calweb.cue.org/index.html

Sponsor: Computer-Using Educators

Subject Area(s): Using the Internet   **Subcategory:** Projects

Grade Level(s):

Description
The California Web Project uses the communication resources of the Internet and a focus on California in order to weave contributions together under various themes such as history, geography, agriculture, science, conservation, business, government, politics, cultures, music, and art.

Commentary
Browse the projects by school name, city, or grade level...or search by curriculum area, community theme, or a California theme. There are lots of ideas for things teachers might do with students in their classrooms.

Site: Electronic Emissary

URL: http://www.tapr.org/emissary

Sponsor: Judi Harris, University of Texas

Subject Area(s): Using the Internet   **Subcategory:** Projects

Grade Level(s):

Description
Dr. Judi Harris and her staff act as electronic emissaries by locating Internet account-holders with subject matter expertise relevant to their curricula who are willing to volunteer some of their time to share their knowledge via electronic mail. This telecommunications project not only matches classrooms and subject matter experts, but also provides training and guidance so that the process proceeds smoothly.

Commentary
Begin by reading general information about the project which includes some examples of matches between classrooms and subject matter specialists. Readers of this page may search the database of experts, submit a match request for their classrooms, and/or volunteer to serve as an Electronic Emissary subject matter expert.

Site: Global Schoolhouse

URL: http://k12.cnidr.org/gsh/gshwelcome.html

Sponsor: National Science Foundation

Subject Area(s): Using the Internet   **Subcategory:** Projects

Grade Level(s):

Description

The Global Schoolhouse project was partially funded by the National Science Foundation and supported also by many local and national businesses. It ended officially in December of 1994. It was designed to show the uses of the Internet in classroom teaching, particularly in enabling collaboration by students and classes that are geographically separated from each other.

Commentary

Links to many of the participating schools and teachers are available and can be found here, as can the final reports and evaluations for the project.

Site: Global SchoolNet Foundation

URL: http://www.gsn.org/indexhi.html

Sponsor: Global SchoolNet Foundation

Subject Area(s): Using the Internet   **Subcategory:** Projects

Grade Level(s):

Description

Global SchoolNet arranges materials in several formats so that teachers can locate resources with ease. There are articles, contests, events, lists, projects, and more. One section, the Global Schoolhouse, contains Internet resources for teachers to use. Look at K-12 Opportunities, which is searchable by keyword, and the Projects Registry, where you can find information on curriculum projects or add your own project to the list.

Commentary

This is one of the best places to look for ongoing projects which will help link your classroom to others around the country...and around the world. Since 1985 Global SchoolNet Foundation (GSN) has made a significant impact in the instructional applications of telecommunications.

Site: iEARN: Youth Making A Difference In The World Through Telecomm.

URL: http://www.iearn.org/iearn

Sponsor: I*EARN

Subject Area(s): Using the Internet   **Subcategory:** Projects

Grade Level(s):

Description

I*EARN is a nonprofit, international organization which connects schools and youth service organizations around the world. The overall goal is for young people to undertake projects designed to make a meaningful contribution to the health and welfare of the planet and its people—and share these strategies and successes via the Internet.

Commentary

The I*EARN globe points to the many countries around the world in which there are projects. The project also sponsors international meetings in various countries. There is substantial information about various projects posted and a listing of sponsoring organizations.

Section 10. Using the Internet

Site: Intercultural E-Mail Classroom Connections

URL: http://www.stolaf.edu/network/iecc

Sponsor: St. Olaf College

Subject Area(s): Using the Internet   **Subcategory:** Projects

Grade Level(s):

Description

The Intercultural E-Mail Classroom Connections mailing lists are provided as a service to help teachers and classes link with partners in other countries and cultures. Since its creation in 1992, the project has distributed over 19,000 requests for e-mail partnerships. Readers may subscribe to a mailing list, read about projects, and participate in discussions.

Commentary

Perhaps the most useful part of this project is the section for teachers seeking partner classrooms for international and cross-cultural electronic mail exchanges. This is an easier-to-manage option than the attempt at penpals for individual class members. The related resources will direct you to other mailing lists and language resources.

KIDPROJ

Site: KIDPROJ

URL: http://www.kidlink.org/KIDPROJ

Sponsor: KIDLINK

Subject Area(s): Using the Internet   **Subcategory:** Projects

Grade Level(s):

Description

Teachers and youth group leaders from around the world plan activities and projects for their students' participation. Participation in projects is limited to kids between the ages of 10 and 15 years old. A listing of the present projects provides information for participation. Some basic information must be provided in English, but there is support for projects in native languages.

Commentary

Take the Webmaster's recommendation and begin your browsing with the "Getting Started" section. The international flavor of this site will be a welcomed classroom addition for many teachers. There is the opportunity for kids to correspond with other kids in their native language as well as participate in many cross-cultural projects involving games, family history, songs, etc.

Site: National School Network Testbed

URL: http://copernicus.bbn.com/testbed2/bts/bts.html

Sponsor: National Science Foundation

Subject Area(s): Using the Internet   **Subcategory:** Projects

Grade Level(s):

Description

The National School Network Testbed works with schools and communities to explore networking as a tool for school change. At this site, you will find summaries of projects going on in various locations, with information provided about the school involved and anecdotal records for each.

Commentary

If you are a teacher, scroll through the list of school projects for some inspiration for things you might try in your classroom. There are unfortunately a few dead links, but enough are alive and well to make the search worthwhile.

Section 10. Using the Internet

Site: Online Class

URL: http://www.onlineclass.com/

OnlineClass **Sponsor:** TBT International

Subject Area(s): Using the Internet   **Subcategory:** Projects

Grade Level(s):

Description

The Online Class Schedule is posted before the school year begins, and this year includes such assorted topics as "Mythos: Zeus Speaks!" for grades 3-8, "Blue Ice: Focus on Antarctics" for grades 4-12, "The North American Quilt: A Living Geography Project" for grades 4-12, "DoodleOpolis: Adventures in Urban Architecture" for grades 3-8, and many more. Print materials are provided, and there is a fee for joining a project.

Commentary

This is a well-organized site, and the projects sound intriguing. The focus on "content over technology" is sound as are the recommendations from several organizations. Individual teachers may want to explore this guided approach to integrating telecommunications into the classroom.

A Project of
Computer Learning Foundation

Site: Our Town

URL: http://www.computerlearning.org/ourtown.html

Sponsor: Computer Learning Foundation

Subject Area(s): Using the Internet   **Subcategory:** Projects

Grade Level(s):

Description

This Web site contains the projects conceived and developed by teachers and their students in order to convey historical and current information about their town. The project leaders provide guidelines for conducting the research and a place to display the results. There is a charge for the development kit, which includes tutorials and Web page software.

Commentary

Towns from Rock Hill, South Carolina to New York City have participated in this project with online information about their towns. There is a competition with prizes, but most interesting is the opportunity to upgrade the interactive capabilities of your pages as teachers, and students become more proficient in their Web page skills.

Site: Projects & Programs

URL: http://www.gsn.org/project/index.html

PROJECTS & PROGRAMS **Sponsor:** Global SchoolNet

Subject Area(s): Using the Internet   **Subcategory:** Projects

Grade Level(s):

Description

The centerpiece of this home page is the Internet Project Registry, designed for teachers searching for appropriate online projects to integrate into their required coursework. Projects are listed by the month in which they will begin, usually with about four months of anticipation time. Teachers may also subscribe to the moderated Hilites mailing list to receive timely notice of projects which will be implemented.

Commentary

Responding to a request for participation is a logical first step for a teacher who would like to begin using Internet projects in his/her classroom. There are links to related resources with the opportunity to post projects you develop at this site.

Section 10. Using the Internet

Site: Welcome to NASA's Quest Project

URL: http://quest.arc.nasa.gov

Sponsor: Education Program, National Aeronautic and Space Administration

Subject Area(s): Using the Internet   **Subcategory:** Projects

Grade Level(s):

Description
The mission of this site is to provide support and services for school, teachers, and schools, to fully utilize the Internet as a basic tool for learning. There are hot topics involving space, a schedule of online events, online interactive projects, and information about the video series and other NASA resources for use in the classroom.

Commentary
The search capacities at this site are really exciting. It is possible to search for projects, resources, events, plus hundreds of other keyword concepts related to space exploration. Teachers will also be interested in online educational opportunities and links to other resources.

NCSA
UNIVERSITY OF ILLINOIS AT URBANA-CHAMPAIGN

Site: Education and Community (NCSA)

URL: http://www.ncsa.uiuc.edu/Edu/MSTE/nationalprojects.html

Sponsor: National Center for Supercomputing Applications

Subject Area(s): Using the Internet   **Subcategory:** Research

Grade Level(s):

Description
The National Center for Supercomputing Applications is primarily involved in developing and optimizing code of high-performance computers. The Center has an outreach component which provides services to K-12 teachers, such as Web page design, training of technology trainers, and high school math instruction.

Commentary
Math teachers will want to check out the courses and tutorials available for them. Most provide university credit and are Web-based. The Interactive Statistics module looks especially interesting, and registration can be accomplished as a guest or for credit.

Site: All-in-One Search Page

URL: http://www.albany.net/allinone/

Sponsor: William D. Cross

Subject Area(s): Using the Internet   **Subcategory:** Search Engines

Grade Level(s): Middle School, High School

Description
This is a mega-search engine site, allowing users to search over 200 Web-based search engines using a consistent interface. Any one of the eleven general sections can be clicked on to expand it into subsections which are also searchable.

Commentary
Since users need to understand basic search techniques in order to use these advanced procedures, this site is not for beginning Web searchers.

Section 10. Using the Internet

Site: AltaVista Search

URL: http://www.altavista.digital.com

Sponsor: Digital Corporation

Subject Area(s): Using the Internet   **Subcategory:** Search Engines

Grade Level(s):

Description

This search engine allows you to search various string types to find sites that contain the keywords you enter. It is one of the most powerful search tools available on the Internet with submenus which are clearly categorized. Just for fun (or sometimes for good information), the 100 hottest Web sites are posted as well as Dilbert cartoons.

Commentary

At a recent national technology conference, teams from AltaVista, Lycos, and Yahoo competed with a scavenger hunt list to determine which search engine (or team) was fastest. Yahoo withdrew early, and AltaVista was the winner. This is a favorite search engine of many people.

Site: Argus Clearinghouse

URL: http://www.clearinghouse.net/

Sponsor: Argus Associates

Subject Area(s): Using the Internet   **Subcategory:** Search Engines

Grade Level(s):

Description

Describing itself as "The Internet's Premier Research Library," this site is intentionally limited to Internet-based resources. Searching from this site will not locate any print material, only computer-based information, all of which has been evaluated and rated by "Digital Librarians."

Commentary

The focus here is on quality of information more than quantity. Where most search engines would return thousands of hits from a simple search string, this site will frequently return fewer than ten. But because all the sites have been evaluated ahead of time, the odds of one of the "hits" being of interest is high.

Site: Ask Jeeves

URL: http://www.askjeeves.com

Sponsor: Ask Jeeves, Inc.

Subject Area(s): Using the Internet   **Subcategory:** Search Engines

Grade Level(s): Middle School, High School

Description

Ask Jeeves uses revolutionary search software that not only understands plain English but also steps you through the search process. For example, if you Ask Jeeves "What's on TV tonight?", he will provide you with a way to select your time zone and the type of program you are looking for. Ask "What is a cell?" He will help you refine your question—were you asking about a Biology topic, a battery cell, or perhaps a cell of a spreadsheet?

Commentary

Named after the unflappable British servant from literature, Jeeves can be your very own information valet. Ask Jeeves has been created using knowledge of a team of researchers, so using Ask Jeeves is like having the world's most knowledgeable Internet librarian at your side. Jeeves uses your choices to provide answers and automatically search other Internet databases.

Section 10. Using the Internet

Site: DejaNews

URL: http://www.dejanews.com/

Sponsor: DejaNews, Inc.

Subject Area(s): Using the Internet   **Subcategory:** Search Engines

Grade Level(s):

Description

Usenet is a collection of newsgroups on the Internet. It is the largest discussion and electronic publishing forum in the world. Deja News provides an easy way to search Usenet, much as Alta Vista, Lycos, and other search engines do for Web sites.

Commentary

This Web site is supported by sponsors and investors. Searching is very easy and quick, since all 175 gigabytes of information is indexed. Be aware that while a valuable source, newsgroups are not censored, so there is a chance that profanity and other inappropriate material may be encountered.

Site: Dogpile

URL: http://www.dogpile.com

Sponsor:

Subject Area(s): Using the Internet   **Subcategory:** Search Engines

Grade Level(s):

Description

Dogpile is a multi-search engine with a built-in timer. When you tell it to search, you not only indicate what to search for but also how much time to take doing it. If you tell it to search for 30 seconds, it finds as many hits as it can in that time and then shows them to you.

Commentary

Dogpile simultaneously searches other Web search engines as well as Usenet, FTP, and newswire resources. You can then continue searching using the site(s) that produced the best results using your search terms.

Site: Excite

URL: http://www.excite.com/

Sponsor: Excite, Inc.

Subject Area(s): Using the Internet   **Subcategory:** Search Engines

Grade Level(s):

Description

This general-purpose search engine site is divided into channels, two of which are Careers & Education and Computers & Internet. Other channels include topics of general interest. There are some interesting side trips you might enjoy taking such as "Rate Your Relationship" and "Play the Physical Fitness Challenge."

Commentary

The "Power Search" option allows users to perform advanced searching in a very simple and easy-to-understand manner.

Section 10. Using the Internet

Site: Four11: The Internet White Pages

URL: http://www.four11.com/

Sponsor: Four11 Corporation

Subject Area(s): Using the Internet   **Subcategory:** Search Engines

Grade Level(s):

Description

This search engine is specialized for helping you to locate e-mail addresses and telephone numbers for individuals. The sponsoring company says it has the largest database of e-mail addresses available, with over 10 million records in it. There is some valuable information here for making phone calls via the Internet.

Commentary

The centralized directory uses "USL" (User Location Service) to notify you when someone you wish to talk to over the Internet comes online, and to provide their e-mail address. There is also a link here to the Four11 Yellow Pages directory search. This site contains a number of "Free Offers" which might be distracting to students.

Site: GOTO.com

URL: http://www.goto.com/

Sponsor: GOTO.com

Subject Area(s): Using the Internet   **Subcategory:** Search Engines

Grade Level(s): Middle School, High School

Description

This is a very easy-to-use search engine suitable for Internet beginners. It is divided into these sections: People, Places, Products, Hobbies, and Searches. The People section, for example, contains a list of famous people, including musical groups, and clicking on an entry executes a search on that name. The other sections work in a similar fashion, and it is also possible to type in a search string.

Commentary

The GOTO.com Website uses a search engine that is the commercial version of the World Wide Web Worm (WWW Worm), which was originally designed and built by an Internet pioneer, Oliver McBryan. It was purchased by Idealab in 1997 and renamed "GOTO." Idealab is the parent company of GOTO.com.

Site: Hotbot

URL: http://www.hotbot.com

Sponsor: Wired Magazine

Subject Area(s): Using the Internet   **Subcategory:** Search Engines

Grade Level(s):

Description

Wired Magazine's audience is primarily high-technology professionals, and this well-organized Web site is particularly suited to the interests of this group. In addition to sections on technical topics such as Web tools and Programming, there are business-oriented topics such as SEC Filings and Initial Public Offerings.

Commentary

Some unusual search options characterize this search engine site. It is possible to search not only by keywords, but also by date, geographic location, and type of media (image, audio, video, Shockwave). When searching for North American data, it is possible to filter for the type of Web site (com, net, edu, org, or gov) on which the data is stored.

Section 10. Using the Internet

Site: InfoSeek

URL: http://www.infoseek.com

Sponsor: Infoseek Corporation

Subject Area(s): Using the Internet   **Subcategory:** Search Engines

Grade Level(s):

Description
This general-purpose search engine also includes specific sections to allow searching for Company Information, Imageseek (browsing or searching for images), Usenet Search, Yellow Pages, White Pages, and E-mail Addresses.

Commentary
The Infoseek Directory, a collection of over 500,000 Web sites rated by the Infoseek staff, is also available here along with a collection of reference resources and the Infoseek Investor, a source for stock market and related data.

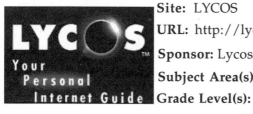

Site: LYCOS

URL: http://lycos.com

Sponsor: Lycos, Inc.

Subject Area(s): Using the Internet   **Subcategory:** Search Engines

Grade Level(s):

Description
Lycos is one of the major search engines on the Internet. In addition to possessing the usual search capabilities, it suggests ways to search for people, their telephone numbers, and even their e-mail addresses. Once you have located someone, you can get Lycos to draw a map that shows where that person lives and even get directions to go there!

Commentary
Lycos uses some special "Expert System" searching software and can find some sites that can be difficult to locate using standard search engines.   There are sections that search for information about specific cities in the United States, Canada, and the United Kingdom. There are also Lycos sites in France, Germany, Sweden, and the United Kingdom.

MAGELLAN
INTERNET GUIDE

Site: Magellan Internet Guide

URL: http://www.mckinley.com/

Sponsor: The McKinley Group, Inc.

Subject Area(s): Using the Internet   **Subcategory:** Search Engines

Grade Level(s):

Description
The key feature of this general-purpose search engine site is a set of options on what to search. The first option is to search the entire Web, over 60 million sites. The second option is to search only reviewed sites, over 60,000 Web sites reviewed by Magellan's experts. The last and most interesting option is to search only "Green Light" sites; these are sites that, when reviewed, were found to contain no content intended for mature audiences.

Commentary
The "Green Light Sites Only" option allows use of this search engine with all students. Note that Magellan does not guarantee that other sites linked to from Green Light Sites are free of adult topics or unregulated content. A mechanism for reporting findings of inappropriate material via e-mail is included at the site.

Section 10. Using the Internet

Site: NetScape Net Search

URL: http://home.netscape.com/escapes/search/ntsrchrnd-1.html

 **Sponsor:** Netscape Communications Corporation

Subject Area(s): Using the Internet   **Subcategory:** Search Engines

Grade Level(s):

Description

Rather than being a search engine itself, this site is an index to resources for searching and is divided into areas for search engines, Web guides, white and yellow pages, specialized searches, and a "help and information" section with tips on how to use the site.

Commentary

This approach to Internet searching is an advanced one and will probably be useful for students and adults who already have some experience with Web searching. But for experienced searchers, this site is a good "jumping off" place to start searching from, since it links to most of the other major search engine sites and is updated frequently.

Site: Newstracker Top Stories

URL: http://nt.excite.com

Sponsor: NewsTracker

Subject Area(s): Using the Internet   **Subcategory:** Search Engines

Grade Level(s):

Description

This site searches hundreds of Web periodicals and displays headline stories at the top of the page. Ongoing coverage of previous day's headline stories is also presented. Additionally, the site is searchable by keywords, and a list of the periodicals searched is available. There is also a "Daily Excite Poll" feature, and the "Newsstand" section provides links to other major online news Web sites.

Commentary

This is a great place to get ideas for current events projects or to search for breaking news stories for the school newspaper. The online help system is an excellent guide to searching both this site as well as other Internet sites. Up to 20 custom search topics can be created and tracked.

Site: Search Engines Front Page

URL: http://www.whereis.com/

Sponsor: Web Publishers

Subject Area(s): Using the Internet   **Subcategory:** Search Engines

Grade Level(s):

Description

This Web site is a "front end" to other major search engine sites. Enter the search criteria here, and the site will send it to a page on which a number of search engines are listed. From that page, it is possible to run the search against those sites in any required sequence.

Commentary

Though powerful, this approach to Internet searching is an advanced one and will probably be useful for students or adults who already have some experience with Web searching.

Section 10. Using the Internet

Site: Switchboard

URL: http://www.switchboard.com/

Sponsor: Database America Companies

Subject Area(s): Using the Internet   **Subcategory:** Search Engines

Grade Level(s):

Description
This search engine is specialized for locating people and businesses. It can also help discover e-mail addresses. Students can see how many other people with the same name in their state are listed here and find out if their parents are listed.

Commentary
The sponsor sells sales leads and other data to businesses and provides this free site as an example of how their technology works. It is a valuable site for locating contact information for people as well as businesses.

Site: WebCrawler

URL: http://webcrawler.com/

Sponsor: Excite, Inc.

Subject Area(s): Using the Internet   **Subcategory:** Search Engines

Grade Level(s):

Description
This search engine's home page has a convenient list of 15 categories from Art to Travel. You can link to a category, such as "Computers" or "Education," before beginning your search. The "Education" section is further subdivided into 12 subcategories ranging from "College Bound" to "Teaching Aids." Each section has a featured Web site that changes every week.

Commentary
Being able to link into progressively smaller sections and subsections makes this an easy-to-use search engine, especially for beginners.

Site: WhoWhere?

URL: http://www.whowhere.com/

Sponsor: WhoWhere? Inc.

Subject Area(s): Using the Internet   **Subcategory:** Search Engines

Grade Level(s):

Description
This search engine is specialized for locating people and has a very easy-to-use interface. Advanced searching is also supported. Addresses, phone numbers, and e-mail addresses can also be searched.

Commentary
There are links to many other related services from this site as well as links to Spanish and French language versions of this site.

Site: Yahoo!

URL: http://www.yahoo.com/

Sponsor: Yahoo! Inc.

Subject Area(s): Using the Internet   **Subcategory:** Search Engines

Grade Level(s):

Description

This is the Computers and Internet list for the popular Yahoo! search engine. Searching is narrowed to categories falling under this heading, such as Computer Science, Conventions and Conferences, Desktop Publishing, Graphics, Hardware, Internet, Magazines, Multimedia, Operating Systems, Programming Languages, Training, Year 2000 Problem, and others.

Commentary

This is a general-purpose search engine site that is very popular. It is divided into a number of sections including one on Education and another on Computers and the Internet. Also see the Yahooligans! for Kids site, a simplified version of this site for lower-grade children, and the Yahoo! People Finder, a site specialized for locating individuals, both of which can be linked to from this site.

Site: Color In Web Documents

URL: http://www.he.net/info/color/

Sponsor: Hurricane Electric

Subject Area(s): Using the Internet   **Subcategory:** Web Page Design

Grade Level(s):

Description

With these resources and the browser, Netscape, the computer user can control the background color, text color, link color, and visited link color. RGB values are given for dozens of colors, so that one can change the font color in the middle of a document.

Commentary

This site is for the Web page designer who is interested in precise colors within the Web site. For the rest of us, it is fascinating to learn about all of the color options and their names. This site might have some general applications in the art classroom.

Site: Designing Universal/Accessible Web Sites

URL: http://www.trace.wisc.edu/world/web/index.html

Sponsor: University of Wisconsin Trace Research and Development Center

Subject Area(s): Using the Internet   **Subcategory:** Web Page Design

Grade Level(s):

Description

A number of areas of concern regarding World Wide Web accessibility may be found in the index of this site along with links to information about designing accessible HTML pages, browsers with built-in voice and access features, and accessible Web site guidelines.

Commentary

The Trace Research and Development Center is concerned with accessability by people with disabilities in numerous venues. Its home page <http://www.trace.wisc.edu> may also be of interest to visitors of this site.

Section 10. Using the Internet

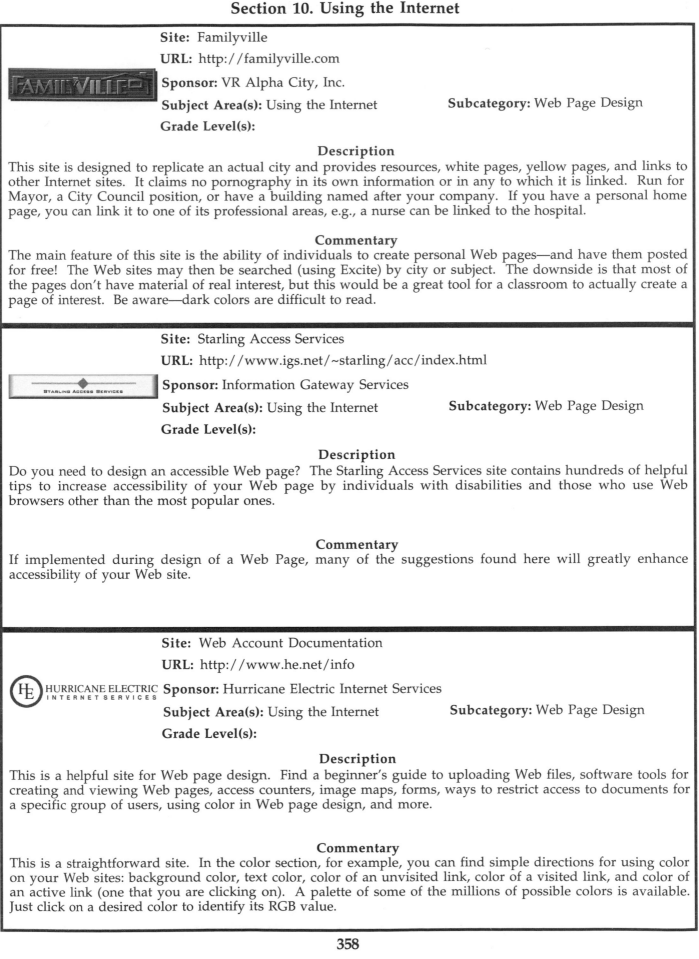

Site: Familyville

URL: http://familyville.com

Sponsor: VR Alpha City, Inc.

Subject Area(s): Using the Internet   **Subcategory:** Web Page Design

Grade Level(s):

Description

This site is designed to replicate an actual city and provides resources, white pages, yellow pages, and links to other Internet sites. It claims no pornography in its own information or in any to which it is linked. Run for Mayor, a City Council position, or have a building named after your company. If you have a personal home page, you can link it to one of its professional areas, e.g., a nurse can be linked to the hospital.

Commentary

The main feature of this site is the ability of individuals to create personal Web pages—and have them posted for free! The Web sites may then be searched (using Excite) by city or subject. The downside is that most of the pages don't have material of real interest, but this would be a great tool for a classroom to actually create a page of interest. Be aware—dark colors are difficult to read.

Site: Starling Access Services

URL: http://www.igs.net/~starling/acc/index.html

Sponsor: Information Gateway Services

Subject Area(s): Using the Internet   **Subcategory:** Web Page Design

Grade Level(s):

Description

Do you need to design an accessible Web page? The Starling Access Services site contains hundreds of helpful tips to increase accessibility of your Web page by individuals with disabilities and those who use Web browsers other than the most popular ones.

Commentary

If implemented during design of a Web Page, many of the suggestions found here will greatly enhance accessibility of your Web site.

Site: Web Account Documentation

URL: http://www.he.net/info

Sponsor: Hurricane Electric Internet Services

Subject Area(s): Using the Internet   **Subcategory:** Web Page Design

Grade Level(s):

Description

This is a helpful site for Web page design. Find a beginner's guide to uploading Web files, software tools for creating and viewing Web pages, access counters, image maps, forms, ways to restrict access to documents for a specific group of users, using color in Web page design, and more.

Commentary

This is a straightforward site. In the color section, for example, you can find simple directions for using color on your Web sites: background color, text color, color of an unvisited link, color of a visited link, and color of an active link (one that you are clicking on). A palette of some of the millions of possible colors is available. Just click on a desired color to identify its RGB value.

Site: Web Reference

URL: http://webreference.com

Sponsor: Athenia Association

Subject Area(s): Using the Internet   **Subcategory:** Web Page Design

Grade Level(s):

Description

This reference is designed for Web page designers from intermediate to advanced skills. It contains links to many other sites which teach Web page design, animation, agents and robots, and coding, with a host of illustrations. There is a news feature of articles related to the Internet. Several locations contain an extensive glossary.

Commentary

This is a 1997 award-winning site as recognized by several publications. The claim to having more than 700 links is easy to believe. This site is fun (for looking at interesting sites and animation) and highly informative (for the individual interested in developing Web sites). It appears to be monitored and updated regularly.

Site: Web Weavers Page

URL: http://www.nas.nasa.gov/NAS/WebWeavers/tools.html

Sponsor: NASA

Subject Area(s): Using the Internet   **Subcategory:** Web Page Design

Grade Level(s):

Description

NASA has gathered some excellent resources for those creating Web sites and interested in tools for Web design. Find HTML guides; style guides from Apple, Sun, and others; tools and techniques for scanning, using translators, and more; tips for creating tables, frames, and forms; a variety of icons and graphic images; a section on VRML, Java and JavaScript; and links to popular online magazines and news about the Web.

Commentary

This is a rich site for those interested in Web design and has many useful links for those just wanting to better understand the Internet. A great place to start is with one or more of the HTML Guides: The Classic "Beginners Guide to HTML", A Page for the Newbies (containing a helpful glossary), and HTML: An Interactive Tutorial for Beginners.

Site: Writing Accessible HTML Documents

URL: http://www.gsa.gov/coca/WWWcode.html

Sponsor: Center for Information Technology Accommodation

Subject Area(s): Using the Internet   **Subcategory:** Web Page Design

Grade Level(s):

Description

Accessibility to visual and auditory information can present a challenge for individuals with sensory impairments. The examples of inaccessible and accessible codes found here provide needed guidelines for those posting graphics, pictures, maps, and audio clips on the Internet.

Commentary

It is helpful to keep in mind that a Web site is intended for the use and enjoyment of those who visit it, which may include vision-impaired users. The samples here are very representative and good examples of how to achieve this goal.

Site: B & R Samizdat Express

URL: http://www.samizdat.com/

NO GRAPHIC FOUND

Sponsor: Barbara and Richard Seltzer, B & R Samizdat Express

Subject Area(s): Using the Internet   **Subcategory:** World Wide Web Indexes

Grade Level(s):

Description

This husband-and-wife team have collected a variety of Internet resources in an attempt to make it easier for teachers, librarians, and others to find things they can use. "Internet-on-a-Disk" is their electronic newsletter containing articles and updates of current happenings on the Web. A unique feature of this site is the dozens of links to Internet resources for the disabled.

Commentary

"Please Copy This Disk" is a feature describing the hundreds of electronic texts available on the Web. Many are available through this service for $10 for people who have no desire (or no capability) for an extensive download. Also find hundreds of links from this award-winning site. This is a wonderful example of what individuals can do with the Internet!

Site: The Virtual Tourist

URL: http://www.vtourist.com/vt/

Sponsor: Kinesava Geographics

Subject Area(s): Using the Internet   **Subcategory:** World Wide Web Indexes

Grade Level(s):

Description

This Web site provides a geographic directory of World Wide Web servers worldwide. Click on a region of the map to identify servers from that state or country or region.

Commentary

This site, despite the name, does not contain information about tourism, such as information about specific cities, countries, states, and regions.

Site: The WWW Virtual Library

URL: http://www.w3.org/vl/

Sponsor: Arthur Secret and a host of volunteers

Subject Area(s): Using the Internet   **Subcategory:** World Wide Web Indexes

Grade Level(s):

Description

This is the mother of all subject catalogs on the World Wide Web and one of the original uses for the Web as it was first envisioned. Choose to see links and resources arranged by category, Library of Congress classification, statistics on popularity by access, Top Ten most popular fields, or service type. This is the place to come to find other sites covering just about any topic you can imagine, and the newest links are identified.

Commentary

Students may well study about this site in school, and they can find out all about it at the actual Web site. The WWW Virtual Library Project was started at CERN in 1991 by Tim Berners-Lee to keep track of the development of the World Wide Web that he had just created. Today, it is maintained by Arthur Secret and a lengthy list of volunteers.

Site: Yanoff's Internet Services List

URL: http://www.spectracom.com/islist

Sponsor: Spectracom

Subject Area(s): Using the Internet   **Subcategory:** World Wide Web Indexes

Grade Level(s):

Description

Find an extensive set of links arranged alphabetically by category—from Agriculture to the WWW. Resource links point you across the Internet and not just on the Web.

Commentary

This site has not been updated since 1996, so some links may prove dated, but it is probably worth checking out the available links on topics of interest.

WWW

OTHER RESOURCES

> ➤ GLOSSARY OF TERMS TO KNOW

> ➤ SEARCHING ON THE INTERNET: A PRIMER

GLOSSARY OF TERMS TO KNOW

acceptable use policy (AUP)—an agreement or contract schools may use to outline specifically how the Internet, the World Wide Web, and accompanying computers and software will be used in an educational setting.

access—to be able to connect a computer to another computer or a network of computers in order to send or retrieve information.

baud rate (or *bps*)—the speed of your modem—actually, the number of bits per second that a modem can transmit or receive; the higher the speed, the faster you will be able to access information. Some sites on the Internet may recommend downloading files only if your modem baud rate is above a certain speed.

bookmark—a feature of your browser that lets you store the addresses of Web pages you frequently visit or want to save in a handy list. Bookmarks save you time in returning to sites you want to visit frequently.

browser—a software program that allows you to navigate the World Wide Web.

bulletin board—a computer program running on a host computer where users can read and post messages.

cyberspace—a common label given to the Internet; the online "place" where telecommunications happens, according to William Gibson, the science fiction novelist who coined the term.

domain name—the registered part of a URL address.

download—the transfer of a file from the Internet or some other host computer to your own computer.

e-mail—text messages that are sent from an electronic mailbox on your computer to one or more other electronic mailboxes using a messaging computer program on one or more intermediate host computers. Most of the time, the host computers are on the Internet, but that is not required. For example, you may have an e-mail system at school or at work that sends messages among users at that location using a local server that is not connected to the Internet.

ftp—File Transfer Protocol, which is the Internet standard for transferring files. Whenever you download software from an Internet host, you are using ftp.

hit list—when you enter search terms into a search engine, the list of addresses of sites that match your search criteria is called a hit list, and the entries on that list are called hits.

home page—the first page you see when you access a site on the World Wide Web. The home page is also the first page you see when you start up your browser, whether it is connected to the Internet or not. Most browsers allow you to change your home page to whatever you want it to be, usually in a menu item called "Preferences".

hotlist or hotlink—a quick connection via hypertext between pages of information; a hotlist may be a list of someone's favorite Web site addresses. Your Web browser helps you create your own, and you will also find Web sites that are merely hotlists of other sites on specific topics or areas of interest.

HTML—HyperText Markup Language, which is an Internet standard for displaying pages in a Web browser on any kind of computer. An HTML page created on a Windows computer should look exactly the same on another Windows computer, a Macintosh, or a UNIX machine.

http—HyperText Transfer Protocol, which is an Internet standard protocol for addressing Web sites; all URL Website addresses begin with "http".

hyperlink or hypertext—words that provide a connection or link to other pages on the Internet and World Wide Web; they are typically in another color and often underlined. In many cases, the text will change colors once accessed to indicate links you have already looked at.

Information Superhighway—a term coined by Vice President Al Gore to refer to the high-speed, fiber-optic communications system that will eventually become the core of the information infrastructure in the United States.

Internet—a worldwide mega-network of connected computers and other networks that allow users to access and share information.

Internet Service Provider (ISP)—a commercial organization that sells access to the Internet.

Internet site—a host computer connected to the Internet that has information that can be accessed.

jump—move from one location to another using hypertext.

keyword—a word that can be searched for in a document.

link—the hypertext connection between two different documents.

logging off—disconnecting from a computer network.

logging on—connecting to a computer network.

modem—a hardware device that is used to connect a computer to a network or another computer via a telephone line; internal modems are installed inside a computer, while external modems are separate boxes outside the computer but connected to it.

network—a group of computers connected to one another, usually by some kind of cabling. Almost all networks have one or more "host" computers (or "servers") which store data and programs that are accessed and used by the other network computers.

newbie—the name used to describe a new Internet user.

offline—disconnected from a network.

online—being connected to a network.

search engine—a kind of computer program running on a server; a tool that helps you search the Internet for information you need. The Internet sites that provide this kind of tool are also referred to as search engines.

surf (the Net)—to browse Internet sites. Sometimes "surfing" means exploring in some kind of casual or semi-random fashion.

telecommunications—the use of phone line, satellite, and/or microwave to transmit information over long distances.

upgrade—new or updated version of software or hardware.

upload—the transfer of a file from your computer to a host computer.

URL (Uniform Resource Locator)—the unique Internet address for a specific Web site; all Web page URLs begin with *http://*.

Web browser—a software application that allows you to view Web pages on the Internet.

Web site—an organized collection of Web pages on a host computer. Web sites are maintained by companies, government agencies, universities, associations, or by individuals.

World Wide Web (WWW)—also called the Web; the graphically-oriented part of the Internet, consisting of an enormous collection of documents stored on computers worldwide. The World Wide Web provides easy navigation and searchable access to multimedia information available on the Internet. In prior times, much of the data on the Internet was text-only and not on the Web, but today almost all of what users access is on the Web.

SEARCHING ON THE INTERNET: A PRIMER

If you have been using the Internet for awhile, you probably already are comfortable using some of the search engine sites such as Alta Vista, Lycos, Excite, and others; and if that is the case, you probably don't need to read this primer. Though there are some differences among search engines, this primer will focus on the general kinds of searching that you can do to find information on the Internet.

Several major search sites are listed in this Directory in the "Using the Internet" section. In those listings, you will find some additional information regarding how they can be used by students, teachers, and parents to do online research. You may want to check that section to see if there are any sites that you have not yet tried.

But if you are new to the Internet, then you will benefit from reading this primer now, because searching on the Internet can be somewhat intimidating, especially at the very beginning.

So what is a search engine? A search engine is a computer program that lives on a host computer on the Internet and is a tool you can use to locate information on the World Wide Web. You type specific words or phrases into the search engine, and it returns the location of Web sites it knows about that match the search criteria you typed. Every search site works a little bit differently from the others, but don't worry about that right now because what follows are some tips that will work with most every search engine.

1. The "Simple Search" Method:

In your browser, there is a line where you type a URL (Uniform Resource Locator), or Web site address, in order to access a site. Suppose you want to find the Web site for Compaq Computer Corporation. Try just typing the word "Compaq" into the URL space and then pressing the "Enter" or "Return" key on your keyboard. Most browsers will take the word you typed and reconstruct it as <http://www.compaq.com>, which is the correct Internet address for Compaq's main website. This does not work for every site you might want to visit, but when it does, it sure is easy! Try it with "Apple" (for Apple Computer) and see what happens.

2. Finding Search Engine Websites:

Most browsers have a "Search" button on their menu bars. This search button can be used to access some of the various search engines. Or you can also just type the search engine's URL into the browser, if you know it.

3. *Single-term Searching:*

Just type the keyword you want to search on in the space provided in the search engine and then press the "Go" or "Search" button to execute the search. This is the simplest kind of search, though it usually produces a list of far too many "hits," or documents and resources matching the keyword you requested.

4. *Multiple-term Searching:*

Multiple-term searching is a little bit more tricky. If you are looking for social studies information, for example, and you type the words "social studies" into the search field, the search engine reads or interprets this search request as though there is an "or" between the two words. So it goes out and finds every Web site that has either the word "social" *or* the word "studies" in it—as well as all of the sites that have both words.

What you are really looking for are all the sites that contain *both* words—or even both words together. Try the search again and this time use the following search string—"social and studies." This will return a hit list of all the sites that have both words in them, but not necessarily with one word right next to the other one.

5. *Using Quotation Marks in Multiple-term Searching:*

If you type "social studies" with the quotation marks around the outside, then the search engine typically knows that you are looking for websites that have those two words right next to each other and in that sequence, and it will give you those results.

Some search engines will give you additional opportunities to refine your search, offering you options to narrow or limit the search by specifying that you want only "exact phrases" or only resources with "all the words" specified or similar options. You should look for these to assist in narrowing your search.

Most search engines have an online help system to help you learn advanced searching techniques, and there are a wide variety of books and classes offered on the topic as well. After experimenting with the techniques in this primer, you may want to go on to more advanced training.

INDEX